CORNISH STUDIES

Second Series

TWELVE

INSTITUTE OF CORNISH STUDIES

University *of* Exeter
IN CORNWALL

EDITOR'S NOTE

Cornish Studies (second series) exists to reflect current research conducted internationally in the inter-disciplinary field of Cornish Studies. It is edited by Professor Philip Payton, Director of the Institute of Cornish Studies at the University of Exeter in Cornwall, and is published by the University of Exeter Press. The opinions expressed in *Cornish Studies* are those of individual authors and are not necessarily those of the editor or publisher. The support of Cornwall County Council is gratefully acknowledged.

Cover illustration: St Piran's flag and the kilt in Cornish National Tartan (courtesy of the *Cornish Guardian*)

CORNISH STUDIES

Second Series

TWELVE

Edited by

Philip Payton

UNIVERSITY
of
EXETER
PRESS

First published in 2004 by
University of Exeter Press
Reed Hall, Streatham Drive
Exeter, Devon EX4 4QR
UK
www.exeterpress.co.uk

British Library Cataloguing in Publication Data
A catalogue record for this book is
available from the British Library

ISBN 0 85989 756 7
ISSN 1352-271X

Typeset in 10/12pt Times by Kestrel Data, Exeter

Printed and bound in Great Britain by
Antony Rowe Ltd, Chippenham

Contents

REVIEW ARTICLE

INTRODUCTION

One of the important roles performed by the series *Cornish Studies* over the past decade or so, in the exercising of academic leadership in our subject area, has been the suggestion of new conceptual and methodological directions. As well as the continued emphasis on the comparative and the interdisciplinary—or at least the multidisciplinary —there has been an attempt to demonstrate the relevance to the current practice of Cornish Studies of social theory and of recent advances in cultural studies, the social sciences and other areas of academic endeavour.

This approach has been associated especially with the work of Bernard Deacon, one of the leading architects of the 'new' Cornish Studies practised today. In an article in *Cornish Studies: Eight* (2000), Deacon argued that studies of Cornwall should be sensitive to issues of scale—from the local to the global—and that, instead of addressing just one 'Cornwall', Cornish Studies should be alive to the existence of various possible 'Cornwalls': temporal, geographical, cultural, and so on. More recently, in *Cornish Studies: Ten* (2002), he has gone further. In deconstructing the 'rhetorically defined space' that constitutes 'new' Cornish Studies, he has insisted that Cornish Studies thus defined should be seen as an on-going struggle for space and that this—the normative project—should be understood and recognized by those who observe or seek to engage with the subject area. He has also repeated the call for a similar recognition of the inherent heterogeneity of Cornwall and Cornishness, emphasizing again the place of micro-history in tackling this diversity.

In this volume, Deacon takes a third step towards the development of 'a more self-critical Cornish Studies project'. Here he argues persuasively that Cornish Studies practitioners should engage with the concept of 'discourse'—a term that, as he puts it, began to seep into the social sciences in the 1980s—by applying 'critical discourse analysis': a means of 'combining social theory with a normative ontology'. In practice, this involves identifying 'discourses'—some taken for granted, others hotly contested—and then subjecting them to critical deconstruction aimed at unlocking their assumptions, motivations and meanings. Thus, for example, as Deacon notes, one might select 'Celtic Cornwall' or 'romantic Cornwall' or 'Cornwall as an English county'—each of them powerful discourses of Cornwall and Cornishness—and then applying critical analysis to begin to dissect and understand them. Other discourses important within a Cornish Studies context might be, as Deacon suggests, those of 'regionalization' or 'regeneration' or 'sustainability': the discourses of the planners and policymakers. Moreover, if Cornish Studies is serious in its attempts to become more self-critical and to acknowledge its normative assumptions, then its own 'foundation myths' are a discourse ripe for analysis and should be laid bare for academic scrutiny.

As this volume attests, there is evidence that Deacon's recent and current calls for new directions are already being heeded. Jonathan Howlett, for example, sets his contribution—'Putting the Kitsch into Kernow'—firmly within the methodological context of 'new' Cornish Studies. Demonstrating how significant imagery and 'seeing' can be in the construction of discourses such as those identified by Deacon, Howlett deconstructs a portfolio of powerful visual material which, he contends, 'has been manipulated into forms that can best be described as "kitsch" '. As a result of this process, he argues, 'the way in which the Cornish see themselves and are seen by others has been profoundly altered—and not always for the better'. Indeed, there has been a general 'enkitschment' of Cornish culture, he says, a phenomenon that has occurred largely in response to the demands of the tourist industry and the needs of consumers from outside Cornwall. The effect of this on Cornwall and Cornishness has been often deleterious: 'at its best kitsch is no more than sentimental and nostalgic but at its worst it is demeaning and alienating'. But, argues Howlett, kitsch is here to stay. What is important, then, is for us to cope with kitsch, to understand the process by which it has become so all-pervasive and—in recognizing the salience of 'seeing' in our experience of culture building—to initiate a debate on Cornish culture: 'a debate in which the lived visual experience meets the studied and analytical'.

Sharon Lowenna, in her article, comes close to laying bare the foundation myths of the Cornish Revival—one of the most powerful discourses of modern Cornwall—or at least to placing the origins of the Revival within the context of the ideological predilections of Henry Jenner, L.C. Duncombe-Jewell and their milieu. Henry Jenner is honoured routinely as the 'Father of the Cornish Revival', and 2004 marks the hundredth anniversary of the publication of his enormously important book *A Handbook of the Cornish Language.* However, as Robert Morton Nance once hinted and as Sharon Lowenna makes plain, Jenner came to matters Cornish relatively late in his life. When he did so, he placed his Cornish interests within a wider paradigm that had been almost a lifetime in the making, setting his Cornish enthusiasms within a framework of Jacobitism, Legitimism and the Celtic Right that had already moulded his religious and political beliefs and formed his circle of friends—including the eccentric L.C. Duncombe-Jewell.

Unearthing much new and often surprising material, Lowenna sheds light on hitherto shadowy areas of Jenner's life, in the process providing fresh insights into the origins and political-religious foundations of the Cornish Revival, ranging widely from the *Firefly* fiasco and the Carlist plot of 1899 to links with William Butler Yeats and the antics of Lord Semphill. As Lowenna concludes, her portrait allows us to resist 'the dangers of hagiographizing Jenner as *fons et origo*' of the Revival and prevents 'the eclipsing of less dominating figures of the Revival through misplaced reverence'. As she says: 'It is healthy to view Jenner in the round'. Certainly, her intervention injects precisely the kind of explicit self-critical analysis demanded by Deacon but often avoided by contemporary adherents of the Cornish Revival who are anxious to protect the assumptions—and reputation—of their project.

Like Howlett and Lowenna, Garry Tregidga and Lucy Ellis in their contribution also rise to the challenges offered by Deacon, searching for a genuine interdisciplinarity in their work and deploying the methodology of the micro-study. Describing the activities of the Cornish Audio Visual Archive project (CAVA), they show how they 'draw on the disciplines of oral history, anthropology and sociolinguistics to provide a framework for analysing the creative potential of group dialogue'. Arguing that this, in contradistinction to traditional oral history methods, allows communities to create their own cultural narratives independent of the control of the interviewer, they then proceed to put their concepts into practice—in a case study of a recording made by residents of a Cornish china-clay village. Ranging from memories of the 1913 clay-workers' strike to definitions of 'a typical Cornishman', the residents deal themselves with issues of community conflict and consensus. They venture into thorny areas of individual and group identity that leave far behind the stereotype of oral history as merely 'the recording of nostalgic and cosy reminiscences about the past', an exploration that has relevance for understanding the present and future as well as drawing a more insightful picture of past events.

Intriguingly, the perspectives offered by Tregidga and Ellis find an

echo in Alan M. Kent's 'Drill Cores', an article which focuses on a
recently discovered manuscript of Cousin Jack stories in Michigan but
which raises far wider questions about the significance of Cornu-
English dialect as a signifier of identity—in Cornwall itself and in the
Cornish diaspora overseas: in the present as well as in the past. Kent
recounts how, while conducting research on Cornish literary traces in
North America, he stumbled across a rich but hitherto unnoticed
collection of Cornish-American narratives—'Drill Cores'—compiled
by the late Walter F. Gries and edited by the late Donald D. Kinsey.
He places these stories within the traditions of 'orality' and 'story-
telling', emphasizing their cultural geographic and materialist contexts,
and, although these narratives were committed to paper rather than
sound recording, Kent draws an explicit comparison between them and
the recent CAVA collections.

   These narratives are not the simple yarns or jokes popularly
imagined to have been the stock of Cousin Jack stories but rather
represent 'a dynamic continuum of oral culture': one that in nineteenth-
century Cornwall had increasingly replaced the traditional 'drolls', and
which overseas was adapted and metamorphosed in response to new
conditions. Such is the importance of these narratives, Kent argues,
that we should reconsider the place of Cornu-English dialect in the
repertoire of Cornish cultural identity, not least in relation to
the routinely privileged position of the Cornish language itself. Again,
this is evidence of a more reflective, more self-critical Cornish Studies
of the type advocated by Deacon: in this case a willingness to both
admit and query the centrality of the Cornish language in the Revivalist
construction of Cornwall.

   As Tregidga, Ellis and Kent all acknowledge, oral tradition can tell
us as much about the present (and future) as the past. This is made
evident in Kayleigh Milden's 'Are You Church or Chapel?' where she
employs oral testimony 'to explore the diversity of socio-religious and
spatial identities that encompass the subject of Cornish Methodism'.
As she explains: '[o]ral narrative research opens up new possibilities in
the study of Cornish Methodism, by revealing a multiplicity of religious
experience that lies beneath rigid methodological categories'.
Specifically, Milden investigates Methodism's role as an 'ethnic
religion' in Cornwall. There is a paradox here, for despite the apparent
ethnic dimension to Cornish Methodism, Methodism as a movement has never been aligned—overtly or otherwise—with Cornish
nationalism. The explanation, according to Milden, is the prominence
of a 'chapel and locality' identity in popular Methodism—an observation that recalls Deacon's insistence upon the heterogeneous nature of
Cornwall and the importance of diverse localities. However, Milden

also observes that the picture is becoming increasingly complex. As identities become more fluid and interchangeable—with individuals capable of adopting different identities in different social contexts—so the propensity for people to assume a number of spatial and ethno-religious identities according to time and place has increased. In this way, Milden concludes, Cornish Methodism is often 'manipulated' to 'represent a variety of cultural, spatial and spiritual identities'.

Graham Busby, in his 'The Contested Cornish Church Heritage', also alights on the complex relationship between religion, place and identity in contemporary Cornwall. His focus, however, is on the medieval buildings of the Anglican Church in Cornwall and their iconic status as architectural expressions of 'Celtic Cornwall': a discourse that has a particular appeal for a certain type of heritage tourist seeking the spiritual dimension of the Celtic 'other'. Busby's research has concentrated on three representative Cornish churches—Gunwalloe, St Just-in-Roseland, and Lanteglos-by-Fowey—and he has discovered, as he explains in his article, that constructions of 'Celtic Cornwall' are important to visitors at each site. Yet most visitors, when pressed, are hard-pushed to define the 'Celtic' qualities, attributes or features of these sites, and appear to be influenced strongly by literature that merely asserts this 'Celticity'. Cornwall as the 'Land of Saints', a sense of 'continuity' in the landscape, and an atmosphere of 'simplicity' within the churches, are also read as signifiers of a 'Celtic Christianity', although, paradoxically, there is often little appreciation of those features (such as the *lan*, or raised churchyard) that might actually be said to evidence a 'Celtic' dimension. For most visitors, Busby concludes, their identification with 'Celtic Christianity' is the consequence of 'a psychological construct rather than an evidence-based one': telling us as much about those individuals as about the church sites themselves.

Cornish churches slip easily into constructions of 'Celtic Cornwall' but the game of cricket—so quintessentially 'English' and redolent of Imperial cultural influence—sits less happily within the discourse of Cornwall as a Celtic nation. While rugby football has been synthesized within the discourse—*vide* the astonishing phenomenon of 'Trelawny's Army'—and has taken its place convincingly alongside hurling and wrestling as a genuinely 'Cornish' pursuit, the position of cricket remains equivocal. Yet, as Ian Clarke makes clear in his article, the history of cricket in Cornwall is in several respects distinctive and exhibits clear contrasts with that of south-east England: the geographical and cultural home of 'village cricket'.

Moreover, as Clarke shows, locality—the spatial dimension of heterogeneous Cornwall—was especially important in the development of cricket in Cornwall, complementing considerations of class and religion. Cricket was introduced to Cornwall by the gentry, who had first encountered the game up-country and were attracted by its 'gentility', resulting in its appearance at Truro and Bodmin, while the presence of outside military units in Cornwall during the Napoleonic Wars also encouraged the sport. Thereafter, as Cornish Methodists increasingly opposed traditional 'pagan' sports, so the 'civilized' game of cricket gained middle-class adherents in towns such as Helston and Penzance. By the 1830s there were locational networks appearing across Cornwall—in the Penwith peninsula, in south-east Cornwall around Liskeard, Looe and Lostwithiel, and in North Cornwall at Launceston, Camelford and Bude. In this way, cricket was established as an integral part of the Cornish social and sporting scene.

There may be doubts about the precise nature and location of cricket within the spectrum of Cornish culture but there can be no dispute about tin mining. In particular, South Crofty—closed in the late 1990s but still the object of hope for those who foresee a twenty-first-century rebirth of Cornwall's ancient industry—is symbolic of all the triumphs and disasters of Cornish mining, its head-frames continuing to define the Camborne-Redruth skyline. For external observers, the final phase of the mine's existence was dominated by the fluctuating price of tin on the international market—and the willingness or otherwise of the British government to support the Cornish industry. But within the industry itself a further concern of considerable magnitude was the discovery of radon gas in the mine and the subsequent debate over the health threats it posed and the manner in which these should be managed.

Although Sandra Kippen and Yolande Collins, in their article examining this debate, display admirable technical knowledge of the radon issue, their aim is not to assess the relative strengths and weaknesses of the several medical and scientific arguments. Rather, their article builds upon a wider debate in the social sciences in which it is argued that ostensibly 'neutral' and 'factual' medical knowledge will be deployed in markedly different ways 'by different groups through their own discourses to further their own agendas'. At South Crofty, the two groups operating within different discourses and for their own agendas were, predictably, the managers and the miners themselves. As Kippen and Collins show, following the discovery of the gas, the understanding, interpretation and use of medical and epidemiological evidence by these two groups evolved in very different directions. On the one hand, on the basis of evidence of the 'threat', South Crofty put into place—at a time of considerable financial stringency—a series of expensive measures to deal with the gas. But, on the other hand, when miners sought to use exactly the same evidence to demonstrate unsafe exposure to the gas and to claim compensation for related illness, their case collapsed. As Kippen and Collins conclude: 'the social and political use made of medical knowledge is not necessarily in a direct relationship with the "facts" as known and propagated by medical science'. Instead, '[f]acts are selected and emphasized in accordance with the social and political function of whichever group is using them'. Their article illuminates a hitherto little known and little understood episode in the closing years of a great Cornish mine. But, as Kippen and Collins observe, their work in unravelling competing discourses has far wider comparative value: 'The story of South Crofty is only one of innumerable stories, providing a micro-view of the wider social perspective of power and use of knowledge.'

A further aspect of the industrial history of modern Cornwall that is little known and little understood is the National Dock Labour Scheme (NDLS) as it applied to Cornwall. Formed in 1947 and growing out of its pre-war and wartime predecessors, NDLS reflected the practical necessities and ideological aspirations of the moment. Often discussed in the context of its application to the major docks elsewhere in the United Kingdom, NDLS in its Cornish guise has been almost always overlooked. Yet, as Terry Chapman demonstrates, its operation in Cornish ports—small by the standards of docks within the scheme elsewhere, with only relatively few dockworkers being managed—had a particular Cornish dimension. Thus NDLS in Cornwall becomes a micro-study of considerable comparative value, a case-study of the scheme's operation in a distinct and discreet region which exhibited both typical and atypical features as far as the scheme was concerned.

The scheme was, Chapman argues, flawed from the start—however necessary and 'inevitable' it appeared at its inception—and was the subject of continuing tension until the Thatcher government's emphasis on denationalization and deregulation rendered it redundant. It was finally abolished in 1989. In its Cornish context, the UK national dock strike in 1970 was a particular illustration of the importance of the local dimension in the history of NDLS: in this case the allegedly disastrous prospects facing the china-clay industry as a result of the strike, when 6,000 clay workers marched in protest against the 100 strikers at the ports of Par and Fowey. In the fifteen years since the end of NDLS, Chapman notes, the authorities managing Cornwall's ports have had to contend with increasingly conflicting demands: cultural, residential, recreational and commercial—including the property development potential of their valuable waterfronts. He notes wryly that a 'joined up' UK national transport policy might yet emerge from

'New' Labour. But if it does so, the maritime component is unlikely to resemble the erstwhile NDLS: the 'future control of manpower in British trading ports seems unlikely to bear the currently unfashionable corporatist stamp of the National Dock Labour Scheme'.

An important contribution to the industrial and labour history of Cornwall, Chapman's article should also be seen as a major new addition to Cornish maritime history. Following the recent opening of the *National Maritime Museum Cornwall* at Falmouth, there has been a renewed emphasis on the maritime dimension of Cornwall's past. A leading figure in this activity is Helen Doe, and in her article in this edition of *Cornish Studies* she combines her interest in Cornish maritime history with a micro-analysis of political conflict in one Cornish port—Fowey—in the years from the late eighteenth century until the Great Reform Act of 1832. The political issues and practices were familiar ones in Cornwall in the period, and have been discussed elsewhere, but there were particular dimensions—such as Naval patronage and the competition for Naval contracts—that gave them a distinctive local flavour at Fowey.

Yet, despite this local colour, while individuals might benefit from political preferment or patronage, the wider community of Fowey did not. As Doe remarks: 'the main parties were too busy fighting elections and spending large sums of money on the electoral battles to assist the town in capitalizing on its geographic benefits of a large deep-water harbour and closeness to the mines'. At the time, tangible evidence such the building of new ships (an important indicator of economic activity for contemporary business interests) seemed sufficient to convince some observers of the lasting benefits of patronage and preferment. But, as the unresolved rivalry between Austen and Rashleigh attested, political conflict could have serious deleterious consequences for Fowey: such as when Austen was forced in 1830 to construct a new harbour at Par as an outlet for his local copper mines. Par grew rapidly to challenge Fowey in both ship-building and trade, including the export of china clay as the industry developed later in the nineteenth century and in the twentieth. Thus the intensely local obsessions of one particular locality came to affect the strategic interests of Cornwall as a whole at a time of vigorous industrial expansion.

In the post-industrial age, Cornwall's strategic interests also seem sometimes to be at the mercy of the more parochial preoccupations of the local political elite. It is instructive to note, for example, that the decisive move that clinched official visibility—if not actually official status—for the Cornish language came from agencies outside rather than within Cornwall. Specifically, it was the response of Kenneth

MacKinnon—long recognized as a specialist in language planning issues, and an advisor to the Scottish Executive on Gaelic—to an approach from the Government office of the South West that led to his *Independent Academic Study on Cornish* in 2000. Subsequently, with the evidence of the study to hand, the British government decided that it would include Cornish amongst the indigenous United Kingdom languages that it would recognize in its signing of the European Charter for Regional or Minority Languages. This was a process that MacKinnon has described in his article 'Cornish at its Millennium' in *Cornish Studies: Ten* (2002): it was a development that would also prompt Cornwall County Council to initiate its own Cornish-language strategy in 2004, a direct result of MacKinnon's intervention and the government's action in response to it.

The year 2004 has also seen the publication of the New Testament in Cornish (in Kernewek Kemmyn, to be precise). Although undoubtedly a huge feat, as well as evidence of deep spiritual commitment, some observers have noted wryly that alas it has come 500 years too late (publication of the Bible in Cornish at the Reformation might have done much to stem the retreat of the language). Moreover, its appearance before a largely secular audience—which rarely reads the New Testament in English, let alone other languages—is unlikely to stir the popular enthusiasm for Cornish that the Revivalists seek but which remains elusive. However, this impressive labour of love is evidence of the fact, that, as Alan M. Kent has noted, although Revived Cornish has yet to break through in popular consciousness and usage, the Cornish language remains a central tenet of the Cornish Revivalist construction of Cornwall. Put another way, to return to Deacon's analysis, the publication of the New Testament needs to be understood within the discourse of Cornish Revivalism: a particular view of Cornwall in which the language is its principal feature.

Intriguingly, Kenneth MacKinnon's article in this edition of *Cornish Studies* sheds important light on how this discourse has developed in recent years. As MacKinnon explains, as part of the background research for his 2000 study he conducted a series of focus group meetings for Cornish-language speakers and learners and for representatives of the three language varieties. His findings are an incomparable resource for understanding the motivations and aspirations of the Revivalists. He has observed, for example, the importance of the 1549 'Cornish Holocaust'—as it was dubbed by some focus group attendees—in shaping attitudes to a language that was, in the estimation those attendees at least, put to flight at the point of a sword. Other attendees were interested in the competitive 'debate' between the three current versions of the Revived Language

—Kemmyn, Unified, and Modern/Late—but avoided the intractable ideological, academic and cultural arguments underpinning the contest by suggesting that these variations might more profitably be seen as 'dialects' rather than rivals.

But most of all, MacKinnon uncovered a new confidence in the language which, despite the fact that breakthrough remained elusive, demanded a new respect for Cornish as a contemporary language and for Cornish speakers and learners. It also demanded that resources be made available to ensure the language's propagation in schools, the media, in other institutions and in public life generally. Such support was the democratic right of Cornish people, it was argued, especially as they had contributed considerably to the UK Treasury and might reasonably expect a return.

Beyond the discourse of the Revival, there remains other scholarly work in Cornish-language studies. Brian Murdoch, for example, has studied medieval Cornish literature at length and, a German language and literature specialist himself, he is intensely interested in the comparative, European dimensions of Cornish writing. The Bible, as we have observed, was never translated into Cornish. But the bulk of medieval and early modern Cornish-language material is—leaving aside subtexts and plots subversive or otherwise—religious in content and purpose. This is especially true of the great religious cycle, the *Ordinalia*, to which Murdoch returns in his article in this collection. He selects one of the three component parts of the cycle—the *Origo Mundi*—and alights upon one particular scene within it: a version of the biblical story in which King David seduces Bathsheba and has her husband, Uriah, killed. Murdoch sketches the story as it appears in the Bible, observes briefly how it has been treated in other art forms, and then turns to the attention it receives in *Origo Mundi*. He decides that this Cornish treatment is 'a fairly radical biblical adaptation' and that it invites comparison with other medieval writings: a comparison he then proceeds to make and which he concludes by pondering the way in which the essence of the story has been maintained in popular thought until our own time. Here, indeed, is a tenacity that matches the enduring quality of the Cornish language itself.

The discourse of 'Cornwall as a Celtic nation' has underpinned the wider Cornish nationalist movement, exemplified in the political party Mebyon Kernow—The Party of Cornwall. Formed in 1951 as a quasi-pressure group, more cultural nationalist than political nationalist, Mebyon Kernow (MK) was a long time transforming itself into a mainstream political party—in the process engaging in a lengthy flirtation with the Liberals (later Liberal Democrats) as well as spawning splinter groups such as the Cornish Nationalist Party. Moreover,

uncertain of its electoral strategy, MK has attempted electoral interventions on an almost *ad hoc* basis, failing dismally in Westminster
elections but pulling off some stunning coups at local authority level
and in 1979 achieving a memorable 10 per cent of the Cornish vote in
the very first election to the European Parliament.

But whatever its ineptitudes, electoral and otherwise, MK has
been a constant feature of the Cornish political scene for over half a
century and has made a sustained contribution to political debate.
Indeed, it was MK which initiated the post-war demand for a Cornish
University. Although the Combined Universities in Cornwall campus
at Tremough is not yet what MK envisaged, it is without doubt powerful evidence of institutional renewal and a starting point from which a
more overtly Cornish agenda might emerge over time. As far back as
September 1968, in its publication *What Cornishmen Can Do: A Statement on the Economic Development of Cornwall*, Mebyon Cornwall
had identified 'Cornwall's great need for a university' and had looked
forward to the time when such an institution would 'offer Cornish
students the option of studying matters which make Cornwall what it is
and may become'.

Additionally, it was Mebyon Kernow that initiated the slogan 'The
Only Region For Cornwall is Cornwall', the stuff of car-stickers in
Cornwall in the late 1960s and 1970s as various bureaucratic regional
designs threatened to engulf Cornwall in an amorphous 'South West' or
'West Country' construct, a process that appeared to reach its absurd
conclusion in 1993 when impoverished Cornwall—tethered to relatively
prosperous Devon—failed to achieve European 'Objective One' status
despite the fact that this mantle was conferred upon demonstrably
richer Merseyside and the Highlands & Islands. Although promptly
unshackled from Devon, and speedily rewarded with European
regional status and Objective One funding, Cornwall was nonetheless
ushered towards a new regional leviathan after the 1997 general
election: a South West (of England) Development Agency and an
unelected South West Assembly increasingly invested with powers
that had once rested with the democratically-elected Cornwall County
Council. At the same time, Mebyon Kernow had long advocated
internal self-government for Cornwall, demanding a Cornish devolutionary Assembly similar in powers to the new Welsh Assembly or the
Scottish Parliament, a formula enthusiastically endorsed by the 50,000
Cornish people who in the early twenty-first century signed a petition to
that effect: a petition that was subsequently ignored by the government
as it prepared its plans for regional government 'in England'.

It is this curious meld of forward thinking policy-making and
central government indifference that has characterized the half century

experience of Mebyon Kernow and accounts in part for its survival against the background wide-ranging social, economic and political change. The enduring strength of the Cornish identity, and its ability to reinvent itself in the face of such change—so much of it hostile to the idea of 'Cornwall' as a place and as an identity—must also help to explain the stubborn endurance of MK and its refusal to capitulate in the face of massive discouragement: even in the 2004 European elections when the UK Independence Party (so opposed to devolutionary government in Britain) managed to co-opt almost all of MK's anti-metropolitan angst in Cornwall.

Against this background, the appearance of *Mebyon Kernow and Cornish Nationalism*, a new book by Bernard Deacon, Dick Cole, and Garry Tregidga, is timely indeed. It is reviewed here by Adrian Lee, a long standing observer of Cornish voting behaviour and Cornish political distinctiveness, who welcomes the volume not only as a definitive history of Cornish nationalism but as a major contribution to the study of European sub-state national movements. Although Lee is clearly sympathetic towards the treatment afforded by Deacon *et al.*, and perhaps to the claims of Cornwall itself, he suspects that for the time being devolution 'south of the Trent' is a dead issue. Moreover, he reminds us that, despite 'new' Labour's apparent constitutional 'modernization' agenda, the United Kingdom remains one of Europe's most centralized political systems. It exhibits, therefore, a metropolitan indifference—Lee argues—in which elite perceptions of Cornwall (such as they are) are 'shaped through the lenses of the second home, the Padstow restaurant and the St Mawes luxury hotel'. And yet, as Lee also observes, Mebyon Kernow is hardly likely to go away: 'Cornwall remains the only part of the United Kingdom, beyond Scotland and Wales, to have sustained a sub-state nationalist or decentralist movement that is neither ephemeral nor lacking in core support'. Thus, he concludes, 'MK's influence on the Cornish political scene is unlikely to abate'. At the very least, as Cornwall moves more confidently towards meeting the challenges of the twenty-first century, the inherent contradictions of Cornwall's existence are likely to provoke new responses to the fundamental injustices and inequalities that exist west of the Tamar. It will be for Cornish Studies practitioners to chart and explain their progress.

Professor Philip Payton,
Director, Institute of Cornish Studies,
University of Exeter in Cornwall,
Combined Universities in Cornwall,
Tremough, Penryn, Cornwall.

FROM 'CORNISH STUDIES' TO 'CRITICAL CORNISH STUDIES': REFLECTIONS ON METHODOLOGY

Bernard Deacon

INTRODUCTION

In reviewing the 'new Cornish social science' Malcolm Williams sums up part of the goal of 'a relevant Cornish social science' as the ability 'to describe what contemporary Cornwall is like and to understand what people in Cornwall think'.[1] By extending this to past times this could equally be an aim for Cornish historical studies—to describe what Cornwall was like and understand what people in Cornwall thought. And yet such a deceptively simple goal begs a number of questions. First, how precisely do we 'describe' Cornwall, either in the twenty-first or the eleventh century? If we wish to avoid the empiricist fallacy that claims that the 'truth' will emerge un-problematically from the 'facts', any researcher has to pose questions, select facts, choose methods: in short adopt a framework for their study.

Claims for a 'new' Cornish Studies are regularly accompanied by the idea, more often implicit than explicit, that it is—or should be—informed by social theory. This supposed role of theory marks it off from an 'old' Cornish Studies. However, claims for a theoretically informed Cornish Studies are more difficult to substantiate in its practice. Some contributors to *Cornish Studies* adopt theoretical frameworks; others do not. And if we review the whole field of Cornish Studies, what is striking is its eclectic pick-and-mix approach to theory. Theories are chosen for their utility in studying discrete issues within Cornish Studies, depending on the disciplinary origin of the researcher and the topic being investigated. Theoretical choice is not, in contrast, a function of Cornish Studies as a field of study.

In this article I wish to explore one particular branch of social theory in a little more detail, making a plea that it might be seen as particularly suited to the task of developing a critical Cornish Studies. In doing this I want to move on from questions of aims and content to those of methodology. In *Cornish Studies: Eight* I proposed that studies of Cornwall should be sensitive to processes operating at multi-level scales, from the global to the local.[2] An awareness of the issue of scale moves us away from a focus on Cornwall to the unravelling of Cornwalls. Building on this, in *Cornish Studies: Ten*, when deconstructing the rhetorically defined space that comprises 'New Cornish Studies', I called for Cornish Studies to be seen as part of an ongoing struggle for space, and for an explicit recognition of its underlying normative stance.[3] Within this I laid out an agenda of micro-history, cultural studies and 'extraversion', as well as an openness to the heterogeneity of Cornwall and Cornishness. The present contribution can, therefore, be read as the third part of an ongoing reflection on the disciplinary field of Cornish Studies. It is by no means the final word but rather a further effort to tie together some of the issues raised in the two earlier contributions, as we grope towards a more self-critical Cornish Studies project.

In both previous reflections I used the word 'discourse'. But it was employed loosely and descriptively. In doing this I echoed the seepage of the term into the social sciences since the 1980s, 'discourse' becoming a fashionable concept that had 'infected social theory'.[5] But it is time to pin down this concept. Here, I try to do just that, taking the reader on a brief tour around the idea of discourse, resting on Laclau and Mouffe's model.[6] However, rejecting those analysts' over-reliance on discourse, I then propose that Cornish Studies could benefit from engaging with discourse in the guise of critical discourse analysis, which offers a way of combining social theory with a normative ontology (underpinning assumptions that are strongly committed to a particular view of the world). In adopting this approach critical discourse analysis offers intriguing signposts, pointing the way towards a critical Cornish Studies.

WHAT IS DISCOURSE?

This article began with Malcolm Williams's plea to 'understand what people in Cornwall think'. This, indeed, is a perfectly respectable aim as we are surprisingly ignorant about what people think: about Cornwall, about their localities, about their everyday lives.[7] Nonetheless, identifying what people think cannot stop there. In revealing the contents of their thoughts we will inevitably then enquire into questions such as how do they think, where do the things they think come from, what institutions help to transmit the elements with which they think and how do they negotiate these, or what constraints are there to the thoughts they think. And to do this, we have to go beyond Cornwall, to investigate the way people in other places and in external institutions think about Cornwall. Conceptually too, we have to go beyond the thoughts of the individual to the system of thought, or more realistically systems of thought, within which they do their thinking.

And this is where discourses enter the arena. A discourse is a way of understanding and talking about the world that can be distinguished from other ways of understanding the world.[8] The analyst can categorize ways of understanding into several, sometimes conflicting, 'discourses'. Thus there is a 'Cornish nationalist' discourse that 'sees' Cornwall as having been oppressed and exploited by the English for over a thousand years. In contrast there is a 'Cornwall as English county' discourse that views Cornwall as an integral component of England. These are clearly competing discourses and there is not much overlap between them. Each makes up a network of meaning, similar to the structuralist description of language as *langue*, or a structure. Within such a network or structure words get their meaning from what they are not. In the 'Cornish nationalist' discourse Cornwall is not England; in the 'English county' discourse Cornwall is not Devon.

Discourses also clearly do more than just reflect the world: they actively constitute the world they describe. There is only one Cornwall, in the sense of its tangible and physical settlements, fields, roads, moors, cliffs and the like. Yet there are several, sometimes complementary and overlapping, discourses of Cornwall. By ascribing meaning, a discourse helps to construct the social world. And it does more; it makes certain actions relevant or 'practical', while ruling out others. If we take it for granted that Cornwall is an English county then other conclusions follow. If Cornwall is a county then how can it have a nationalist movement? If Cornwall is a county then how can it possibly claim regional status? Counties surely have local identities and not national identities and county councils rather than regional assemblies. Despite the contrast between the glaringly obvious empirical absence of anything resembling a nationalist movement in any English county and the continuous existence of—albeit low-level—political nationalist activity in Cornwall for over a half a century,[9] the existence of Cornish nationalism can still be routinely questioned, ignored or denied. Claims for a Cornish assembly are also dismissed with invocations of a feared domino effect as Devon, Dorset and Rutland all follow suit. The power of the 'Cornwall as English county' discourse thus has major implications for what are seen as practical policy options and poses considerable difficulties for those who think outside its assumptions.

This alerts us to two more aspects of discourses. First, they are engaged in a struggle for meanings. If the meaning of Cornwall can be fixed as 'English county' then the process of loss of decision-making eastwards and the re-centralization that accompanies south west regionalization becomes easier to accept. Second, discourses possess different power resources. Bourdieu has called discourses such as that of 'flexibility' an example of a 'strong discourse', a discourse backed by the strength of banks, multinational companies, politicians and other discourses such as neo-liberalism.[10] In similar fashion, 'Cornwall as English county' is a 'strong discourse', backed by the media, the education system, government and by everyday processes such as counterurbanisation and population change.

All this does not mean, of course, that society is 'just' about discourse. One of the criticisms of post-structuralist approaches is precisely that: that 'reality' is denied and everything is reduced to language, or discourse. The implication is that if we say or write something, the world can become the thing we write or say. If we wake up one morning and believe we are Chinese, Basque or Cornish we will be Chinese, Basque or Cornish. Obviously things are not so simple. Even poststructuralists usually accept that there is such a thing as reality and that language cannot on its own easily change that reality. But they also make the point that we can only access reality through language. It is only by the use of words that we know, or are told, that we are Chinese or Basque or Cornish. While some hermeneutical approaches might deny this role of language, substituting experience for feeling, for a social scientist language is clearly unavoidable when describing and explaining 'reality'. Discourse analysts differ among themselves concerning the role they give to this linguistic structuring of 'reality'. For some, such as Laclau and Mouffe, discourse is stretched to encompass all material practices. Thus the economy is analysed as a set of discursive practices, an economy of signs and symbols.[11] However, as we shall see, not all discourse analysis denies a distinction between discourse/language on the one hand and material processes and practices on the other.

So far, I have written of linguistic 'structures' and of discourses as competing or complementary structures. But this may lead to an over-determinist view of discourses. For, while making up a structure at any given point in time, discourses are also temporary and contingent; they comprise possible networks of meaning but never necessary networks and are always potentially open to change. Possibly the most valuable insight of post-structuralism is that meanings are never permanent but always potentially unstable. A brief backwards glance at Cornish history might illustrate this. In the early nineteenth century the Cornish were described as a dynamic, innovative and industrious people at the forefront of technological change.[12] But this structure of meaning, while fixed for a period in the nineteenth century, changed so that by the late twentieth century, the Cornish were being viewed as undynamic, besotted with the 'dreckly' syndrome and contrasted—explicitly or implicitly—with 'dynamic' incomers. Discourses of the Cornish have clearly changed considerably over the past two hundred years: former meanings have been destabilized and new meanings attached, only perhaps to be discarded in turn.

This potential instability is produced in practice through *parole*, the actual process of language use. While we, as agents, make use of language that comes to us as a structure, with pre-given rules and constraints that we cannot entirely ignore, we also have some opportunity to use that structure in different ways, to re-negotiate existing meanings and to attach new ones. Discourses are, in other words, always to some extent malleable. I say 'to some extent' because our ability as agents to change the meanings of discourses, particularly 'strong' discourses, is clearly limited by a variety of social positioning: such as our ethnicity, gender, place of residence, educational background, class, status, or institutional location.

HOW DO DISCOURSES WORK?

We have seen that discourses are aspects of the linguistic construction of the world, doors of perception through which we access and construct reality. But how does discourse work? Laclau and Mouffe provide various concepts with which we can model discourse in practice. This might best be illustrated visually.

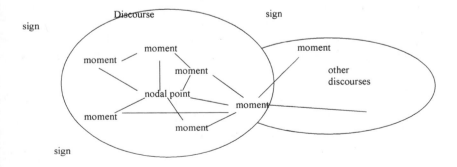

Language is composed of signs—words or groups of words. But these signs are empty until contrasted with other signs. For example the word *kye* in the Cornish language is meaningless until we know that it equates to 'dog' in English. But what is a dog? Dog takes on its meaning through contrast with cat or horse. Similarly *kye* gains meaning in relation to *cath* or *marth*. For Laclau and Mouffe particular meanings emerge when signs are linked to other signs within discourses, and then they become 'moments'. These moments articulate with each other. Thus within the 'tourist' discourse of Cornwall, the sign 'Celtic' becomes a moment attached to 'romance', 'tradition', 'King Arthur', 'standing stones', 'jewellery' and so on. But within a discourse of Cornish nationalism, 'Celtic' may resonate rather differently, articulating with 'rebellion', 'internationalism' and 'language', amongst other moments. The nodal point of a discourse is that privileged sign around which others crystallize. In the 'neo-liberal' discourse, 'market' is the privileged sign; in a 'Cornish nationalist' discourse, 'Cornish nation' becomes the privileged sign.

Discourses attempt to transform signs that are outside their boundaries into the moments of a discourse, articulating them with other signs and achieving a degree of closure, putting a temporary stop to the fluctuating meanings of signs. Thus, in a 'tourist' discourse of Cornwall, the sign 'romantic' is linked to 'Cornwall' in order to achieve 'romantic Cornwall', a moment that then articulates with other moments such as standing stones, cliffs, deserted engine houses, Tintagel and so forth, so that this relationship begins to appear naturalized, to be taken for granted. The signifier Cornwall then becomes inevitably and invariably associated with romance. However, this signifier remains a floating one, subject to different meanings in different discourses and at the core of a struggle between discourses to establish meaning. The way that different discourses define the same signs in differing ways can therefore become a subject of investigation. We might thus identify a 'south west regional' discourse, which positions 'Cornwall' differently, accepting some moments, such as 'rural' or 'romance', but excluding others such as 'nation'.

To sum up, discourses are systems with which we represent the world. They can be analysed semiotically (how their language is articulated and how meanings are made). Furthermore, this semiosis 'has real effects on social practice, social institutions and the social order more generally'.[14] It is thus 'performative'; people and groups act out the consequences of discourses in real life, taking actions on the basis of the discourse they use to understand the world. For example, if one summer a number of accidents at strategic points on the A30 produced a major gridlock on Cornwall's main roads, this could be explained by means of a number of discourses. It could be seen as an act of God, or as the result of the lack of sufficient road space, or as the effect of population growth and tourism, or as the result of longer-term changes in transport and the growth of car ownership and mobility. Each discourse carries its own policy implications. For the first, there might be little to do but pray; for the second the answer would be to build more roads; the third implies policies that result in more sustainable development and an alternative to tourism, and the final discourse might look to broader policies necessary to change life-styles and make us less dependent on road travel.

But there remains the question of how far discourses can be bracketed off, or separated, from those 'social practices, social institutions and the social order more generally'. For some discourse analysts, such as Laclau and Mouffe, everything is a discursive practice and everything is mediated by language. Cornwall's roads may be jammed with traffic but we can only understand that congestion through using one discourse or another. Others demur. For them distinctions can be made between the semiotic order of discourse and other social practices that cannot just be analysed discursively. Laclau and Mouffe's approach to discourse, for these analysts, remains linguistically reductionist and underplays the non-discursive constraints on discourse.

WHAT IS CRITICAL DISCOURSE ANALYSIS?
The brand of discourse analysis that retains an opening towards broader social theory is critical discourse analysis (CDA), especially that of Norman Fairclough, and this is the social theory that might offer particular methodological appeal for those seeking a critical Cornish Studies.[15]

For Fairclough, discourses do help to constitute the social world but they are also themselves constituted by wider social practices. There is, therefore, a dialectical relationship between discourse and society. In adopting this approach CDA steers a course between those who claim that discourses arise from the material world and are, to a varying extent, unproblematical representations of that social world, and those who claim that everything is discursive, including material practices. Instead discourse can only be analysed within its broader, though not determining, social context.

CDA also offers a model for analysing discourses. Discourse has three dimensions. First, there is a communicative event, for example a written text, interview, speech, visual image, or newspaper article, during which the discourse is actively reproduced and sometimes transformed at the micro-level. Second, we find an order of discourse. The latter comprises the semiotic order, defined as the network of social practices within which the text is located. There is for example an order of discourse of the academy, or an order of discourse of the media.[16] Orders of discourse contribute to social relations, reproduce systems of knowledge and help to construct social identities. For Fairclough this means that discourse has a relational function, an ideational function and an identity function. An order of discourse can be conceptualized in turn as containing particular discourses, genres and styles. We have seen that discourses are the ways we represent the world. Genres are ways of acting and interacting with other people by speech or writing or other forms of communication. For example, the interview is a characteristic genre of the order of discourse of the media. Styles or voices are the ways of identifying or constructing the self, both individually and as part of social or institutional identities. Thus there appears to be a particular style of Cornish patriotism that entails bedecking oneself with symbols: tartan ties and caps, St Piran's flags, black and gold articles of clothing and so on. Finally, discourse is never just text, but is also context; there is a broader aspect of social structuration within which or together with which we can place the orders of discourse.

Practically, this all means that communicative events have three levels of analysis—the text, the discursive practice and the social practice. Analysis might proceed along all three levels. For example, in 2004 Cornwall Arts Marketing (partly funded by Objective One money) collaborated with the *Guardian* newspaper to produce a special supplement on 'Cornwall's creative scene', or artistic sector. This put forward a discourse of artistic culture in Cornwall, attempting to promote this culture as a dynamic aspect of Cornwall's future; 'artists have the potential to be an economic engine of Cornwall's future'.[17] The supplement—the communicative event—might be analysed in a number of ways.

First, we could focus on the way it uses language, the grammar and metaphors it employs, the sentences it constructs. At the level of the text we could, for example, investigate transitivity, how events are connected. Does the document use passive or active forms of sentences, does it mask agency? Thus it is stated that artists are 'struggling to work in a county with soaring property prices'.[18] Soaring property prices appear to be a natural event with no obvious cause, a bit like the weather. By nominalizing the phrase 'soaring property prices', no agent is directly implicated in the process. Yet rising prices are separated textually from mention of the 'increasingly affluent visitors who now see Cornwall as a fashionable holiday destination'.[19] The agency of those visitors who then decide to use their greater economic resources to buy property in Cornwall is thus masked and the indirect role of cultural tourism in generating higher property prices is also rendered indistinct and unavailable for discussion.[20] Or we could probe its modality; the degree of affiliation there is to statements made. Are claims made as if they are expressions of the truth or is there some hedging? Discussing surfing culture, a gallery owner in Newquay claims, 'it really is laid back down here'.[21] This is a statement made in the form of a truth claim, asserting the laid-backness of Cornwall, rather than expressing this more tentatively, as by saying 'sometimes we can begin to believe it's really laid back down here'.

Second, we could focus on its discursive practice, on the origins of the assumptions and ideas in it, on the processes of its production and consumption, on its links to other discourses, such as the discourse of 'neo-liberalism' or 'Cornwall as English county'. The 'down here' phrase used by the gallery owner betrays a naturalized and taken-for-granted view of Cornwall as periphery, as somewhere 'on the edge', as does the very title of the supplement—'Living on the Edge'. Other discourses interact and inform the 'artistic culture' discourse. For example, the Principal of Falmouth College of Art is quoted as saying 'the current debate requires institutions to connect with this really strong tradition of cultural activity'.[22] This statement would seem to bring the artistic discourse close to the demands of the campaigners for a Cornish Assembly. However, the same interviewee is also quoted elsewhere as saying 'the south-west region has more arts practitioners per head than any other part of Britain apart from London, and within that region Cornwall is the hotspot'.[23] The 'Cornwall as English county' discourse here combines with the discourse of 'English regionalization' to put implied constraints on the sort of institutions that Cornwall might require.

In probing the assumptions of the text, gaps could also be identified. The director of Tate St Ives is reported as seeing 'a natural difference between the approach of artists who are drawn to live in the rural south-west of England and that of the ultra-hip art crowd in London'.[24] As well as being replete with discursive modalities—is the London art crowd really 'ultra-hip'?—and dominant discourses, for example of 'deep rurality' and 'English regionalization', this phrase also constructs two groups: those who come to live in Cornwall and those who stay in London. In doing so, it ignores a third group, those who were born and/or grew up in Cornwall and choose to stay in (or come back to) Cornwall. This is even more striking as in its earlier pages the supplement makes great play of the role of a 'revitalised sense of Cornish identity and pride' and of native-born artists.[25]

Finally, we might identify the social practice to which the artistic discourse belongs, using wider social theory, for example relating to cultural governance or, more generally, to cultural studies theories, that would allow us to relate it to other practices and to other fields. Here, we might be drawn to sociological theories about sub-cultures, or to economic approaches to regeneration and theoretical takes on the relationship between economics and culture, or perhaps political models such as network analysis, that would direct our attention towards the networks of individuals, groups, institutions, quangos and government departments that sustain the arts sector in Cornwall and in the south west of England.

For the critical discourse analyst all texts draw on particular social and institutional practices as different discourses and genres are articulated together. This interdiscursivity, a form of intertextuality (of relying on and being influenced by a chain of already existing texts) provides the space in which change occurs. Discursive transformations happen when combinations of discourses are used creatively and when discourses are articulated in new ways. For example, the South West Regional Development Agency (SWRDA) and the South West Regional Assembly (SWRA) have spent thousands of pounds on a South West England Brand Centre.[26] This body is engaged in discursive work, creating a logo, images, narrative, even a 'tone of voice' for businesses in the 'south west' of England to 'talk the same language and begin a conversation with people about the story of South West England'.[27] In doing so discourses are being stitched together to try to create something new. Thus a 'neo-liberal' discourse of global competitiveness is articulated with a traditional 'tourist industry' discourse and a discourse of regionalization. And other discourses are in turn joined onto these. For example, the South West England Brand Centre's website informs us sagely that the preferred 'tone of voice' for talking about the south west should be 'plain speech with attitude . . . we use (polite) slang expressions like "party on".[28] This somewhat desperate effort to combine neo-liberalism with a version of retro-1980s Californian surfer dude discourse also indicates that it is one thing to combine discourses, another thing altogether for the new meanings to become successfully fixed. It is at this point that we would need to turn to social theory to assess the constraints and opportunities for such a newly configured discourse.

In what sense critical?
In the previous example I came close to the 'critical' aspect of CDA. Broadly, CDA has been described as taking up social questions, exploring how changes take place at a micro-level and 'how discourse figures in relation to other social elements in processes of social or institutional change'.[29] But it is with regard to what questions are taken

up, and why, that the critical element of CDA enters into things. For CDA aims 'to uncover the role of discursive practice in the maintenance of unequal power relations, with the overall goal of harnessing the results of critical discourse analysis to the struggle for radical social change'.[30] It focuses on those representations and constructions of social groups which have detrimental consequences for those groups, on how these representations are constructed and the role they play in furthering the interests of certain groups.[31] In common with other deconstructionist social analysis 'an important discourse analytical aim is to unmask and delineate taken-for-granted, common-sense understandings, transforming them into potential objects for discussion and criticism and, thus, open to change'.[32] Returning to my earlier example, if Cornwall is seen unproblematically as an English county, then this will have consequences for demands for constitutional change and for devolution of decision-making to a Cornish level. But if that representation is deconstructed and revealed as a historical construct then it is potentially opened up for discussion and debate.

It is in this sense that CDA is not 'neutral' but is committed to social change through opening up possibilities. Fairclough argues that people have a right to know what insights discourses give them, what insights they are cut off from, whose discourse it is, what they gain (or lose) from its use, what other discourses are available and how dominant discourses have become so dominant.[33] This knowledge makes it easier to manage change, endowing individuals with the potential for greater agency and empowering them as citizens.

However, in taking this stance CDA at times skirts close to the argument that insists that there is a 'truth' out there; thus we are informed that CDA is concerned with 'truth, truthfulness and appropriateness of texts, their production, and their interpretation'.[34] At other times the word 'misrepresentations' is used. At first glance, this does not look to be too far away from approaches such as the ideology critique favoured by Marxist-influenced social theorists of the 1970s. Ideology critique sees language as masking reality. The reality is then revealed by the social researcher, armed with expert knowledge (Marxist theory) unavailable to the ordinary person. But social constructionists have heavily criticized this position. According to discourse theory, the elevated observer can only exchange one discourse for another, as the inevitably discursive construction of 'reality' makes the latter unattainable. Adopting this social constructionist stance, it is difficult to see how one construction can be 'truer' than another because there is no point outside discourse from which to evaluate or critique individual discourses. Critics of discourse analysis regularly point to this peril of 'relativism', where there is no single truth, but where all statements are the result of historical and social positioning.

Perhaps a search for the 'truth' is too ambitious an aim. Embracing a degree of relativism, CDA has nevertheless been described as adopting a modified ideology critique, one where discourses are more or less ideological, depending on how far they contribute to relations of domination and give distorted representations of reality.[35] However, access to the truth is not viewed as a (social) scientific privilege. The aim is rather more modest than the definition of truth; as we have seen it is instead to 'denaturalize . . . taken-for-granted understandings of reality',[36] and in doing so to expose new areas to political debate, one in which any citizen has the right to be involved and to be heard, not just the researcher.

But which discourses and what understandings of reality are we to deconstruct? Taken-for-granted or naturalized discourses, the ones most urgently in need of deconstruction, are exactly those discourses the researcher may not think of as problems. CDA in itself gives little guidance on which discourses are the best candidates for deconstruction, other than those that maintain unequal power relations, which leaves the potential field of research fairly wide open. However, while CDA of itself might not direct us, Cornish Studies can. Concerned with Cornwall and its people, a critical Cornish Studies could, without much difficulty, identify a number of discourses for deconstruction, some of which have already been mentioned here, such as those of 'regionalization', of 'romantic Cornwall', of 'Cornwall as English county'. There are also discourses endemic to policy-makers, such as those of 'regeneration', 'sustainability' and 'community'. These, trotted out casually and almost never closely examined, would benefit from some sustained critical analysis. Other taken-for-granted discourses, such as 'Celtic Cornwall', could also be candidates for deconstruction. And Cornish Studies also provides the standpoint from which to critique these discourses. This is unmistakeably a critique from the periphery.

It is feminist research that here comes tantalisingly close to Cornish Studies research. Some feminists have argued that, as women are an overlooked group, their peripheral position viz-a-viz an androcentric centre means that their research is bound to be normative, criticising that which oppresses women. This has led to the emergence of feminist standpoint theory.[37] From this perspective women's experiences, to a degree outside or peripheral to that society, provide the standpoint from which to research a patriarchal society. In parallel, it has been proposed that 'ethnic minorities' can also 'on the basis of experience, deliver standpoints from which the dominant understandings can be identified and criticised'.[38]

This sounds familiar to those of us working in the Cornish Studies field, where otherwise naturalized discourses, such as those of 'English regionalization' or 'English nationalism', automatically present themselves as problems. However, Jørgensen and Phillips point out that standpoint theory comes with its own health warnings.[39] One is that it constructs the world in terms of us and them, in the process homogenizing the oppressed group and underplaying differences among that group. This is exactly the aspect of Cornish Studies that I have already indicated that we need consciously to move away from, from an over-determined 'Cornwall' to a sensitivity towards differing 'Cornwalls'.[40] The distinction between a 'them' and an 'us' also requires resisting as it can reproduce the naturalized distinctions of the centre and other simplistic categories of dominant discourses (categorization clearly evident in the occasional Cornish versus English bunfights that break out in the letters pages of the local press— exhilarating in their way but doing little to move debate beyond stereotyped ethnic battle lines).[41]

Standpoint theory, research from a situated position to some extent outside structures of domination, provides the Cornish Studies researcher with a position from which to view the world critically. But this healthy scepticism towards the taken-for-granted discourses of the metropolitan centre needs to be coupled with a strong reflexivity, an awareness of our own cultural and social location. Furthermore, it should not prevent us from trying to work across difference. For instance, research on the discourse of Englishness and its consequences in constructing Cornishness should not be confined to the external. It would have to embrace the Englishness within Cornishness and the Englishness within all of us (to some degree). For a discourse of Cornishness has clearly overlapped, sometimes considerably, with a discourse of Englishness, an under-stressed yet central aspect of the Cornish identity in terms of understanding its difference from other British identities. CDA, however, can allow us to isolate the role of discursive practice, denaturalize the moments and articulations of that discourse, uncover the processes that determine its meaning and as a result empower individuals by yielding knowledge which opens up the space for discussion. In Cornwall such space often appears especially constricted and stifled as a result of the lack of a critical public domain and the institutional vacuum that allows taken-for-granted discourses to thrive in unquestioned luxury.

CDA METHOD AND ITS PROBLEMS
But, moving from the level of principle to that of practice, how do we actually go about CDA? The challenge of CDA research is to 'analyse

empirically the many ways in which [a discourse] is constituted, reproduced and modified within the very process of communication'.[42]
Through an iterative analysis, moving between linguistic analysis and
wider social theory, the aim is to 'find out how the world (or aspects of
it) is ascribed meaning discursively and what social consequences this
has'.[43]

To do this CDA imports a method of explanatory critique from
critical realism.[44] This posits four stages. The first is to identify a
problem, for example this could be the process of top-down regionalization that defines the space open to Cornish decision-making. The
second stage is to identify the network of social practices that gives rise
to this. This would involve isolating the peak regional institutions (such
as Government Office South West, SWRDA and the SWRA) and
identifying the discourse of regionalization and of Cornwall that
is reproduced within those institutions.[45] Thirdly, we can consider
whether the problem sustains the system and if so, how. Who gains
from the process of regionalization? And finally, the researcher
identifies the possibilities of overcoming the problem. In traversing
these four stages the researcher moves between linguistic analysis of
texts, their production and reception, social theory relevant to their
context and the institutional practices that give rise to them.

There are, of course, weaknesses associated with CDA, just as
there are with any form of social theory; areas under-conceptualized,
gaps unaddressed. For example, the distinction between discursive
and non-discursive practices, the way they connect and the way we
differentiate between them remains somewhat unclear in practice.
CDA also stands accused of a weak understanding of group formation
and agency.[46] In relation to this, although CDA directs attention to
research on both the production and consumption of texts, the weight
of research has in fact tended to be placed on the production of texts,
rather than their consumption. And yet in consuming texts, agents
always have the possibility of re-negotiating, to a degree, meanings
of discourses. An analysis that avoids this potential re-negotiation
remains in danger of adopting an over-structural approach to
discourse.

CONCLUSION

Fairclough has claimed that everyday life has become more textually
mediated and that people's lives are increasingly shaped by
representations produced elsewhere, affecting 'even who they are and
how they [should] see themselves'.[47] While now generalized, this is a
familiar process for Cornwall and its people. From the rebellious
periphery of the sixteenth century through the super-loyal royalism of

the later seventeenth century, the West Barbary of the eighteenth, the representations of the Newlyn School of the late nineteenth, and the tourist-business-induced imagery and romantic novelists of the twentieth century, Cornwall has been awash with metaphors and buffeted by a veritable storm of signifiers. Both Cornwall and the Cornish people have been and are being discursively constructed in a number of often conflicting ways. The result is a confusing kaleidoscope through which 'real' Cornwalls are glimpsed only hazily and intermittently.

However, these discursive constructions make Cornwall particularly suitable for the application of CDA. CDA could be employed both to deconstruct historical representations and narratives and contemporary discourses of Cornwall. It could also generate reflection on some of our own foundational myths, opening up the space for a discussion of alternatives. Moreover, in terms of the content of a Cornish Studies research agenda, its implications are profound. For, if discourses are produced elsewhere then that 'elsewhere' has also to enter the frame of analysis. This demands that researchers raise their eyes beyond Cornwall while at the same time, to avoid the problem of over-homogenizing Cornwall, remain sensitive to differences within it. Furthermore, in its call for a dialectic between detailed textual analysis and social theory, CDA would appear to meet the multidisciplinary or multiperspectival aims of the 'new' Cornish Studies, as well as those I have previously offered in *Cornish Studies: Ten*. CDA could thus act as a unifying approach for a critical Cornish Studies, bringing the rhetoric of the 'new' Cornish Studies together with a critical practice and providing a methodology to match its preferred content.

NOTES AND REFERENCES

1. Malcolm Williams, 'The New Cornish Social Science', in Philip Payton (ed.), *Cornish Studies: Ten*, Exeter, 2002, p. 61.
2. Bernard Deacon, 'In Search of the Missing "Turn": The Spatial Dimension and Cornish Studies', in Philip Payton (ed.), *Cornish Studies: Eight*, Exeter, 2000, pp. 213–30.
3. Bernard Deacon, 'The New Cornish Studies: New Discipline or Rhetorically Defined Space?', in Philip Payton (ed.), *Cornish Studies: Ten*, Exeter, 2002, pp. 24–43.
4. This turn from Cornwall to Cornwalls is being reflected in the work of the Cornish Audio Visual Archive and Cornish Communities research programmes at the Institute of Cornish Studies.
5. Norman Fairclough, Bob Jessop and Andrew Sayer, 'Critical Realism and Semiosis', *Journal of Critical Realism*, 5.1, 2002, 2–10.
6. Ernesto Laclau and Chantal Mouffe, *Hegemony and Socialist Strategy: Towards a Radical Democratic Politics*, London, 1985.

7. Here, research in Cornwall lags well behind that in other places, such as Brittany. See Ronan Le Coadic, *L'identité Bretonne*, Rennes, 1998 for an in-depth ethnographic study of attitudes of Bretons to their culture and identity.

8. The following account draws heavily on Marianne Jørgensen and Louise Phillips, *Discourse Analysis as Theory and Method*, London, 2002, an excellent introduction to what can often seem an impenetrable and jargon-laden area of study.

9. See Bernard Deacon, Dick Cole and Garry Tregidga, *Mebyon Kernow and Cornish Nationalism*, Cardiff, 2003.

10. Pierre   Bourdieu,   'L'Essence   du   Neo-Liberalisme',   *Le   Monde Diplomatique*, March 1998.

11. For a non-poststructuralist text that seems to make similar assumptions see Scott Lash and John Urry, *Economies of Signs and Space*, London, 1994.

12. For an example see J.D.Tuckett, *A History of the Past and Present State of the Labouring Population, volume 2*, London, 1846, pp. 536–7.

13. And for an example of this see Cornwall County Council's contribution to the *European Development Fund, County of Cornwall: A National Programme of Community Interest 1988–1991*, Brussels, 1987, para 1.2.8.

14. Fairclough *et al.*, 2002.

15. Norman Fairclough, *Language and Power*, London, 1989; *Critical Discourse Analysis: The Critical Study of Language*, London, 1995; Lilie Chouliaraki and Norman Fairclough, *Discourse in late Modernity: Rethinking Critical Discourse Analysis*, Edinburgh, 1999.

16. Norman Fairclough, Simon Pardoe and Bronislaw Szerszynski, 'Critical Discourse Analysis and Citizenship', in A. Bora and H. Hausendorf (eds), *Constructing Citizenship*, Amsterdam, 2003.

17. *Guardian, Living on the Edge*, 12 June 2004, p. 13.

18. *Guardian*, 2004, p. 13.

19. *Guardian*, 2004, p. 11.

20. Imagine the different meaning produced if the sentence were constructed actively: 'increasingly affluent visitors now see Cornwall as a fashionable holiday destination and those who buy second homes help make property prices soar'.

21. *Guardian*, 2004, p. 14.

22. *Guardian*, 2004, p. 11.

23. *Guardian*, 2004, p. 10.

24. *Guardian*, 2004, p. 13.

25. *Guardian*, 2004, p. 3.

26. South West England Brand Centre, 'Welcome to the South West England Brand Centre'; available at http://www.southwestbrand.info. Accessed 23 December 2003.

27. South West England Brand Centre, 'Tone of Voice Guidelines'; available   at   http://www.southwestbrand.info/guidelines/tone-of-voice/index. Accessed 23 December 2003.

28. South West England Brand Centre, 'Tone of Voice Guidelines'.

29. Fairclough *et al.*, 2003.
30. Jørgensen and Phillips, 2002, p. 64.
31. Norman Fairclough, 'Global Capitalism and Critical Awareness of Language', *Language Awareness* 8.2, 1999, 71–83.
32. Jørgensen and Phillips, 2002, p. 178.
33. Fairclough, 1999.
34. Fairclough *et al.*, 2002.
35. Jørgensen and Phillips, 2002, p. 181.
36. Jørgensen and Phillips, 2002, p. 185.
37. Dorothy Smith, *The Everyday World as Problematic: A Feminist Sociology*, Boston, 1987.
38. Jørgensen and Phillips, 2002, p. 192.
39. Jørgensen and Phillips, 2002, pp. 192–93.
40. Deacon, 2002. For an example of work within the Cornish Studies field that shows this sensitivity see Amy Hale, 'Whose Celtic Cornwall? The Ethnic Cornish meet Celtic Spirituality', and Alan Kent, 'Celtic Nirvanas: Constructions of Celtic in Contemporary British Youth Culture', in David Harvey, Rhys Jones, Neil McInroy and Christine Milligan (eds), *Celtic Geographies: Old culture, New Times*, London, 2002, pp. 157–70 and pp. 208–26.
41. See for example *West Briton*, 13 May, 20 May, 27 May 2004.
42. Fairclough *et.al.*, 2003.
43. Jørgensen and Phillips, 2002, p. 145.
44. For critical realism see Andrew Collier, *Critical Realism*, London, 1994.
45. For a preliminary analysis of the role of the peak institutions of the new regionalization see Bernard Deacon, 'Under Construction: Culture and Regional Formation in South-west England', *European Urban and Regional Studies* 11(3), 2004, pp. 213–25.
46. Jørgensen and Phillips, 2002, p. 90.
47. Fairclough, 1999.

PUTTING THE KITSCH INTO KERNOW

Jonathan Howlett

INTRODUCTION

New Cornish Studies has over the last few years developed a solid underpinning of theoretical knowledge to support a wide field of enquiry. It is by adopting the various models of Cornwall that have thus emerged, that investigations such as that conducted in this article can be moved forward. Numerous visual images of Cornwall have been produced during the last hundred years, and a selection is examined here. They correspond closely, it is argued, to the models of Cornwall that have emerged from recent research. It is intended, therefore, that this article should contribute to and further stimulate debate on how 'the visual image' contributes to the cultural climate of Cornwall today. The main contention is that much of this visual material has been manipulated into forms that can best be described as 'kitsch'. As a result of this process, the way in which the Cornish see themselves and are seen by others has been profoundly altered—and not always for the better.

'Seeing' has a primacy in our ways of understanding that it is easy to overlook in our contemporary culture, with its overt dependency on language. Our eyes come first as a means of processing complex conscious and unconscious acquisition of information. Language is something painfully and methodically learned to give meaning to that information. Examination of how profoundly this process and its results influence how we act, think, vote, and view our prospects is something that should be of consuming interest to us all. Failure to acknowledge this influence on our lives can have far-reaching effects on how we perceive ourselves and on how we reach decisions about our lives and community. One way to model such a concept is to refer to the work of the film set designer. A vital element of his or her task is to ensure that just before the 'take' the set is 'dressed'. Mostly it is assumed that this process is to make the illusion convincing for the audience, and indeed that is one aim of the process. But another is to aid the actors in developing characterization. Nothing is left to chance when it comes to sustaining the illusion of reality for actors and audience. This kind of visual material is mostly absorbed at an unconscious level by the brain via the normal pathway from the eye. What if there were other visual pathways of which we have little or no conscious awareness? How might these affect our overall visual model of our environment? Just such possibilities were outlined by Professor V. Ramachandran in the Reith Lectures for 2003.[1] Such research is only in its infancy and to make great claims would be premature. It would appear, however, that there is emerging evidence of a scientific nature that will enable visual artists and image makers to support the case for visual information being a major—if not *the* major—shaper of social and cultural identity.

KITSCH AND KERNOW

Two important points should be noted about the place of kitsch, the first being in the political sphere. Kitsch has always been seen by some critics as a throwaway item, something not to be taken seriously. But it should only take a little reflection to see that the use of kitsch to manipulate serious culture can have long-lasting results. One that springs to mind is the 'entkitsching' of German culture by the Nazis in the 1930s. So effective was this that some seventy years later the playing of Wagner's music in Israel is still a matter of bitter debate.

The second factor is that in the last few years serious academic attention has been paid to kitsch: in particular in major publications by Tomas Kulka and Celeste Olalquiaga. The great power inherent in kitsch, they argue, is its ability to reduce genuine sensation and sentiment to a tawdry cheapness and to replace 'the subtlety and ambiguity of art with instantly recognisable stereotypes'.[2] The apologists of kitsch defend it on the grounds of its mass availability and democratic accessibility. Such a defence is intended to disarm opposition by labelling it 'elitist' before debate can be initiated. Tomas Kulka makes no pretence of trying to defend attacks on kitsch against the charge of elitism. According to him: '[t]he term has its established use; it denotes objects that have widely popular appeal, yet despite this are considered bad by the art-educated elite.'[3] He argues that value judgements are part of a culture's way of setting its own internal standards, and that they have a great deal to do with competence. Kitsch is in fact something that is 'done' to the consumer by its makers and purveyors. Validation of kitsch by its consumption can only be sustained as long as people continue to believe in its value.

'Kitsch hustles . . . the manner and razzle dazzle of presentation'[4] but it lacks substance, much like the 'Cool Britannia' art of the 1990s. Walter Benjamin identified the consumerisation of culture and fine art as a destructive force in 1936, though he eschewed the word kitsch. In Benjamin's view endless copying and repetition of an original work erodes its 'aura', the magical sense of being in the presence of something profound and truly meaningful. In the 1960s the original marble statue of Michelangelo's David resided quietly in the Accedemia in Florence where it could be viewed in quiet solitude. Today the same room heaves with cultural pilgrims all getting their 'quick fix', in Benjamin's terms, a huge degradation of the experience possible when confronted by such a work.

1. *This fridge magnet with its camp appearance is the epitomy of kitsch in the terms of Kulka's definition: it degrades the image by repetition and by subverting its meaning. The serious intent, what Benjamin called the 'aura', is stripped away by this transformation. (author's collection)*

In 1967 the *Book of Kells* was displayed in a simple wooden display case in a quiet foyer in Trinity College Dublin. Today a multi-million-Euro business herds a crocodile of reverential pilgrims into the darkness where they have two minutes to shuffle solemnly round the bomb-proof, climate-controlled case housing the 'heritage icon'. Outside, of course, the visitors can buy an endless amount of trivia as souvenirs. Kitsch's 'instantly recognizable stereotypes' need no explanation; their visual impact says it all.

Olalquiaga identifies melancholy and nostalgia as defining emotions of kitsch. Peter Wollen in his review of her book challenges the hypothesis, asking: '[h]ow certain can we be that the emotional triggers of melancholy and nostalgia are as distinct . . . as she claims'.[5] Indeed, nostalgia would seem always to be tinged with melancholy: Olalquiaga describes melancholy as essentially the 'shattered and dispersed' remnants of memory, along with a dismissal of the past as any sort of perfection and a looking to the future 'not yet within grasp.'[6] Kulka places a new condition on defining repetition in kitsch: '[k]itsch imitations involve distortion.'[7] This may hold true in the case of mass-produced souvenirs, but it is not so true where the repeated image is achieved by photographic means. For example, the reproduction of one of Walter Langley's fine portrait heads of Newlyn fishermen on a beer bottle label with the marketing name of 'Strong Sou'Wester' turns the Langley painting into kitsch by usage and context without distortion. It is this sort of usage that has taken some cultures, Cornish among them, to the verge of becoming a simplistic simulation of themselves.

It was increasingly clear as the nineteenth century drew to a close that the Cornish mining industry had little hope of widespread or sustained revival, and that the fishing industry was also endangered. The sheer lack of other choices or resources after the First World War ensured that the tourist trade was an option gladly seized upon by one and all, from leading Cornish figures to those who hoped to be able to let the spare room to visitors from June to September. 'Selling Cornwall' was the thing to do, from the publicity department of the Great Western Railway to the local town clerk. The means of that selling was to trade upon the past, the romantic past, the brave heroic past and the tranquil past, untouched by shells and barbed wire. One effect of selling that past to the visitor was that the people themselves began to see it as 'the way we were', and the only way they could be. Taking visitors on a fishing trip meant one had to continue to act like a fisherman, even if all one really did was to take visitors on fishing trips. Elsewhere, others had to elaborate a quasi-medieval Celtic and mysterious past, a supposed reflection of what had been the 'real Cornwall'. Above all, the tourists were to be given what they wanted.

This may have been a successful tactic in the development of the tourist industry but, then as now, it was hardly a positive strategy for the future when adopted by the community as a whole. In their important examination of the heritage aspect of the tourist industry in Cornwall, Kennedy and Kingcome[8] offer remarkably similar analyses to those proposed by Kulka. 'Kitsch always means what it says', writes Kulka, 'and says it literally. There are no two ways of reading kitsch. (Once kitsch is interpreted ironically, or as a parody, it ceases to be kitsch.)'[9] Kennedy and Kingcome add: 'historical reality is reduced to fragmentary images, which are the visual equivalent of sound-bites. These replications and reproductions are without humour. They are adopted in all seriousness, brimming with verisimilitude and an apparently convincing dedication to truth'.[10] This 'seriousness' in replication is potentially devastating, locating 'Cornishness' in a world of nostalgic kitsch such as that described by Olalquiaga, where cultural fossils become the fetish objects of an imaginary contemporary culture. She describes this nostalgic kitsch as essentially 'bad' kitsch, 'unable to leave the past, it is trapped in a re-creation that fails to engage or transform'.[11] The re-creation does not of course have to be as literal as the Poldark or Geevor mining theme parks; it may well be the imagined re-creation of the fishing industry when confronted by the 'realism' of the Newlyn School paintings.

In determining the kitsch quality of the commercial images, the seriousness of their purpose must not be underestimated, even if in a wiser and more cynical world we can see how inflated or distorted some of the messages are. In particular the publicity departments of the railway companies that sold the Cornish Riviera had a very serious intent, to sell tickets and thereby bring holidaymakers to Cornwall. The degree of negotiation with town councils meant that consideration had to be given to local sensibilities in the production of some of the railway posters and other literature. Even if the images were in one sense 'idealized', everyone had to some extent to believe in or identify with the images offered, and thus collude in the realization of the ideal for the visitor. This raises the issue of just how much did the Cornish really believe in the kitsch simulation that was on offer to then, and indeed to what extent do they today? Just how many of the images created—then or now—have a tongue-in-cheek element that in Kulka's terms would disqualify them from classification as kitsch? But even if a self-mocking irony is readily apparent to the Cornish, what if this is not detected by the in-coming consumer: do the images become kitsch all over again? Certainly, there is an undercurrent of subversive meaning in many of the images presented today, and the Cornish do seem to take pleasure in mocking both the visitor and the stock images of themselves as presented to the visitor.

Much more ambivalent are the sort of early kitsch attractions that have themselves now become part of the history of tourism and of cultural misappropriation. Glasscock's King Arthur's Great Hall is the best Cornish example here. That it was kitsch is not difficult to establish. The outwardly sincere belief that Glasscock held in his project confirms it as being kitsch, even if his private motivation may have been less high-minded. Now the Great Hall has become an attraction in its own right as a museum of 1920s' kitsch, worthy for preservation as part of the heritage industry.

EXAMINING THE FISH CELLAR

The representation of a key marker of Cornish culture—the fishing industry of west Cornwall and its communities—by sophisticated in-migrant painters in the late nineteenth century has been an important element of Cornish self awareness ever since. The importance of the fishing industry in Cornwall was sufficiently great in nineteenth-century perceptions that the Cornish coat of arms has as one of its supporters a sou-wester clad fisherman. Such prominent symbolic usage of a fisherman indicates the conscious awareness in the community of the vital importance of the industry.

The use of fishing communities on the fringes of society and geography as metaphors for a lost ethos of simplicity, bravery, hardiness, and piety is a theme running strongly in nineteenth-century social awareness. It stands in stark contrast to the widely held middle-class belief current in the latter part of that century that the urbanization and industrialization of the working class had produced a degenerate, puny and 'devious and cunning'[12] population. Illustration of this is found in H. G. Wells's novel *The Time Machine* with his creation of the degenerate Morlocks, and confirmed by the miserable health of many volunteers at the time of the Boer War. In contrast, the painters of the rural fishing communities offered up a pre-industrial people as an embodiment of lost virtues. This engaged artists in a variety of locations across Europe. Walter Langley travelled to paint fishing communities in Holland in the same timeframe as he was recorded as a Newlyn painter; Stanhope Forbes began in Brittany before Cornwall. Even the second generation of Newlyn artists began in other similar communities. Laura and Harold Knight had begun painting in Yorkshire fishing villages and in Holland long before setting foot in Cornwall. The painters did not see the Cornish fishing communities as particularly unique, they were just one of a number of painting opportunities or—as Bernard Deacon has it—'spatial possibilities'.[13] It was the Cornish themselves who perhaps chose to see these representations as making themselves 'special'. There is early anecdotal evidence of both conflict and collusion with the painters. Forbes was unable to paint on Sundays as his landlady would 'turn me out'.[14] One painter who broke the Sabbath had his painting slashed, and models refused to work for Sabbath breakers.[15] The use of a notorious drinker to represent the minister in Titcomb's painting 'Primitive Methodists' seems to have produced no documented outrage and infers a degree of collusion, hinting that the flattery of being depicted as pious outweighed the rather contradictory morality of the model. Both parties in the process of making paintings—artists and subjects—strove to cast the visual material in the mould they separately desired.

The result was a body of visual representations of people, place, custom and tradition that purported to show authentic images of West Cornwall in the 1880s and 90s. Compared to the idealized and sensationalized 'history' painting of the time, it is indeed verist in its intention. However the 'reality' displayed is one edited via the artist's eye: the message to be read is carefully crafted by all the skill of the painter's art. It is in the omissions and in the subtle hints that the message for the intended middle-class and urban audience is encoded. Whether it is in the direct pathos of Langley's 'Women must weep' or in the religious iconography of candle and the Raphael print on the wall in Bramley's 'Hopeless Dawn', the message was clear: 'grief and loss, faith and endurance' are what go to make nobility of soul. You cannot find that in the urban stews of the Midlands and London. The Cornish were perhaps particularly susceptible to the presentation of themselves as God-fearing and pious, the strength and depth of Methodism in Cornish working-class culture was the root of that feeling. How much they played up to it and how the images became a wish-fulfilment are open to conjecture: it is highly probable that in the work of the painters the Cornish villagers saw themselves as they wished to be and be seen.

The biblical theme reaches its apogee in the late Stanhope Forbes painting 'The Seine Boat' of 1904, depicting a fishing method that was in serious decline in the face of more modern and efficient means. The picture is retrospective and reflective. Bearded patriarchs, two younger men and a boy gaze out to sea for sign of a pilchard shoal. A strongly evangelical culture could read this as an apostolic metaphor; Mount's Bay becomes the Sea of Galilee. They are no longer fishermen, they are fishers of men. Perhaps some imagined not the pilchard shoal but a figure walking across the water to the waiting boat. This sort of

2. *The Seine Boat: use of this Stanhope Forbes painting as a cover picture for the magazine* Cornwall Today *edges it into the realm of nostalgic kitsch. (Private Collection, Bridgeman Art Library)*

imagery massages not only pride in skills and tradition but more perhaps spiritual pride in one's own piety. Social historians have shown how often Cornish pride colours stories of miners in and outside Cornwall, with their ludicrously boastful claims of prowess and worth when compared to non-Cornish competitors. What is also so strongly contributory to the powerful imagery in the picture is the complete lack of modernity. Nowhere is there anything that indicates a technological world different from that of 1800: it is a timeless image and it is that sense of time standing still that was to 'sell' Cornwall so successfully in the years to come. When he produced this painting, Forbes had been in close contact with the people of Newlyn and Paul for twenty years: to a great extent this picture shows just how far the people of Newlyn had projected their self-image into Forbes's work.

Another late Newlyn painting, by William Titcomb—'The Church in Cornwall, Rogation Day Procession' of 1906—shows a very different scene and is seldom reproduced. The picture makes a strong visual link with religious practice in Catholic Brittany. The surpliced choir, processional cross and priest in embroidered cope (modelled by Bernard Walke) are a far remove from the religious practice of most

West Cornish fishing villages in the late nineteenth century. This is the Catholic-Celtic Cornwall of the middle-class Revival; part of the so-called invented tradition constructed by scholars and enthusiasts in the pursuit of a post-industrial Cornwall. Yet this picture is almost certainly unfamiliar to many that know and admire the Newlyn school, and we must ask why? It is profoundly atypical of the consensus of what goes to make up Cornishness. It is by no means an inferior painting but it has not captured the popular imagination, either inside or outside Cornwall. It is perhaps significant that the final version exhibited in the RA in 1906 now resides in middle-class Cheltenham's art gallery. It reflects a minor strand in the social fabric: after all it was Walke's church of St Hilary that was ransacked by an angry Kensitite mob in 1932 'smashing its candles and pictures and carrying off its statues'.[16]

In *Eyewitnessing* Peter Burke makes the following statement: 'paintings . . . allow us, posterity, to share the non-verbal experiences or knowledge of past cultures'.[17] But what sort of past culture? Imagined, partly imagined, or perhaps even real? Certainly the culture of Catholic-Celtic Cornwall is partly imagined and it certainly was not real for most working-class fishermen and their families. On the other hand, the culture of the fishermen was equally unreal for the majority of the middle-class. The plein-air painting of the late nineteenth century is indeed a partly imagined world: the material of that world may have been real but the conditions and the attitudes of that physical world have been manipulated. The fact that many of the painters had been pupils of Herkomer—who was perhaps the most socially responsible and socially honest painter in the late nineteenth-century English art establishment—helped to avoid many of the worst excesses of late Victorian idealization, sentimentality and stereotyping.

One thing we cannot do with pictures is *smell* them, and if one thing is certain it is that the streets of Newlyn were not the squeaky clean ones we see in paintings. Roger Langley in his book on his grandfather Walter Langley quotes from the 'Perambulating Contributor' to the *Cornishman* newspaper, who was writing at a time when the first painters appeared in the town:

> Several times I have been shocked and disgusted with the state of the thoroughfares, mud and filth and rotten fish lying about and trampled under foot. And then the smells! In certain conditions of the atmosphere the effluvia are something appalling and anyone . . . would barely survive the stinks and stenches which . . . pollute the live air. But the inhabitants go about . . . with wooden noses for all it affects them. The

sanitary condition of Newlyn is truly woeful . . . a continual
menace to the well-being of the district.[18]

Written perhaps as early as 1880 the picture conjured above
does not sit easily with the romantic constructs of the paintings: even
the earlier, more 'gritty', representations let alone the increasingly
'bowdlerized' confections supplied for the growing middle-class market
within a very few years. The early and highly-charged Newlyn paintings
such as Forbes's seminal 'Fish sale on a Cornish beach' of 1885 and
Langley's 'Men must work and women must weep' of 1883 show their
figures dressed in the roughest and coarsest working clothes.

*3. 'Women must weep'.
Walter Langley's famous
painting is strong on realism
and poverty as well as
emotion. This was not due to
last in the face of consumer
tastes more inclined to
decorative sentimentality.
(Birmingham City Museum &
Art Gallery)*

By the end of the decade much more decorative work is apparent;
just as modern TV 'soaps' artificially raise the material culture of their
characters so do the later Newlyn pictures. Frank Bramley's 'Domino'
of 1886 and Edwin Harris's 'The Lesson' of 1889 both depict situations

*4. Harris's 'The Lesson' is everything that the Langley is not: decorative and
sugary it imposes middle-class values and tastes on a working community.
(Private Collection on loan to Penlee House, Penzance)*

where costume and furnishing indicate a middle-class setting.
Bourdillon's 'Jubilee Hat' of 1887 is unashamedly sentimental, if still
believably set in a fisherman's cottage.

The second generation of painters—who loosely grouped themselves around S.J. 'Lamorna' Birch—were all much more interested
in middle-class subjects and concerns: whether in depicting slightly
romantic and 'gypsyish' scenes or straightforward images of blissful
middle-class holidays that they just happened to paint in Cornwall.
Their works do not really contribute to the visual image of the Cornish
in the way that the early pioneers did. They are depicting the incomer
at play: even when they are painted by Cornishman Harold Harvey
there is this very middle-class and English timbre to them. The use of a
careful repertoire of stock emotions, that is such a hallmark of kitsch,
was important to the nineteenth-century painters too. The carefully
constructed images of piety, courage, fortitude, and healthy vigour
would not easily survive the squalor that was the physical accom-
paniment to all that they wished to depict. Poverty equals simplicity in

5. *GWR* Holiday Haunts *cover for the 1930 edition. The bearded patriarches of the 'Seine Boat' have now become the tourist attractions that the visitors require. The process of 'entkitschment' is well underway. (National Railway Museum)*

their canon, not squalor. It was not only the physical squalor of the industry itself but also, just occasionally, the curtain lifts on more serious degradation. Drink, no matter what Methodists might maintain, was an ever-present problem. More sinister were the hints unearthed in the letters of one of the visiting continental painters at St Ives. The wife of the Swedish painter Anders Zorn seems to have had her eyes and ears open. 'Emma [Zorn] was shocked to find that boys of 18 or 19 years were made to marry 14 year old girls to keep them from being corrupted'.[19] We have become all too aware today that sexual abuse ran beneath respectability in nineteenth-century society, and there is no reason to think Cornwall any different.

So how is it that those very images, made for the most part over 100 years ago, can now be part of a kitsch construction of Cornwall? The way to access this change in emphasis and meaning is to begin by looking at the meaning intended at their inception. In the main the great set-piece pictures of the Newlyn School hark back to a pre-industrial ideal, rural England: I use 'England' deliberately here because it is a Cornwall *in* England that the external audience in the 1880s and 90s would have thought of. The fact that that England was an imaginary and perfect construct did not matter at all. It was an England on the margins and untainted by the Industrial Revolution. The awakening of Cornish consciousness by the mid twentieth century meant that the same images could now hark back to an ideal and 'lost' Cornwall, a perfect time before the age of 'making do' or 'getting by'. In the visual motifs of the late nineteenth century, Cornwall was a romantic, sanitized, neatly-packaged dream that the Cornish could ingest comfortably: 'that nostalgia, which has underlain all my experience of life'.[20] The big difference was that now the paintings were not just meaningful to the fishing communities or the wealthy patrons who had purchased them: now they had a resonance for all Cornish people and became a visible sign of that departed prowess and greatness. To the visitor they became the never-never land that had generated the pretty villages in which they came to stay. The few remaining fishermen, especially any bearded patriarchs, became attractions in their own right.

The GWR guide book *Holiday Haunts* of 1930 has just such an image on its cover, where a seated and suitably bearded old fisherman is playing the ancient mariner to a group of small children. Degenerating over the years to stock characters in Rupert Bear books or for selling fish fingers, the Cap'n Birdseye figure was to be the fate of fisher folk. All of this can easily be subsumed into a heritage version of Cornwall, with a romantic attractiveness that the original participants would not have known.

CAMELOT

Trying to pin down and identify Arthurian images specific to Cornwall and Cornish culture is a lot harder than one might expect, after the wealth of fishing imagery. The problem is twofold. First, the Arthurian material relating to Cornwall is mostly nineteenth-century and, second, its initial impetus was via literature not the visual arts. The publication of Tennyson's 'Idylls of the King' in the mid nineteenth century was the starting point for a massive outside interest in that part of the Arthurian cycle that related to Cornwall. The flood of images that followed, often from the pre-Raphaelite painters—Rossetti, Millais, Dyce, Hughes and Burne-Jones—did not require the artists to visit Cornwall. Theirs' was a studio art constructed lovingly and in exquisite detail in London. They expressed no concern with any genuine attempt to place their work in anything other than a reconstructed medieval fantasy. The Arthur they painted was the Arthur of Sir Thomas Malory and had no connection with the mysterious sixth century figure that so tantalized scholars. Furthermore, the real subject matter of the paintings was the sexual and moral politics of the nineteenth century, man as hero and noble soul, woman as seducer and sorceress. There was little that was going to enter Cornish consciousness: the images were crafted to appeal to an almost exclusively metropolitan and middle class audience.

What did eventually catch the Cornish imagination was perhaps the serious archaeology that began in the early twenthieth century to try to add fact to the myths, stories and legends. The discoveries at Tintagel and Castle Dore—which showed real evidence of important activity in the fifth-sixth centuries—brought the prospect of a 'real' Arthur and a 'real' Tristan and Isolde to the attention of the public and the media. This, of course, was meat and drink to the Celtic Revivalists in the early part of the twentieth century, and firmly equated their reconstructed Celtic Cornwall with an Arthurian past when most of the evidence for such a claim was largely conjectural. Attempts to visualize

6. *St Piran's flag and the kilt in Cornish National Tartan: a statement of modern Cornishness that by and large seems a 'no go' area for the marketing fraternity.*
(Cornish Guardian)

the Celtic past—whether re-constructed or not—have been often difficult in Cornwall: unlike in Scotland, there has been no recent tradition to draw upon.

The prohibition of Highland tartan in 1746 and its subsequent re-habilitation begun by Sir Walter Scott and the early nineteenth-century romantics provided a ready visual peg on which to hang identity and culture, one that today's Scots view with considerable ambivalence. There was nothing comparable for the Cornish, and so in 1948 E. E. Morton Nance invented a Cornish National Tartan to give a visual and Celtic dimension to Cornish costume. This has had enormous success and is now something of which most Cornish people are aware as a visual badge of Cornishness. Equally successful has been the adoption of St. Piran's flag as the national emblem of modern Cornwall. Because of the repeated use of Arthur as a unifying strand in the monarchy's and later the government's 'British Project',[21] it is much more difficult to attach images of Arthurianism to Cornwall: the result is that the effect on Cornish visual awareness is diffuse. Arthur is disputed territory with Scots, Welsh, Bretons, and even English claiming him as their own. It is only the Tristan legend that can be located firmly in Cornwall and this has produced some limited visual imagery, though once again for external consumption and often with reference to Wagnerian opera.

Direct images of the Celtic and Arthurian Cornwall in the work of any of the painters involved in Cornwall are few. The obvious example is that of Elizabeth Stanhope Forbes who not only produced finished paintings in a largely romantic and pre-Raphaelite idiom but also wrote and illustrated *King Arthur's Wood*, a romantic fairytale for children. This was published in 1904 ahead of Rackham's *Rip Van Winkle* and Dulac's *Arabian Nights*,[22] which while putting her in the forefront of that particular genre probably had little impact outside the middle class. Although we now tend to view such work as mannered and perhaps sentimental, the kitsch effect of Forbes's work is a drop in the ocean of Arthurian kitsch, which suffused middle-class iconography and literature. Any enkitschment of Cornwall is only by association with a wider Arthurian kitsch. Until, that is, we look at the epicentre of Arthurian kitsch, the whole ambience of Tintagel itself. From plastic swords in the English Heritage gift shop at the foot of the castle to the cast resin dragons and statuettes of Merlin that cram the shelves of its gift shops, Tintagel is a whirl of consumer kitsch and—of course—straightforward bad taste.

The crowning glory of it all, however, is a wonderful palace of kitsch, something that Umberto Eco would recognize as a true 'authentic fake': namely the building now occupying the site of the old

7. *Stained glass by Veronica Whall and high-quality painting by W. Hatherall
were commissioned in all seriousness for King Arthur's Great Halls by
Frederick Glasscock.*
(King Arthur's Great Halls, Tintagel)

manor house, King Arthur's Great Halls. This extraordinary
agglomeration of art, craftsmanship and sheer hocus-pocus is a classic
of early twentieth-century romantic muddle-headedness. Frederick
Glasscock—who had made himself a millionaire out of a successful
recipe for custard—built it in the late 1920s and early 1930s. What
confirms the whole enterprise and its magnificently decorated building
as kitsch is the utter seriousness with which it was built and equipped.
Glasscock was not in the tourist business: he was directing a one man
crusade backed by his own money to build an organization called 'The
Fellowship of the Knights of the Round Table of King Arthur', based
on elements of Freemasonry and the Scouting Movement. Almost all
that you see today on visiting the Hall is exactly as Glasscock intended.
The specially commissioned retro pre-Raphaelite paintings executed in
the early 1930s reinforced the messages of a romantic Arthur, and
are used extensively in their Tintagel Castle guidebook by English
Heritage: perpetuating the Anglo-Medieval Arthur. The seventy-three
stained glass windows were designed and executed by Veronica Whall,
a pupil of William Morris. The brochure for the Halls describes them as
'the best post pre-Raphaelite windows anywhere'. It is this high-quality
applied art and a total lock of irony or mockery that assure the Halls its
place in the pantheon of kitsch. One American visitor quoted and used
in the publicity material claims it is finer than anything in Florida. In
a sense, Glasscock out-performed the masters of kitsch across the
Atlantic, and in the terms of Olalquiaga's definition created an outstanding example of nostalgic kitsch: a 'perfect memory of something
that never really happened'.[23] The present owners of the Halls are
the Freemasons of Tintagel and have been since 1952. The current
Director and his team have put together a visitors' brochure that
indicates they are well aware of the kitsch element in the Halls' own

history and in the Arthurian 'industry' as a whole. They suggest Geoffrey of Monmouth's 1190 History of the Kings of Britain had more than a hint of 'An early marketing scam'[24] and ask 'Where was Camelot (Hollywood?)'.[25] They conclude by emphasizing 'this unique building, with its compelling aura'.[26]

The latter is a contentious stance, if one is to take Benjamin's argument about 'auras' seriously. Certainly, the art work is of a high enough quality to be worthy of consideration. But it is the entkitschment of it in Glasscock's project that jeopardizes our taking it as seriously as perhaps it deserves. Who was meant to be influenced by this kitsch, fake Arthurian world? Almost certainly not the indigenous Cornish but rather the visitor and the credulous: and in the 1920s they were mostly the middle class. The Arthur presented by the assemblage of viewpoints and attractions at Tintagel, then and now, has almost nothing to do with any 'real' Dark Age leader and a lot to do with anglocentric myth making; it is an outside projection onto Cornwall. Nonetheless it is a very effective one and represents a kitsch tradition over which the heirs of a dim and distant Celtic tradition have no control. In early August over the last few years a 're-enactment' of the Battle of Camlann—Arthur's alleged Last Battle—has been performed, complete with mock medieval tents, armour and all the trimmings. No doubt it was much enjoyed by all, participators and spectators alike, and the tills of Tintagel rang merrily. All good fun we might say, but suppose that—like the re-enacted Battle of Stamford Hill at Stratton—it becomes a 'traditional' annual event and Arthur dies perennially at the hand of Mordred on a make-believe battlefield. What does the repetition do to any remaining vestige of real historical continuity and connection? Any meaningful aura that the location might have had is swamped by the razzmatazz of the show, which must of course go on.

BRANDING THE PROJECT: 'CORNISH' WITH EVERYTHING

The first moves to 'sell' post-industrial 'Cornwall' and 'Cornish' as desirable marks of distinction for products and services, came from the railways that were anxious to sell tickets and keep profits up. The earliest poster in a recent exhibition at Penlee House dates from 1904 and indicates an early partnership between hotelier and railway. Marketing phrases are always indicative of an underlying concept that is used to sell the product. One of the earliest to emerge is credited to Cornwall's most famous son in the late nineteenth and early twentieth centuries, Sir Arthur Quiller-Couch: or 'Q' as he was know to millions through his successful fictional work. He realized that one option for a Cornwall faced with ruination as the mining industry imploded was the tourist trade, and he emphasized the need to do it well and with style and quality. It was his description of Cornwall as the 'Delectable Duchy' that provided one of the most enduring phrases to be applied to Cornwall. The underlying concept here is one with an aristocratic slant implying quality in all things and monarchical connections: it is essentially a backward-looking construction. The most successful and powerfully effective concept was that developed by the Great Western Railway in its promotion of the 'Cornish Riviera'. The first tranche of advertising focused on the idea of likening Cornwall to the Mediterranean and produced a poster comparing Cornwall to Italy and the concept of exotic 'otherness'. Most people had, of course, never seen Italy and so market credulity could be exploited. In terms of kitsch, this early imagery ranks quite strongly and in matters of fashion and taste kitsch can be deemed to be a 'dumbed down' version of the 'real' product for mass consumption by the middle classes.[27] The 'real' location is the actual Riviera in France or Italy to which the wealthy go, and the substitute for mass travel and the middle class is the 'Cornish Riviera': with a few gratuitous palm trees to convince the sceptical. The point is one not dissimilar to Umberto Eco's concept of the 'authentic fake' which, with determination and re-enforcement, gradually becomes authentic. While we no longer believe that west Cornwall is a parallel to the Ligurian coast, we do all have a solid concept of a Cornish Riviera with a mild climate and palm trees and perhaps a certain faded elegance in some of its older hotels. The kitsch has become a reality.

A wonderful example of kitsch and changing meanings is in the example of the cast-iron badge that used to grace the front of the 'Cornishman' express train: a rather feminine pixy in figure-hugging yellow tights sits, with legs wide apart on an enormous and priapic toadstool. We have to accept that no one saw or was willing to see the sexual symbolism in this badge: either at the time of its design or subsequent usage. But the fact is that today its meaning has totally changed and such a design would be unusable and unacceptable.

The publication of S.P.B. Mais' book *The Cornish Riviera* in 1924 (it was into its third edition by 1934) celebrated Cornish exoticism. The volume's coloured frontispiece showed the now ubiquitous palms, and the thrust of its advertising was a combination of 'difference' and nostalgia. Almost all of the visual material for tourist initiatives was by this time in the form of highly coloured and high-quality posters. The public were appreciative of the developing styles in artwork, so much so that the London and North Eastern Railway was able to stage successful exhibitions at its stations from 1923 and in the New Burlington Galleries in 1928: they attracted great acclaim. An overview of the genre in the years before nationalization describes the critical debate that flourished over the merits of abstraction v. realism, and recount Tom Purvis's assertion that the key to a good poster was 'simplicity and clarity in getting the message across'.[28] This phrase in itself takes us to the criteria for kitsch: this is a call for instant and effortless identifiability, relying on stock images and triggering stock emotions with minimum exposure. The designers could not assume that travellers spent hours lingering on railway platforms just to view the posters. However, they could always buy a poster for their very own and thus relive the holiday pleasure every day. In his brief and sometimes acerbic little book on the railway poster *Happy Holidays*, Michael Palin points out the absence of modernity in the great majority: 'landscapes are delightfully proportioned and quite free from any stain of progress', and again 'It's a Utopia, a Britain . . . in which the Industrial Revolution never happened'.[29] An examination of the GWR and subsequent British Railways posters reveal a lack of

8. A typical and very fine example of the GWR poster. Note the absence of modernity and the prominence of the traditional fishing boats that were by the time of the poster becoming ever scarcer.
(Penlee House, Penzance)

modernity: the emphasis is on tranquillity and old fashioned simplicity. Boats are sailed not powered, crowds are absent and the sea calm, and, as Palin points out, the train is conspicuous by its absence.

The failure of modernity in English art between the world wars is closely connected to a 'turn to an internal life': modernism is abandoned in favour of 'evoking a fictionalized or idealized vision of a pre modern world'.[30] Although the GWR was not noted for modernist posters, they did employ McKnight Kauffer, a leading modernist graphic designer, and two innovative posters for Cornwall and Devon by Ronald Lampitt received critical acclaim. Lampitt use a style evident in some of Matisse's early work, but it was not repeated. The kitsch landscape vision of the railway poster was admirably suited to nostalgia and made people feel good about a sort of fuzzy, harmless nationalism: good 'because they responded spontaneously, but also because they know they are responding in the right kind of way. They know they are moved in the same way as everybody else.'[31] The tendency of kitsch to require collective amnesia is part of the power it wields. We know that the actuality is not like the railway poster but we go along with the fiction all the same. We do so because it is more comfortable that way, because we can share the comfort with our fellows and not upset people with a blunt appraisal of the true nature of things. The railway poster meets Kulka's tests of kitsch with ease. It does not transform or enrich our enjoyment of the real Cornwall: in fact the poster is more likely to reaffirm our fixed model. Given the holidaymaker's determination to have a good time and enjoy him or herself, it is unlikely that the discrepancy will intrude into consciousness. Railway posters up until the 1950s were quite outstanding as examples of the commercial artist's work: and they were first-class kitsch.

The holiday postcard is a powerful visual tool in promoting locations and creating longing. The vast majority of cards are photographic and factual 'views'. However, even there the eye of the photographer has selected and edited for the delight of the viewer and the profit of the promoter. A recent trend has been to create the 'art' postcard with a more carefully themed or composed image. Interestingly, this seems to have begun in Tuscany in Italy in the late 1980s and gradually spread until the same stylistic approach can be seen from Siena to Sennen. Of more interest on this context is the humorous postcard. There is, of course, the universal 'McGill' card with its puns and clumsy *double entendre* that can be found in any seaside resort from one end of the British Isles to the other. There is a whole other sub genre where the target for the humour is the local inhabitant: on the surface the majority of these cards continue the fine old tradition of stereotyping the rural dweller as comic and grotesque.

9. *The grotesque and exaggerated rural inhabitant as imagined by the*
sophisticated townee.
(J. Hinde & Co, Redruth)

The 'Local Pasty Poachers' is typical of this approach, and
examples in Scotland parallel this: with a haggis replacing the
pasty. This is a distinctly metropolitan view, rendering the Cornish as
undesirable and comic 'others', except when providing the butt of the
jokes for the visitors. Cornwall as remote and distant is also part of the
same strand, and postcards depict holidaymakers arriving exhausted
and with their car worn out at the door of their B&B (complete with
'yertiz' on the signboard). The kitsch element here is to instantly give
the recipients a warm sense of superiority. It confirms their opinion
of the locals as being entirely justified, and allows the senders an
adulatory pat on the back for heroically battling to reach the far, and
exotic, west.

Of more interest than these mild examples are the much more
controversial series of 'Classic Cornwall Cards' published by Ashley
Peters and originating from Penzance.

These cards are controversial because the images are staged
photographs and, therefore, have an aura of realism that the cartoon
drawing does not. In fact, the cartoon can distance itself by being
merely a representation and not an actuality, and through stylization it
removes some of its potential to shock. The Classic Cornwall Cards

10. Two typical 'Classic Cornwall' cards. But are they kitsch? More plausibly they are mocking the kitsch representations of Cornwall, but how aware of this post-modernism are the visitors buying them?
(Classic Cornwall Cards, Ashley Peters, Penzance)

confront this and set out to shock by giving the viewer no chance to avoid the reality of the mockery. We are all inured by now to nudity —or at least semi-nudity—in newspapers and advertising: provided the bodies are young and beautiful. What shocks us is the ageing, sagging flesh with its discolouration and blemishes: it is perhaps uncomfortably close to our own appearance and that disturbs us. The sexual innuendo is little different from the 'McGill' cards and the mockery of the locals—as witless or credulous—is the same as the

11. The high or low point of the genre depending on your point of view.
(Classic Cornwall Cards, Ashley Peters, Penzance)

previous two examples from J. Hinde. It is the uncompromising nature
of the photograph that upsets us, but is it kitsch or simply bad taste?
Does the Cornish origin of the work reveal a post-modern self-
mockery and a hidden contempt for the external gaze? In terms of
kitsch, we can begin by applying Kulka's criteria to see if there is any
correlation. Yes: there is instant identifiability, but stock characters
with their emotional associations are used as well. Fishermen's caps,
pipes and beards are much in evidence: in fact some of the protagonists
could have walked out of the 'Seine Boat', stripped off and been ready
for the 'shoot'.

'The Beast of Bodmin' card uses a stereotypical caveman with the
addition of phallic sausages. The stock emotions are reversed ones:
the viewer may indeed feel revulsion. But more significantly he or she
feels superior and can look down on the grotesque Cornish and feel
good about himself/herself by denigrating others while enjoying a
good laugh. In no sense does this material enrich or broaden our
understanding or experience. It reinforces attitude and prejudice, and
in fact if we were to meet a bearded fisherman on the quayside at
Newlyn we would instantly be reminded of the postcards, and the real
fisherman diminished. The evidence would seem to position the cards
in the world of kitsch and contribute to the reduction of traditional
Cornish culture as a parody of its former self. If the cards were
produced outside Cornwall they would be an insensitive and
exploitative lampoon. But since they originate inside Cornwall and
seem to be produced by Cornish people, we should perhaps look for
a different shade of meaning. Is this a way of mocking perceived
prejudices by reflecting them back at the prejudiced; or is it a way of
disguising true feelings by hiding behind what others want to see?

In a large photofeature in *Cornish World*[32] the attempt by Martin
Ellis of Cadgwith to establish a viable modern seine net technique for
catching pilchard is recounted. It is all very traditional and 'Cornish'
but the opening pages of the article present Martin in a very different
way, one of self-mockery and comic dismissal. Is this just clever self-
promotion or something more profoundly disturbing? It is in fact an
acting out of the mock-heritage role assigned to the Cornish and
the fishing industry in particular. Why when something innovative,
environmentally sustainable, and combining the best of the new with
the old is created, is it presented in a parody of a Captain Birdseye
commercial? I believe it is because that without the golden touch of the
icons of the commercial world, we cannot activate the icons of our own
heritage: they have lost the validity to stand alone and they are now
validated by their consumer potential.

It is now to the consumer products that I want to turn. There is

12. *One of the most successful users of folklore in a commercial context has been Skinners of Truro: they are to limits, and Cornish Tartan and Bards are seen as definite 'no go' areas.*
(Skinner's Brewery, Truro)

considerable use of Cornish culture in the visual kitsch used to market some consumer products within Cornwall. The kitsch ranges from gentle romantic landscape on Furniss Cornish Gingerbread tins to the confrontational 'Knocker' who 'flashes' on the label of Skinner's Knocker beer. The criteria of 'easy identifiability' and a 'stock emotion' characterize successful commercial material just as much as they apply to kitsch: unsuccessful variants simply vanish. The images do not enhance or enrich our experience of Cornishness, and it would be ludicrous to suggest that they do. However, it may give added enjoyment to drink a locally produced beer with a distinctive name that links it to the folktales of Cornwall. The serious folktale has been pressed into service to sell a local product and has been used consciously to do so: this may offend the humourless ultra-nationalist or fastidious scholar but it does have the added advantage of reaching an audience that might otherwise have remained untouched. The young surfing visitor is less likely to buy one of the many booklets on Cornish

myths and folkstories than buy beer: and he/she may just read the
label. Such a trivial and flippant representation of a national cultural
material need not be detrimental and can be of value. The sexual
innuendo can offend and one supermarket chain did not stock
'Knocker'as the buyer found the label too offensive. Skinners
responded by relabelling the bottled beer as St. Piran's Ale: same beer,
different label, with a wonderfully witty image of the saint surfing in on
his millstone. Cornish culture here has been entkitsched, and, yes,
there is a degree of trivialization of some very rich and valuable
cultural material. But the use redeems itself, perhaps, by increasing the
accessibility of that same material. Kitsch only becomes reprehensible
when it undermines—ethically and morally—as Nazi kitsch did with its
racial and social intolerance. Similarly, kitsch of the southern United
States was reprehensible, with its portrayal of the African-American as
a comic and rather stupid but loveable servant.

13. *Redruth Brewery's can for its quality bitter brewed to coincide with the*
1997 Keskerth Kernow march.
(beer can, author's collection)

Of a completely different nature is the labelling on Redruth
Brewery's Cornish Rebellion Traditional Bitter. This was first brewed
for the 1997 celebrations and the march to Blackheath to com-
memorate the 1497 rebellion and to draw attention to Cornwall's
current social and economic problems. I am interested here in the

canned version, for the labelling differs significantly from the bottled: there being a larger surface area for the designer to work with. Unlike Skinner's, there is a determined seriousness to this design. Saddled with a brewery emblem of the Lamb and Flag (St. George's), the designers reduced the emblem to a minute size and instead went for as many Cornish 'national' markers as they could fit on. This was all combined with a colour scheme of the 'national' colours of black, gold and white. The image of marching rebels was produced in a mock fifteenth-century woodcut style, with a Cornish language motto above and its translation in 'olde English' below. Behind all this was a 'mock' hand-written document, in grey on the black ground. This gave a brief account of the rebellion and even managed to squeeze in the final and famous last words of Myghal an Gof. Despite this pretentious and complex imagery, the result is to give a sensation of luxury high quality and a feeling that only a superior and intellectual elite could successfully decode such a text: exclusive kitsch at its best.

Foodstuff manufacturers have also employed the Cornish brand strategy. Although they occupy a very different market sector in most instances, when compared to the brewers, they have used some of the same elements: especially in the tradition and nostalgia presentation of their products. In the case of Furniss, they have also made a clear distinction between products that they see as essentially English as opposed to Cornish, though what interests us here is the use of kitsch or nostalgia-slanted imagery. On recent packaging, there is prominent use of the Cornish shield and fifteen bezants, together with the motto

14. *A piece of geniune Cornish National Tartan and a plastic pasty: all officially approved on one single item a greetings card. This is a delightful and humorous piece of kitsch with an unintended (?) twist in the company name:*
Wasteland Arts.
(Wasteland Arts and Cornwall County Council)

from the Cornish coat of arms. There is also a map of Cornwall littered with tiny St. Piran's flags to mark the towns, and the words Cornwall or Cornish are used eight times. There is little that is overtly kitsch here or even a particularly nostalgic: the nostalgia is reserved for varieties of biscuits aimed at a wider market and where, interestingly, the word Cornwall does not appear at all, not even on the company's address.

The pasty is not only a significant cultural icon—used in effigy when slung below the crossbar at Twickenham—but is now a rapidly growing fast food. Pasty shops exist in locations as diverse as London, Brighton, Oxford, and Stirling. Ginster's, with a complete distribution system throughout the British Isles, has marketed and advertised its products assertively. It uses a St. Piran's cross as part of the company logo, and has produced some delightfully kitsch advertising copy in which a moonlit view of Mount's Bay has a crescent 'moon' in the form of a silvery pasty. The Ginster's advert was one of a series in which the pasty was used as a surreal replacement in an otherwise straight photographic image. The Proper Cornish Pasty Company played the traditional game in authenticating their product. On the card sleeve in which the pasty comes, are a whole battery of visual reminders of Cornish origins: including the County Council logo from its Approved Origin Scheme. The final kitsch twist here is the personalization of the product by the excerpt from the (spurious?) Mrs Tresidder's diary of 1824: written in mock dialect. Behind all this is a pastel coloured Cornwall, suitably nostalgic for the consumer. While no one part of this assemblage is particularly kitsch, the result is a folksy kitsch presentation of a straightforward food item as something infinitely desirable and special.

The food and drink market is hugely influential in determining whether the visitor feels he/she has had a good time. A hard sell approach during the short summer season is predictable but what also seems to be achieved is the presentation of Cornwall as a producer of high-quality goods and services that requires the sustaining of a particular image all year round: not just in the summer season. A successful marketing image of that sort is likely to be kitsch, particularly as it is based on the selling of Cornish goods rather than the selling of the Cornish as warmly welcoming hosts: the approach which the Irish have used.

SELLING OUR BIRTHRIGHT, DEMEANED BY THE MARKET PLACE?

The collection and analysis of images of contemporary Cornwall and the Cornish is a complex and sometimes bewildering task. The use of the past and the appropriation of established imagery for new and commercial purposes have been a strong strand in the story. The fact that the various models of Cornwall—the working-class industrial, the Catholic-Celtic, and the literary romantic—can be paralleled by accompanying visual material has made it possible to untangle parts of this complicated whole and make apparent the meanings in a process that is essentially subliminal.

The problem with kitsch is that people like it, and it becomes difficult to attack its artistic and cultural poverty without becoming open to the charge of elitism identified above. The lack of broadly agreed standards or even criteria in which to locate kitsch in today's post-modernist climate further compounds this problem. However, by deploying Kulka's arguments, it is easy to see that a great deal of the identified models of Cornish culture have been adapted for the purposes of commerce and a tourist market. As part of this adaptation, they have been rendered down to the very essence of kitsch and often served up in a manner redolent of the theme park. This may indeed be good for commerce and for people's pockets but is it good for the Cornish in Cornwall? If all that matters is the wage packet at the end of the month—regardless of self-esteem or privacy—then everything is up for sale and it probably does little harm. If, however, self-esteem, peace of mind, and (for want of a better term) some sense of spiritual awareness are important, then the entkitschment of things and ideas that we cherish and revere has potentially serious consequences.

The entkitschment of the several models of Cornish culture and their visual constructions has taken place at an ever-increasing intensity over the last hundred years. The location of this process in the marketing of Cornwall as a holiday environment and as a brand for products and produce is largely positioned in the tourist context and in perceived markets outside Cornwall. Actually, inside Cornwall it is noticeable that the coastal fringe—with its intense tourist activity—is significantly more likely to display the kitsch results of this process. Inland towns and villages, with a greater emphasis on agriculture and an enduring non-tourist economic base, are almost devoid of much of this evidence. Thus there is a clear spatial dimension to entkitschment which would seem to identify it as a representation of a Cornwall wholly serving a transient and external audience.

THE INVISIBLE CORNISH

Too often the abiding perception of Cornwall is of a location devoid of its inhabitants. How often do we hear from visitors: '*I love Cornwall*'? But seldom do we hear: '*I do like the Cornish*'. The most extreme manifestations of such attitudes sees the Cornish as a species of troglodyte, who under cover of darkness empty the bins and clean the amenities ready for the visitors. This sort of dismissal is well documented and can be traced in a wide variety of literary and artistic activity: in the writings of D.H. Lawrence, for example, or in films such as 'Straw Dogs' where the Cornish are presented as a brutalized people strongly reminiscent of the American 'red neck'.

The entkitschment process of romanticising the land while reviling the inhabitants is of course not unique to Cornwall: both Ireland and Scotland, for example, have suffered similar experiences.

COPING WITH THE KITSCH THAT WE HAVE ADOPTED

The definitions of kitsch that Tomas Kulka formed do indeed describe much of the visual material examined above. How has this happened to Cornish culture? Have the Cornish been ruthlessly exploited by the sophisticated and metropolitan centre, or have they done it to themselves? The answer is, of course, 'yes' to both propositions. In the 1950s the word 'global' meant the world-wide power and interests of nations: summed up symbolically by the Stars and Stripes versus the Hammer and Sickle. Today, those of the multinational corporation have by and large replaced the interests of the nation state. This change of meaning has permeated whole cultures—Cornish being one of many—with the necessities of the 'market place'. The kitsch representation of Cornwall began when the tourist industry replaced heavy industry as the best chance of earning a livelihood within Cornwall. The fact that the Cornish themselves are exploiting their own culture in this way is not surprising . But what is new is the loss of control of image making. Long gone are the days when a town council could influence the sort of image portrayed on a major advertising campaign. Today, marketing decisions and trends are decided in boardrooms often thousands of miles away: the best that most small commercial entities can do is to acquiesce and imitate. The reality is that Cornwall is a small commercial entity, much smaller in terms of wealth and resources than most multi-national corporations.

Like it or not, if a Kitsch Kernow is what sells, then it is perhaps important to try and manage that kitsch as sensitively and as creatively as possible. An important step in that management is to raise the level of awareness of the images being projected. Limited ethnographical research seems to indicate wide awareness of the high-profile impact of television and a much lower one of the steady erosion of cultural values by the more traditional media of the press and periodicals and the messages in commercially-linked ephemera. It is possible to retain pride and dignity in a culture while still using that culture commercially: at its best kitsch is no more than sentimental and nostalgic but at its worst it is demeaning and alienating. Acceptance of how we might take responsibility for the visual representations of our culture and for implementing it successfully, is a challenge to be met at all levels of artistic, commercial and social endeavour. In the harsh environment of a global economy, maybe we can see it as something more positive than 'making do'.

In conclusion, it is inevitable that we must accept the reality of kitsch and its place in the economics of mass tourism. If we reject that then we may be faced with the rejection of our past. Rejecting the culture that 'we were' because we are unable to accept its metamorphosis will leave us with the prospect of 'a cultureless, post-industrial journey into the unknown'.[33] This is not comfortable or encouraging to envisage. David McCrone's last paragraph in *Scotland the Brand* could well read very pertinently, with the substitution of Cornwall for Scotland:

> Scotland is, currently at least, a stateless nation in which there is very little democratic control over the means of its own cultural reproduction. Its capacity to shape its representation is severely limited. Until such time as this is regained, then the charge that Scotland exists simply as 'land of dreamtime' will remain.[34]

Written in 1995, before devolution, this statement is particularly relevant in the debate on regional government within the British State. Culture, even one with a strong kitsch element, should be something we construct for ourselves: not something we have constructed by others. The complex ambiguity of our experience of culture building is beautifully described in John Berger's *Ways of Seeing*. He states that seeing establishes our place in the surrounding world and that although we might describe that world via language it does not alter the fact that we are visually imbedded in it. The difficulty of reconciling these two processes produces a dynamic tension, out of which a more successfully unified debate on Cornish culture might flourish: a debate in which the lived visual experience meets the studied and analytical.

NOTES AND REFERENCES

1. V. Ramachandran, *The Emerging Mind* Reith Lectures 2003. www.bbc.co.uk/radio4
2. C. Brown, *Star Spangled Kitsch*. New York, 1975, p. 105.
3. T. Kulka, *Kitsch and Art*. Philadelphia, 1996, p. 12.
4. C. Brown, 1975, p. 105.
5. P. Wollen, 'Say Hello to Rodney', in *The London Review of Books*, 17 February 2000, p. 3.

6. C. Olalquiaga, *The Artificial Kingdom*, London, 1998, p. 228.
7. Kulka, 1996, p. 81.
8. N. Kennedy and N. Kingcombe, 'The Disneyfication of Cornwall—Developing a Poldark Heritage Complex', in *International Journal of Heritage Studies*, 14:1, pp. 45–59.
9. Kulka, 1996, p. 97.
10. Kennedy & Kingcombe, p. 53.
11. Olalquiaga, 1998, p. 293.
12. Stedman Jones: quoted by A. Howkins in D. Morley and K. Robins (eds), *British Cultural Studies*, Oxford, 2001, p. 148.
13. B. Deacon, 'Imagining the Fishing', in *Rural History*, 2001, pp. 159–78.
14. T. Cross, *The Shining Sands*, Tiverton, 1994, p. 55.
15. C. Fox, *Stanhope Forbes and the Newlyn School*, Newton Abbot, 1993, p. 20; Deacon, 2001, p. 170.
16. P. Payton, 'Paralysis and Revival: The Reconstruction of Catholic-Celtic Cornwall', in E. Westland (ed.), *Cornwal:. The Cultural Construction of Place*, Penzance, 1997, pp. 25–39.
17. P. Burke, *Eyewitnessing*, London, 2001, p. 13.
18. R. Langley, *Walter Langley: Pioneer of the Newlyn Art Colony*, Bristol, 1997, p. 51.
19. Cross, 1994, p. 99.
20. A.L. Rowse, *A Cornish Childhood: Autobiography of a Cornishman*, London, 1942, p. 13.
21. L. Colley, *Britons: Forging the Nation 1707–1837*, London, 1992.
22. J. Cook, M. Hardie and C. Payne, *Singing from the Walls*, Bristol, 2000.
23. Olalquiaga, 1998, p. 293.
24. D. Hutchinson (ed.), *One Man's Dream* (guidebook for King Arthur's Great Halls), Tintagel, 2000, p. 4.
25. Hutchinson, 2000, p. 4.
26. Hutchinson, 2000, p. 27.
27. J. Gronow, *The Sociology of Taste*, London, 1997.
28. B. Cole and R. Durack, *Railway Posters 1923–1947*, London, 1992, p. 18.
29. M. Palin, *Happy Holidays: the Golden Age of Railway Posters*, London, 1998, p. 6.
30. D.P. Corbett, *The Modernity of English Art 1914–1930*, Manchester, n.d., pp. 156–57.
31. Kulka, 1996, p. 27.
32. *Cornish World*, 29, pp. 8–15.
33. D. McCrone, A. Morris and R. Kiely, *Scotland – The Brand*, Edinburgh, 1995, p. 196.
34. Mcrone, Morris & Kiely, 1995, p. 209.

'NOSCITUR A SOCIIS': JENNER, DUNCOMBE-JEWELL AND THEIR MILIEU

Sharon Lowenna

INTRODUCTION

The starting points for this study are two questions that puzzled Robert Morton Nance in his article 'Gwas Myghal [Henry Jenner] and the Cornish Revival':[1] why did Cowethas Kelto-Kernuak have so brief an existence, and why did it take a further twenty years to see the language revival make much progress? It is instructive to remember that the bulk of Henry Jenner's commitment to the Cornish language occurred relatively late in his life when he was already retired. This study, therefore, examines Jenner's earlier life and preoccupations, contextualising the view that Jenner's Grand Bardship marked the culmination of his lifelong politics. It explores Cowethas Kelto-Kernuak and the establishment of Gorseth Kernow within wider European and Pan-Celtic political currents, and seeks to counterpoint other extant accounts[2] as an interventionist strategy for re-appraising the 'received wisdom' on the Cornish Revival. Addressed in relation to Jenner, Duncombe Jewell and their milieu are Anglo-Catholicism, Jacobitism, hermeticism, and their links to the 'Celtic Right'.

THE LEGACY OF BISHOP JENNER

Jenner Snr (Bishop Henry Lascelles Jenner) was an ordained Anglican with a deep commitment to High Church Ritualism. Politically, in his own son's words (Henry Jenner): 'Most advanced High Churchmen of the period could be characterised as extreme Tory in their political views.'[3] Bishop Jenner was a member of the Order of Corporate Reunion (OCR)[4] formed in 1874 by the Rev. F.G. Lee to promote the reunification of Anglicanism with both Roman Catholicism and the

Eastern Orthodox Church. As Anglo-Catholicism is a key influence on the Cornish Revival, it is important here to differentiate between 'Catholicism' and Tridentine Roman Catholicism as the OCR was in no way *ultramontane*. Anglicanism was held to be more faithful to early Christianity and more 'catholic' than Roman Catholicism. The nineteenth century and early twentieth century were contentious for Anglican unity as a number of high-profile Anglicans converted to Roman Catholicism. These included Robert Hugh Benson, son of Anglican Archbishop Edward White Benson, who became a Roman Catholic priest in 1904 and subsequently Monsignor in 1911. There was, however, a less well-known phenomenon of conversion the other way. The First Vatican Council pronouncement of Papal Infallibility in 1870 led to disaffected Roman Catholics throughout Europe joining the 'Old' Catholic Church with its affirmation of Celto-Gallicanism.

The OCR promoted a return to pre-Reformation worship, before centralist Papal authority arrogated the *a priori* autonomy of divinely ordained monarchies. Its commonalities with Eastern Orthodoxy lay in pre-Nicene Christianity, that is, before the split between Eastern and Western Church traditions. Its theology stems, therefore, from the Eastern Church legacy to Celto-Gallican liturgical practices. In that knowledge, it is interesting to note that the Troparians of the Orthodox Church Kalendar include St Kea and St Cuby.[5] A return to the mysticism and discipline of the pre-Reformation 'Church Militant' was manifested in ornate vestments, elaborate communion practices, burning of incense, and strict liturgical scholarship. Anglican Ritualism linked these to a reverence for medievalism and painstaking antiquarian researches that traced the validity of Apostolic succession.[6] Everyone connected to the Order of Corporate Reunion was sworn to secrecy, and F.G. Lee destroyed all papers relating to the Order prior to his death.[7] Jenner Snr was also an active member of the *Societas Sanctae Crucis* (Society of the Holy Cross); its primary mission was to 'maintain and extend the Catholic Faith and Discipline' in adhering to Catholic practices in the Celebration of the Holy Eucharist. In 1867, the *Societas Sanctae Crucis* sent a laudatory address to Archbishop Gray of Cape Town, congratulating his actions for the trial of Bishop Colenso *in absentio* for heresy.[8]

Bishop Jenner's son (Henry Jenner) grew up steeped in his father's staunch Anglo-Catholicism, even sometimes adopting the High Church 'Old Style' Julian Calendar dating of letters. Bishop Jenner sent his son to St Mary's College, Harlow—an ultra-conservative public school for 'sons of the extremer members of the Catholic party in the Church of England'.[9] His formative years were troubled, as his father became embroiled in his own battle for a colonial Bishopric. Henry

Lascelles Jenner was consecrated as Bishop of Dunedin, New Zealand, in 1866.[10] His selection and consecration took place in England, allegedly without the full consultation or consent of Church authorities in Dunedin itself. However, Bishop Jenner was embarrassingly rejected by Dunedin for his Ritualist notoriety. Despite visiting New Zealand to put his case personally, Bishop Jenner did not find favour with the majority of Dunedin diocese and was humiliatingly rejected once again. Anglican authorities in England prevaricated, but were not prepared to foist him on Dunedin in the teeth of such strong opposition. Despite this, he refused to give up his claim to the See and was eventually defeated in 1871. Throughout, he refused to believe that his was a lost cause and insisted on using the full title of his never-to-be-sat-on Dunedin See. It was not until 1888 that he attained a Bishopric, leading a small congregation of the Old Catholic Church in Paris.[11]

Clearly, title and standing were important to Bishop Jenner. In 1848, for example, he had founded his own confraternity and order of chivalry, entitled The Sovereign Sacred Religious and Military Order of Knights Protectors of the Sacred Sepulchre of Our Lord Jesus and of the Most Holy Temple of Sion. It later merged with two other spurious Jacobite orders—the Realm of Sion and the Order of the Sangreal —into a 'federal chivalric condominium' called the Sovereign Order of the Realm of Sion.[12] These kind of revived 'ancient' Orders commonly embodied exclusivity, invented ceremonial, grand titles and deference to an absolutist 'Grand Master' or Hierophant. It is outside the intent of this study to rehearse the putative links between Chivalric Orders and the Knights Templar, 'true' Merovingian bloodlines, Scottish Rite Masonry and Arthuriana. Neither is there scope to explore the over-lapping discourses of Sang Real (Holy Blood) and San Greal (Holy Grail).[13] It will suffice to highlight a European-wide nineteenth-century resurgence of arcane ideas that rallied elites to secret societies and mysticism. In this philosophy, the Glorious Revolution of 1688 that brought the Protestants William and Mary to the throne in Britain had usurped the true Anglo-Catholic Church and the 'holy' bloodline of the Stuart monarchs. Sympathies lay with James I of England and VI of Scotland who asserted his regal absolutism. James being 'Jacobus' in Latin, the term Jacobite was used. As a consequence, King Charles I was revered as Saint and Martyr for the regicide that resulted from his refusal to relinquish his Divine Right of Kings.

JENNER THE JACOBITE

In 1897, the Marquis de Ruvigny et Raineval explained Legitimism as an overarching term that supported restoration of 'legitimate' (holy blood) monarchies, be they Jacobite, Carlist or Miguelist.[14] The

Jacobite basis of the Divine Right of Kings also pertained to Legitimist support for the 'Carlist' Pretender to the Spanish throne (Don Carlos VII) and the 'Miguelist' Pretender to the throne of Portugal (Dom Miguel). Given fervent monarchist and anti-modern sympathies, Coulombe states that it is not surprising that 'the noted Cornish language scholar and nationalist Henry Jenner was one of the major revivers of nineteenth-century Jacobitism.'[15] It is, though, a misreading of Jenner to characterize him as merely a 'romantic' Jacobite, for Legitimism politically was ultra-monarchist and anti-democratic.

Henry Jenner, the Marquis de Ruvigny and Bertram, 5th Earl of Ashburnham, were the prime initiators of the Exhibition of the Royal House of Stuart at the New Gallery in Regent Street in 1889. The Earl of Ashburnham was President of the General Committee.[16] Together with other Fellows of the Society of Antiquaries, Henry Jenner of the British Museum is listed as member of the Catalogue Committee and Executive Committee with special responsibility for manuscripts and printed books. Mr and Mrs H. Jenner are listed as loaning personally owned relics of the Martyred King Charles I, as is the Rev F.G. Lee of the Order of Corporate Reunion. Amongst gentlemen patrons are F.A. Lumbye and E.R. Crump Esqs, *confrères* of Jenner and Ashburnham in the Jacobite Society of the Order of the White Rose (OWR). Ernest Crump was the OWR's Registrar—a respectable solicitor and self-styled Jacobite 'Chevalier'[17] who had cultivated a likeness to Charles I by wearing a Van Dyke beard and melancholy expression. When Lumbye wrote to Jenner enquiring after a Legitimist Kalendar that the British Museum had misplaced, Jenner could not shed any light. He did, however, make the startling admission that he had personally suppressed British Museum materials in the past, but this was not one of those occasions.[18]

Patron of the Exhibition of the Royal House of Stuart was Queen Victoria, who generously lent several Stuart artefacts even though she was a Hanoverian usurper. The Exhibition adopted the affectation of Legitimist titling of more than a thousand exhibits, entering the names of post-Stuart monarchs in parentheses and thus implying Queen Victoria's lack of legitimacy. The direct Stuart claim descended from Charles I's daughter whilst Victoria was merely descended from his sister. Moreover, the Stuart heir embodied absolutist divine right whereas Victoria's line held the throne as constitutional monarch only, by narrow Parliamentary consent of 1688.[19] When Jenner was presented to Queen Victoria as one of the promoters of the Stuart Exhibition, she snubbed him as she immediately turned her back on him, saying curtly: 'I have heard of Mr Jenner.'[20]

A commemorative Pedigree Chart of the House of Stuart was on sale, compiled by the Portcullis Poursuivant-of-Arms. Thus the accession to the throne by William and Mary was refuted in favour of the Legitimist accession of 'James III and VII' and heirs. The 'rightful' Queen of England and Scotland was Her Majesty Queen Mary Theresa Henrietta Dorothea, Archduchess of Austria-Este-Modena, and consort of Ludwig III of Bavaria: the 'Queen across the water—Mary IV and II'. Mary Theresa and the Bavarian Court in Munich seem to have taken a diplomatic view of Legitimism, neither encouraging nor denying her claims. The Legitimist heir-apparent to the thrones of England and Scotland was Mary Theresa's eldest son Crown Prince Rupprecht of Bavaria. Rupprecht was not Pretender Prince of Wales, as that is a title that can only be conferred by the Sovereign. He was however Jacobite Duke of Cornwall, by hereditary right.

Exclusive Jacobite drawing room cliques (dismissed by Jenner) existed to extol Charles I.[21] These included the Forget-Me-Not Club (in memory of Charles I's last exhortation before his beheading: 'Remember!'), the White Cockade Club and the Society of King Charles the Martyr. They observed Jacobite anniversaries, wearing mourning on 30 January and decorating with funerary wreaths the statue of Charles I then in Trafalgar Square. The Society of the Order of the White Rose was founded in 1888 by the Earl of Ashburnham and was presided over by Jenner as Chancellor. Jenner intimated in personal letters, however, that he preferred his involvement in Legitimist politics to remain publicly low-profile. He was variously documented at different times under *ex officio* titles such as 'the Recorder' and 'Thesaurarius'. Lord Ashburnham had wanted *de jure* recognition of Legitimist titles and Chivalric rank. He himself had been honoured as Knight of the Golden Fleece and of Franz-Joseph, Knight Grand Cross of the Sovereign Order of Malta, Knight of the Teutonic Order of the Levant, Knight Commander of the Order of Saint Gregory, Grand Master of the Sovereign Order of Saint Thomas of Acre and Regent of the Confraternity of the Knights of the Realm of Sion.[22]

The Society of the Order of the White Rose was unashamedly elitist and exclusive. A criticism printed in *The Globe* in 1888 accused it of making no effort to increase its members and holding aloof from the outer world. Jenner's published refutation stated:

> The Order does not consist of Roman Catholic ladies; for many of its members are Anglican gentlemen . . . [with] no idea of setting forward the Church of Rome . . . The Order is in no sense a public society. The general public are not invited

to join in it; nor would they find admission thereto an easy
matter.[23]

In the *White Cockade Journal*, the Honourable Mrs Ermengarda
Greville-Nugent, Foundress of the Society of King Charles the Martyr,
Companion and Senator of the Order of the White Rose, wrote
an article on the OWR's history. After explaining its hierarchy of
Chancellor, Recorder, Registrar, Herald, Proto-Notary, Senate and
Companions of the Order, she described the ceremony for admission
of Companions-Elect.

> The Chancellor (Mr Jenner, whose imposing height and
> long beard, added to his dignified presence, made him well
> fitted for his role) sat on a raised throne-like chair, with the
> Senators in a semi-circle to right and left of him. Opposite sat
> the Registrar at a table on which was the parchment Roll to
> be signed by the Companions-elect. 'White Rose Herald',
> Cyril Davenport, Esqre, of the British Museum, was charged
> with emblazoning their coats-of-arms upon the Roll. Having
> signed, each Companion-elect was conducted to kneel before
> the Chancellor's 'throne'.

Jenner's role was to submit each genuflecting Companion-manqué to
the Order's confidential list of ritual questions, such as:

> Do you believe the Revolution of 1688 to be a National
> Crime?
> Do you believe in the Hereditary Divine Right of Kings,
> wholly independent of the Will of the People?

The Chancellor then pinned the badge—a silver rose on a white
ribbon—on the breasts of the neophytes and, pressing their right hands
between his palms, impressively said, 'Remember!'[24]

The Royalist, first published in 1890, financed by Jenner[25] and
edited for a while by L.C.R. Duncombe-Jewell, carried articles on Irish
and Welsh Jacobitism, Jacobite secret ciphers, and the distinction
between Cornish and English identity.[26] The Legitimist Ensign even
ran an anti-Hanoverian poster campaign in London on the eve of
Edward VII's coronation in 1902.[27] More hard-line activist organizations were the Thames Valley Legitimist Club and the Legitimist
League; the latter described as 'a secret society which takes care to
allow as little of its doings as possible to transpire to the public'.[28]
Extremist Legitimist groups certainly did exist with the serious aim of

dynasty change, largely in support of the Bourbon Pretender to two thrones—as both King Don Carlos VII of Spain and as Charles XI of France. A clandestine group in turn-of-the-century Paris operated for the restoration of Don Carlos, and for the Legitimist claim of Dom Miguel to the throne of Portugal. The group's other Rightist strong-holds of support were Normandy and Brittany. These Carlists in France were known as the Blancs d'Espagne.[29] Carlist clubs thrived in parts of Spain and Carlist newspapers were regularly published. Don Carlos was therefore regarded as Legitimism's brightest hope for regaining his throne. Indeed, in 1898, *Pearson's Magazine* stated that 'very active measures are now being taken to prepare for a favourable moment, when Don Carlos will give the signal for the resumption of hostilities'.

THE *FIREFLY* PLOT

Lord Ashburnham was involved in a scandal in 1899, in which Henry Jenner was also implicated. On 15 July 1899 Vincent English (Vice-Chairman of the Thames Valley Legitimist Club) was caught attempting to smuggle a large cache of firearms into Spain, which would have initiated a long-planned Carlist *coup d'état*. International censure[30] was exacerbated by the fact that Lieutenant English was a serving Royal Navy officer. Dom Miguel, the Portuguese Pretender, had a residence on the coast at St Jean de Luz, close to the French-Spanish border. This royal residence was put into the service of Spanish Carlist insurgents. Two substantial deliveries of guns were transferred from the yacht *Firefly*[31] at St Jean de Luz under cover of darkness, but a third nighttime run was intercepted. *Firefly* was boarded, her crew arrested, forced into the port of Arcachon and her illicit cargo impounded. The gunrunning vessel had been purchased and refurbished by Ashburnham; he had also financed the weapons and ammunition obtained from Germany. Solicitor E.R. Crump's brief was to obscure any documentary evidence of Ashburnham's role. Crump also had to address the international legalities necessary to have *Firefly* and her crew released from arrest, on payment of a substantial fine. Her cargo of rifles and ammunition was of course confiscated. The large number of Carlist Papers of the Ashburnham Family Collection[32] shed light on the extensive planning involved. Telegraphic cables and letters in secret code indicate coordination in Paris, Venice, Madrid, Cerralbo, Santander, and St Jean de Luz. Docu-ments also evidence that Jenner was the 'Firefly Plot' cryptographer and probable Carlist liaison to Germany. One of Jenner's letters to Ashburnham evaluates different cipher manuals,[33] the pros and cons of dot ciphers versus square alphabet ciphers, and recommends the use of Jenner's own sophisticated secret codes system. Jenner's encryption instructions are to fasten tracing paper on to the key alphabet and symbols, and to use red and black ink for clarity of decryption. His code appraisal also points out that 'Jewell's other cipher seems to turn out exactly like the ordinary easy ones'.[34]

Duncombe-Jewell's active involvement in the Firefly Plot is confirmed by a letter he wrote later to Jenner of their work for Ashburnham's *Blancs d'Espagne* in preparation for the abortive Carlist rising. He reminds Jenner of his commitment in 'carrying out delicate and not always safe missions' on the Continent.[35] Whilst Ashburnham's and Lieut. English's involvement could not be kept out of the press; Jenner was able to cover up his own complicity. He instructed Lumbye:

> As for if anyone went to Munich or not, you know nothing . . .
> If you think it advisable you might say that while I was abroad
> last year you sent all my letters at frequent intervals to
> addresses all of which were in Switzerland and none in
> Bavaria, and received postcards and letters from me from
> Switzerland only.[36]

Firefly's crew pay list includes a 'C. Alexander'.[37] Intriguingly, this is one of the many, many aliases of Alexander Crowley—better known by his Celticized name—Aleister Crowley. Crowley's autobiographical writings[38] explain his seduction by Legitimism and the Celtic Church. At Cambridge, he says,

> My reactionary conservatism came into conflict with my anti-
> Catholicism. A reconciliation was effected by means of what
> they called the Celtic Church . . . My innate transcendentalism
> leapt out towards it. The *Morte d'Arthur, Lohengrin* and
> *Parsifal* were my world. I not only wanted to go out on the
> quest of the Holy Grail, I intended to do it.
>
> I became a romantic Jacobite . . . I wished to place Mary IV
> and II on the throne. I was a bigoted legitimist. I actually
> joined a conspiracy on behalf of Don Carlos, obtained a
> commission to work a machine gun, took pains to make
> myself a first-class rifle shot and studied drill, tactics and
> strategy. However, when the time came for the invasion of
> Spain, Don Carlos got cold feet. The conspiracy was disclosed;
> and Lord Ashburnham's yacht, which was running the arms,
> fell into the hands of the Spanish navy.

For his efforts, Crowley received a Carlist knighthood. He took his admission to the Order with absolute seriousness, keeping ritual vigil in a wood all night over his armorial bearings.[39] After this disappointing Legitimist foray, Crowley (at this time a man of some means) retired to his newly purchased home—Boleskine House near Loch Ness—to work mystic rituals.

THE HERMETIC ORDER OF THE GOLDEN DAWN

This interest had led Crowley to join an occult fraternity—the Hermetic Order of the Golden Dawn—in November 1898. Heading the Order of the Golden Dawn was another ultra-Jacobite, Samuel Lidell MacGregor Mathers. Mathers had established the elaborate rituals, Mystic Circumnambulations and hierarchical degrees of the Golden Dawn based on Masonic-Rosicrucian practices, allegedly derived from a German occult Order's 'Cypher Manuscript' of dubious provenance. He took as his Golden Dawn *nomen incognito* the Gaelic motto 'S Rioghail Mo Dhream: Royal is my Tribe'.[40] Mathers and Crowley apparently first met in May 1899, just weeks before the ill-fated *Firefly* sailed out of Dartmouth to rendezvous with her cargo of rifles.[41] Mathers and Crowley were among a number who had studied medieval manuscripts and grimoires in the British Museum at the time Jenner was Keeper of Manuscripts there. The *soi-disant* Sobieski Stuarts spent a great deal of time researching genealogies and clan tartans in the Reading Room in 1870s,[42] and in the late 1880s and 90s William Butler Yeats was a frequent researcher. Sir E. Wallis Budge, Keeper of Egyptian Antiquities, was also rumoured to be a member of the Hermetic Order of the Golden Dawn. Other known members included the Rev J.C. Fitzgerald of Falmouth (Frater 'Deus Meus Deus'),[43] and heiress Annie Horniman, who supported Mathers financially and was later benefactress of Yeats and the Abbey Theatre, Dublin (Soror 'Fortiter et Recte'). Her father was the Liberal Member of Parliament for Falmouth and Penryn, who was scandalized to receive an anonymous letter informing him of his daughter's involvement with 'a Secret Order which has for its object practising so-called witchcraft of the Middle Ages'.[44] How one became a member of the Hermetic Order of the Golden Dawn is, of course, cloaked in mystery. Firstly, one had to be recommended by an existing member or trusted simpatico, such as Arthurian enthusiast Ralph de Tunstall Sneyd, author of *Vivien and Merlin*.[45] Next one's background and suitability were thoroughly investigated, followed by a personal interview conducted by one Frater and one Soror of the 'Inner' circle. Finally, an 'astral' or 'psychic' interview was undertaken.

Mathers's authoritarian direction of the Golden Dawn accrued from the 'Secret Chiefs' of the Order, channelling their esoteric knowledge through him alone. He and his wife Moina moved to Paris in 1891, where he was heavily involved with Legitimist politics. There, Mathers assumed the Jacobite title of Count MacGregor, Earl of Glenstrae,[46] and Annie Horniman became perturbed by Mathers's Jacobite obsessions, which she regarded as a major distraction from his Order of the Golden Dawn responsibilities. As Ellic Howe has observed:

> There are a number of obscure references in various letters to Mathers' 'political' activities. It seems Count MacGregor de Glenstrae was involved in some kind of Celtic lunatic fringe and hoped for a restoration of the House of Stuart. Yeats provided a clue in Autobiographies: 'Mathers imagined a Napoleonic role for himself, . . . a Highland Principality, and even offered subordinate posts to unlikely people.' . . . Celtic loyalties as well as Magic brought Yeats and Mathers together. He went to Paris in 1896 to consult Mathers about the ritual for a projected Order of Celtic Mysteries. . . . Yeats says of Mathers 'At night he would dress himself in Highland dress, and dance the sword dance, and his mind brooded on the ramifications of clans and tartans. Yet I have at moments doubted whether he had seen the Highlands, or even, until invited there by some White Rose Society, Scotland itself.'[47]

It is clear that the break-up of the Golden Dawn can be attributed largely to Mathers' prioritizing of Legitimism. At one point he even declared his political and military activities were at the behest of 'the Secret Chiefs'[48] and the work was so dangerous that he feared assassination.[49] Mathers's leadership of the London Temple of the Golden Dawn became increasingly bizarre. He brooked no questioning of his authority and threatened critics with occult warfare. Crowley was initiated in Paris by Mathers into the Higher Degree of Zelator, which the London Temple refused to recognize. Mathers then authorised Crowley to go to London to occupy the Golden Dawn headquarters on his behalf. This interjection resulted in the notorious 'Battle of Blythe Road'. Crowley arrived in Highland dress, and wearing a black mask of Osiris over his face. Yeats had the police called and Crowley was forced to leave. Members of the Golden Dawn met in emergency session the same day to formally suspend Mathers, pending ratification by the entire College of Adepti. An interregnum Order was mooted—free from Mathers' dictatorship—to be convened under the camouflage name of The Research and Archaeological Association.[50] The Blythe Road schism in the Golden Dawn eventually led Yeats and the anti-Mathers faction to establish the Stella Matutina Temple. Mathers's vitriolic letter to Yeats asserts that there is just one sin to top Yeats's treachery: 'now it only remains for you to betray your country to the Saxons with whom you seem so proud to associate yourself!'[51]

Yeats's exploration of Irish Celticity is well documented. That he had links with Cornish Revivalists warrants further research. John S. Kelly's *A W.B. Yeats Chronology* cites a meeting in 1902 between Yeats, Annie Horniman, and Duncombe-Jewell,[52] and Yeats's publication of his poem 'Bressel the Fisherman' in the *Cornish Magazine* in 1898 was the first time it appeared in print.[53] The Irish-Celtic Revival at this time epitomizes a contested space in which notions of 'Irishness' were subject to competing political appropriations. *Celtia* 1901–4 evidences a wide spectrum of Irish delegates to the Pan-Celtic Congresses, from republican future insurgents of the 1916 Easter Rising to Anglo-Ascendancy figures of the Celtic Right. Irish Nationalism and Home Rule were not congruent with Republicanism. It was possible to desire secession from Britain but to remain Imperialist and to imagine an Ireland federated to the British Empire. Equally, rule by restoration of dispossessed royalty was not out of the question. Neither was rule by a leisured and lettered class, purged of democratic laxity. Yeats's brand of Irish nationalism was increasingly right-of-centre politically, and his anti-democratic views would lead him into his flirtation with 1930s' fascism.

DUNCOMBE-JEWELL AND COWETHAS KELTO-KERNUAK

Celtia does not seem to evidence a diverse range of political stances in the Cornish delegation to Congress, as a staunchly establishment and Anglican bloc represented Cornwall. One delegate, though, stands out as something of a misfit. Around the turn of the century, Duncombe-Jewell made a living as freelance journalist for right-of-centre publications such as the *Morning Post* and *Daily Mail*. In fact, his accomplishments at the *Daily Mail* have become a much-quoted exemplar in the history of journalism.[54] In 1898, he was assigned to cover the story of the launching of HMS *Albion* on the Thames. Confronted back at the *Daily Mail* office as to why his filed story contained no reference to the thirty people who had drowned at the event, Duncombe-Jewell's alleged response was: 'Well, I did see some people bobbing about in the water as I came away but . . .'.

Duncombe-Jewell's apparent absence from the 1901 Census is because he had become a war reporter. Like the more famous Winston Churchill, he was acting *Morning Post* correspondent covering the South African War.[55] He returned to Britain before the war's end to collaborate with Jenner again in Jacobite and Celtic politics. Together

with establishment figures such as Sir W.L. Salusbury-Trelawny and
Thurstan Peter, they founded Cowethas Kelto-Kernuak in August
1901, making the announcement in the 1902 Congress issue of *Celtia*.
Celtia 1901–4 demonstrate their effective lobbying on behalf of
Cornwall to be admitted to Congress as the sixth *bona fide* Celtic
nation. Duncombe-Jewell's enthusiastic Secretaryship of Cowethas
Kelto-Kernuak is on record and—tellingly—his arguments for the
inclusion of Cornwall include the (unsupported) statement that
the Cornish Celts had ever fought for the causes of 'the Catholic Faith
and Legitimate Monarchy':[56] a reference, presumably, to the 1549
Prayer Book Rebellion and Cornish Royalism in the Civil War.

Duncombe-Jewell's writings in *Celtia* celebrate some notable
Cornish authors such as Arthur Symons, close friend of Yeats and
another contributor to the *Cornish Magazine*. Also listed are two
Anglo-Cornish writers with sustained right-wing politics—the Hon J.F.
Rennell Rodd and Mr Herbert Vivian. Sir Rennell Rodd, when British
Ambassador in Rome in 1915, informed the Foreign Office of Emily
Hobhouse's 'unpatriotic' pacificist activism in Italy.[57] He later became
a member of the fascist January Club.[58] Herbert Vivian was an
affirmed Legitimist and seems to have shared many acquaintances
with, and the preoccupations of, the Celtic Right. There is *en passant*
reference to Vivian's presence in Venice[59] in Lord Ashburnham's
Carlist papers, some years before the *Firefly* scandal. Herbert Vivian's
magazine *The Whirlwind* had attracted liberal criticism in 1890 for
anti-semitism because of its statement that 'the proper way to deal
with Jews is a rigorous boycott'.[60] In 1933, Vivian published *Kings in
Waiting: A Survey of the Monarchist Position in Europe*, with a study of
Mussolini's Fascist Italy following in 1936.[61] Furthermore, he was
for many years a close friend of Aleister Crowley. Vivian reviewed
Crowley's book *Konx Om Pax* and included an appreciation of him in
his own autobiography.[62]

Duncombe-Jewell's spirited defence of Cornwall's Celticity is
his *tour-de-force*, though his idiosyncrasies threatened to compromise
Cornwall's acceptance by the Celtic Congress. His eccentric crusade for
'authentic' Celtic-Cornish costumery of blue kilts and conical hats,
and his tendencies to personalize debate, attracted some disapproval.
Perhaps as a consequence of Congressional rebuke, Duncombe-Jewell
abruptly disappeared from Cowethas Kelto-Kernuak sometime in
1903, leaving Jenner to follow through with Cornwall's case.
Duncombe-Jewell re-surfaced again shortly after in an unexpected
place: the Scottish residence of Aleister Crowley. Crowley's account
relates how he invited L.C.R. Duncombe-Jewell to Boleskine House
for just a week, but instead he became settled there as Crowley's

general factotum. Duncombe-Jewell at this time began calling himself Ludovick Cameron, 'being a passionate Jacobite and allegedly having a Cameron somewhere in his family tree'. Jewell a.k.a. Cameron was 'very keen on the Celtic revival and wanted to unite the five [sic] Celtic nations in an empire. In this political project he had not wholly succeeded: but he had got as far as designing a flag.' L.C.R.D.J. Cameron was present at the 1903 marriage vows of Crowley and Rose Kelly, compensating for what he saw as a lack of gravitas in the standard civil ceremony: 'Duncombe-Jewell excelled himself. The ordinary oath was not for him. He produced a formula the majesty of which literally inhibited the normal functions of our minds. It was the finest piece of ritualistic rigmarole that I ever heard in my life'. In July the following year, Crowley and Rose's short-lived daughter—Nuit Ma Ahathoor Hecate Sappho Jezebel Lillith—was born. Duncombe-Jewell remarked later that she had died of 'acute nomenclature':[63] which is perhaps ironic coming from Ludovick Charles Richard Duncombe-Jewell Cameron.

It is more than likely that his identity change to Cameron was helpful in evading his creditors. Jewell/Cameron demonstrated a flair for debt evasion and sponging money throughout his life. Far from Henry Jenner lacking knowledge of the whereabouts of L.C.R.D.J. Cameron, Jenner and he continued to meet and correspond for another thirty years until Jenner's death. Much of the copious correspondence from Cameron comprises begging letters and unfulfilled promises of 'the cheque's in the post' variety. It is marked that, over a long period, Cameron's vague threats to re-locate to Cornwall are always accompanied by yet another request to 'Hal' for money.[64] If Jenner wished Cameron to stay away from Cornwall, it must have been at some considerable personal expense. In 1915, Jenner was even advised by Cameron's father to put a stop to Ludovick's scrounging. Ronald Jewell expressed his regret that his son was in so much financial debt to the Jenners and ends his letter: 'We pray daily that God will deal with him in His Grace and Mercy and deliver him from the Snare of Satan.'[65] Between 1908 and 1918, Cameron was a contributor of articles to the *Occult Review*[66] on such diverse topics as 'Superstitions Connected with Sport' and the 'Mystery of Lourdes'. R.H. Benson too was an *Occult Review* contributor, as were several members of the Temples of the Golden Dawn and Stella Matutina, and an anonymous writer with the nom-de-plume 'One and All'.

Jenner's published output up until the First World War was varied in subject, and in 1904 his *Handbook of the Cornish Language* came into print. Morton Nance reminds that the publication of Jenner's *Handbook* was a:

tremendous advance from his position in 1877, since which
date he had practically done nothing at Cornish . . . The
Handbook was not followed up, as intended, by a volume of
reading-lessons, exercises and vocabularies that would have
completed it as a means of instruction. The collapse of the
Celtic Cornish Society was partly to blame for this.[67]

As Duncombe-Jewell's language advocacy in 1902 had emphasized
its 'study and preservation' rather than any intention of imminent
popular revival, the collapse of Cowethas Kelto-Kernuak was not
perhaps as much of a setback as Nance believed. Jenner's work
on Cornish chiefly comprised scholarly and antiquarian interests.[68]
Those continued in collaboration with such people as Thurstan Peter,
Canon G.H. Doble and Thomas Taylor; all three expressed Jacobite
sympathies.[69]

JENNER IN RETIREMENT

In 1907 Jenner wrote the Cornish Gorseth ceremony, 'just in case'.
It was adapted from the Welsh Gorsedd, but has curious and
unmistakeable echoes of the Order of the White Rose ceremonials. On
his retirement to Hayle in 1909, Jenner's Cornish-language interests
were well balanced with work on Arthuriana, folk legends, Legitimism
and Anglo-Catholicism. Jenner's contribution to *The Fairy Faith in
Celtic Countries*[70] was on pisky legends in Cornwall; the anthology
itself evidencing the *volkisch* preoccupations of Pan-Celticism. The
Grail legends and their link to Joseph of Arimathea are particularly
pertinent to Jenner's Celtic Church and Old Catholic leanings. In the
1909 *Catholic Encyclopedia*, Arthur F.J. Remy explains that the Grail
legends claimed for the history of the Church in Britain an origin as
illustrious as the Church of Rome, but independent of it. The Grail
legends, therefore, challenged Roman primacy and legitimated the
theology of Anglo-Catholicism in Britain.[71] Jenner also undertook paid
freelance writing for the *Catholic Encyclopaedia* from 1907 to 1913,
where his wide knowledge of pre-Reformation Catholic theology
provided highly specialized articles on Orthodox and Celto-Gallican
liturgy.[72] The British and Foreign Bible Society[73] was another
organization enlisting his knowledge of Georgian, Arminian, Coptic,
Nestorian, Syrian, Samaritan, Abyssinian, and Ethiopic Churches. His
Legitimist commitment had not waned as correspondence and
publications in the Truro archives identify Jenner as the author of
numerous pieces including, for example, an Anglo-Catholic Sequentia
'Sancta Caroli Martyrium'[74] and a Carlist poem 'Dios, Patria, Rey'.[75]
Mr and Mrs Jenner were invited to subscribe to an appeal from

the Society of King Charles the Martyr for a memorial donation to Falmouth's Anglican parish church that has Charles I as its patron saint.[76] The portrait, in the style of Lely, remains in the Church of King Charles the Martyr. The church continues to hold its Patronal Service each year on the anniversary of the regicide. It is also pertinent to note that the motto of Falmouth Town Council is 'Remember!'.

Jenner's Legitimist Papers from the Edwardian period contain an enlightening manifesto of the Thames Valley Legitimist Club.[77] It sets out its Principal Objects[78] as asserting Christian, Monarchist, and Royal Prerogatives, and confirms the Legitimist aim to 'oppose in every way Republicanism, Atheism and Socialism'. In 1910, Jenner was still corresponding with the Marquis de Ruvigny and, the same year, the Earl of Ashburnham again enlisted Jenner's assistance in verifying the credentials of a Captain Gallenga who was volunteering for discreet Carlist missions overseas.[79] Genealogical research into royal bloodlines continued too. The *Fiery Cross* reviewed Jenner's study 'Who is the Heir to the Duchy of Brittany?'[80] Jenner's answer was: Her Majesty Queen Mary Theresa, consort of Ludwig III of Bavaria. The *Fiery Cross* explained that Mary Theresa was therefore heir to 'all Celtia, with Saxondom and Normandy thrown in'.[81] Nor was Jenner's Jacobitism pure intellectualism. The Jenner Papers[82] include many exchanges with the Bavarian Royal House and Court. Warm letters, postcards and photographs were sent to him from Queen Mary Theresa, Ludwig III, Princess Hildegard, Princess Louis, Princess Adelgunde, Baroness Wullfen, and Countess Durckheim. The Royal household in Munich also received Carlist, Miguelist, and Jacobite visitors of Jenner's acquaintance such as the Marquis de Ruvigny.[83] These royal letters (right up to the outbreak of the Great War in 1914) make friendly references to several occasions the Jenners stayed with the Bavarian Royal Family in Munich and at their summer Palace of Leutstetten near Berchtesgaden. Not too far over the Austrian border, the Portuguese Pretender Dom Miguel (a serving officer in the Austrian army) also lived in exile,[84] where his 'Miguelista' adherents—servants of Michael—paid court.

Jacobite circles in 1914 were presumably quite shaken when war was declared as Crown Prince Rupprecht joined Ludendorff's Command on the Flanders front. Jenner blamed the Prussians for the Great War, considering that the Bavarians and Austrians had no choice but to follow their lead.[85] Jenner's son Bernard served in the British Royal Navy, seeing action in the Heligoland engagements. Despite that, Jenner received warnings that known Legitimists were under surveillance, suspected by intelligence authorities of being in communication with Munich.[86] Reconciling his anti-Hanoverian stance with

patriotic allegiance to the British monarch was not a quandary for
Jenner, as any monarchy was better than none. He became Hon.
Secretary of Hayle Belgian Refugee Relief Committee, though he says
the 'only thing to do is let them blether, and then go & do as I think
best'.[87] He resigned in mid-1915. He was also a recruiting officer.
In a tortuous ethical segue, he squared his Jacobite conscience by
explaining that he was not required to swear an oath to serve King
George V—only the recruit was. He complains also that neither he nor
a fellow recruiting officer have been made JPs: 'but as the two of us are
neither Radicals nor Methodist class-leaders, there is not much chance
of such a thing in Cornwall'.[88] In July 1914, Cameron wrote asking the
Jenners for left-off clothes, socks and shoes. Early in 1915, Jenner
informed Lumbye that 'Jewell alias Cameron has got a commission in
the Cameron Highlanders and either has gone to the front or will go
shortly.'[89] Whether Cameron did or did not go to the front, in the
winter of 1916 he and Jenner enjoyed some amiable time together in
Bath.[90] By early 1917 Cameron was out of uniform again, begging for
money and Bernard's old overcoat as he had none.[91] The War meant
that the Order of the White Rose was moribund. By 1924, when a
revival of the OWR was mooted, Jenner had lost enthusiasm in favour
of his Cornish interests. Approached to hand over OWR property, he
seemed willing to do so, but only after his careful weeding of the
correspondence files. He did not consent to hand over his OWR
Chancellor's Badge of Office as it was his personal property; he had
commissioned it personally from a Masonic jeweller whom he knew.[92]

JENNER AND THE CELTIC RIGHT

Throughout Europe, the first quarter of the twentieth century was
marked politically by conflict between reactionary and Leftist
ideologies. In Russia in 1908, the Monarchist Right formed the
anti-semitic and anti-bolshevist Union of the Archangel Michael,[93] but
the 1917 Russian Revolution manifested a severe threat to anti-
democratic and anti-socialist sensitivities. This led to a number of
far-Right groups in Britain being established in the inter-war years.
The British Fascisti, for example, was formed in 1923 to oppose
Socialism and Communism[94] and was followed in 1934 by the aristocratic January Club.[95] In France, the fascist Croix-de-Feu[96] and Action
Francaise[97] were the Rightist spearheads of 'the nationalism of the
blood and soil'. Spanish nationalism was developing along the divisive
lines that would lead to the Spanish Civil War; Catalan fascists in the
early 1930s had their Parsifal and Grail cults centred on Montserrat[98]
and, after Franco seized power, he united the fascists of the Falange
with the Carlist-Monarchists, forming the *Falange Española*

Tradicionalista.[99] Gwyn A. Williams's study *When Was Wales?* identifies a marked right-wing tonality in Welsh nationalism of the period, typified by Saunders Lewis and Ambrose Bebb. With others, they formed Plaid Genedlaethol Cymru (Welsh Nationalist Party) in 1925. Lewis was deeply conservative, a monarchist, and a believer in leadership by a synarchy of elite and cultured gentry. Williams says Bebb, after studying at the Sorbonne, 'burst on the scene in the early 1920s virtually as a spokesman for Action Francaise with a Breton accent' and declared, 'it is a Mussolini that Wales needs!'[100] Umberto Eco perceptively observes that popular anti-semitism can find fertile soil in 'crude forms of racism of the neo-Celtic kind', but intellectual anti-semitism was 'certainly fuelled by Catholic legitimism'.[101]

Jenner's authoritarian outlook bears self-evident similarities. In a response to a misguided appeal for him to espouse Socialism, his politics are made quite explicit:

> I must decline under any circumstances to support the Labour Party, whose ascendancy would in my opinion be disastrous to the country . . . [as] one of the many bad features and modern developments of that hateful thing, democracy . . . Perhaps we differ in our primary conception of politics. I hold that the object is to secure the best possible government, not the representation of everybody.[102]

That Jenner was a fascist admirer is confirmed in 1923 by his approval of both Mussolini's Fascisti pact with King Victor Emmanuel III in Italy in 1922, and the dictator Primo de Rivera's *coup d'état* in 1923 achieved in accord with the Spanish King Alfonso XIII. He says:

> Two de facto Kings, those of Italy and Spain, have recently shown by their support of Fascism (for the Spanish revolt is on Fascist lines, though it does not call itself so) that they can rise to the occasion and assert themselves, very much to the advantage of their countries, and a similar thing might happen here if 'King Labor' [sic] were to get the upper hand . . . the struggle is not between rival dynasties but between any sort of dynasty at all, any sort of decent government, on the one side, and Labour, Socialism, Communism, Bolshevism etc on the other.[103]

Jenner busied himself in Cornwall in a variety of honorary positions.[104] These must have accrued respectability and credentials at the time when the planning for the Cornish Gorseth was becoming well advanced. At a crucial point L.C.R. Cameron then intervened, jeopardizing Jenner's respectable standing. In October 1924, Cameron wrote a lengthy and extraordinary letter to Jenner.[105] In contrast to the tone of previous letters, which were self-pitying, the tone is ebullient. His letter is a barely-veiled threat to expose Jenner's role with Lord Ashburnham in the *Firefly* scandal. Ashburnham had died in 1913 and Cameron had persuaded his heir and niece, Lady Catherine, to consider letting him write 'the Life' of the 5th Earl. Cameron described his planned biography as including 'a history of the last futile struggle of Legitimism in Europe' and reminded Jenner of their close work together through the Order of the White Rose and Carlist movements. Cameron was clearly aware of the power he had to make or break reputations, using the dead Earl as example. He suggested Ashburnham's attitude on Legitimism, the Boer War and the Irish Question could perhaps be passed over lightly, and that the Earl's private life was a subject requiring Cameron's 'extraordinary delicacy of treatment'. This affirmation of control by Cameron is, unsurprisingly, followed by a bald statement on his need for money. Another letter to Jenner follows shortly in which he confirms his access to the relevant incriminating documents and his intention to take up Lady Catherine's suggestion that he write the proposed 'Life of Ashburnham' at the Earl's stately home, Ashburnham Place in Sussex. Cameron's opportunism is justified, he feels, by poverty inappropriate to his station and the need for a 'warm home for winter'. This L.C.R.D.J. Cameron is a far cry from the one wheedling for hand-me-down clothes. He grumbles that Ashburnham Place is no longer kept up in the Earl's former grand style though he will require Jenner to finance £10 for a dress suit, shirts, and shoes, plus £20 to tide him over, plus another £3 or £4 needed to appease creditors. Whether Jenner complied with Cameron's princely demands is not ascertained, but no 'Life of Ashburnham' appeared.

The establishment of the Cornish Gorseth and the assistance of the Welsh Gorsedd are well known. At the 1928 Treorchy Gorsedd, eight Cornish were embarded. The Horn of Plenty of the Welsh Gorsedd was donated by the late Lord Tredegar, whose heir was yet another intimate of Aleister Crowley.[106] Jenner's scholarly justification of Boscawen-un as venue for the first Gorseth Kernow included an Arthurian legitimation,[107] and Hugh Miners pays tribute to the help of D. Rhys Phillips ('Beili Glas')[108] who was, like Jenner, a librarian and archivist. Miners also notes Rhys Phillips's suggestion of the Cornish Gorseth becoming a Welsh subsidiary 'somewhat after the manner of the one recently established in Staffordshire by de Tunstall Sneyd and others.'[109] Given Tunstall Sneyd's presence on the periphery of the Hermetic Order of the Golden Dawn (see above), his esoteric activities are not unexpected. In the mid-1920s, 'Thor's Cave' in the East Staffordshire Peak District, 'took centre-stage in the re-enactment of Druidical ceremonies initiated by the eccentric Ralph de Tunstall Sneyd, Bard and self-styled Knight of the Round Table. Held in a mixture of Sanskrit, Welsh, English and Latin, these celebrations of the "Bardic Circle of the Imperishable Sacred Land" attracted crowds of up to 2,000.'[110]

Rhys Phillips also urged the Cornish Gorseth to enhance its pedigree by bestowing honorary bardships on members of the aristocracy.[111] The Minute Books and Papers of Gorseth Kernow[112] do reveal a tendency to propose gentry as Initiates and even those necessitated 'their suitability to be enquired into'. Selection was in camera and not made by reference to any discernable criteria.[113] Under Jenner's Grand Bardship, the very first aristocrat made Gorseth Kernow Bard of Honour at the Merry Maidens in 1932 was the Master of Sempill.[114] A flamboyant aviator, Lord Sempill arrived by air wearing a Scottish kilt.

Colonel William Forbes-Sempill, 19th Baron Sempill, served with distinction during the Great War. From 1920 to 1922 he acted as expert to Japan in training aviators at Kasumigaura and he kept in close touch with the Japanese throughout the 1920s and 1930s. British Foreign Office files deemed 'classified' for seventy-five years[115] show that on his return from Japan, between 1922 and 1926, Sempill sold secrets of British aeronautical construction to the Japanese naval attaché in London, Capt. Teijiro Toyoda. A memorandum from Vernon Kell (Head of MI5) read: 'The question of prosecuting Sempill has been considered on more than one occasion.' He escaped incarceration under the Official Secrets Act only because a trial would have disclosed MI5's covert surveillance of Japanese diplomatic mail. Unaware that his actions as a traitor had been discovered, Sempill was attempting to become aeronautical adviser to the Greek military when MI5 called him to a revelatory meeting in March 1926. Confronted with the evidence against him, Sempill admitted his actions and was made aware that he had been very lucky not to be charged and imprisoned. The Japanese subsequently increased air combat capacity in conjunction with German manufacturers Junkers and Rohrbach, facilitated by the Japanese–German Axis alliance. This nascent Japanese air force grew eventually to attack Pearl Harbor and, towards the end of his life, Japan awarded Lord Sempill the Order of the Rising Sun. One incident places Sempill in Cornwall the year after his meeting with MI5. On Boxing Day 1927 he telephoned a report on the loss of the *Lady*

Daphne, a china clay transport, to the RNLI. Sempill is described as 'a frequent visitor and subsequent resident of The Lizard'.[116]

Throughout the 1930s, Sempill was increasingly associated with extreme Right and anti-semitic groups such as The Link and the pro-Nazi Anglo-German Fellowship.[117] In October 1933, the year after his Gorseth embarking, Sempill was also honoured with an invitation to join the German airship *Graf Zeppelin* during her transatlantic voyage to the Chicago World's Fair.[118] The aristocratic glamour of the guests-of-honour aboard gave much needed international prestige to the regime of Germany's new Chancellor. It also distracted from the accusations of Nazi human rights abuses in the wake of the Reichstag fire eight months before. A recently released list of Nazi sympathisers in the British establishment includes Lord Sempill and William Joyce (later 'Lord Haw-Haw') as members of the Right Club: a secret organization set up by Archibald Ramsay MP 'to oppose and expose the activities of Organised Jewry'. Unlike the populist British Union of Fascists led by Sir Oswald Mosley, the Right Club was deliberately exclusive. The infamous 'Red Book' detailing the Right Club's membership 'offers a chilling insight into the virulence of the anti-semitism which was rife among peers, MPs, knights of the realm and other leading society figures', and included a handwritten copy of Ramsay's vicious anti-semitic lyrics 'Land of Dope and Jewry'.[119] What Gorseth Kernow made of all this is unclear: although it always made plain that it was 'non-political'.

CONCLUSION

Without Henry Jenner there still may have been a Gorseth Kernow. There was little doubt, however, that—with Jenner—it would be firmly stamped with his mark. For Jenner personally, the founding of Gorseth Kernow was an actualization of will, and a belated platform for his values of doctrinaire exclusivity, the cult of personality, and obfuscated processes of honours conferral. The Gorseth at its foundation was not going to approve or facilitate a popular Cornish Revival, for it was not intended to so do. These considerations do not lessen Jenner's achievements in the field, but do go some way to account for their specificity. Descriptions and photographs of him presiding as Barth Mur (Grand Bard) have an uncanny way of articulating his likeness to Saint Nicholas or Moses.[120] Both, of course, connote the authoritative Patriarch of Eastern Orthodoxy or Old Testament. However, the dangers of hagiographizing Jenner as *fons et origo* are to allow the eclipsing of less dominating figures of the Revival through misplaced reverence. It is healthy to view Jenner in the round and to remember that, historically, it is in the nature of the political Right to represent itself as 'non-political'. It is, however, difficult to deny that 'Dalleth Gorseth Kernow' was consciously constructed as political practice, and over-determined by Jenner's background and caesarism. With that caveat, Morton Nance's assessment of Jenner's contribution to the Cornish Revival now seems even more astute: 'In it he found something entirely after his own heart, which in a few years made realities of many things of which he had dreamed, but scarcely hoped that he might live to see.'[121]

NOTES AND REFERENCES

1. Robert Morton Nance, 'Gwas Myghal and the Cornish Revival', *Old Cornwall* 2:8.
2. Most recently, David Everett's 'Celtic Revival and the Anglican Church in Cornwall, 1870–1930', in Philip Payton (ed.), *Cornish Studies: Eleven*, Exeter, 2003.
3. Henry Jenner, *George Knottesford Fortescue: A Memory*, London, 1913, p. 10.
4. J. Embry, 'The Catholic Movement and the Society of the Holy Cross', London, 1931. Project Canterbury
   http://justus.anglican.org/resources/pc/ssc/embry/chapter17.htm
5. A Troparian is a short hymn celebrating a Saint or an important event and is used in the daily offices and liturgies of some of the Orthodox Churches. *Troparian of St Cuby* By thy journeyings, O Hierarch Cuby, thou dost teach us the virtue of making pilgrimages. Wherefore, O Prince of Ascetics and all-praised Wonderworker, we entreat thee to intercede for us that Christ our God will not find our lives to be utterly worthless and will show us great mercy. *Troparian of St Kea* Thou wast unsparing in thy missionary labours in Brittany and Cornwall, O Hierarch Kea. As thou didst make the flame of the Orthodox Faith burn brightly in the face of defiant paganism, pray to God for us, that we devote our lives to confronting the paganism of our times for the glory of Christ's Kingdom and the salvation of men's souls.
   http://users.netmatters.co.uk/davidbryant/C/TropKon/Nov.htm# Nov5
6. P. Herring, 'Tractarians and Ritualists', *Ecclesiology Today* 29, September 2002, p. 51. http://www.ecclsoc.org/ET.29.pdf
7. F.G. Lee Collection, Pitts Theology Library Ms 212, http://www.pitts.emory.edu/Archives/text/ms s212.html
8. Embry, 1931.
9. Henry Jenner, *George Knottesford Fortescue: A Memory*, n.d., p. 14.
10. John H. Evans, 'Bishop Jenner and the Diocese of Dunedin', *Journal of Religious History* 4:4 1967.
11. Philip Schaff, 'Old Catholics', *The New Schaff-Herzog Encyclopedia of Religious Knowledge, Vol XIII*,
    http://frnesmith.tripod.com/new_schaff.htm
12. Revived and Recently Created Orders of Chivalry,
    http://www.heraldica.org/topics/orders/bg-orders.htm

13. See M. Baigent, R. Leigh and H. Lincoln, *The Holy Blood and the Holy Grail*, London, 1982.
14. Melville Henry Massue, Marquis de Ruvigny et Raineval and Cranstoun Metcalfe, 'Legitimism In England', *The Nineteenth Century Review*, Sept 1897, E-text http://www.jacobite.ca/essays/ruvigny.htm
15. Charles A. Coulombe , 'God Bless the Prince of Wales', *Monarchy*, Journal of the International Monarchist League, June 1994, E-text http://www.monarchy.net/articles/P_wales1.htm
16. Ashburnham's father, the 4th Earl, had collected an extensive library of early books and medieval manuscripts that Henry Jenner had had scholarly access to—including the famous Stowe Missal. On inheriting, the 5th Earl had this famous library catalogued, broken up and auctioned. Parts were purchased by the British government (the Stowe collection shared between the British Museum and Dublin), the German government (part of the Libri and Barrois collection, all, save one MS of thirteenth-century German ballads, resold to France), the Italian government (the rest of the Libri collection) Mr Yates Thompson (the MSS known as the Appendix) and Mr J. Pierpont Morgan (the Lindau Gospels).
    http://68.1911encyclopedia.org/B/BO/BOOK_COLLECTING.htm
    and Catalogue of Irish Manuscripts in the Royal Irish Academy
    http://www.ria.ie/library&catalogue/pdf/
    atalogue%20of%20iri sh%20manuscripts.pdf
    I have not followed up to ascertain if the Ashburnham Collection contained any manuscripts in Cornish. Given Jenner's connection, it might be a fruitful lead in tracing lost or unknown Cornish fragments.
17. Jenner Papers, Courtney Library, Royal Institution of Cornwall (RIC), Truro, and Henry Jenner, 'Sobieski Stuarts', *Genealogical Magazine*, Edinburgh, 1897.
18. Jenner to Lumbye, 17 August 1899, RIC Jenner Papers, Box 13, Pack 5:2.
19. A. Grueber, H. Jenner, T. Humphry Ward, Catalogue of the *Exhibition of the Royal House of Stuart*, The New Gallery, Regent Street 1889 and Murray G.H. Pittock, *Celtic Identity and the British Image,* Manchester, 1999, p. 73.
20. B. Waters, 'New Kings on Old Thrones', *Pearson's Magazine*, February 1898.
21. 'The Forget-Me-Not Club really amounts to little more than a coterie of ladies and gentlemen holding very informal drawing room meetings . . . The FMNC name is just another floral title to which none of us object.' (NB Jenner himself was a member of the conservative Primrose League), RIC Jenner Papers, Box 13, Pack 5, Jenner to Lumbye, 2 December 1911.
22. Revived and Recently Created Orders of Chivalry,
    http://www.constantinianorder.org/history.htm and
    http://www.heraldica.org/topics/orders/bg-orders.htm
23. c. 6th July 1888. Unsigned, but appended 'Jenner' in Ashburnham's hand, Ashburnham Family Archive: Carlist Activities, File Refs: ASH/2903,

2904, 2906, 2909, 2918 East Sussex Record Office, Lewes. These Ashburnham Carlist Papers are as yet unsorted.

24. White Cockade Journal, June 1928, in Ashburnham Carlist Papers, Lewes.
25. Jenner to Lumbye, 5 November 1924, RIC Jenner Papers, Box 13, Pack 5:2.
26. Pittock, p. 73 and LCRDJ Cameron to Jenner dated 'xiv:XI:1924', RIC Jenner Papers, Box 7, Pack 4.
27. Pittock, p.73.
28. Waters, 'New Kings on Old Thrones'.
29. Waters, 'New Kings on Old Thrones'.
30. *The Times*, 19 July 1899, p. 8, *Seizure of a British yacht*. 'The Spanish consul at Arcachon officially confirms the report of the seizure at that port of the British yacht Firefly, 133 tons, having on board 4,000 rifles, supposed to be intended for the Carlists. It is alleged that the yacht belongs to an Englishman representing Don Carlos in England. There were 15 men on board, and the name of her commander is given as Mr Vincent English. The vessel is stated to have come from Dartmouth. The rifles seized are described as being of the chassepot pattern.' (Reuters)
31. Not the same as the racing yacht *Firefly* owned by the Falmouth based artist Henry Scott Tuke around the same time.
32. Ashburnham Carlist Papers, Lewes.
33. 'La Cryptographie Militaire' 1883, 'Handbuch der Kryptographie' 1881, 'De la Cryptographie' 1893, 'Tratado de Criptografia' 1894.
34. Jenner to Ashburnham dated Ash Wednesday 1899, Ashburnham Carlist Papers, Lewes.
35. LCRDJ Cameron to Jenner, dated xxij:X:1924 RIC Jenner Papers Box 7 Pack 4.
36. Jenner to Lumbye, Aug 1899, RIC Jenner Papers, Box 13, Pack 5:2.
37. *Firefly* crew pay list 26 August 1899, Ashburnham Carlist Papers, Lewes.
38. Alexander Crowley (Aleister Crowley). *The Spirit of Solitude: An Autohagiography*, 2 vol. Mandrake Press: London, 1929. Subsequently re-titled *The Confessions of Aleister Crowley*, e-text: http://www.hermetic.com/crowley/confess/index.html
39. Crowley, *The Confessions of Aleister Crowley* Ch. 13 p. 120.
40. Ellic Howe, Foreword to *The Magicians of the Golden Dawn: A Documentary History of a Magical Order 1887–1923*, London, 1972.
41. Howe, p. 194.
42. Henry Jenner, 'Sobieski Stuarts', *Genealogical Magazine*, Edinburgh, 1897.
43. Howe, p. 274.
44. Howe, p. 234.
45. Howe, p. 185.
46. Howe, p. 226.
47. Howe, pp. 112–114.
48. Howe, p. 141.
49. Howe, p. 191.

50. Howe, p. 226.
51. Howe, p. 238.
52. John S. Kelly, *A WB Yeats Chronology*, London. 2003, p. 83. 17 November 1902: 'In the evening Pixie Smith, AEFH (Annie Horniman), Sturge Moore and Duncombe-Jewell at WBY's 'Monday Evening'. Index entry reads 'Duncombe-Jewell, Ludovick Charles Richard (1866–1947), soldier, war correspondent and champion of Cornish'.
53. W.B. Yeats, p. 461 in A.T Quiller-Couch (ed.), *The Cornish Magazine*, Vol. 1, July–December 1898. It was re-titled 'The Fish' and published in the anthology *The Wind Among the Reeds* the following year.
54. Cited in David Randall, *The Universal Journalist*, London, 2003.
55. The Queen's South Africa Medal, no bars, was awarded to 'Mr LCR Duncombe-Jewell, Morning Post', and turned up for sale on the Internet in 2003. http://www.medalsofwar.com/camp.html, US$ 2,275.
56. *Celtia*, October 1901, p. 153.
57. Renell Rodd to Eric Drummond (Foreign Office), 18 June 1925, cited in John Fisher, *That Miss Hobhouse*, Secker and Warburg, 1971, p. 237.
58. Subsequently 2nd Baron Rennel, Partner in Morgan Grenfell & Co, member of the aristocratic 'January Club', founded in 1934 'in sympathy with the fascist movement.' In Ted Grant, *The Unbroken Thread: The Menace of Fascism*, written 1948, published Fortress Books 1989, E-text http://www.tedgrant.org/works/4/8/fascism.html
59. Unsigned letter to Ashburnham from Venice, 31 October 1891, Ashburnham Carlist Papers, Lewes.
60. *Liberty* VII, 13 September 1890, pp. 6–7, cited in *The Debates of Liberty: Liberty's Connection to Other Publications*, unpublished manuscript by Wendy McElroy, E-text
http://www.zetetics.com/mac/libdebates/apx1pubs.html
61. Herbert Vivian, *Kings in Waiting: A Survey of the Monarchist Position in Europe*, London, 1933, and Herbert Vivian, *Fascist Italy*, London, 1936.
62. Herbert Vivian, *Myself Not Least, Being the Personal Reminiscences of 'X'*, London, 1925, cited in *Friends and Acquaintances of Aleister Crowley*, http://www.redflame93.com/VIVIAN.html
63. Crowley, *Confessions*, ch. 50 p. 409,
http://www.hermetic.com/crowley/confess/chapter50.html
64. For example, 'I suppose they will let me write in the workhouse, for the sake of the money my work will bring them; and I shall be able to write as well from Liskeard as anywhere.' LCR Cameron to Jenner, 9 January 1910, RIC Jenner Papers.
65. Ronald Jewell to Jenner, 9 October 1915, RIC Jenner Papers, Box 7, Pack 4.
66. LCR Cameron, 'Superstitions Connected with Sport', *Occult Review*, May 1908. LCR Cameron, 'The Mystery of Lourdes', *Occult Review*, Sept 1908, cited in Ralph Shirley, *An Index to the Occult Review 1906–28*. E-text *http://www.austheos.org.au/indices/OCCREV.HTM*
67. Nance, *Gwas Myghal and the Cornish Revival*.
68. One of the few references to a revival of spoken Cornish in the RIC

Jenner Papers is a suggestion to Jenner from Richard Hall for a revival of 'the old tongue'. Jenner Papers, Box 9, Pack 11.

69. Doble to Jenner, 22 August 1924, RIC Jenner Papers, Box 7, Pack 12. Peter to Jenner, 19 November 1913, RIC Jenner Papers, Box 7, Pack 8. Taylor to Jenner, 2 October 1916, RIC Jenner, Papers, Box 7, Pack 8.
70. Walter Yeeling Evans Wentz, *The Fairy-Faith in Celtic Countries* London, 1911.
71. Arthur F.J. Remy, 'The Holy Grail', *The Catholic Encyclopedia*, Vol. VI, 1909, http://www.knight.org/advent/cathen/06719a.htm
72. Henry Jenner, 'Ambrosian Liturgy and Rite,' *The Catholic Encyclopedia*, Vol. I, 1907, E-text www.newadvent.org/cathen/01394a.htm Henry Jenner 'Celtic Rite', *The Catholic Encyclopedia*, Vol. III, 1908, E-text http://www.celticorthodoxy.org/document011.shtml Henry Jenner, 'Liturgical Use of Creeds', *The Catholic Encyclopedia*, Vol. IV, Robert Appleton Company, 1913 edition, 1908, E-text www.newadvent.org/cathen/04479a.htm Henry Jenner, 'East Syrian Rite', 1913, E-text http://church-of-the-east.org/library/Syro%20Chaldean.htm
73. BFBS to Jenner, RIC Jenner Papers, 3 August 1909, Box 7, Pack 4.
74. Sequentia includes the pre-destined 'Thus the bardic verse fulfilling . . .'
75. Mrs E. Greville-Nugent to Jenner, 15 December 1912, RIC Jenner Papers, Box 13, Pack 7; see also M.K. Flynn, *Ideology, Mobilization and the Nation: The Rise of Irish, Basque and Carlist Nationalist Movements in the Nineteenth and Early Twentieth Centuries*, London 2000, p. 101, 'In keeping with their nineteenth-century slogan, *God, Patria and King (Dios, Patria, Rey)*, Carlists more often used the term *patria*, rather than *nacion.*'
76. Greville-Nugent, ibid.
77. RIC Jenner Papers, Box 7, Pack 9.
78. *Legitimist Ensign* 4, 4th May 1910.
79. Ashburnham to Jenner, 20 Novemeber 1910, RIC Jenner Papers, Box 6, Pack 2.
80. *The Fiery Cross* takes its name from the Jacobite Highland symbol that rallied defence forces to race and clan. The Fiery Cross symbol and use of robes were exported by emigrants to America in the nineteenth century, and were appropriated in the former Southern Confederacy States by the *White Brotherhood*, the *Knights of the White Camellia and the White Rose*, and the *Ku Klux Klan*. (Encyclopedia Britannica, Eleventh edition, Vol. XV, Cambridge, and New York.)
81. *The Fiery Cross*, October 1909, RIC Jenner Papers, Box 13, Pack 9.
82. RIC Jenner Papers, Box 13, Pack 2.
83. News on de Ruvigny, which Jenner got 'from Jewell', date 3 October 1911, RIC Jenner Papers, Box 13, Pack 5:2.
84. *Great Orders of Chivalry*, http://www.chivalricorders.org/orders/ortu gal/vilavic.htm
85. Jenner to Lumbye, 18 February 1915, RIC Jenner Papers.
86. Ibid.

87. Ibid.
88. Ibid.
89. Ibid.
90. L.C.R.D.J. Cameron to Jenner, 25 October 1916, RIC Jenner Papers, Box 7, Pack 4.
91. L.C.R.D.J. Cameron to Jenner, 18 February 1917, Box 7, Pack 4.
92. Jenner to Lumbye, 5 November 1924, RIC Jenner Papers, Box 13, Pack 5:2.
93. Michael Kellogg, *Hitler's Russian Connection: White Émigré Influence on the Genesis of Nazi Ideology, 1917–1923*, http://www.sscnet.ucla.edu/soc/groups/scr/kell ogg.pdf
94. Troy Southgate, *The Rise and Fall of English Fascism between 1918–45*, Historical Pamphlets Series No. 30, http://www.rosenoire.org/articles/hist30.php and '1900–1931 First wave Britain's early fascists', *Searchlight Magazine*, http://www.searchlightmagazine.com/stories/century/1900-1931.htm
95. *The Times*, 22 March 1934.
96. English translation: 'the Fiery Cross'. It benefited from the Roman Catholic Church's proscription prohibiting practicing Catholics from supporting *Action Francaise*. Many conservative Catholics instead became members of the *Croix de Feu*, including the young Francois Mitterand. http://www.encyclopedia4u.com/c/croix-de-feu.html Also, Archives Nationales de France 451AP/81 à 451AP/93: *Le mouvement Croix-de-Feu 1929-36, http://www.archivesnationales.culture.gouv.f r/ chan/chan/fonds/xml_inv/EtatsdesfondsAP/idx_corpname.html#IC*
97. *Encyclopedia of the Holocaust*, New York, 1990, cited: http://motlc.wiesenthal.com/text/x01/xr0109.html
98. *Catalunya, Parsifal and the Escamots.* http://wais.stanford.edu/Spain/ spain_catalun yaparsifalandtheescamots71103.html
99. http://en.wikipedia.org/wiki/Spanish_Civil_War
100. Bebb did oppose Nazism later, and the pro-Hitler attitude of some Breton nationalists in 1939.
101. Umberto Eco, 'The Poisonous Protocols: the distinction between intellectual anti-semitism and its popular counterpart', *Guardian*, 17 August 2002.
102. RIC Jenner Papers, Box 7, Pack 5: This is a draft letter to an unnamed recipient, in Jenner's hand, undated.
103. Jenner to Lumbye, 27 October 1923, RIC Jenner Papers, Box 13, Pack 5:2.
104. Jenner to Lumbye, 5 November 1924, RIC Jenner Papers, Box 13, Pack 5:2.
105. L.C.R.D.J. Cameron to HJ xxij:X:1924, RIC Jenner Papers, Box 7, Pack 4.
106. 'Lord Tredegar: A Biographical Sketch', http://www.redflame93.com/Tredegar.html
107. Henry Jenner, 'The Gorsedd of Boscawen-un', Paper—Federation of Old Cornwall Societies, 25 June 1927.

108. Hugh Miners, *Gorseth Kernow: the First 50 Years*, Gorseth Kernow, 1978.
109. Rhys Phillips to Robert Morton Nance, November 1928, cited in Miners, *Gorseth Kernow*, p. 17.
110. Tourism promotional material for Dovedale District, http://www.simonholtmarketing.com/PDFs/MVVC%20Thor's%20Cave.pdf
111. Miners, *Gorseth Kernow*, p. 25.
112. The Minute Books and Papers of Gorseth Kernow (Cornwall Records Office File Ref: X1104) are embargoed from public scrutiny for thirty years from the date of their donation in 1999. My thanks to Rod Lyon, Grand Bard, for eventual permission to consult these unsupervised.
113. Minutes, Gorseth Kernow, 20 April 1929.
114. Minutes, Gorseth Kernow, 23 July 1932.
115. Public Records Office release of MI5 material (KV 2/871-874), 7 May 2002, http://www.pro.gov.uk/releases/may2002-mi5/list.htm and Will Hollingworth, 'British Lord was spy for Japan', *The Japan Times* Online, 5 January 2002, http://www.japantimes.co.jp/cgi-bin/getarticle.pl5?nn2002010 5a3.htm
116. http://www.elevator-world.com/magazine/archi ve01/9708-001.htm
117. Public Records Office—KV 2/872, papers showing Sempill's affiliation to fascist groups, http://www.pro.gov.uk/releases/may2002-mi5/list.htm
118. *Passenger Files: Francis T. Turner, Colonel William Francis Forbes-Sempill and Charles Dollfuss*, http://sts.stanford.edu/dymaxion/crash.htm
119. Paul Lashmar, *Independent on Sunday*, 9 January 2000, http://www.independent.co.uk/news/UK/his_Britain/nazilead090100.shtml see also Richard Griffiths, *Patriotism Perverted: Captain Ramsay, the Right Club and British Anti-Semitism, 1939–40*, London, 1998.
120. Miners, *Gorseth Kernow* pp. 25–26.
121. Nance, *Gwas Myghal and the Cornish Revival*.

Postscript: There are two letters in the Jenner Papers from L.C.R.D.J. Cameron that ante-date Jenner's death. Ever the fantasist, he asked Kitty Jenner for an advance of money against a screenplay he had written as a guaranteed box-office success (11 February 1935). The other letter (24 March 1935) is an obsequious enquiry if Kitty might recall a 'box of books Hal wished me to have . . .'

Acknowledgementss: RIC Courtney Library (Truro), East Sussex Records Office (Lewes), Morrab Library (Penzance), Kresenn Kernow (Redruth), Falmouth College of Arts. Individual thanks for comment and encouragement: Jason Whittaker, Russell Clarke, Barry Cooper, Peter Hayes and—as always—Neil Kennedy.

TALKING IDENTITY: UNDERSTANDING CORNWALL'S ORAL CULTURE THROUGH GROUP DIALOGUE

Garry Tregidga and Lucy Ellis

> Interdisciplinary work, so much discussed these days, is not about confronting already constituted disciplines (none of which, in fact, is willing to let itself go). To do something interdisciplinary it's not enough to choose a 'subject' (a theme) and gather around it two or three sciences. Inter-disciplinarity consists in creating a new object that belongs to no one.
>
> Roland Barthes, *Jeunes Chercheurs*

INTRODUCTION

The Cornish Audio Visual Archive (CAVA) is developing against a background of changing perceptions in oral history. For instance, inter-disciplinary approaches can set in motion a view of the archive as not solely a collection of reminiscences about the past but also as a means to understand those present-day social and cultural processes under-way in Cornwall that have immediate relevance to its people, such as the maintenance of cultural identity, accent change, and the impact of increasingly heterogeneous communities. On a practical note there is perhaps an even more basic issue in relation to the collection of data, with traditional assumptions about the neutrality of the interviewer now being challenged by a variety of new approaches. This paper is an interdisciplinary consideration of these debates within the context of Cornish Studies. In the first section we draw on the disciplines of oral history, anthropology, and sociolinguistics to provide a framework for analysing the creative potential of group dialogue. It will be suggested that this particular approach offers an opportunity for communities to create their own cultural narratives free of the external control of an interviewer. These conceptual ideas are then related to a case study of a recording made by residents of a Cornish village. Historical events are recounted from living memory and interpreted through a discussion of the underlying themes of communal conflict and consensus. This approach also lends itself well to a consideration of the behaviour and attitudes of group participants in relation to contemporary issues. By addressing such a broad range of topics and perspectives this article seeks to establish a powerful interpretative framework for current and future Cornish study within CAVA.

REASSESSING THE INTERVIEW PROCESS

The way in which an interview should be conducted is a basic and contested issue for oral historians. For many orthodox practitioners the purpose of a recording is simply to offer a personal insight into a specific historical event. This reflects the established view of oral history as simply a device whereby eyewitness accounts are combined alongside written sources to provide fresh insight into a debate on a particular historical topic or event. In these circumstances the interviewer should adopt a detached role, merely asking a few questions and allowing the interviewee to provide the facts. Carolynne Kieffer, an American sociologist, concluded in 1993 that 'the oral history interview is not meant to be a dialogue. It is rather a narrative description —typically, but not necessarily, chronological—of individual and group experiences in a particular time and place. The interviewer is present only to direct the course of this description when and if necessary'.[1] Prominent oral historians in Britain have expressed a similar view. A typical example can be seen in the following comments by Robert Perks, curator for oral history at the British Library's National Sound Archive:

> Do not ask too many questions or try to impress by using long words, your aim is to get them to talk, not to talk yourself. Do not interrupt answers: always wait for a pause. Make sure they can tell you what they think matters most; and never cut them off in mid flow. It is important that you listen intently and maintain good eye contact. Respond positively and regularly by making appropriate non-verbal signs of encouragement. Body language like nodding and smiling is much better than 'ers' and 'ums' and 'reallys'. It is vital to be relaxed, unhurried and sympathetic. Do not contradict: be tolerant of prejudices.

Try to avoid revealing your own opinions as it can influence
what you are told.[2]

However, there are indications that a reappraisal of interview
technique is now starting to take place. Locally, this can be seen in the
work of Treve Crago at the Institute of Cornish Studies. Whilst accepting that a conventional approach is more likely to result in a 'clear
good quality recording' and is certainly preferable for new students of
the discipline, his personal style of interviewing tends to ignore many
of the 'golden rules'. Using examples taken from his own research,
Crago pointed to the benefits of a proactive approach. He concluded
that 'it is unavoidable that the interviewer is going to have to speak at
some point'.[3] This echoes the experience of Alessandro Portelli who
believes that a sound recording is actually generated or 'co-created'
between two individuals and it is inevitable that even the mere
presence of the interviewer will have an impact on proceedings. Portelli
concluded that the 'fiction of non-interference' actually turns the
recorded 'dialogue into two monologues; informants supply a
monologue of brute facts, while historians and anthropologists will
supply later—from the safety of their desks—a monologue of
sophisticated ideas that the informant never hears about'.[4] The logic of
this statement is that only by directly engaging with the interviewee can
we supply an ethical and democratic context for recording and then
interpreting personal testimonies. In these circumstances the concept
of a silent role for the interviewer is not really possible:

> There is no oral history before the encounter of two different
> subjects, one with a story to tell and the other with a story to
> reconstruct. We tend to forget, however, that the first person
> who speaks in an oral history interview is usually not the
> interviewee, but the interviewer. In a very concrete sense,
> the source's narrative can be seen always as a response to the
> historian's initial questions: 'When were you born?' 'Tell me
> about your life'? 'Who was the union secretary at that time?'.
> By opening the conversation, the interviewer defines the
> roles and establishes the basis of narrative authority. In fact,
> although an oral autobiographical narrative may look on the
> surface very much like any other autobiographical *text*, it
> constitutes a very different autobiographical *act*, because the
> basis of authority is different. Autobiography (especially if
> written for publication) begins with a person's decision to
> write about herself or himself, but in the interview, the

initiative is taken by the interviewer, from whom the legitimacy to speak is ostensibly derived.[5]

While arguing that historical testimony will always be interpreted through the prism of the interviewer's presence, Portelli implies that there can never be an un-reconstructed interviewee. As a result scholars are now starting to explore the dialogic interaction that takes place in a recorded interview. A good example of this can be seen in Louise Ryan's narrative work on the experiences of female emigration from Ireland to Britain in the 1930s. Locating herself within the interview process Ryan compared and contrasted her own story with that of the interviewees. At one level she could clearly relate to their experiences since there were obvious similarities in terms of gender, nationality, and the fact that she was also an economic migrant who had moved away to London in search of employment. This common bond was recognized by the interviewees and one member of the group even admitted that she could only tell her story to 'another Irish person'. Yet there were important differences in terms of age, education, and occupation. These personal factors were compounded by the wider socio-economic changes that have taken place since the inter-war period. Ryan's subjective attitudes to being Irish were shaped by her personal experiences in the 1990s 'of a prosperous, lively, energetic, optimistic and dynamic Celtic tiger'. The economic and cultural renaissance of Ryan's Ireland was in stark contrast to the testimonies of the ten elderly Irish women that she interviewed; they remembered 'not just the economic problems but also the social attitudes, the strict conventions and lack of hope of the bleak 1930s'.[6] For them, this was an image that had been frozen in time. These 'interpersonal dynamics' lay at the heart of Ryan's study and it provides us with a useful comparative case study of what might be described as the interpretative revisionist approach to the role of the interviewer.

The enormous importance and significance of Ryan's 'common bond' with her interviewees for the data she obtained is really only hinted at within this revisionist approach. What does it mean to share a cultural background with your interviewees and what are the implications for your study? Methodological discussion within anthropology considers this very issue and provides a theoretical and conceptual framework for the notion of the 'indigenous fieldworker'. The central task of anthropological fieldwork is ethnography which is the work of describing a culture. Branslaw Malinowski states that good ethnography should grasp 'the native's point of view'.[7] 'Classic' anthropology is still practised in societies foreign to the fieldworker where the culture under scrutiny stands in contrast to that of the observer and hence is more easily observable. However, if the field-worker is also 'the native' then a set of fascinating practical and theoretical questions arise. There must be a deeper understanding of the process by which the indigenous fieldworker makes sense of their data. Being *of* the culture and *observing* it at the same time demands a compartmentalization of the mind and a set of strategies to cope with the 'closeness'. Reflection on the ethnography gained and experiences from the field are but two areas requiring a process of 'disassociation' on one or more levels. For CAVA at the Institute of Cornish Studies these are important considerations for Cornish fieldworkers making oral history recordings with the people of Cornwall where Cornish culture and history are the objects of study. These ideas present both a challenge and an opportunity for exploration as the archive develops its research potential as a major academic resource.

The use of 'auto-ethnography', the study of the self as well as the other, has become more acceptable to the extent that anthropologists sometimes use their own experiences as ethnography. Nelson Graburn sounds a note of caution and states that autobiographical ethnography is only of any value to the ethnography of other people if these others are of the same social background (nationality, ethnicity, class, gender and so forth) as the author. The issue here is one of cultural similarity and difference and its relationship to information gathered from in-formants. In line with the former, the ethnography of the 'Us' is advantageous to the observer 'in that the objects of his academic gaze are likely to feel no threat from one of their own, and that he knows their subculture so well he can use his research instruments with great care and sensitivity.'[8] Another practical advantage comes with easy access to informants and the social networks that informants partici-pate in. The re-positioning of anthropology with respect to its 'objects' of study that Graburn talks of is discussed by Clifford in the light of the many restrictions placed on anthropological fieldwork by indigenous governments at national and local level. For instance, an outsider studying native American cultures may be required to testify in support of land claim litigation if research is permitted to continue. Clifford comments that these historical pressures on what can and cannot be said about a people means that:

> Anthropology no longer speaks with automatic authority for others defined as unable to speak for themselves ('primitive', 'pre-literate', 'without history'). Other groups can less easily be distanced in special, almost always past or passing, times —represented as if they were not involved in the present

world systems that implicate ethnographers along with the peoples they study. 'Cultures' do not hold still for their portraits. Attempts to make them do so always involve simplification and exclusion, selection of a temporal focus, the construction of a particular self-other relationship, and the imposition or negotiation of a power relationship.[9]

Thus, an ideological shift brought about by the dismantling of colonialism has led to a view of communities of interest in the context of the present as well as the past. This revisionist approach is absolutely germane to the work of CAVA and provides a framework for research currently underway at the Institute of Cornish Studies whereby the past has a relevance for present and future issues such as housing in Cornwall, accent change, kinship structures and cultural identity.

The foregoing discussion of the role and identity of the fieldworker provides an apposite framework for our analysis of recent experimental work by CAVA. While discussing the oral history interview Portelli suggests that in some circumstances 'a critical, challenging, even a (respectfully) antagonistic interviewer may induce the narrator to open up and reveal less easily accessible layers of personal knowledge, belief and experience'.[10] Yet an alternative option is to go even further by replacing the central position of the interviewer through the medium of group dialogue. The way in which a narrative is shaped in a recorded interview is determined by the controlling influence of the researcher. Regardless of 'old' or 'new' approaches to oral history it is still this individual who identifies and establishes the subject for discussion. This particularly applies to the responses given to specific questions: replies are influenced by the words, style, and outlook of the interviewer. Indeed, it is this person who effectively dictates the agenda during a recording session. This means that an issue or event of minor importance to the narrator (for example, politics) might be elevated in a recorded discussion over other more important topics to the narrator (such as religion). The real identity of an individual or a community only emerges when the narrator is able to control the narrative. In these circumstances part of the work of CAVA should be directed at providing alternative opportunities for groups to simply engage in natural conversation about Cornish culture. Free of the control of the interviewer, three or four individuals can discuss a range of subjects on an informal basis. The story that is created is not imposed or limited by an outside influence (i.e. the interviewer) since the group itself generates the momentum. Even the formal nature of the session is likely to be reduced since groups are less likely to be aware of the presence of recording equipment.

These issues have been given much attention within the study of sociolinguistics—the interaction between language and society. The work of William Labov represented a watershed for this area of enquiry and his methodological contribution in the form of the 'Observer's Paradox' made possible the study of language in its social context. He states that 'the aim of linguistic research in the community must be to find out how people talk when they are not being systematically observed: yet we can only obtain these data by systematic observation'.[11] Elements of systematic observation include the presence of recording equipment and the presence of the interviewer. The way people talk when they are not being observed, or as Labov puts it, 'that vehicle of communication in which they argue with their wives, joke with their friends, and deceive their enemies', is referred to by sociolinguists as the 'vernacular'. The vernacular is a type of speech which is of special interest to linguists. Unlike more formal styles of speech (for example interview-style or reading aloud) its definitive quality is that minimum attention is given to it on the part of the speaker. Observation of the vernacular provides the most systematic data with which to analyse linguistic structure. Other, more formal, styles give rise to irregular phonological and grammatical patterns, with a great deal of 'hypercorrection'. Since the conventional interview is public speech—monitored and controlled in response to the presence of an outside observer—techniques must be used to lift the subject and interviewer out of the constraints of the one-to-one confrontation. One of several techniques suggested is to use the normal interaction of the peer group to control speech. Labov's methodologically ground-breaking work in South-Central Harlem involved the study of local non-standard adolescent speech.[12] Data was collected from peer-group interaction through long-term participant observation and, as a result, the negative effects of formal observation was kept to a minimum. This discussion shows us that methodological and theoretical re-working, in the context of a re-assessment of the dialogic process through which data is acquired, is not exclusive to oral history.

Another way in which ideas from language studies can illuminate the interviewer–interviewee relationship for oral history is the theory of *accommodation* as proposed by Howard Giles and Peggie Smith.[13] The 'controlling influence' of the interviewer finds a parallel in this theory which seeks to formulate the way in which speakers often try to accommodate to the expectations that others have of them when they speak. Accommodation is one way of explaining how individuals and groups can relate to each other. An individual can try to induce another to judge him or her more favourably—to gain social approval —by reducing differences between the two and this is called *convergence* behaviour. As an alternative, if a speaker desires to be judged less favourably the shift in behaviour is away from the other's behaviour—this is *divergence* behaviour. A good example of convergence occurs when a speaker tries to adopt features of the accent of a listener or that used within another social group. Giles and Nikolas Coupland explain accommodation as a 'multiply-organised and contextually complex set of alternatives, regularly available to communicators in face-to-face talk. It can function to index and achieve solidarity with or dissociation from a conversational partner, reciprocally and dynamically.'[14] Robert Le Page highlights this definition in the direction of the way in which accommodation can create the speaker's identity: 'we do not necessarily adapt to the style of the interlocutor [conversational participant], but rather to the image we have of ourselves in relation to our interlocutor.'[15] Thus speaking is not only for the purpose of involving others socially, but it is also a personal act in that it helps create and project an identity in a particular set of circumstances. Identity becomes the central concern when we consider two different types of convergence—upward convergence and the more rare downward convergence. The former takes place as people with more broadly based social networks meet people with a higher social status. This is the mechanism that underpins most accent change which is the move towards accent standarization. Here people abandon their regional speech variants to fall in line with the more prestigious standard variety of spoken English. Downward convergence occurs when a higher-status person accommodates to a lower-status person. There is obvious potential here for the application of this framework to the oral history interview situation. Below, we illustrate the phenomenon of downward convergence in action in the context of group dialogue.

CONFORMITY AND CONFRONTATION:
THE CONVERSATIONAL DYNAMICS OF IDENTITY

Over the past four years CAVA has been conducting a series of experiments in the field of group dialogic studies. Empirical evidence for this article is drawn from a group recording carried out in a community building in one of the Clay Country villages of Mid-Cornwall. A free-style approach was adopted whereby members of the local community had the opportunity to create and articulate their own cultural narratives without the outside control of an interviewer. As a result the recorded discussion covered a broad range of topics that simply emerged during the course of their extended conversation. There were three core participants in the discussion (Courtney Grose, Frederick Thomas, and John Retallick) with occasional contributions from a fourth person (Peter Hamilton). Significantly, there was no formal 'interviewer' on this occasion, with another member of the community acting as the facilitator of the event.[16]

Before considering the recording, however, it should be pointed out that the concept of group dialogue is problematic for many oral historians. After all, the presence of more than one narrator can be confusing for somebody listening to a sound recording after the event, while a single person might also dominate the narrative in a group setting and prevent other individuals from making a meaningful contribution. Moreover, the creation of a shared narrative can make it difficult for those oral historians who wish to focus on a standard life story approach to reconstructing the past. In these circumstances it is perhaps not surprising that relatively little discussion has been given to the potential of group dialogic studies. Those oral historians who have considered the subject tend to hold mixed views. A good example is Paul Thompson, a leading figure in the development of oral history in Britain, who wrote in 1978 that 'sometimes a group, for example in a public bar, may be the only way into a hidden world of a common work experience of sabotage or theft, or the secret devices of poachers in the countryside'.[17] Yet in a more recent article written in association with Hugo Slim, Olivia Bennett, and Nigel Cross, he adopted a distinctly critical attitude:

> Groups can bring out the best and the worst in people. Sometimes, by taking the focus off individuals, they make them less inhibited, but the opposite can occur just as easily. A group may subtly pressurise people towards a socially acceptable testimony or a mythical representation of the past or of a current issue which everyone feels is 'safe' to share and which may be in some sense idealised. Communal histories gathered in this way can involve a powerful process of myth construction or fabulation which misrepresents the real complexity of the community. At worst, this can develop into a persistent false consciousness which can only tolerate the good things, and remembers 'how united we all were', or which exaggerates the totality of suffering and recalls 'how bad everything was'. The voices of the less confident, the poorer and the powerless, are less likely to be heard, and so the variety of experience and the clashes and conflicts within a community may well remain hidden.[18]

This quote from Thompson *et al.* provides a framework for analysing the dynamics of the Clay village recording. It raises a number of issues relating to both social and ethnic representations of community life that can usefully be investigated in a Cornish context. In the first place there is some evidence from the recording to support Thompson's view that a group setting can lead to a nostalgic reconstruction of the past. Thomas, for example, presents an idyllic story about his childhood. He recounts that 'we was all happy. They never had kiddies there if they didn't love 'em, you know. I can't remember my mum or dad . . . putting a heavy hand on [any] of the kids'. Similarly, Retallick suggests that 'you haven't got the togetherness or friendship or whatever you like to call it in the villages today as what you had back then'. This sweeping statement is then endorsed by the other two characters despite contradictory evidence elsewhere in the same recording, notably in relation to the bitter divisions caused by the 1913 clay strike. The natural desire to conform in a domestic conversational setting can be put forward as an explanation. This can clearly be seen in relation to their discussion of illiteracy in Cornwall before the Second World War, with Grose's initial use of a closed question effectively preventing any meaningful discussion:

CG: Well, course in the old days, boy, you had the dust beat out your ass with a stick if they couldn't do it and therefore nobody couldn't do it. I can't remember going to school with anybody that couldn't read and write, can you?

JR: No.

CG: Some weren't all that good scholars but they could all read and write . . . and do simple sums.

JR: If they weren't all that good at spelling they could read and they could write.

Yet on reflection the illiteracy discussion can also be seen as undermining Thompson's arguments on group dialogue. Grose's reference to the harsh disciplinarian approach shown towards young people is in stark contrast to the personal memories of Thomas. Although 'a socially acceptable testimony' is imposed in this particular instance, it suggests that the presence of other narrators means that it is quite likely for conflicting perspectives to emerge during the course of a recording. After all, a nostalgic account is equally possible in a conventional interview. As with any primary source it is the task of the scholar to probe beneath the surface and in this case the existence of multiple voices at least enables the possibility of different perspectives. Thus, at one stage Thomas recounts that when he went to school in the St Austell area in the second decade of the twentieth century he never saw any children 'hungry or poorly clothed'. Though clearly not wishing to totally contradict Thomas's position, Grose then offers a useful corrective by pointing out that conditions would have been different in the impoverished mining communities of West Cornwall. It is a reminder that the flow of a conversation can easily change according to the circumstances and characters involved.

Indeed, a careful analysis of the recording points to underlying tensions beneath the surface. Contrary to the official view outlined earlier one might argue that researchers can gain a surprisingly unique insight into the 'real complexity of the community' through a consideration of group dialogue. This is perhaps most evident in relation to the group's reconstruction of the events surrounding the 1913 clay strike. Grose and Retallick were not even born until several years after the strike took place but in both cases they were able to recount stories passed on by their fathers and other individuals living at the time. Grose's family had been traditionally employed in a pit management role with the clay industry, while Retallick's father was one of the pickets in 1913. These contrasting roots of cultural memory resulted in significantly different narratives from the period. For Retallick the emphasis was on the violent confrontations between the police and the strikers. He recounted stories based on specific clashes linked to the physical injuries sustained by his father. Grose, however, focused on the outside interference of flying pickets in those village communities that still wished to carry on working during the strike. Not surprisingly, these two approaches led to confrontation during the course of the discussion. In the following extract Grose attempts to build up the case against industrial action only to be swiftly undermined by Retallick's one-line interruption:

CG: I think that most of the pits in the Bugle area wanted to work on. Didn't want to come out. But, of course, flying pickets, the idea that it's peaceful persuasion is all bull shit really . . . Then it got like a stand-off between the men in the district, when the flying pickets was coming and wanted everybody to go out because unless its solid 'tin' effective and the local fellas wanted to say, 'Look, here in Bugle most of us want to work and we're going to work and that's the end of that'. Well, then it come to strife between 'em and then, of course, the pickets said that we want to stop the pumping engines . . .
JR: Father was one of the pickets.
CG: Yeah [silence].

The example demonstrates how sudden changes in style and language reveal issues of symbolic importance. Grose attempts to regain the dominant role in the discussion by recounting another anti-strike story. In this case a local clay pit was owned by a German firm that was already paying its workforce a higher wage than the figure demanded by the strikers. A group of flying pickets arrived at the works only to be confronted by the 'Cap'n', the traditional symbol of local authority in the industry, and he quickly defuses the situation. Using humour and language for effect Grose adds that 'Cap'n said, "Oh, get away on with 'e, . . . they baint gonna follow your crowd. They're getting more than that now [laughter]." ' Once again Grose is 'fighting the battles' of an age before his own lifetime. Retallick responds in a similar fashion by pointing to an incident in which the pickets had placed nails on the road from Roche to Nanpean in order to puncture the bicycle tyres of the police. The action results in a brief and humorous victory over the forces of authority as the police are forced to carry their own bicycles rather than leaving them for the pickets. It is significant that this symbolic exchange of stories took place nearly ninety years after the actual event. Such a vibrant reconstruction of the past in the context of the present suggests that further study is required in order to investigate the wider cultural implications of the strike in the decades that followed. What can be established is that recorded dialogue between two or more narrators of a similar age can reveal the underlying tensions in a society more effectively than a conventional interview.

Interestingly, the one individual that was alive at the time was relatively silent on the subject. Thomas was a young child in 1913 and might have been expected to make a contribution to the discussion, particularly since his father became a trade union secretary in the industry. Louisa Passerini's pioneering oral narrative work incorporates a variety of perspectives drawn from psychoanalysis in order to explore 'the un-said, the implicit, the imaginary'. Focusing on the experiences of working-class men and women in Fascist Italy she concluded that silence could be evidence of 'a profound wound in daily experience'.[19] Entire life stories were recalled without a single reference to the period from the rise of Mussolini to the events of the Second World War. It is quite possible that Thomas's silence might be a similar example. At a later date he was interviewed separately on the events of 1913 and on that occasion presented an alternative narrative covering the hardships experienced by local working-class families as a result of the strike. Rather than a heroic struggle against the forces of authority and capital, Thomas perceived the strike in terms of the disillusionment of workers forced to return to the pits in order to provide food for their families. His moving statement that 'it went on so long that people got [silence] hungry' contrasts strongly with his public narrative less than two years earlier of an idyllic childhood. By investigating this complex exchange of words and silences we can obtain a broader picture of the cultural dynamics of a community. Peter Burke points out the need for 'an awareness of linguistic conventions and variations' on the part of historians. Not only does language study offer 'a means to the better understanding of oral and written sources', it offers an alternative approach to the history of communal culture and everyday life.[20] On the subject of silence, we must also make reference here to the fact that the 'interviewer' is, for almost the entire duration of this Clay Country recording, completely silent. From our extended methodological discussion in the previous section we can see that the controlling influence of the interviewer is overcome by almost dispensing with him/her altogether.

Much of the discussion of the recording concerns the extent to which group dialogue is a medium which *expresses*, or by contrast, *suppresses* the complexity of community life. Thompson describes the latter process as hiding 'the clashes and conflicts within a community' in favour of socially acceptable testimony or at worst a 'persistent false consciousness . . . [which] remembers "how united we all were"'. The interpretation of excerpts of the recording so far has shown both processes in action. Conflict is evident with reference to the Clay strike and, powerfully, through the use of silence within group dialogue. We now turn to Thompson's contention that group dialogue can enforce 'communal histories' whereby 'the voices of the less confident, the poorer and the powerless are less likely to be heard'. One group participant (Hamilton) stands apart from the others in the sense that he is a relatively recent resident of the village. A tension of a different kind is illustrated by the following exchange where the group attempt to define a typical Cornishman:

CG: If he's like no other bugger you met you know he's a Cornishman.
PH: I heard one story that if you find a hole there's always a Cornishman at the bottom of it.
[silence]
CG: Well . . . that's a *mining* 'ole.

The break in flow of the conversation here and the correction imposed by Grose serves to effectively distance Hamilton from the power centre of the group foregrounding his status as in-migrant to the village. Another example from the recording sees Hamilton using language to reposition himself towards the centre of the group using 'accommodation' behaviour, more specifically 'downward convergence' as outlined above. The topic of discussion is the pattern of changing tenure over the years in a particular part of the village.

CG: Yeah, 'e live up beside Freddie Thomas . . . yeah . . . they got two daughters.

PH: Roger Wells used to live across there and then he went up Trescoth.

While Hamilton's contribution to the group reconstruction of housing patterns from memory is confined to the very recent past, the grammatical construction of his utterance betrays a desire to be seen as belonging to the dense social fabric represented by the other members of the group. The use of 'went up Trescoth' shows the lack of the preposition 'to' which is a feature of the Cornish dialect and is one which survives today in the speech of young people. In line with our earlier description of accommodation this represents a personal act in that it serves to create and project an identity. It can also be thought of as code-switching where the adaptation that takes place is to an image the speaker has of himself in relation to his interlocutor/s. What makes this example of accommodation so interesting is that, technically speaking, it demonstrates downward convergence. This is so because the accent/dialect profile of the speaker in question is closer to the standard form of spoken English than the Cornish variety spoken by the other members. By using the grammatical form 'up Trescoth', the speaker is consciously substituting a non-standard form for the more standard 'up to Trescoth'. Relatively unusual though the adoption of regional features may be, the context of the conversational setting exerts an exceptionally strong, positive identity around Cornishness. A more convincing analysis of the type of accommodation behaviour we see here, then, is perhaps to view it as not downward but upward convergence toward the local prestige variety of English. Lesley Milroy considers the set of dialect and accent features associated with regional varieties of English to be *vernacular norms* which are 'perceived as symbolising values of solidarity and reciprocity rather than status, and are not publicly codified or recognised'.[21] This statement finds an echo in Peter Trudgill's formulation of *covert prestige* and its role in regional norm-maintenance against a tide of linguistic change.[22] These theories help us to understand why regional accents and dialects survive at all.

A model of human interaction from the discipline of sociology developed by Mark Granovetter—*social networks*—can provide a useful framework for understanding the social structure of communities and for illuminating the type of dialogue dynamics we have discussed here.[23] The type of network that underpins the group dialogue of the recording is a *dense multiplex* network. If you participate in a dense network then the people you know and interact with also know and interact with one another. If you are also a participant in a multiplex network then the people within it are tied together in more than one way, that is, not just through work but also through social activities. People who go to school together, marry each other's siblings, and work and play together are said to be involved in dense multiplex networks. These are said to be found at the extremes of the social-class structure. An important characteristic of them is that they are indicative of strong social cohesion, produce feelings of solidarity, and support individuals in identification with others within the network. We have described here some definitive properties of traditional rural communities in Cornwall. A further property of dense multiplex networks is their maintenance of a stable set of linguistic norms, or vernacular norms, as described above. The relevance is clear for our discussion of language use within the recording as Cornish dialectal and accent norms are exhibited in their traditional form.[24] These are the vernacular norms bearing covert prestige. Importantly, they motivate the accommodation behaviour shown by Hamilton.

Language variation studies have used the concept of network and

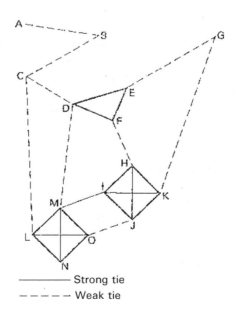

1. *Idealized representation of a language situation where individual members differ in the relative strength of tie (adapted from Milroy & Milroy, 1992).*

relative strength of network tie to understand linguistic change within a community over time.[25] Figure 1 shows a visual representation of a notional network. If the particular language situation of our group dialogue were to be represented as a network, Hamilton represents a relatively weak tie (see dashed lines on Figure 1 below) and the other members of the group represent the relatively strong ties within dense networks (represented by solid lines). Weak ties are crucial in that they diffuse innovative accent forms to close-knit groups over time (as shown by the diagram). While linguistic change is not the focus of the present discussion and, while the time frames are different, these ideas allow us to see that Hamilton's accommodation behaviour, in the context of the recording, goes against the accepted linguistic function of weak ties i.e. displaying conformity rather than innovation.

The foregoing discussion has highlighted some aspects of community conformity and conflict to arise from the Clay Country group dialogue recording. The preparation of this article has brought into focus the need for us, as researchers in the field of narrative studies, to develop a notion of *sensitivity*. For instance, an understanding of shared consciousness based on community (Retallick's 'sense of togetherness'), Cornishness, and other cultural pivots requires sensitivity to meet the challenge of increasingly heterogeneous local communities undergoing rapid social change. In group dialogic studies this concern is of particular importance in relation to the final stages of interpretation and presentation. Community narrative might remove the fieldworker from the initial collection of data but sensitivity is still required in dealing with the analysis of data and the subsequent issues that arise. We must therefore remember Portelli's earlier warning of turning a recorded 'dialogue into two monologues'. The role of the researcher in group dialogue needs further study since, as was mentioned earlier, narrators can create a 'monologue of brute facts' only for the scholar, possibly now totally removed from the recording session, to apply 'a monologue of sophisticated ideas that the informant[s] never hear about'. One might add that we need sensitivity in our methodological approach to all oral history interviews. The first section exemplifies the considerable value and importance of an exploration of the interview–subject relationship for future research within CAVA. These considerations lead us to believe that sensitivity is a multi-dimensional concept requiring further investigation.

CONCLUSION

We began this analysis of Cornwall's oral culture by highlighting the potential of CAVA as a means to understand those present-day social and cultural processes underway in Cornwall that have immediate relevance to its people. Oral history should not just be concerned with the recording of nostalgic and cosy reminiscences about the past. Indeed, the real aim of CAVA is the creation of a unique resource that can reveal the complexities of the past, present, and future. Our work here is set firmly in the revisionist paradigm where, as Clifford puts it: 'Cultures do not hold still for their portraits'. An interdisciplinary approach is central to a revisionist agenda and our analysis of group dialogue has taken us to a closer understanding of two major areas of enquiry: issues of conformity or conflict with implications for cultural identity and methodological issues related to the fieldworker-subject relationship. By exploring the conversational dynamics of identity scholars can obtain further insight into underlying issues of both historical and contemporary significance. In terms of methodology we have drawn on debates within oral history, anthropology, and sociolinguistics to discuss the overarching theme of the influence that the presence of the fieldworker/interviewer brings to interactions with subjects/informants. Notable amongst these debates are interviewee-as-narrator, the indigenous fieldworker, the Observer's Paradox and accommodation theory. On the face of it this presents a useful comparison of approaches but the challenge ahead, initiated here, is to go further and to fuse them into a really meaningful framework for future research with which to understand both Cornwall's oral culture and matters of contemporary social and cultural importance.

NOTES AND REFERENCES

1. C. Kieffer, *Oral History in Your Community*, Missouri, 1999. http://muextension.missouri.edu/explore/aging/gg0008.htm
2. R. Perks, *Oral History: Talking about the Past*, London, 1992.
3. T. Crago, ' "The Myth of Non Interference": A Personal Reappraisal of the Role of the Interviewer in the Process of Oral History', in *Cornish History Network Newsletter*, 10, March 2001.
4. A. Portelli, *The Battle of Valle Guilia: Oral History and the Art of Dialogue*, Madison, WI, 1997, p. 12.
5. Portelli, 1997, p. 9.
6. L. Ryan, ' "I'm Going to England": Women's Narratives of Leaving Ireland in the 1930s', *Oral History*, 30: 1, Spring 2002.
7. B. Malinowski, *Argonauts of the Western Pacific: an Account of Native Enterprise and Adventure in the Archipelagoes of Melanesian New Guinea*. London, 1922.
8. N.H.H. Graburn, 'The Ethnographic Tourist', in M.S.E. Dunn, *The Tourist as a Metaphor of the Social World*, London, n.d., p. 26.
9. J. Clifford, 'Introduction: Partial Truths' in J. Clifford and G.E. Marciss, *Writing Culture*, California, p. 10.

10. Portelli, *Battle of Valle Giulia*, p. 12.
11. W. Labov, *Sociolinguistic Patterns*, Oxford, 1978, p. 209.
12. W. Labov, P. Cohen, C. Robins and J. Lewis, *A Study of the non-standard English of Negro and Puerto Rican Speakers in New York City*, 2 vols, Philadelphia, PA, 1968.
13. H. Giles and N. Coupland, 'Accommodation theory: optimal levels of convergence', in H. Giles and R. St Claire (eds), *Language and Social Psychology*, Oxford, 1979, pp. 45–65.
14. H. Giles and N. Coupland, *Language: Contexts and Consequences*, Buckingham, 1991, pp. 60–61.
15. R. Le Page, 'The Evolution of a Sociolinguistic Theory of Language', in F. Coulmas (ed.), *The Handbook of Sociolinguistics*, Oxford, 1997, p. 28.
16. The oral narrative extracts in this article come from a single recording (CAVA/M/MP1, December 2000, Institute of Cornish Studies). Pseudonyms are used for the four narrators.
17. P. Thompson, *The Voice of the Past: Oral History*, Oxford, 1978, p. 174.
18. P. Thompson, H. Slim, O. Bennet and N. Cross, 'Ways of Listening' in R. Perks and A. Thomson (eds), *The Oral History Reader*, London, 1998, pp. 114–25; see also K. Howarth, *Oral History: A Handbook*, Gloucester, 1998, p. 125.
19. L. Passerini, 'Work Ideology and Consensus under Italian Fascism', *History Workshop Journal*, 8, 1979, p. 92. Passerini's work is discussed in A. Green and K. Troup, *The Houses of History: A Critical Reader in Twentieth-century History and Theory*, Manchester, 1999, p. 232.
20. P. Burke, *The Art of Conversation*, Cornell University Press, 1993, p. 1.
21. L. Milroy, 'Social Network and language Maintenance', in A. Pugh, V. Lee and J. Swann, *Language and Language Use: a Reader*, London, 1980, p. 35.
22. P. Trudgill, 'Sex, Covert Prestige and Linguistic Change in the Urban British English of Norwich', *Language in Society*, 1, 1972, pp. 179–95.
23. M. Granovetter, 'The Strength of Weak Ties: A Network Theory Revisited', in P.V. Marsden and N. Lin (eds), *Social Structure and Network Analysis*. London, 1982.
24. For a description of the vernacular norms for Cornish English (the accent variety of English spoken in Cornwall) see J. Wells, *Accents of English*, Cambridge, 1982, or A. Hughes and P. Trudgill, *English Accents and Dialects*, London, 1996. Interactions between social change in Cornwall and accent patterns amongst young people of Cornwall are discussed in L. Ellis and M. Ireland, 'Accent Change in Cornish English and Implications for Regional identity', paper presented to the UK Language Variation and Change Conference, University of Sheffield, September 2003.
25. J. Milroy and L. Milroy, 'Speaker-innovation and Linguistic Change' in J. Milroy, *Linguistic Variation and Change: On the Historical Sociolinguistics of English*, Oxford, 1980, pp. 176–91.

'DRILL CORES': A NEWLY-FOUND MANUSCRIPT OF COUSIN JACK NARRATIVES FROM THE UPPER PENINSULA OF MICHIGAN, USA

Alan M. Kent

INTRODUCTION

Cornwall, and other territories in these islands, are slowly but surely finding a renewed interest in what is colloquially termed 'Dialect', or perhaps more appropriately 'non-standard' Englishes. This regained gaze has not only fallen upon Dialect and non-standard Englishes in Cornwall; it has also alighted upon the many storytellers indigenous —such as Will Coleman and Trev Lawrence[1]—and visiting,[2] as well as mixed-ethnicity storyteller groups,[3] who have all viewed Cornwall as a profitable 'mine' of Celtic imagination and mystery; not to mention resolutely Cornish humour, and genuine, unadulterated 'folklore', 'myths', 'narratives', and 'urban legends,[4] all told in Cornu-English. Gradually too, at the various Cornish gatherings around the world, we are witnessing a rise in narrative performances by an increasingly mobilized global Cornish—politically and culturally aware—who are claiming and reformulating their heritage.[5] This chapter re-examines the genre of 'dialect' folk narrative known as 'Cousin Jack stories' in the light of a newly-found manuscript. That manuscript not only provides us with a remarkable resource of nineteenth- and twentieth-century folktales, but also re-opens the important issue of Dialect studies within the new Cornish historiography.

In a long-forgotten March 1953 issue of the *National Geographic* magazine is a feature titled 'Work-hard, Play-hard Michigan' by the journalist Andrew H. Brown. Tucked away in the feature is a section of popular post-war 'encountering natives' anthropology titled 'Meeting a 'Cousin Jack''' which, given the context of the full article, emphasizes the apparent exotica and difference of this ethnic group. Brown is being shown around the Upper Peninsula of Michigan by Jack Bowen of the Cleveland-Cliffs Iron Company at Ishpeming, and the writer records the moment when he first encounters a Cousin Jack:

At the Mather Mine, A shaft, we watched miners scramble off the lift cage at the end of their shift. Bowen stopped a man of rugged build and introduced him to me.

'This is Billy Richards,' said Bowen, 'one of our miners whose ancestors came from Cornwall.'

Cornish Miners are known locally as 'Cousin Jacks.' Top-notch men underground, their forefathers came to Michigan when Cornwall's tin mines petered out.

At Ishpeming I looked up Walter F. Gries, superintendent of Cleveland-Cliff's welfare department.

'Ever hear of a Cornish pasty?' (Gries pronounced it 'pass-tee.')

'Never have,' I answered.

'Well, the pasty helped build this country. Come home with me and I'll have Mrs. Gries make you one . . .'

. . . Upper Peninsula's iron and copper mines, and lumbering, attracted not only Cornishmen but also Finns, Swedes, Irishmen, Italians, and French Canadians. Their dialect stories are part of local folklore.[6]

This article is concerned with the 'dialect stories' and 'local folk-lore' of Walter F. Gries. By necessity, my introduction to his work is autobiographical. As I have outlined in my 2004 work *Cousin Jack's Mouth-organ: Travels in Cornish America*,[7] I had originally journeyed to the Upper Peninsula to investigate the life and work of another Cousin Jack storyteller, William Jack Foster—although, as it turned out, Foster had died in April 2003. The remaining legacy of his story-telling is found on a video recording at Calumet's historic theatre, in which he 'recalls the hard life and times of miners and their families in the Copper country'.[8] In the video he is dressed as a Cousin Jack, complete with pasty pail and miner's hard hat, and tells a number of stories about the Keweenaw Peninsula (part of the Upper Peninsula of Michigan), though perhaps none of them sound as specifically Cornish as one might expect. William Jack Foster, however, was well-known in and around Calumet for his work, and it was disappointing not to have met him. It certainly seemed as if I would not find the Cousin Jack narrative legacy I was interested in researching.

However, on the final day of my time at Eagle Harbor on the Keweenaw Peninsula, one of the members of the Ellis family with whom I was staying—Tom Ellis Jr., had a recollection that, within his house, he had what he initially thought was 'a play' about the Cousin Jacks of the Upper Peninsula. Ignited with interest that there might be a surviving drama about the Cousin Jacks I asked Tom to find the manuscript for me, and in the early hours of the morning he located the text. The manuscript was called *Drill Cores: Folklore of Michigan's Upper Peninsula from the Collection of Walter F. Gries.*[9] It was actually not a drama (the confusion has arisen because of one of the lead headings which read 'The characters on stage'), but a collection of folklore and Cousin Jack narratives, edited by Donald D. Kinsey from an archive and earlier manuscript of Walter F. Gries, the superintendent of Cleveland-Cliff's welfare department, whom Andrew H. Brown had met back in 1952. Walter F. Gries was Tom Ellis Jr's grandfather. A very brief perusal of the manuscript told me that I needed to study the text further, so Tom photocopied the manuscript for me to take back to Cornwall. I have since learnt that Kinsey and Gries's text is perhaps far more significant than I first thought, and in fact the manuscript is at present the best surviving record of Cousin Jack narratives in the USA.[10]

PENINSULA VOICES: CULTURAL GEOGRAPHY, CULTURAL MATERIALISM

The development of the field of so-called 'cultural geography' is a useful theoretical platform from which to consider *Drill Cores*, and has already proved a useful critical tool within the new Cornish historiography.[11] Far from offering only 'a sense of place and space', this critical methodology allows us to work beyond the conventions of the usually delineated strands of literary and geographical theory, and work in a multi-disciplinary manner, realizing the limitations and strengths of both fields. In their influential 1994 study, *Worlds of Desire, Realms of Power: A Cultural Geography*, which develops the earlier works of Edward Said's *Orientalism* (1978) and in certain respects Benedict Anderson's *Imagined Communities* (1983),[12] Pamela Shurmer Smith and Kevin Hannam emphasize:

> the interaction between metaphor and materiality, showing
> not only that the way in which people think the world has very
> real repercussions for the way it is, but also that the way in

> which they experience their environment has implications for
> how they construct metaphors . . . We do not believe that
> culture and communications are mere epiphenomena of
> material reality but neither do we believe that culture is a
> superorganic thing which writes upon landscapes.[13]

With this critical position we can progress beyond nineteenth-century
preservationist 'folklore' collection and limiting modernist anthropology to demonstrate how a manuscript such as *Drill Cores* can show
how places, spaces, and environments are endowed with a range of
sometimes interlocking, sometimes conflicting meaning, relating not
only to the transnational Cornish but to other peoples and ethnic
groups of the Upper Peninsula. The 'construction of metaphor' in
particular has profound relevance to the way in which any Cornish
'folk' narrative is told, as does the 'material reality' of the moment of
production; for example, the reason why Gries's Cousin Jack narratives
are spatially located in the world of men and men's work, and as we
shall see, how certain archetypes of Cousin Jack characters and their
ideological positions have developed.

   The other critical context for the reading of *Drill Cores* is one that
I have outlined previously: that of cultural materialism. I have long
argued that scholars of Celtic literatures, whether in indigenous Celtic
languages or in imperialist 'replacement' languages like English in the
Atlantic archipelago, or French in Brittany, need to promote the use of
'other tools and methodologies' within the field, so that 'it can benefit
from cultural materialist, new historicist and feminist perspectives,
drawing on applicable developments in studies of other literatures'.[14]
It is cultural materialism in particular which is profoundly relevant
here, since as its major proponents—Jonathan Dollimore and Alan
Sinfield—argue:

> Culture does not (cannot) transcend the material forces and
> relations of production. Culture is not simply a reflection of
> the economic and political system, but nor can it be in-
> dependent of it. Cultural Materialism therefore studies the
> implication of literary texts in history.[15]

We are, therefore, concerned with the implication of the Cousin
Jack narratives of Gries, and their position in history—both at the
moment of production and their subsequent interpretation by successive generations of listeners, and now readers. A related point is worth
making here. In 2000 I argued that the next step for the new Cornish
historiography had to be 'to evaluate how Cornish men and women

wrote about the territories to which they emigrated, and how their descendents now perceive their relationship to Cornwall'.[16] Such a realization has come at the same time as the CAVA (Cornish Audio-Visual Archive) project, which endeavours to develop the field of oral history within new interpretative methodologies. This has evolved into the *Cornish Braids* project, which ventures to 'create a multi-generational profile of Cornish life in the twentieth century . . . investigating key strands of cultural activity'.[17] Since emigration is a key strand of cultural activity in Cornwall, the oral narratives of Cornishmen and women in the USA are also applicable and appropriate, as Garry Tregidga has demonstrated in his construction of research links with the University of Boulder, Colorado. And given this cultural need, *Drill Cores* becomes a highly suitable case for academic treatment.

THE UPPER AND KEWEENAW PENINSULAS OF MICHIGAN

The cultural geographic and materialist context for *Drills Cores* is the Upper Peninsula of Michigan, and then more specifically the Keweenaw Peninsula. As a state, Michigan is composed of two halves, separated by the Straits of Mackinac and the Great Lakes of Lake Michigan and Lake Huron. The southern 'oven-glove'-shaped peninsula is mainly an agricultural region, but is dominated by the city of Detroit, which as Rowse argues, has 'a large Cornish population'.[18] The Upper Peninsula is more isolated, relying economically on timber and mining. It borders Lake Superior, and the Canadian province of Ontario, and the state of Wisconsin to the south west.

Jutting north into Lake Superior, on the Upper Peninsula's northern coast is the Keweenaw Peninsula. In dimensions, the Keweenaw is virtually the size and shape of Cornwall—horn shaped, and tailing towards the ports of Eagle Harbor and Copper Harbor. Both the Upper and Keweenaw Peninsulas have attracted numerous Cornishmen and women since mining began in the region in the middle of the nineteenth century. Culturally, therefore, many Cornish men and women were travelling from one peninsula to another; and we might legitimately offer a hypothesis that some were attracted to the Keweenaw for that very reason: it reminded them of home.

The classic study of the region is Angus Murdoch's 1943 work *Boom Copper: The Story of the First U.S. Mining Boom*, which explains how the first really experienced miners to work the Keweenaw were the Cornish, who were apparently astounded at the huge chunks of 'native' copper to be found there.[19] The Cornish arrived in the late 1840s and early 1850s, initially working the famous 'Cliff' Mine, then later moving to the massive Central Mine, which they headed to 'like homing pigeons'.[20] Within his study of mining processes, Murdoch also outlines the importance of Cousin Jack's Cornu-English:

> Central, in fact, was so Cornish that a native-born American visitor often wished he'd brought an interpreter with him. Cornish crake is founded on the English language, but with such picturesque adaptations that it can sound like a foreign tongue. A Cousin Jack miner might 'feel some foolish' if he didn't 'beat' his hand drill 'brave and true' into the 'keenly' lodes underground in the 'wheal'.[21]

Although Murdoch established scholarship on the Keweenaw, his successor is Arthur W. Turner. His 1994 book *Strangers and Sojourners: A History of Michigan's Keweenaw Peninsula* is now the standard academic work on the region.[22] Turner, following the work of Cornish-based scholars such as John Rowe,[23] begins by examining the famous Cliff Mine, which was the area in which the anti-Cornish school-teacher Henry A. Hobart once worked. Hobart found the Cornish 'coarse, dirty and rough' and 'likes hogs in every sense of the word'.[24] Despite this contrary view, the Cornish quickly became the managerial class on the Peninsula, as in other locations across the world.[25] Other useful contexts for the reading of Gries's narratives can be found in the recently collated *Historical Diaries of the Copper Country 1845 to 1910*. An anonymous Copper Country marshal gives a flavour of the region in 1898, when Cousin Jack culture was at its height in Calumet, with Ed Hocking likely (as his name suggests) to have Cornish origins:

> March 23, 1898: Ed Hocking, the baseball magnate of Hancock, 'stole' into Calumet last night and attempted to 'kidnap' Calumet's best pitcher for his team.
> March 27, 1898: I was soundly booed. The big Cornish style wrestling match, with a purse of $200, for the world championship, was staged at the Armory Opera house. The two wrestlers fought to even-up after two hours. At 11.55 p.m. I stepped onto the stage and gave the men five minutes to decide the matter. This raised a howl of dissension. At midnight I called the match a draw. Today I am the most unpopular man in the country.[26]

These two entries alone tell something of the dominance of Cornish culture in and around Calumet. As Turner has shown, Calumet was one of the largest cities in America at this time[27]—and was filled with Cousin Jack culture, and no doubt the telling of many narratives. Such incidents formed the metaphorical base for the Cousin Jack stories which evolved in Gries's collection. Calumet is a core cultural-geographic touchstone. For many of the miners, it represented civilization, even though paradoxically, in other ways it was another typical American mining frontier town.

Another context for the reading of Gries's narratives is Newton G. Thomas's accomplished 1941 novel *The Long Winter Ends*.[28] Indeed, the dialogue of both texts could easily sit in each other's narrative. Newton G. Thomas was born in Stoke Climsland in Cornwall in 1878 and journeyed to Michigan's Upper Peninsula as a child. This was a generation later than the original, initial Cornish migration, although not at such a distance that the stories could not be passed on. Thomas worked for the majority of his life teaching dentistry and histology at the University of Illinois, but he never forgot Cornwall and the Upper Peninsula he knew as a boy. The novel tells the story of a year in the life of a young emigrant miner named Jim Holman who leaves Cornwall to work in the copper mines of the Upper Peninsula. He spends his first year living in a boarding house (crucial Cousin Jack narrative space) with other Cornish miners, and it is within this context that Cousin Jack culture is most effectively explored.

It is naïve to believe that this culture is an exact transposition of Cornish culture 'plonked down' in places where the Cornish settled. Like Cornish culture itself, Cousin Jack culture has its own internal differences, politicization and iconography—which though related to Cornish life, was infused with new influences, reflecting the cultural geographical context of the new location. This issue is a considerable thematic device in *The Long Winter Ends*, since despite a Gries-like attempt to preserve the Cornish continuum in America, finally, Jim Holman neglects this in favour of a future which is Americanized. From a folkloric viewpoint, this may seem something of a pity, but in the context of a realist novel like *The Long Winter Ends*, the 'reality effect'[29] is resolutely historically accurate. That was the choice many Cornish emigrants made; a choice in the long-term that would actually cause the decline and near-extinction in the number of Cousin Jack stories being told and re-told. The modern re-invention of Cornish-America could not have been perceived by those tellers, whose often stoic narrative 'voice-scapes' had begun to be viewed as irrelevant as the third generation Cornish became more integrated into post-war America.

Thomas's novel has been long criticized for its alleged inauthenticity,[30] particularly in terms of Thomas's written depiction of Cornu-English, but this criticism is wrong-headed, since it is clear that the

Cornu-English being spoken in America had its own nuances and was actively being embellished by American English, not to mention the other ethnic groups operating around the mines of the Upper Peninsula.[31] This is to be expected, since Cornu-English does not stand still (even though, paradoxically, many of its practitioners wish it would), and Thomas's novel and Gries's narratives are examples of this progression. Likewise, present Cornu-American dialect words and writings have developed from earlier periods, incorporating new concepts and revising old ones. A.L. Rowse seems to agree. He comments that Thomas 'gets the dialect absolutely right'.[32] In the novel, though, there is an on-going debate about speaking 'proper' ('Cornish bayn't the best Henglish that's spawk'),[33] which appears the product of the Cornish miners' concerns over literacy and the need to 'make do':

> "Tis diff'runt 'ere,' Jim said. 'People be more edicated. Life be aysier, an' aour hard lines wouldn' suit. I bayn't gifted with spaych'. He hesitated. 'Bein' laughed at wouldn' keep me awake. 'Tedn' that. I bayn't fitted for un. I do w'at I can w'ere I can'.[34]

Thus, despite Jim being a member of the second generation of Cornish miners who headed to the Upper Peninsula, the culture in which the novel operates is a resoundingly illiterate one. Only by the end of the story can Jim read ('This was the longest letter Jim had ever received, and he spent the whole evening on it before he was sure he had its meaning')[35] This illiteracy, however, was the same culture that had so nourished and sustained the classic Cornish folk narratives over several centuries. Therefore, the prominence of 'orality' and 'story-telling' is related to a lack of written culture, and it is re-infused with energy when new cultural situations arise; what Shurmer Smith and Hannam term 'the interaction between metaphor and materiality'.[36] A comparable situation is perhaps the contemporary rise of interest in Cornu-English as a new 'cultural weapon' of Cornish difference,[37] given the relative failure of the Cornish language as such a 'weapon' —at least on a mass scale—by the end of the twentieth century.[38] Relating this back to the narratives of Gries, he understood that the Cousin Jack narratives of America could preserve Cousin Jack difference, in an America which was perceiving Irish and Scottish ancestry as 'Celtic' but neglecting the Cornish input on American culture. In his own words, he wanted to show how 'the pasty helped build this country'.[39] Useful context for this is given by Shirley Ewart and Harold T. George in their 1998 work *Highly Respectable Families: The Cornish of Grass Valley 1854–1954*,[40] where they note the historical invisibility of the Cornish in Census Returns and other records, since they were recorded as simply being 'English'.

WALTER F. GRIES AND DONALD D. KINSEY

The corpus of stories contained in *Drill Cores* is remarkable and to understand their production, some knowledge of the teller/author, and the editor, is necessary. The teller and author, Walter F. Gries, was born of German extraction in Lake Linden on the Keweenaw in 1892. His father was John Adam Gries, and since his father's middle initial was 'A' he was given the nickname 'Axle Grease'.[41] Walter's mother, Ida Johanna Tappe Gries, lived to survive Walter by only six months. For much of his life, Walter F. Gries lived at Negaunee, and as Brown's article demonstrates, he was most recently the superintendent of Cleveland-Cliff's welfare department.

However, he had held many important public offices in his life, including service as a school teacher, principal, welfare agent, warden of Marquette prison, State Welfare Commission member, President of the Michigan School Commissioners' Association, and Michigan Welfare Agents' Association. He was also Vice-President of the Michigan Education Association and President of the Bay Cliff's Health Camp for a number of years. This biographical information is important, since it shows how fully involved Gries was with the community of Keweenaw and the Upper Peninsula. He was never at arm's length to the society, and so understood its lifestyle and language. Gries was forced to retire early, ironically due to chronic diabetes.[42] His plan had been to assemble all the Cousin Jack stories he had into an anthology. It was not to happen, since just as he started work on the project, his condition worsened and he died. The year was 1959. Kinsey's editing of *Drill Cores* identifies the transnational nature of Gries's experiences in the Upper Peninsula, an illuminating point worth bearing in mind, in the light of any perceived narrow cultural nationalism, as the following sequence demonstrates:

> Howard Medlyn was Walter's Cornish barber in Ishpeming. He knew that Walter was German. He was telling the boys that this was Walter's nationality. They would tell Howard that he was 'bit orf in the 'ead!'
> ''cud'n be German! 'Ow cud h'any bloody German talk like a Cousin Jack—an' 'e do talk like un!'
> But if you want to talk like an immigrant national, all that is needed is to spend your childhood as one of them. Their dialect grows with you, as a natural part of your own speech.[43]

Clearly Gries had spent so much time in the company of the Cornish, that he had gained an ear for their way of speaking. It was an ear that was to serve him remarkably well over the next few decades, and why we should guard against ethno-linguistic categories of identity.

Although Kinsey was slightly younger than Gries, the life of Donald D. Kinsey (*c.* 1902–1965) is less well-documented. Jean and Tom Ellis recollect that he originated from the farming region of the Lower Peninsula, and that he worked as an agricultural company representative and merchant.[44] In his spare time he developed, through Gries, an interest in Michigan's folklore. Kinsey and his wife often visited her sister at Eagle Harbor; this sister was married to Walter Gries's wife, Velta. Kinsey, his wife, and children lived in Grand Rapids.

THE 'DRILL CORES' MANUSCRIPT: CONTEXT AND DESCRIPTION

A 'drill core' is the term applied to a cylindrical boring sample of rock, usually cut out by a diamond drill. It reveals a picture of what lies below the surface, and shows the depth, richness, and extent of the lodes underground. It is mining which forms the metaphorical base for the manuscript and the tales contained within, which in Gries's view show the 'depth, richness and extent' of Cornish narrative skill. An alternative explanation for the title of the manuscript, however, could be that Gries saw 'Core' as a pun on the usual Cornish miner's name for a shift—also known as a 'core', when miners would be working at drilling rock. As Orchard argues:

> Miners usually work but 6 hours at a time, and consequently four pares of men are required for the whole time—forenoon core, from 6 a.m. to noon; afternoon core from noon to 6 p.m.; first core by night from 6 p.m. to midnight; and last core by night from midnight to 6 a.m.[45]

It is likely that such traditional practices continued in the Upper Peninsula, as in Cornwall. This shift pattern is certainly the case in Thomas's *The Long Winter Ends*, and again forms the time-frame for many of the Cousin Jack narratives Gries told.

Including the preliminaries, the typewritten manuscript is printed on 123 pages. Not all of the manuscript, however, is devoted to Cousin Jack stories. It begins with Kinsey's dedication to Gries, who is described as a 'Good Friend and delightful companion, host and 'open sesame'to many of my delightful years in the Northern Peninsula of Michigan'.[46] Chapter 1, 'Sirens Sing from a Northern Shore', is introductory and it recalls the year 1929, when Kinsey first travelled to the Upper Peninsula as a newlywed husband, with his bride. Kinsey's technique in the chapter is to express the isolation of the Upper Peninsula ('The cement pavement ended at Alma. I carried two reserve cans of gas in the trunk. I expected that rural gas stations would pull down the shades early at night. They did.'[47]). The trip Kinsey takes is across the Straits of Mackinac, at the far northern end of the Lower Peninsula of Michigan. Here, he exclaims, is 'romantic history', and is where he first met Walter Gries. Kinsey gives a context for the construction of the Cousin Jack stories:

> Through Walter Gries I learned the history and lore of the Upper Peninsula. I read his library of lore with avid interest. We fished the lakes and streams, explored the old copper mines, picked thimbleberries for jam and blackberries for pies. We gathered pine knots from decaying beams of old mine shaft houses to make hot fires for baking in the old kitchen range. We made canes in variety. Some of the canes were ready-cut by beavers while working around their dams. We explored the old Copper Falls Mine where the beaver dam had burst spreading copper stamp sand over the valley like a grey Sahara.[48]

In very many ways, Kinsey's description has all the feel of a transplanted Cornish industrial landscape. Not only are the derelict mines (picked over by those who ought to be preserving them), but there is also industrial pollution on a large scale. Walter Gries kept a 'log' of his activities at his summer camp, which clearly became the recording device for remembering the Cousin Jack stories. Now in the hands of Tom Ellis Jr, I have seen this log.[49] It is a fascinating document in itself, since clearly Gries worked as a cultural magpie during the early twentieth century, recording snippets of narrative, dialogue, ideas, newspaper cuttings (that he had written) and mining history which formed or enhanced the narratives he both created and embellished. Kinsey gives the original context for its use:

> The log served a delightful purpose. The family and friends would sit around the fire of an evening, get out the log and recall past hours of fun and humor. This often triggered the demand for an hour or so of Walter Gries' wonderful skill in telling folklore stories of the mining country.[50]

Kinsey, however, also contributed to the log, so it seems it had a wider social function as a community recording device—a kind of primitive piece of proto web-space 'guest book' onto which visitors could sign. Kinsey made a contribution in 1937, its flavour paradoxically somehow even more 'Cornish' and more romantically 'Celtic' than what was being expressed in Cornwall itself at that time:

The smack of Cornish pasties on the tongue,
Savory and hot, with crust of golden brown;
Spiced with old Cornish tales, told round the fire
At evening when the cool has settled down;
The pleasing cup of friendship that we drew.[51]

Chapter 2, 'The Life of the Story is in the Man', introduces the first Cousin Jack narrative. Its telling is unique within the context of the wider manuscript since one can see the combined voices of the more refined Kinsey with the Cornu-English of Gries. The overall, almost Chaucerian effect of 'teller' and 'tale' is not completely dislocating, but one can clearly see where Kinsey hands over to the earlier teller, symbolized here by the change to italics:

The house of the newlywed miner stood on the hill near the church. Let's call him Freddy Trembath. Freddy has found something lacking in his newly wedded state. Cornish wives are usually industrious and dutiful. They are excellent cooks. It was their custom to arise early, kindle the fire, bake a pasty for their ''andsome' and cook him a hearty breakfast. But Mary Jane was on the lazy side. Freddy soon found that she loved to lie abed of a morning. Day after day Freddy went on shift without his pasty and only a pick-up breakfast. The boys at the mine remarked on Freddy's cold lunch of bread and beef, and began to twit him about it. Freddy would blush and mutter to himself. Finally he poured out his problem to his 'pardner', Billy.

'I dawn't knaw w'at I'm gawn to do 'about Meeary Jane. 'Er dawn't git h'up an' light the fire an' bake me a pasty like a good woman oughter. 'Er lies abed 'alf the moornin. H'I'm afeared to take on 'about h'it, cos she might get mad. W'at shall h'I do?'

Billy gave Freddy some 'fatherly' advice about how to handle women. Freddy went off shift at mid-morning the next day. When he reached home, Mary Jane was still snoozing in bed. Freddy filled a bucket with ice cold water from the well. He stood at the foot of the bed and shouted, 'Fire! Fire! Meeary Jane!'

Startled, Mary Jane rose bolt upright in bed. 'Where? Where's they fire, Freddy?'

Freddy cut loose with the pale of ice water.

'Ef 'ee 'd like to knaw, h'it's in h'every bloody stove on the 'ill but aours!'[52]

This tale is the first in the collection, and despite the mix of narrative voice, the subject-matter has all the hallmarks of a classic Cousin Jack story. The importance of mining and of an appropriate diet for the physicality of the work is brought home again and again within Gries's corpus. In all Cousin Jack narratives, the pasty is the only appropriate food—nothing else will suffice (not even fuggan or saffron cake). The role of the 'pardner' is often extenuated, and here, supplants the place and function of the wife as listener and companion; perhaps because of the time spent together and the danger almost constantly faced underground. Thus women's roles are reduced in dramatic status, but they are highly defined in the domestic sphere, and can be positive, if only in the sense of duty and industry. None of Gries's narratives ever deal with sexuality (nor do others within the wider corpus), but the tales could be and frequently were sexist. This was because they were told almost always within a male context. 'On the 'ill', meanwhile, defines the Cornish cultural-geographic context. The impression is that such behaviour would not matter if it happened 'off the 'ill'. The verb phrase for *throwing*: 'cut loose' seems to have a greater place in the adit or shaft than in the bedroom, but obviously this heightens the dramatic and comic effect of the tale. The alliterative effect of '*h'it's* in *h'every* bloody stove on the *'ill*' brings about a poetic finality to the story.

This somewhat typical tale enables Kinsey to spend time reflecting on Walter F. Gries. Gries had been in the business of collecting and collating Cousin Jack stories for some years. In the log is a note: 'Do you suppose there will ever be a book published that will set down the Cornish stories or 'plods'that have been going the rounds of the mining regions these many years? There are lots of these yarns, but few have every seen printer's ink.'[53] Unfortunately, Gries carried many stories in his head. They never needed writing down, but as Kinsey explains, 'a tape recording which Mr. Rhynie Hollitz of Shaker Heights, Ohio, was kind enough to send'[54] contained several additional tales, which Kinsey was then able to transcribe in the present manuscript of *Drill Cores*. In the same chapter, a good deal of the text is devoted to the Italians, who also, of course, worked as miners in the Upper Peninsula. Much Italian folklore is recorded in this chapter; the manuscript littered with Anglo-Italian phrases such as 'If we getta chance to put-a Georg-a Wash and Garibaldi togedder, we could lick-a da whole-a worl'!' and 'Now-a what you tink for dat?'.[55] Chapter 3, A Cosmopolitan Touch, begins with a re-examination of Gries's German heritage, but it evolves into a close study of the other large ethnic group of the Upper Peninsula—the Finns (who worked in mining alongside the Cornish); ending with a section on the French Canadians (who tended to work in lumbering).

Chapter 4 is titled 'Cornishmen: One and All' and, with a few minor diversions, pages 47 to 123 are devoted to the folklore and stories of Cousin Jacks. Chapter 5 is devoted to 'The Cornish Pasty' while Chapter 6 is called 'Deep Levels Underground'. Although all of these chapters contain a range of Cousin Jack narratives, it is Chapter 7 ('The Cap'n Dick Commentaries') where the focus entirely swings onto such stories. The language of this Chapter is given illumination in Chapter 8, which is labelled 'Dialect Dawdling'. This chapter is important since, as we shall see, it is one of the few pieces of text (within a limited few contemporary exceptions) in Cornu-English literature, where the authors discuss the grammar, punctuation, and structure of 'Dialect'. In perhaps a response to the usual hard lot of the woman in Cousin Jack narratives, Chapter 9 explores in more depth 'The Joys and Tribulations of Cousin Jenny and the Kids'. Chapter 10 meanwhile, continues on from 'The Cap'n Dick Commentaries' by offering further Cousin Jack narratives, but more wide-ranging in subject-matter than mining life alone. The manuscript has no conclusion or after-word. It finishes simply with 'A Tender Cornish Tale', an appropriately sentimental ending.[56]

The manuscript contains over fifty separate Cousin Jack narratives in total. Not even the other masters of Cousin Jack narratives in the USA—D.E.A. Charlton (who wrote between 1920 and 1940) or Charles E. Brown—can equal this.[57] The original dates of the stories are extremely difficult to deduce, though clearly from the mining practices some of them were culled from a narrative base that was more nineteenth-century than earlier twentieth-century. However, a modern component or idea winds its way in occasionally. The Ellis family estimate that the bulk of the composition of the stories within the manuscript occurred in the pre-Second World War period (matching Charlton and Brown's assemblies), though *Drill Cores* itself and the editing work of Kinsey took place in the early 1960s, just after Gries's death. Clearly, however, the great age of the transcription of the Cousin Jack stories was the 1930s.

DROLLS, COUSIN JACK STORIES AND PLODS

The structural origins of many Cousin Jack narratives (including those of Walter F. Gries) appear to lie in the earlier 'folk' narrative of Cornwall,[58] which, paradoxically, were appearing at home and across the globe at almost exactly the same time at which traditional drolls were in decline.[59] According to Henry Jenner, the Cornish word 'daralla' is perhaps the origin of the word Droll,[60] and it is to collectors such as Robert Hunt, William Bottrell, H.J. Whitfield and Margaret Courtney that we are indebted since they prevented much further loss by freezing the droll or story in printed form[61]—effectively what Gries and Kinsey have also completed.

There were a number of socio-cultural and geopolitical reasons why the drolls of the previous ages started to decline in the nineteenth century. Certainly, the growth of mass literacy, revivals in Methodism, and alternative pastimes contributed to decline.[62] But it might also be postulated that these drolls they were being replaced in Cornish culture by the Cousin Jack Stories whose success and popularity reflected their essential modernity; that is, they were the product of a complex industrial society—so patterning the growth of the novel. They were relevant to many Cornish and transnational Cornish people's experience (as opposed to say, for example, the 'swirling mist' narratives of saints, King Arthur and mermaids), and were appealing because they were amusing and humorous, and most vitally, self-deprecating, firmly tongue-in-cheek, and poked fun at themselves and anyone else ripe enough to be satirized. Put another way, it can be argued that as traditional pre-industrial Cornish culture was eroded in the nineteenth century, so the Cousin Jack story took on a function as the new droll of modernism.

However, the relatively quick decline of Cornish involvement in overseas mining caused the Cousin Jack genre itself to implode, with a limited number of survivors such as William Jack Foster, D.E.A. Charlton, Charles E. Brown, Walter F. Gries, and Donald D. Kinsey continuing to tell the stories into the late twentieth century. The embers of that moment of production might be this article itself, as well as certain rekindled interest amongst the newly mobilized and politically active global Cornish.[63] That said, in my visit to the Upper Peninsula in 2003, I was told by the successors to Gries's generation that a succession of Cousin Jack narratives had been handed down. However, the oral corpus of the tales was much reduced. The following is an example:

A Cousin Jack goin' down Petherick Hill met another one

comin' up. The first Cousin Jack said to the second one, 'Why are you walkin' s'fast? Where 'ee goin'?'

'I'm goin' over the doctor', said the second Cousin Jack.

'What fur?'

''Tidn fur me. 'Tis fur me wife . . .'

The first Cousin Jack stood thoughtfully for a while.

'I'll tell 'ee what. I'll join 'ee. I dun't like the look of mine either . . .'.[64]

This shows the explicit need in the Cousin Jack corpus for a final punch-line; the narrative working its way towards a joke. It is the logical (or illogical) thinking Cornishman who provides the mechanism of the humour and the creation of the intended effect on the listener.[65] This 'logicality' may even extend to something in the Cornish mindset, concerned with the application of technology on emotional life and relationships: an 'industrial Celt' world-view that suggests that if it works in the mine, it will work in other contexts too. The Cousin Jack is capable of dealing with modernity and transition in this way. Thus the narrative corpus is a coping-strategy against dislocation. This is why the concept of 'advice' from older miners to the young is so important in Gries' stories. The meeting of the two Cousin Jacks is important too. It takes place at Petherick Hill; again instantly Cornish narrative space. Given the fact that this story was outlined to me by Phil Medlyn,[66] who is strongly connected to the Keweenaw, this narrative would seem to be strongly linked to the corpus in Gries and Kinsey. Doctor stories are common, perhaps because of the need to regularly consult the mine doctor, and because new ailments were presenting themselves to the Cornish in new places. In the mine, the doctor was the difference between life and death.

It is clear though that certain varieties of Cousin Jack tales exist in the world corpus, as can easily be seen in the work of the cartoonists Oswald Pryor[67] and Ian Glanville. Both of these cartoonists have focused on Cousin Jack 'down under' in Australia. Glanville believes that the lasting success of the Cousin Jack story in comicbook format may be attributed to:

> their reliability, customs, traditional food, music, sport, a strict adherence to their religious beliefs, and of course the unique Cornish wit! The Cornish (Cousin Jack) style of humour is basically the misplacement of words, or their use in such a manner that the result is quite different to what the speak intended.[68]

Glanville believes that the central plank of Cousin Jack narrative humour to be located around malapropism, which is also a theme within Gries and Kinsey, and to a certain extent crops up in the narrative of Thomas's *The Long Winter Ends*. Glanville's archetypal characters are of interest to us. In his comic books, these are Cousin Jack himself, the Cap'n, the old-timer named Herb, 'laad' the kettle-boy, Parson, Thomas the cynic, Hardluck the traveller, Missus ('Jenny'), the schoolmistress, William and Richard (young boys), the doctor, Zack, mining engineers and the occasional Irishman ('Paddy'). These in themselves are actually based on older nineteenth-century stereotypes—established in the fictions and narrative poetry of writers such as John Tabois Tregellas and William Bentinck Forfar;[69] although Tregellas and Forfar themselves also looked back to earlier repre-sentations of the Cornish 'type' established by satirists like Andrew Boorde,[70] and, as Stoyle has demonstrated, the propagandists operat-ing against the Cornish during the Civil War.[71]

Nonetheless, Glanville's character base facilitates much comedy. For example, Cap'n appears to 'knaw best' but is always outwitted by the on-the-ground miner: Cousin Jack. Mining engineers and pro-fessors, who think they know tin or copper, usually end up the worse for wear. Thomas and Parson have endless debates on Methodism, with Thomas and his world-weary ideas most often coming off best. The intellectuals and the pompous are ripe for satire, as are the Irish, who are regarded as inferior in industry and religion. Not only is this the domain of straightforward comedy, but also an exploration of the ethnic tensions that dominated mining camps.

Virtually all of these archetypes can be found in realist novels from Cornu-centric writers such as Daniel Mason in his 1996 novel *Cousin Jack*,[72] but also in the wider American literary canon; for example in the short stories of Bret Harte.[73] Indeed, the archetype of the 'wild' Cousin Jack can now be seen in such diverse cultural activity as *Tommyknocker* soda, manufactured in Denver, but sold at many Cornish locations in the USA; *Golden Nuggets* breakfast cereal (1970–79 and 1999–present)—advertised with a bushy-bearded Cousin Jack named Klondike Pete ('Yee har!'), with mining wagon, pick-axe, and 'hoss'—and on pasty manufacturers' packaging all over the USA.

Much of this is connected to the original imaginings of Cousin Jacks, which may have started with real incidents in the rough and tumble world of the mining camps, with the persistent threat of danger underground from rock collapse and explosions, and the inevitable loneliness caused by the separation from the host culture.[74] The gritty realism, down-to-earth style, and lack of interest in 'refinement'—not to mention poverty and poor sanitation—created a certain resilience in the metaphorical base of the stories, far removed from the early drolls. Gries and Kinsey have perceptive views on the two main types of Cousin Jack stories to be told:

> Cornishmen recognize a difference between 'stories' and 'plods'. The 'story' is based on some actual incident. Characters may be changed, but the core of the event goes on being told. The 'plod' was the pure invention of someone's lively imagination. The humor in Cornish stories and plods has a flavour all its own. It often mixes with pathos or pokes fun at the naïvety and the frailties of human living. That makes it very human.[75]

'Plods' are actually discussed within *The Long Winter Ends*. Here the plod would seem to be a kind of ballad (in itself a narrative), but Thomas then relates this to the wider position of the Cousin Jacks in the Upper Peninsula:

> Tom went for his concertina, and after a little searching of the keys found the air and harmony. Jake and Jim listened in amazement. 'There 'tis,' Tom said, and repeated it.
> The three were silent for minutes. Then Jake spoke.
> 'Thicky be some plod!' He blew a mouthful of smoke into the air and watched it as if his thought expanded with it. 'Some plod,' he repeated. 'Fancy Ol' Parent or Uncle Ned —our fathers—plannin' for their boays t'go t'Parliament.' He stopped for his idea to take root. 'Us was born t'labor like a hox to the plow. 'Ere a boay say, 'I will be this or that,' an' go after un.' Jake's eyes glowed: Jim and Tom waited. 'Our fate was Cornish: thicky boay's dream be American. Thicky tale be a capsheaf to Allen's argymint, shore nuff!'[76]

Although here the plod is used in a more positive way—conferring the status of 'some plod' on the teller ('some' always in Cornu-English adding expertise or skill), there is something of an echo of Gries and Kinsey's view in more recent dialect stories and poems, which I have identified elsewhere.[77] In effect, many of the dialectician narratives, regularly winning prizes in Gorseth competitions today,[78] are the cultural equivalent of Gries and Kinsey's 'plods'.

Plods should not be seen as a completely negative concept, however. Trev Lawrence's regular BBC Radio Cornwall afternoon show Cornish stories (which sometimes feature Cousin Jacks) may be termed 'plods' in that they are pure invention,[79] though Lawrence draws astutely on the shared folkloric heritage; making them less plods than those I have termed the 'Tyin' the Dunkey to the Carn' narratives which appear elsewhere.[80] Problematically though, such 'plods' tend to draw on archaic language within Cornu-English, and in many cases are pure invention (i.e an unrealistic, exaggerated dialect which was not the way the Cornish spoke or continue to speak) while, by contrast, the Cousin Jack narratives retain their core narrative values. But in their re-telling they are updated to suit modern Cornu-American speech patterns, and their materialist setting. In this way, their metamorphosis and adaptation makes them closer to Brunvand's 'urban legends'.

The trend towards the amusing and humorous, including the self-depreciating humour, has brought about both cultural benefit and harm. The stock-in-trade innocent and naïve Cornishman has been the popular face of both historical and contemporary dialecticians. For those outside of the parent culture this is redolent of yokelism, while for those inside the culture the imagined Cornishman or woman does not always bear any relationship to the way Cornishness is perceived by them. The borders are muddied even further when it comes to the way that contemporary comedians such as Jethro tell their jokes.[81] However, Jethro can legitimately claim 'Cornishness' and popular success, which is not the case for the much criticized 'comic' portrayals of the Cornish and their dialect in BBC's Dawn French vehicle *Wild West*.[82] Television and film in general are a long way from realistically presenting Cornu-English because there is not yet the ethnic acting base to facilitate it.

DIALECT AND DISSENT

Given the importance of Cornu-English dialect as a signifier of Cornish difference, particularly since the decline of the Cornish language, there has been surprisingly little serious socio-linguistic study of this method of communication in Cornwall and—as I shall argue—even less in transnational Cornish communities. An exception from the nineteenth century is the useful 1846 volume of Uncle Jan Trenoodle's *Specimens of Provincial Cornish Dialect*.[83] Uncle Jan Trenoodle was the pseudonym of William Sandys (1792–1874) who is best known now for his work on Cornish Christmas carols and music,[84] but who also worked as the Commissioner of affidavits in the Stannary Courts. Sandys offers many examples of dialect usage, and his observations on structure and lexical choices are still pertinent. Another important volume was Fred W.P. Jago's *The Ancient Language and Dialect of the Cornwall*, which was published in 1882,[85] Jago completing much useful work on the survival of Cornish-language words employed in English in Cornwall: many of which continue to be used today.

The single most important twentieth-century contribution has been the work of Ken Phillipps (1929–95) in two studies, *Westcountry Words and Ways* (1976), and *A Glossary of the Cornish Dialect* (1993).[86] Phillipps's relevance will discussed below. More recently, important work has been completed by Andrew C. Symons in short studies in *An Baner Kernewek/The Cornish Banner*, which deserves wider recognition.[87] These scholars being the exception, other studies in the twentieth century have tended to be focused on dialect survival words,[88] effectively vestigial terms, and have, in general, been anti-quarian in style and methodology. However, still the most commonly consulted work on Dialect is Martyn Wakelin's 1975 work *Language and History in Cornwall*, which drew heavily on the 1967 Southern Counties' *Leeds Dialect Survey*,[89] and although this text has some flaws, its breath of coverage has yet to be equalled: particularly in terms of the phonological, morphological, and lexical features of Cornu-English.

The analysis of dialect within the academic community in Corn-wall has not been completely barren however. Much useful work on dialect was completed by the Institute of Cornish Studies in the period 1973–86, under the leadership of Professor Charles Thomas, culminating in the breakthrough 1978/79 *Sociolinguistic Survey of English in Cornwall*, which was co-ordinated by Rolf Bremann. Bremann advanced two hypotheses:

1. Among the present population of Cornwall there is still a marked social stratification in the use of English.
2. There is less variation in pronunciation in West Cornwall than in East Cornwall.[90]

His analysis of the tape-recorded interviews showed that:

1. In West Cornwall, as well as in East Cornwall, the pronunciation of upper social classes show less variation from the prestige variant RP ('Received Pronunciation') than the pronunciation of lower socio-economic groups.
2. In West Cornwall, all three social classes in the survey show less variation from RP than the corresponding groups in East Cornwall.[91]

These were interesting finds for anyone concerned with Cornu-English speech patterns across the territory, not least because the 'West' has often been regarded as more Cornish than the 'East'. Bremann had less to say about dialect itself, however. Given the

evidence of this survey, it is interesting to speculate on what a similar
—but necessarily more ambitious and complex—survey of global
Cornu-English might reveal. Does, for example, the Cornu-English of
the Upper Peninsula have more variation from RP than, say, the
Cornu-English of Yorke Peninsula in South Australia, and how do
these forms relate to American and Australian Englishes?

At home, the important arguments had actually been made prior
to the Second World War: by Arthur Wilfred Rablen (1917–73) in a
1937 essay titled 'Cornish Dialect Words'. In this essay, Rablen undertook a progressive and wide-ranging study of dialect. In Charles
Thomas' words: 'it marks a very notable contribution'.[92] Curiously
enough, much of Rablen's argument is applicable in consideration of
the Cornu-English features of Gries's narratives; particularly in terms
of the technical terms used in the mining process, which effectively
emigrated across the Atlantic with the miners who spoke them. Rablen
makes a pertinent observation about the use of dialect after such
'travel':

> By Travel I mean also that sons and daughters go away from
> home, and by being laughed at, learn which of their words and
> senses are dialectal. They return in pride of knowledge
> and annoy the people who have never been away by their
> comments on rural usage. Thus social snobbery awakes
> linguistic consciousness.[93]

The Cousin Jack narratives work in complete antithesis of this. In
the case of the mining communities overseas, social snobbery did not
awake linguistic consciousness, and the miners that Gries knew did
not have to modulate their speech according to the other speakers and
listeners. In this sense, then, we can hypothesize that Cousin Jack
narratives ought to be a cultural location where genuine dialect continued longer than in Cornwall itself. In Cornwall, linguistic consciousness has been further raised by the post-Second World War
in-migration. This process has led to the current position where
Cornish children often resist speaking 'naturally', a result of peer group
pressure and the media's continual erosion their grammar and lexicon.
This is not just the case in Cornwall; it is happening to other dialects
across these islands, Europe and the rest of the world. It is also
happening to children and speakers in the Upper Peninsula, and it
takes a good deal of linguistic dissent to retain the unmodulated voice,
or modulate (as many Cornish do on a daily basis) between non-dialect
speakers (usually at work or in education) and dialect speakers whom
they are comfortable with. We may contrast this twenty-first-century

situation with Gries's un-modulated phonetic of two Cousin Jacks observing for the first time an American Football match:

I took nawtice that the ground was a bit of a muck. Right opperzyte where us stood to, there was a paund o' water.

I remarked to Percy, 'Daun look very much a place for playin' vootball.' I said, 'Part o't look zif it had been ploughed up.'

'Aw, that's nort,' he saith. 'They weun matter that. I've seed it tain times wiss'n that.'

Wull, him-by everybody beginned to shout, an' us zeed a string o' chaps comin' out from the previllion an' runnin' on to the vield. Butifule an' clane they looked, with nice new jerseys. Wull, they sticked theirzells in their proper plances, an' Percy was indicatin' 'em all by name an' telling us what they was an' where they come from. I cude'n volley what he said so very well, but some was halves, sim-so, an' some was dree-quarters, an' there was one stood by hizzell. I reckon he must a-bin a whole wan. Wull, an' there was wan chap dressed in black cloas. He wad'n much of a player; he wad'n. I never seed 'en titch the ball wance. All he de'd was to rin about blawin up a li'l tin trumpet like a cheel to a crissmas party. He aunly got in the way o' the rest, he did, an' 'winder they did'n putt'n off the vield. He putt me in mind o' thik stoobid valler into the circus, what rins about makin' up a terrible amount o' vuss but daun' do nort to assist.

I cude'n attempt to describe the match to 'ee. My ole hand goes all to bewilderment when I tries to piece it out. O' court, I did'n understand the rules an' that makes all the difference. I tried to vathom what they was about of, but so-fur as I cude zee, their aunly objic was to tear wan-tother limb from limb. They was rishin' after wan tother zif they was tryin' to ketch a pickpocket. If a chap aunly picked up the ball, an rinned off wi' it, dree or vower bulkin gurt fallers wude jump right pon tap o'n. Wan chap half so big again as tother rished up an ketched 'en round the neck an' drowed 'en so far as he cude zee 'en right into the fulfh. About a score o'm stooped down an putt their hands together an' started shovin' jis like so many sheep. Then all-to-wanse, half e'm wude go down in the much an' tother hald wude zit on 'em. Then wan chap wude get the ball an' way-da-go. An' bevore he'd gone a yard, dree or vowe more wude jump 'pon the back o'n like terriers on a rat, an' down thik lot wude go. An' bim-bye they'd screal up

again, mud an' muck from haid to voot. You cude see 'em
pickin' 'en out from their eyes so's they cude zee who to jump
on nex.

Caw, my dear 'art alive. What haivin' an shovin', pullin' an'
scraalin'. Rinnin', ketchin', tweetin', all to a mass; down in the
mud, up in the air, round and round, in an' out, worms, toads,
spaniels, cats, spittin' an' pankin', kickin' an' wrastlin'; haids
an' veet, arms an' laigs, a movin; mole heap, a yard from the
line, a ninch from the line, he's over! No he id'n, yes he is . . .
An' if they chaps have ever got theirzells properly clane again
'tis a winder to me.[94]

Ken Phillipps would instantly recognize not only the lexical
choices here but also the grammar. Unlike most other observers of
Cornu-English, Phillipps is not reticent in dealing with grammar, and
that is why his contribution had been so important in our understanding of Conru-English at home *and* away. As he argues, 'the
occasional rule occurs'. In summary, his conclusions include Cornish
dialect's propensity towards:

Reversals
Archaisms
The retention of thou and ye (thee and ye ['ee])
The use of double plurals
Irregular use of the definite article
Use of the definite article with proper names
The omission of prepositions
The extra 'y' suffix on the infinitive of verbs
They is used as a demonstrative adjective
Frequent use of the adverb 'up'
The use of 'some' as an adverb of degree[95]

All of these survived the trans-Atlantic journey to the Upper
Peninsula, and may be found in the above text from Gries and Kinsey,
and in those which follow below. Gries also incorporated a limited
quantity of poetry into his canon, and here, in ''Ansome 'Arry weth the
H'Auburn 'Air', tricks of the narrative trade, not to mention core
elements of Phillipps' observations, are developed in what we might
describe as a 'poetic plod'. The poem works as a tribute to the dialect
stress of dropping of appropriate 'h's and placing them where they are
lacking, ahead of vowels. It seems this signifier of Cornish dialect was
crucial to many of the Cousin Jack storytellers, but in contemporary

dialect writings and the oral continuum it is now seen as less important; a good example of how Cornu-English does not stay fossilized:

'Ansome 'Arry's 'air was h'auburn,
The color of red 'ematite.
'E comed 'ere from dear 'ol Camborne,
Minen core was 'is delight.

'E were praoud of 'is h'adornment,
For h'it's color and h'it's curruis.
'Is friends said t'were a perm'nent,
An' were h'envied by the gurruls.

'Ome, said 'arrym they do call me
'Ansome 'Arry weth the h'Auburn 'air.
H'over 'ere, hawsome dever
They doesn't about one's feelin's keare.

A bloody red'ead 'ere h'I'm called
By they 'oo 'elp me sink a raise.
But most o' they es nearly bald.
H'I shan't keare 'ow much they taise.

A 'ead o' 'air es grand h'I say,
Be 'e light or dark or red.
For they 'oo 'ave no 'air to lay
Es jealous of we 'oo 'ave, 'tes said.[96]

There is not the space here to enter into a full discussion of the effect of such texts, nor all of their dialect origins. One further point is worth making though. Compared to Cornwall, dialect studies of Cousin Jack narratives are embryonic to say the least, with one exception. This is Hadley Tremaine's 1980 study 'Cornish Folk Speech in America'.[97] Tremaine examines survivals in Massachusetts, which 'was settled c.1629 as a plantation of Salem by fishermen from the Channel Islands and Cornwall', but he also considers the Upper Peninsula. He makes the following observation, which is also applicable to the Gries and Kinsey collection:

Most striking is the Cornish habit of mixing up pronouns, perhaps a compensation for the lack of the Celtic emphatics; obliquely, at least Celtic Cornish 'survives' in this tendency.

The effect is coupled with the h-dropping typically, but of course not uniquely.[98]

Tremaine provides an illustrative, very common Cousin Jack story to demonstrate this:

> Harry Soady complains to an old Cornish friend about his use of language. 'I dearly love to visit with the Cornish people. But there's one thing about them that has always bothered me.'
> 'What is it, 'Arry?'
> 'It's the way you Cornish use your pronouns and verbs. You don't seem to have any rhyme or reasons, any rules or regulations for the way you use them.'
> Jimmer said, 'I tell 'ee 'Arry, 'ere's 'ow it is about they pronouns; we got a rule for they.'
> 'You have?'
> 'Yes, we 'ave. We do call anything she excepting a tomcat, and we call 'er 'e.'[99]

There is an inherently Cornish sense of logic within this narrative that it to be found in most Cousin Jack stories. Tremaine was aware of the corpus that existed in the Upper Peninsula, but while he was writing he did not find Gries and Kinsey's collection, despite what he terms leaving 'no menhir unturned'.[100] Paradoxically, and perhaps showing the illogical nature of Cornu-English, Gries and Kinsey's collection, like Thomas' novel, often adds initial 'h's for effect, as can be seen below. Gries has this to say about Cornish dialect:

> There is a juggling in the use of pronouns, as well as a confusion and contradiction in words that often results in astonishing expressions. Yet, the listener knows what the speaker means in spite of the abuse of grammar . . . Cousin Jack and Jenny invented the art of positive contradiction in grammar: 'H'I though t'were she, an' she thought t'were h'I, said Gracie Specott. 'But w'en we got h'up to where we were, we found t'wudn' nayther of us.'[101]

Such grammar is dissenting because it requires the listener to be coded into the 'astonishing expressions'. In essence, modern political and cultural nationalism could learn much from the 'positive contradiction in grammar' since it was actually one of the mechanisms of Cornish independence, both at home and abroad. Hence the way the common story of when an employer asks a Cornishman if he knew of anybody else who could fill a vacancy, the Cornishman would always know of a Cousin Jack who could step into the position. This is symptomatic of something else: there was a linguistic and industrial unity demonstrating independence and difference. Dialect, therefore, could be used much more successfully as the voice of dissent by a larger number of the population within contemporary Cornwall. Its use within dissent in the American mining camps is well-documented in Gries's narratives.

THE CAP'N DICK COMMENTARIES: PUSHING THE 'JACK' ENVELOPE

Given the large number of narratives contained within *Drill Cores*, in an article of this length it would be impossible to analyse and comment upon each of them. Instead, what I have endeavoured to do, is to offer the reader four representative samples of the text, with a copies of the manuscript deposited in the Cornish Centre at Redruth and at the CAVA project of the Institute of Cornish Studies. The interested reader will then be able to find many more samples of such narratives in the MS.

Gries's principle skill was taking the type of Cousin Jack stories that Carlton and Brown told and incorporating them into longer and lengthier narratives. Cap'n Dick is the same archetype as the Cap'n found in the comic books of Ian Glanville. His is the voice of experience in the new territory. Gries labels the first story 'Internal Combustion'. This narrative is very typical of the kind of shorter Cousin Jack story. We notice that the main character is a good Methodist—a teetotaller—who lived in a better age than the present one. 'Fitty', of course, is a popular Cornu-English expression and is often used in conjunction with how one is feeling and, therefore, in the context of medical advice. The New World environment also has to be considered, however, and near Lake Superior beer freezes in winter. Meanwhile, all the linguistic conventions are integrated into the final paragraph of the story—again where alliteration ('bloody blast the beer blaws') pushes the story to an explosion-themed conclusion. Things often 'blaw' in Cousin Jack narratives. Put another way, the story could be told in a much less poetic form, and this is the way in which Gries appears to progress the form. Of course, patterned orality increases the ability to tell the narrative without breaks or pauses, much in the same way that rhyme worked for say, the cast of *Ordinalia*, and for earlier balladeers like Billy Foss and Henry Quick:[102]

Cap'n Dick took a pull on his pipe. I remember Jim Berryman 'oo used to work on the Ridge Mine forty year h'ago. Jim was a tee-totaller. Never touched a drop o' liquor in 'is life. One time h'old Jim wuzn't feelin very fitty, an' 'ee gaws to see the doctor. Doctor said 'ee wuz a but run daown, an' told un to drink a little bee h'each day to brace un h'up. So Jim sent 'is boay to the tavern at Maple Grove, about 'alf mile away to get some o' they stuff. 'Appenend to be one o' they cold Lake Superior days, an' the beer froze solid afore the boay got un 'ome. Jim putt they bottles be'ind the kitchen stove, an' went h'upstairs. Coorse, w'en the beer started to thaw, the bottles busted, an' weth a noise like a bloody blast the beer blaws h'all over they kitchen, h'even h'up to the ceilin', m'son. Jim comes tearin' daown the steers, an' seein the mess all h'over the place, 'ee sez, 'Damme, ef 'e wuz goin' to blaw h'any'ow, et's far better to 'ave un blaw there than h'in my h'insides![103]

Courtship is a typical theme for more advanced Cousin Jack stories and in the following narrative, which Gries titles 'She Hung Him Out to Dry', we witness an inversion of narrative order, for it is the Cousin Jenny who comes out the better off. Here the voice of experience ('M'son') again offers repeated guidance, so that the listener will not make the same mistake as Jan Trembath. The logic here is based on a work-based issue, that the miner will not be wet for work, which would, in actual fact, be much more uncomfortable. However, this apparent logic is not viewed as being very sensible by Mary Jane:

M'sun, did'st ever 'ear tell 'ow Jan Trembath come to lose h'out with Tom Tregillis' daughter, just as 'e 'ad made up 'is mind to marry 'er? Tom lived h'over on the H'east side o' town, an' Jim's Boordin ouse was crosst town, so h'each time Jan gaws to see Mary Jane 'e 'as to walk 'about mile an' a 'alf. One h'evenin w'en Jan wuz sittin' up with she, h'it started rainin', an damme, the 'eavens h'opened. One o' these 'ere cloudburst thee reads of. Water wuz runnin' daown the middle o' the streets. Tom comes in the parlor, w'ere wuz Jan an' Mary Jane, an' sez, 'M'son, naw use thee goin' 'ome along this night an' spoil thy Sunday Cloes. Better for thee to putt h'up 'ere in the spare room. An' 's tells Mary Jane to fix h'up the room a bit. Then 'e gaws h'about to set the rainbarrel for to catch sof' water. W'en Mary Jane comes daown steers, Jan wuz gone. But, damme, 'bout 'alf hour later in 'e comes.

'W'ere 'ast thee been?' says 'er. 'Been 'ome,' says 'e.
'Wot for didst thee go 'ome?'
'Went 'ome to get my h'umbrella,' sez Jan. 'Might be rainin'
w'en I gaws to work in the moornin', an' I feared to get my
good cloes wet.'
An' dost thee knew, m'son, after that 'er would 'ave nuthin'
to do weth 'e?[104]

Another type of Cousin Jack story is given by Gries in the same
chapter. It is titled 'No Power in Pygmies' and comes from a sub-genre
of 'warning' narratives, intended to offer advice to the young underground. Charlton and Brown rarely offer such 'socially responsible'
narratives. The use of the real example of the St Just miners increases
the reality of the tale because it shows internal difference and dissent in
Cousin Jack culture, and that no doubt St Just miners had their own
view of others. Either way, the advice here is about the materialist
'takin' on' of employees in particular contexts. The final line opens the
narrative out for discussion, and also perhaps a response from another
teller, who knew of a disastrous occurrence, and thereby, warning the
listeners of the consequences:

Back in the h'early days, m'son, afore the time o' these
machine drills, there wus some h'art and science to the
swingin' o' a 'ammer and the twistin' o' a drill. Some rivalry
there wuz, too, mongst 'ammermen. Settin' to one side all
h'argument, twas h'admitted that they chaps from daown St
Just was 'ad a pretty way weth a drill. Must be h'admitted,
though, most o' they St Justers wuz such dretful small chaps
that they scarcely h'appeared to be grawed h'up men. W'en
twistin' a drill they never took a full hand 'old, but passed
the steel twixt third and fourth fingers. This 'abit formed a
callous, m'son. Cap'n Tredennick 'ad a geek for the callous
'pon a man's left and afore 'iring 'im. And h'only once ded 'e
make a mistake. That was the time 'e 'ired a teamster 'oose
fingers wuz calloused from 'angin' fast to the lines o' a freight
team. But come Cambourne an' Redruth chaps, Tom
Penglase 'mongst 'em never 'ad a good word for the boays
from St Just.
'Damme,' says Tom, 'saw one o' they little St Just chaps
back in Colorado kill 'isself tryin' to do a man's work.'
'This chap was so bloody short 'e must 'ave 'ad a 'ard time
reachin' 'igh enough to wash 'is own face an h'eyes. 'E wuz
standin' on a stull one day in a 'igh stople tryin' to gad daown

a loose piece of rock from the 'anging. Wuzn't strong enuf nor 'andy enough to 'old the gad while strikin', so h'after 'e 'ad dropped un a score o' times, 'e took bit o' string and tied fast to the gad, makin' the h'other end fast one side o' the stull, and damme, the St Just chap fell h'on the h'other side and 'anged 'isself to death. Wot's think o' that now?'[105]

The final example is a kind of narrative that could be found in other contexts and continents. It is the old theme of the ignorant and illiterate, but experienced miner, versus the sophisticated, educated, but stupid mining professor. This tale is called ''Tis no time for Parting'. The narrative is crammed with beautifully attuned dialect, however, even in Jimmie's interpretation of the way the college professor speaks. In such ways, Gries's stories go beyond the usual tellings and become almost artful in their completion:

> Cap'n Dick took a match, lit his pipe, and took a long pull at it. He let the smoke filter through his moustache as he flipped the match into the stove.
> 'A chap's pretty safe takin' a ride on the cage these days, m'son, for the rope 'olds and the bale usually is in fair shape. The 'oistin' h'engineer must knaw wot 'e's doin'. Tain't much like the h'old days when most places dedn' 'ave moor'n a bucket and rope. Which reminds me o' one time back long we. A party o' these 'ere college professors come h'out to 'ave a geek about the place I wuz workin. Daown they gaws in the bal, and comin' h'out we 'ad to 'oist two o' they at a time in the bucket. Finally, the last chap wuz comin' h'out with Jimmie Trebilcock, and 'e nawticed the rope looked a bit frayed.'
> ''Ow often,'sez 'e to Jimmie, 'dost 'ee change these ropes?'
> 'About once h'every three months,' sez Jimme, 'and we change this one tomorrow—h'if we get h'up safe.'
> 'Well, that bloody professor was a-standin' there on 'is tiptoes, tryin' to make hisself as light as possible.'[106]

TONGUELESS LANDS: DUN'T 'EE WORRY 'BOUT THE DIALECT M'SON

Of late, there has been world-wide interest in the extinction of the world's languages, now reaching the realms of 'armchair travel'.[107] According to Nettle and Romaine, 'ninety percent of them are expected to disappear in the next one hundred years',[108] and they argue that the loss is part of a large picture of collapse in the world-wide ecosystem. It is a loss which is all too familiar within the Cornish context, although the Cornish language has been recovered.[109]

Ironically, some early revivalists of Cornish seemed to have been all too sceptical about the impact and place of Cornu-English, that those who spoke it maintaining the view were 'simple' and un-educated.[110] Within the revival of Cornish, there is still an uneasy uncertaintly over the relationship between Cornu-English and Cornish. It is an ideology that seems to suggest that 'if you are truly Cornish, then you will learn Cornish'; this despite the fact that Cornu-English dialect is the *modus operandi* for most Cornish people. If we are moving into a cultural climate where Cornish is part of the education system, which appears to be an agenda of many activists,[111] then we will need to be careful about alienating the Cornu-English speaking majority—a lesson for which Irish culture paid a heavy price.[112]

An increasing concern is that not only will the world's languages be exterminated, but that, increasingly, the varieties of non-standard Englishes will also disappear. Celtic Englishes have a lengthy history, often working in tandem and in correspondence with that territory's 'English'.[113] In essence, the two have been symbiotic since English first started to be introduced in that area. Some non-standard Englishes, of course, are gaining linguistic ground; for example, it is possible to hear on the streets of St Just-in-Penwith young people using terminology and concepts from 'African-American Englishes' or 'Rap' culture. Likewise, the very thorough integration of the lexicon of surfing into Cornu-English, provides hope for development of dialect, incorporat-ing and blending in these words, as has always been the case.

Gries and Kinsey's *Drill Cores* provides an interesting touchstone for discussion of all of this. The manuscript needs other scholars and interested groups to look over its pages. We can, however, make some conclusions about its relevance and importance to global Cornish culture. *Drill Cores* is a very detailed folkloric record of Cousin Jack culture in the Upper Peninsula of Michigan, which provides us with an increased worldwide corpus of Cousin Jack narratives. The task now is to compile these disparate resources into one body so that the narratives can be cross-referenced, and that we might be able to see patterns of narration developing alongside specific industrial or sociological changes. Major tellers, such as Gries, Kinsey, Foster Charlton, and Brown in the USA, and others in Australia, South America, and South Africa can then be studied and identified.

We also note that the key grammatical and lexical choices of Cornish storytellers survived the crossing and have become enhanced by the new culture. There is no loss of 'Cornishness' in the transition; it is just another form and type of Cornish ideology. Related to this is the

growing need for a new evaluation of Cornu-English. As Phillipps
suggests, that is should be 'valued as a blend of shibboleth and
talisman, to prove one's Cornish identity in a system that by that time
maybe be geared to uniformity'.[114] The same comment may be applied
on those groups around the world who profess Cornish heritage. Only
time will tell if the Cousin Jack narratives are the last 'bright ember' of
oral narrative in Cornish culture, or as I have argued elsewhere,
whether the new narratives of Cornwall will just assume new cultural
forms[115] as technologies and—in Walter Benjamin's terms—the
'mechanical reproduction of art'[116] increases and improves. If the
former is the case, then at least they have not been lost and cannot be
lamented. If the latter is true, then the archetypes of Cousin Jack
culture appear as exciting and dynamic, not to mention as humorous a
medium as any other contemporary ethnic group. I began this article
with Andrew H. Brown's feature titled 'Work-hard, Play-hard
Michigan'. Here, Brown turns to Walter F. Gries's wife, and with the
same anthropological awe, watches her make pasties:

> Mrs. Gries let me kibitz as she rolled out four pieces of
> dough to dinner-plate size. On half of each dough disk she
> piled potatoes, turnips, ion, cubed beef, and pork. Liberally
> seasoned, each structure was topped with a walnut-size chunk
> of butter. Then Mrs. Gries folded over the dough and crimped
> the edges of the half-moons. Slit at the top, the pasties went
> into a hot oven for an hour. The steaming pasties were
> the backbone of a feast rounded out with a green salad,
> chowchow, and strong tea.[117]

This simple act of cooking is for Walter F. Gries and his wife, even in
the early 1950s, an act of dissent, flying—as Yvonne R. Lockwood and
William G. Lockwood convincingly argue about the Upper Peninsula
of Michigan—in the face of globalization and the homogenization of
American culture.[118] This domestic dissent was small but over time
has had wider political implications; particularly in the now active
'memory' of the Cornish in America. As Stephen Hall has recently
shown, pasty-making in itself, as a foodway, is a folkloric act,[119] as is
the passing on of Cornish culture's global impact. The two forms of
subversion ultimately reach fruition in a Gries story called 'Jan wants
New Law' over the genuine nature of the Cornish pasty (a media
debate recognisable in contemporary Cornwall), when several pasty
makers requested appropriate legislation over the making and selling
of pasties in Michigan:

I been readin' the pictures 'pon the paper 'bout this 'ere pasty dinner they ad for the Governor down to Lansen. I can tell 'ee one thing, m'son. Ef our Janie made the pasty, I knaw 'e was a beauty. I seed too 'pon they city papers 'bout 'ow to make a pasty. Ef you do follow the rule which our Janie do follow, 'e'll tun h'out as pretty as can be. I 'spec our Janie 'ave made thousand of hunderts of pasties. She do make et kearful like weth a suet crus' and she do build at h'up so that 'e's filled in between foot and 'angin'. An', mind you, she do knaw that a man's stummick ed'n bo bloody root 'ouse, 'cause she do put plenty o' mayt in un. Us in the h'ron country, we do knaw a good pasty w'en we do see un. And, mind you, this 'ere dicin' of the taties and turmits ean't fitty. Like our Janie, you 'ave to chip 'em fine like so that the gravy 'ave a choice to work through the taties and turmits an' h'onions. One thing I see, too, 'pon the paper, one o' these papers from Detroit, talkin' bout Cornish 'pastry'—now, these knaw a pasty ed'n no pastry. A pasty as a pasty an' that's all there is to un. Es, m'son, it do take one weth experience to learn to eat un. I do see where the Guvnor clunked the 'ole pasty down in no time. The Picture 'pon they paper showed un droppin' a bit o' catsup on un. W'en a man get started h'eatin' a pasty, 'e can't stop. 'E just keeps goorin' down till 'e reach the las' bit o' suety crus'. And before long thee will realize that thee had turned a gert leaky, 'ansome pasty into a man! I shud like to see the Guvnor w'en 'e comes 'ere for a ski tournament. I want to spake to un 'bout 'avin they boays in the Legislater pass a law forbidden the callen of a pasty, a purdy Cornish pasty, a 'pastry'.[120]

As I have argued, such narratives are not provincial or narrow. When compared with Arthuriana, Tristan and Iseult, the medieval dramatic tradition, the folktales, not to mention the historical romantic continuum of Cornwall, the Cousin Jack story might seem slight and unrefined. But as this article has shown we should not be dismissive of it, for its popularity over one hundred and fifty years demonstrates its centrality in the corpus of populist telling and writing emerging from Cornwall. Gries and Kinsey's manuscript should make us revise our view of Cousin Jack stories as just simple yarns or jokes, and relocate them at the contemporary end of a dynamic continuum of oral culture. Likewise, they should also make us reconsider our response to Cornu-English and . . . *h'its use h'as a dissenting voice, m'son.*

ACKNOWLEDGEMENTS

I am indebted to Tom Ellis Jr., Jean and Tom Ellis, Keri L. Ellis, Phil Medlyn, Danny L.J. Merrifield, and the people of Eagle Harbor, Michigan for their assistance in the writing of this chapter.

NOTES AND REFERENCES

1. See Will Coleman, *Brave Tales*, Cornwall County Council, 2002; Trev Lawrence, *Songs, Poems and Legends—A Cornish Miscellany: The Droll Teller in the Last Labyrinth at Land's End*, Penzance, 1989. See also the *Sense of Place* project on www.cornwall.gov.uk.
2. See Mike Dunstan, 'Telling It As It Is: Storytelling in the china clay villages', in Ella Westland (ed.), *Cornwall: The Cultural Construction of Place*, Penzance, 1997, pp. 143–53. See also contributors to Cornwall County Youth Service (ed.) *Strong Talk / Lavar Krev*, Cornwall, 1997.
3. Scavel an Gow, *Dream Atlas*, Linkinhorne, 2002.
4. The latter term was coined by Jan Harold Brunvand. See Jan Harold Brunvand, *The Choking Doberman and other 'New'Urban Legends*, New York and London, 1984.
5. See Cornish American Heritage Society, *11th Gathering of Cornish Cousins 2001*, Mineral Point, WI, 2001; Dehwelans, *Dehwhelans 2004 Programme*, Cornwall 2004.
6. Andrew H. Brown, 'Work-hard, Play-hard Michigan', in *National Geographic* CI: 3, 1952, pp. 299–300.
7. Alan M. Kent, *Cousin Jack's Mouth-organ: Travels in Cornish America*, St Austell, 2004, pp. 296–331.
8. William 'Cousin Jack' Foster, *Boom to Bust: Minetown USA*, Calumet, n.d.
9. Donald D. Kinsey (ed.), *Drills Cores: Folklore of Michigan's Upper Peninsula from the Collection of Walter F. Gries*, MS, n.d.
10. Another useful collection is the work of D. E. A. Charlton, in the *Engineering and Mining Journal* between 1920 and 1940. Charlton tended to use verse more than narrative however. See also D.E.A. Charlton, 'Ruminations of Wilyum Jan: A Cousin Jack comments on events in the mining world', *Explosions Engineer*, April 1923, pp. 37–38. Phil Medlyn and Tom Ellis also offer a selection in Kent, 2004, pp. 315–6. These should be compared with H. Lean, *Book Three of Short Cornish Dialect Stories*, Camborne, 1952.
11. See, for example, Catharine Brace, 'Cornish Identity and Landscape in the Work of Arthur Caddick', in Philip Payton (ed.), *Cornish Studies: Seven*, Exeter, 2003, pp. 130–46; Simon Trezise, *The West Country as a Literary Invention: Putting Fiction in its Place*, Exeter, 2000.
12. Edward Said, *Orientalism*, London, 1978; Benedict Anderson, *Imagined Communities*, New York, 1983.
13. Pamela Shurmer-Smith and Kevin Hannam, *Worlds of Desire, Realms of Power: A Cultural Geography*, London, 1994, p. 4.

14. Alan M. Kent, *The Literature of Cornwall: Identity, Continuity, Difference 1000–2000*, Bristol, 2000, pp. 15–16.
15. Jonathan Dollimore and Alan Sinfield (eds), *Political Shakespeare: New Essays in Cultural Materialism*, Manchester, 1985, p. viii.
16. Kent, 2000, p. 282.
17. Treve Crago, 'Defining the Spectre: Outlining the Academic Potential for of the 'CAVA Movement'", in Philip Payton (ed.), *Cornish Studies: Ten*, Exeter, 2002, p. 262.
18. A.L. Rowse, *The Cornish in America*, Redruth, 1991 [1969], p. 181.
19. Angus Murdoch, *Boom Copper: The Story of the First U.S. Mining Boom*, Hancock, Michigan, 2001 [1943], p. 37.
20. Ibid., p. 202.
21. Ibid.
22. Arthur W. Turner, *Strangers and Sojourners: A History of Michigan's Keweenaw Peninsula*, Detroit, 1994.
23. John Rowe, *The Hard Rock Men: Cornish Immigrants and the North American Mining Frontier*, Liverpool, 1974, pp. 62–95.
24. Turner, 1994, p. 67.
25. Philip Payton, *The Cornish Overseas*, Fowey, 1999.
26. Anon (ed.), *And in Whose Hills You shall Mine Copper: Historical Diaries of the Copper Country 1845 to 1910*, Lake Linden, Michigan, 1996, p. 22.
27. See Arthur W. Turner, *Calumet Copper and People: History of a Michigan Mining Community 1864–1970*, Hancock, Michigan, 2002 [1974].
28. Newton G. Thomas, *The Long Winter Ends*, Detroit, 1998 [1941].
29. A concept devised by Roland Barthes. See Roland Barthes, *The Rustle of Language*, Oxford, 1986 [1967], pp. 141–48.
30. Discussion and correspondence with members of the Cornish Literary Guild, 1991–95.
31. See Kent, 2004, p. 324.
32. Rowse, 1991 [1969], p. 191.
33. Thomas, 1998 [1941], p. 74. 'Bayn't' seems to have dropped out of Cornu-English of late, perhaps because it is now redolent of Mummerset-style comic speech. The author remembers his older relatives in mid-Cornwall often using this word into the early 1990s.
34. Ibid., p. 82.
35. Ibid., p. 356.
36. Shurmer-Smith and Hannam, 1994.
37. See, for example, Alan M. Kent, *The Hensbarrow Homilies*, St Austell, 2002; Les Merton, *Oall Rite Me Ansum! A Salute to Cornish Dialect*, Newbury, 2003; Simon Parker (ed.), *Chasing Tales: The Lost Stories of Charles Lee*, Linkinhorne, 2002; Myrna Combellack, *The Permanent History of Penaluna's Van*, Peterborough, 2003.
38. See the candidates for the Cornish Language Board exams, 1986–91 in Philip Payton and Bernard Deacon, 'The Ideology of Language Revival', in Philip Payton (ed.), *Cornwall Since the War: The Contemporary*

History of a European Region, Redruth, 1993, p. 277. Alternatively, considering the original loss, the revival of Cornish might be said to be one of the most remarkable socio-linguistic phenomena in contemporary European history. See also Philip Payton, 'Identity, Ideology and Language in Modern Cornwall', in Hildegard L.C. Tristram, *The Celtic Englishes*, Heidelberg, 1997, pp. 100–22.

39. Cited in Brown, 1952, p. 300.
40. Shirley Ewart and Harold T. George, *Highly Respectable Families: The Cornish of Grass Valley 1854–1954*, Grass Valley, California, 1998.
41. Kinsey (ed.), n.d., p. 14.
42. This condition is often called 'Cornishman's disease' due to its prevalence amongst the Cornish.
43. Kinsey (ed.), n.d., p. 19.
44. Information supplied by Tom and Jean Ellis of Eagle Harbor.
45. See W.G. Orchard (ed.), *A Glossary of Mining Terms*, Redruth, 1991, pp. 14–15.
46. Kinsey (ed.), n.d. p. 2.
47. Ibid., p. 3.
48. Ibid., p. 8. Thimbleberries were an important treat for the early Cornish settlers of the Keweenaw, and are still picked by Cornish families.
49. Walter F. Gries, *A Bit of Cornish Lore*, MS, n.d.
50. Ibid., pp. 8–9.
51. Ibid., p. 10.
52. Ibid., pp. 12–13.
53. Ibid., p. 14.
54. Ibid., p. 16.
55. Ibid., pp. 20–23.
56. Ibid., p. 123.
57. See Charlton, 1923; Brown, 1940.
58. Usefully summarized in Tony Deane and Tony Shaw, *Folklore of Cornwall*, Stroud, 2003. See also Craig Weatherhill and Paul Devereux, *Myths and Legends of Cornwall*, Wilmslow, 1998.
59. For an analysis see Kent, 2000, pp. 124–32.
60. See Henry Jenner, 'Some Possible Arthurian Place-Names in West Penwith', in *Journal of the Royal Institution of Cornwall*, 1912, p. 87. This correlates with the entry in Richard Gendall (ed.), *A Practical Dictionary of Modern Cornish, Part One: Cornish—English*, Menheniot, 1997, p. 35.
61. See Robert Hunt (ed.), *Popular Romances of the West of England: The Drolls, Traditions and Superstitions of Old Cornwall (First and Second Series)*, London, 1865; William Bottrell (ed.), *Traditions and Hearthside Stories of West Cornwall: First, Second and Third Series*, Penzance, 1870–80; H.J. Whitfield (ed.), *Scilly and its Legends*, London, 1852; Margaret Courtney (ed.), *Cornish Feasts and Folklore*, London, 1890.
62. See Kent, 2000, pp. 95–99.
63. See, for example, Jim Wearne, *Me and Cousin Jack*, Chicago, 1996; Gage McKinney, *When Miners Sang: The Grass Valley Carol Choir*, Grass Valley, 2001; Marion Howard, *The Nightingale Sings*, Mineral Point,

2002. Interestingly, however, there is new Cornu-American interest in the old drolls. See Shirley Climo, *Magic and Mischief: Tales from Cornwall*, New York, 1999.

64. See Kent, 2004, pp. 315–6.

65. For useful observations on the character of the Cornish, see Salome Hocking, *Some Old Cornish Folk*, St Austell, 1903, pp. 167–79.

66. Kent, 2004, pp. 315–6.

67. See Oswald Pryor, *Australia's Little Cornwall*, Rigby, Adelaide, 1962.

68. Ian Glanville, *St Just's Point*, Bendigo, Victoria, n.d., p. 3. This comic book is usefully read in the light of contributors to Stuart Murray (ed.), *Not on Any Map: Essays on Postcoloniality and Cultural Nationalism*, Exeter, 1997; and David Bennett (ed.), *Multicultural States: Rethinking Difference and Identity*, London and New York, 1998.

69. See John Tabois Tegellas, *Cornish Tales*, Truro, c. 1863; William Bentinck Forfar, *The Exhibition and other Cornish Poems*, Truro, c. 1891.

70. Cited in Martyn F. Wakelin, *Language and History in Cornwall*, Leicester, 1975, pp. 206–7.

71. Mark Stoyle, *West Britons: Cornish Identities and the Early Modern British State*, Exeter, 2002.

72. Daniel Mason, *Cousin Jack*, Fowey, 1996.

73. Reuben H. Margolin (ed.), *Bret Harte's Gold Rush*, Berkeley, California, 1997.

74. For examples in the Keweenaw, see Keweenaw County Historical Society (eds), *Central Mine: Years of Hard Work—Lives of Pain and Hope*, Calumet, 1998, pp. 62–3.

75. Kinsey (ed.), n.d., p. 55.

76. Thomas, 1998 [1941], pp. 92–3.

77. See Alan M. Kent, 'Bringin' the Dunkey down from the Carn: Cornu-English in Context', in Hildegard L.C. Tristram (ed.), *The Celtic Englishes IV*, Heidelberg, forthcoming.

78. See Federation of Old Cornwall Societies (eds.), *Cornish Dialect in Prose and Verse: A Selection of the Prize-Winning Entires in the Gorsedd Competitions 1969–80*, Cornwall, 1982. More recently, there have been some notable exceptions to such 'plods'.

79. Trev Lawrence regularly reads Cornish-themed narratives on the Afternoon show on BBC Radio Cornwall. See also Lawrence, 1989.

80. Kent, forthcoming.

81. Jethro, *What Happened Was . . .* , London, 1995; Jethro, *Stark Raving Bonkers! Live Stand Up*, London, 2003.

82. Jonathan Gershfield (dir.) *Wild West—Series 1*, London, 2004.

83. Uncle Jan Trenoodle, *Specimens of Provincial Cornish Dialect*, London, 1846.

84. See Richard McGrady (ed.), *Traces of Ancient Mystery: The Ballad Carols of Davies Gilbert and William Sandys*, Redruth, 1993.

85. Fred W. P. Jago, *The Ancient Language and Dialect of the Cornwall*, Truro, 1882.

86. K.C. Phillipps, *Westcountry Words and Ways*, Newton Abbot, 1976, *A Glossary of Cornish Dialect*, Padstow, 1993.
87. Andrew C. Symons, 'Language and History', *An Baner Kernewek/ The Cornish Banner* 92, 1998; Symons, 'She 'Er and Un', *An Baner Kernewek/The Cornish Banner* 94, 1998; Symons, 'Stress and Intonation Patterns in Cornish Dialect', *An Baner Kernewek/The Cornish Banner* 95, 1999; Symons, 'Models of Language Transfer', *An Baner Kernewek/ The Cornish Banner* 96, 1999.
88. David J. North and Adam Sharpe, *A Word Geography of Cornwall*, Redruth, 1980.
89. Wakelin, 1975, pp. 7–8.
90. Rolf Bremann, 'A Sociolinguistic Survey of English in Cornwall', in Charles Thomas (ed.), *Cornish Studies/Studhyansow Kernewek*, 7, 1979, p. 42.
91. Ibid.
92. See Charles Thomas, 'Dialect Studies, III: Arthur Rablen's 1937 essay', in Charles Thomas (ed.), *Cornish Studies/Studhyansow Kernewek*, 8, 1980, pp. 37–47.
93. Ibid., p. 46.
94. Kinsey (ed.), n.d., pp. 92–3.
95. Phillipps, 1993, pp. 9–13.
96. Kinsey (ed.), n.d., pp. 94–5.
97. Hadley Tremain, 'Cornish Folk Speech in America', in *Midwestern Journal of Language and Folklore* VI: 1/2, 1980, pp. 17–25. For background on the early Cornish in America, see Samuel Eliot Morison, *The European Discovery of America*, New York, 1971. See also Kent, 2004, p. 236.
98. Ibid.
99. Ibid. See also Richard M. Dorson, 'Dialect Stories of the Upper Peninsula: A New Form of American Folklore', *Journal of American Folklore* 61, 1948, pp. 113–50.
100. Tremaine, 1980.
101. Kinsey (ed.), n.d., p. 98 and p. 100.
102. See Deane and Shaw, 2004, pp. 116–22.
103. Kinsey (ed.), n.d., p. 84.
104. Ibid., p. 85.
105. Ibid., p. 89.
106. Ibid., pp. 90–1.
107. Mark Abley, *Travels Among Threatened Languages*, London, 2003.
108. Daniel Nettle and Suzanne Romaine, *Vanishing Voices: The Extinction of the World's Languages*, Oxford, 2000.
109. See Peter Berresford Ellis, *The Cornish Language and its Literature*, London and Boston, 1974, pp. 147–212.
110. See the ideology of A.S.D. Smith, *The Story of the Cornish Language: Its Extinction and Revival*, Camborne, 1947.
111. For comment on this see 'Double Cornish' in Alan M. Kent, *Love and Seaweed*, St Austell, 2002.

112. See Adrian Kelly, *Compulsory Irish: Language and Education in Ireland, 1870s–1970s*, Dublin, 2002.

113. See the arguments in Hildegard L.C. Tristram (ed.) *The Celtic Englishes I*, Heidelberg, 1997 (ed.) *The Celtic Englishes II*, Heidelberg, 2000. For a useful comparison, see M. Wynn Thomas, *The Two Literatures of Wales*, Cardiff, 1999.

114. Phillipps, 1993, p. 2.

115. Alan M. Kent, 'Screening Kernow: Authenticity, Heritage and the Representation of Cornwall in Film and Television, 1913–2003', in Philip Payton, *Cornish Studies: Eleven*, Exeter, 2003, pp. 110–41.

116. Walter Benjamin, *Illuminations*, London, 1970.

117. Brown, 1952, p. 300.

118. Yvonne R. Lockwood and William G. Lockwood, 'Pasties in Michigan's Upper Peninsula: Foodways, Inter-ethnic Relations, and Regionalism', in Stephen Stern and John Alan Cicala (eds), *Creative Ethnicity: Symbols and Strategies on Contemporary Ethnic Life*, Logan, Utah, 1991, pp. 3–30.

119. Stephen Hall, *The Cornish Pasty*, Bridport, 2001.

120. Kinsey (ed.), p. 60.

'ARE YOU CHURCH OR CHAPEL?' PERCEPTIONS OF SPATIAL AND SPIRITUAL IDENTITY WITHIN CORNISH METHODISM

Kayleigh Milden

INTRODUCTION

Much has been written about the cultural distinctiveness of Cornish Methodism; indeed the phrase *Cornish Methodism* has become an entity in itself, taking on its own characteristics and cultural images. But what is so Cornish about Methodism? After all, fundamentally it was an English movement, founded by an Englishman, and retained strong connections with the Established Church. More importantly, what are the social connotations of the 'cultural image' of Cornish Methodism, and how has this affected the religious and political 'DNA' of Cornwall throughout the nineteenth and twentieth centuries? Furthermore, even in the present day, Cornish Methodism remains a profound part of the cultural iconography which 'makes Cornwall different' from other parts of the United Kingdom. Yet Cornish Methodism has many social and spatial identities, which are not always cohesive. These various dimensions of identity need to be explored in order to appreciate the complexities of ethno-religious identity in Cornwall. Oral testimony will be the principal source used in this paper, which will enable us to explore the diversity of socio-religious and spatial identities that encompass the subject of Cornish Methodism. Oral narrative research opens up new possibilities in the study of Cornish Methodism, by revealing a multiplicity of religious experience which lies beneath rigid methodological categories. This article will consider international debates in religion and nationalism, placing the Cornish situation within this theoretical framework. It will explore Methodism's role as an ethnic religion, and consider why despite being a symbol of Cornish nationhood, Methodism has never become involved in a separatist movement en masse. Part of the reason, it will be argued, is the prominence of a 'chapel and locality' identity within popular Methodism, which has at times been incoherent with a 'Cornish Nationalist' identity.

DEBATES IN RELIGION AND SPATIAL IDENTITY

Scholars are divided on the relationship between religion and nationalism. Benedict Anderson links nationalism's 'psychic appeal' to the decline of religion and belief in the afterlife. In his view nationalism substitutes religion with a faith in an everlasting life through membership of a continuing nation, which is not followed as a political ideology but as a 'cultural system with religious characteristics'. Anderson has been challenged on this point, however, as James Kellas has argued, because often religion and political nationalism coalesce together; as in the cases of the Roman Catholic Church and Islam, which have been closely involved with nationalism in Eastern Europe and Asia.[1] Within the United Kingdom, Urwin has asserted that while religion is declining, it still continues to exert some influence on political and territorial identity, adding that there exists a geographical distinctiveness to religious denominations.[2] Moreover, even in 'secularized' nations religion can continue to serve as an ideological tool for the mobilization of national identity. Ina Merdjanova has noted that nationalism is a secular substitute for the major functions of religion but at the same time it uses religion as a symbol of nationhood. This is rooted in the fact that nationalism is not just about 'power relations', but also about identity and culture; or, as Brubaker has termed it, 'nationalism is in principle "a way of seeing the world"'.[3]

Perspectives regarding the function of religion in a Cornwall-wide context also need to be considered. Philip Payton has concluded that the foundations of Cornish nationalism stemmed from the Anglo-Catholic movement of the late nineteenth and early twentieth century. Due to the collapse of the regional mining economy, and the apparent 'paralysis' of Cornish society, Methodism remained a distinctive feature of regional identity, aligned with Cornwall's industrial (rather than its Celtic) past. Payton has argued, however, that the Cornish Celtic Revival was unsuccessful at grass roots level due to the movement's highbrow image, and more importantly the inability to appeal to Cornish Nonconformists, as most of the Revivalists were either Roman Catholics, as Henry Jenner became and as L.C. Duncombe Jewell affected as a 'Jacobite', or High Anglicans like the Rev. W.S.

Lach-Szyrma.[4] The romantic objectives of these early activists was to 'rebuild a pre-industrial Celtic-Catholic culture in Cornwall' as an alternative to a stagnant society based on Liberal-Nonconformity. This was in contrast to the success of the Welsh Revivalists 'who managed to address their aspirations to the Methodist majority'.[5]

The place of religion within that existing culture has been a core theme of Garry Tregidga's work on twentieth-century Liberal politics. He has applied Stein Rokkan's centre-periphery theory within the Cornish context to investigate the power of regional identity on the political composition of Cornwall. Rokkan has demonstrated that provincial districts defend their culture against control from the centre, and that regional political identities are based on three core factors, or 'cleavages': (1) anti-metropolitan hostility; (2) the belief that socio-economic needs or rural communities are neglected by urban-based parties; and (3) the survival of religious Nonconformity. In these peripheries the strength of Nonconformity preserved the prominence of traditional issues and provided a secure base for Liberal and Old Left parties. Tregidga argues that Cornwall's socio-economic independence coupled with the strength of Methodism preserved the prevalence of the Old Left and Nonconformist issues in the periphery, largely differentiating the region from the 'mainstream' state system.[6] As Tregidga has utilized Rokkan's cleavage theory to explain Cornwall's religious-political make-up, so Bernard Deacon has employed the framework of Daniele Conversi's work on cultural core values. Deacon argues that although Cornish culture possesses the 'core values' or pivots put forward in Conversi's thesis: religion (in part provided by regional Methodism), family, race and language, none of these, however, qualify as a 'core value', which may explain the relative weakness of ethno-national mobilization in Cornwall. Methodism might differentiate Cornwall from other areas in terms of actual church attendees but the overall decline in religious attendance, just 12 per cent of the adult population by 1979, suggested 'a less central role for religion'. He concluded that only 'territory' could qualify as a core value for Cornish nationalist politics. Yet this was in itself problematic since 'a core value of territory does not easily lend itself to political mobilization, as it only reacts to perceived threats' to territorial integrity.[7]

New approaches to Cornish Studies, however, are beginning to move away from macro-analysis and consider the micro-level perspective of the sub-regions within Cornwall. This was partly as a result of a debate on the subject instigated by members of the Cornish History Network in 1999. One such advocate was John Probert, who suggested that in 'some senses there is no such thing as Cornwall as it includes such a diversity of regions'. Declaring that in certain cases it was more appropriate to compare Cornish towns with their counterparts outside the region, such as Redruth and Stoke-on-Trent, rather than other local centres, he raised the 'need to put Cornwall into its geographical regions as Braudel has done for France'.[8] A similar perspective is evident in the work of Ronald Perry, who concluded that the mining collapse in the late nineteenth century split the region 'into a patchwork of economic specialisms'. The demise of a core industry created 'opportunities for economic diversification' in the localities, notably the clay industry around St Austell, tourism at Newquay and horticulture in Penwith and the Tamar Valley. This produced 'variations in the positive and negative economic impact of re-adjustment from place to place and from time to time'.[9] For Bernard Deacon this micro-level dimension is central to his view that spatial issues present a useful agenda for the future development of Cornish Studies. Researchers in the field need to recognize that the historical and contemporary life of Cornwall is based on 'processes that operate at different scales: the global, the Cornish and the local'. Writing in *Cornish Studies* in 2000 he remarked that such an approach would go beyond the current tendency to concentrate on Cornwall as a single entity:

> Cornish Studies, 'new' perhaps more than the 'old', prefers to concentrate its analysis on a Cornwall-wide scale, driven by a concern to unpack those factors that produce and reproduce 'Cornwall' and its overall unity. This can lead to a downplaying of analysis at a lower spatial scale, at the levels of communities and districts within Cornwall . . . despite the fact that a Cornish Studies perspective offers a clear opportunity to work . . . with more traditional local history procedures in building on the latter's focus on discrete places and communities and placing them in a broader and more comparative framework.[10]

Despite the recent shift towards micro-level studies, little consideration has been given to religion at a lower spatial aspect. David Easton has analysed sub-regional denominational membership from a statistical perspective,[11] but thought also needs to be given to the subjective nature of religion, politics, and identity at the level of locality. A spatial perspective can usefully be applied to aspects of Cornish Methodist identity. For example, ethnic iconography is often interwoven within the religious oral tradition of a community, which in part, serves as a bastion of 'cultural defence' against the dilution of social and spiritual customs. But for many people the role of

Cornish Methodism in 'cultural defence' may not be a conscious assertion of Cornish Nationalism, indeed they may not have any particular view towards this whatsoever; but it is an unconscious or unthinking 'loyalty' to Cornish traditions, locality and family which enable individuals to comprehend the relationship between the past and the present. These elements of identity need to be explored at the locality level in more detail to establish the multilayered dynamics of Cornish 'nationalism' as a whole.

Although certain nationalist narratives of Cornish Methodism would perceive the movement as a united force against the repression of State religion, in actual fact, Methodism in Cornwall has continued to be a multi-layered movement and is often divided on both 'horizontal' and 'vertical' lines. An 'establishment' strain of Methodism having more in common with Anglicanism that other Methodist groups; in addition there exist divisions between locality and denominational ancestry, and it is often divided on religious, geographical and psychological terms. Since the Methodist Union of 1932, the remaining individual Methodist denominations were merged into one 'united' Methodist Church. However, many Methodists retained a vehement loyalty to chapel and faith, refusing to identify themselves with an amalgamated Methodist Church. Indeed, Cornwall was at the forefront of opposition to Methodist Union.[12] This could be viewed in two ways: firstly an 'ethnic' protest against *Cornish* Methodism being swallowed up into *English* Methodism, and a micro-regional protest at community level, against the merger of local chapels, and the loss of individual identity of these particular chapels. Both of these explanations are probably to some degree true, and Cornwall was anxious to hold on to its religious distinctness at both a Cornish and community level. Nonetheless, it does not necessarily follow that these two 'macro' and 'micro' perspectives were in harmony or united as a cohesive force of opposition to religious 'hegemonization'. The socio-cultural dynamics behind both the universal and localized perspectives of Cornish Methodism will now be discussed in more detail.

CORNISH METHODISM AS AN ETHNO-RELIGION

There exist two contradictory historical perspectives when considering Methodism's relationship to Celto-Cornish nationalism. It could be argued that the effects of Methodism acted as a counter force to Celtic traditions, and never had any considerable connection to Cornish nationalist ideology. Nonetheless, Methodism was co-opted into the Cornish identity, and there is evidence to suggest that the religious domination was not a stranger to Cornwall's Celtic heritage. The nature of these contradictory historical perspectives will now be explored further, in an attempt to unravel some of the paradoxes that surround Cornish Methodism's role as an ethnic religion.

During the nineteenth century Methodism became the dominant religion in Cornwall. The 1851 Religious Census suggests that Methodism accounted for over half of all the religious worship in Cornwall; the religious movement claiming 154,705 of the total attendance figure of 241,494.[13] Methodism flourished during the period of Cornish industrialization, and as David Luker has observed, the religious movement became a 'badge' of regional identity during this period of socio-economic change.[14] What is more, Methodism continued to serve as a fundamental dynamic of Cornish society until at least the 1950s. Therefore it would be expected, perhaps, that Cornish Methodism would have been firmly integrated within the wave of Celtic nationalism which occurred during the decades surrounding the turn of the twentieth century. In Wales, the campaign to disestablish the Church of England encompassed a large majority of Nonconformist communities, whereas in Cornwall, no evidence has yet been found of any large scale agitation for Church disestablishment from the chapels. But arguably Cornwall differed from Wales in a number of socio-religious, linguistic, and demographical factors which marred the progress of a Cornish nationalist movement in the formative years of the Celtic revival. It has been suggested that Methodism was actually a negative force on Cornish ethnicity; the religious movement sweeping away remainders of the periphery's Celtic heritage and older Cornish customs.[15] In contrast the Welsh language was a pivotal part of the Celtic principality, with a strong tradition of Welsh-speaking Methodist Circuits that served to fuse a common sense of ethnicity.[16] The bonds between Welsh language and nonconformity continued to be united as a medium of resistance to the 'Anglicized' landlord hegemony in nineteenth-century rural Wales.[17] But arguably Cornwall did not experience the same level of class conflict between nonconformity and the political establishment. The Liberal Unionists benefited from a number of aristocratic Cornish born MPs who promoted a sentiment of Cornish patriotism, but were still firmly attached to the English State and the Anglican Church. Indeed, it has been argued that the rise of the Liberal Unionists in Cornwall was an obstacle to Celtic separatism: the Unionists regarding themselves as both 'Cornish' and 'English' patriots, and even used anti-Celtic imagery in their speeches.[18]

But on the other hand there is evidence to suggest that Non-conformity did play a significant role in Cornish nationalist issues during this period. Tregidga has argued that the Welsh experience suggests, 'that if a popular nationalist movement had emerged in Cornwall during this period, it would have been associated with religious nonconformity'. Welsh nationalism was directly linked to the political demands of the Free Churches, such as education, temperance, land reform and the disestablishment of the Anglican Church, which were all regarded as nationalist causes. The campaign for disestablishment had also strengthened the links between Welsh nonconformity and the Liberal Party, as they continued to support Church Disestablishment, the issue becoming official Liberal Party policy in 1887. Paradoxically, despite the apparent absence of Nonconformist involvement in Celtic nationalism, many of these issues were of paramount importance in Cornwall as well, and the regional Liberal Party was calling for Cornish Church Disestablishment in the years leading up to the First World War. The Methodists had claimed for many years that they were the real 'Church of Cornwall', and by 1912 Anglicans were warning that there were 'few arguments—if any—which were applied to Welsh disestablishment . . . which could not be applied with equal reason to Cornwall'. Liberal-Nonconformist issues, which dominated much of the regional political framework during the nineteenth and twentieth centuries, also often displayed quasi-ethno-nationalist tones, such as the *Cornish* Sunday Closing Bill of the 1880s and 1890s. Furthermore, it would seem that religious Nonconformity was beginning to be immersed in Cornwall's Celtic culture by the interwar period. Tregidga has noted that the experience of Tyr ha Tavas (Land and Language), a language pressure group formed in 1932, suggests that Nonconformists could now relate to the Revival.[19] Cecil Beer was a leading member of this group, which appeared to be less socially exclusive than other Cornish movements previous to this era:

> Interviewer: Was religion a problem?
> Beer: No, we didn't find that at all. I've got an idea that Jenner was Catholic; I don't know what Morton Nance was. But in Tyr ha Tavas we were nearly all Nonconformists in the group. Hambly was a member of the Society of Friends, the Quakers. In fact, he married one of the Rowntree family . . . I'm a Baptist, several of the others were Methodist and I don't think anybody connected with the original church service [in Cornish] was Church of England![20]

The narrative extract demonstrates that Methodism (and religious Nonconformity) was involved with the Cornish Revival Movement of the interwar period. Indeed, many other prominent figures in the Cornish Movement were Methodists. The Rev. Mark Guy Pearce, author and Wesleyan Minister, and Bard of the Cornish Gorsedd, played an active part in the Revival. Alfred Browning Lyne, editor of the *Cornish Guardian*, county councillor, and President of the Bodmin Free Church Council, was also a supporter of the Cornish Movement, and was keen to link the Celtic Revival to Liberal Nonconformity. But although there may well have been a prominent Methodist leadership in the Revival Movement, and Beer seemed to recall no social exclusion within Tyr ha Tavas, it requires further research into whether this enthusiasm spread to the mass of the Methodist population in Cornwall during this period. The 'organizational' group of Tyr ha Tavas, although largely Nonconformist, consisted of educated Cornish 'exiles' based in London.[21] As a rule the Cornish Revivalists were led by mainly middle-class intellectuals who, it has been argued, had little intention of linking the movement with political motive; their prior aim being centred on the dissemination of Cornish culture and language.

Oral narrative studies of specific individuals can provide further insight into this subject. George Pawley White was a leading figure in the Cornish Revival, and a founder member of the Cornish nationalist movement, Mebyon Kernow. He has also been a Methodist local preacher since 1925, and has worked in various Cornish circuits at the 'grass roots' level. Therefore, it would be expected that he would consciously connect Methodism with both the Cornish Revival and Nationalist movements. Paradoxically, however, it would appear that his views in this subject are much more complex:

> Pawley White: My Cornishness has progressed with my Methodism—if you can say that—with the two things coming together. I used to preach in Cornish in various places . . .
> Interviewer: Do you think there was any connection between Methodism and the Cornish Celtic Revival at the beginning of the twentieth century?
> Pawley White: No . . . there was a general feeling of clannishness—you knew you were Cornish—you were Methodist—but you knew you were Cornish.[22]

Despite intrinsically linking his 'Cornishness' with his Methodism (as well as preaching in Cornish), Pawley White appears to see no connection between the Cornish Revival and the religious denomination, but there only existing a 'general feeling of clannishness'. This would seem to support that theory that Methodism had little impact on the Cornish Celtic Revival. Yet we need to go beneath the surface in order to truly appreciate the complexities of the relationship between the religious denomination and the Celtic Revival. Although Pawley White is a Methodist local preacher, he comes from an educated, middle-class background, which arguably enabled him to become a member of the 'Cornish intelligentsia' who led the Revival movement. Certainly, it would seem that the involvement in the Revival was not always on denominational lines but rather based on social stratum. This was also noted by Brian Coombes, a former Grand Bard of the Cornish Gorseth, who recalls: 'At the beginning it didn't appeal to the grass-roots Methodist population . . . it didn't appeal to the grass-roots Anglican population either—or the grass-roots nothing population'.[23] This demonstrates the dichotomy that exists *within* religious denominations; and within Methodism there are arguably a number of social layers within the body, which continued to divide cultural and spatial perspectives of Cornwall. The 'establishment' Methodism, of which Pawley White comes from, may well have been more attuned to the Anglo-Catholicism of the Revival movement. Methodism itself had always been a 'dual religion', of both the 'proletariat' and 'bourgeois' classes. The religious moment extolled an ethic of social improvement and financial frugality that appealed to entrepreneurial groups.[24] In Cornwall, this 'establishment' Methodism may have fraternized with the Celtic Revival; both of these forces providing a social and intellectual 'respectability' for the nonconformist 'nouveau riche'. Despite Pawley White's comment that Methodism had little to do with the Revival Movement; he concedes that the Wesley guild had strong links with the dispersion of Cornish culture through the Old Cornwall Societies, which were formed in 1920:

> In the early days of the Wesley Guild you had windows opened on various subjects, and Cornishness was one of them . . . the Wesley Guild was in a way, favourable to the Old Cornwall movement, and a lot of people belonged to both. I would say a large proportion of the people that ran the Old Cornwall Societies were Methodists—which is not surprising really as Methodism in those days was *the* thing, especially for business people . . .[25]

This strongly suggests that during the interwar period many Methodists in the Wesley Guild and the Old Cornwall Societies were beginning to explore issues connected with Cornish culture and identity. Once again, it is the middle-class 'establishment' Methodism which was aligned to the Revival movement in its early period; indeed it could be said that leading Methodists played a pivotal role in the dispersion of Cornish culture through the Old Cornwall Societies. Therefore it would not seem unrealistic that many middle-class Methodists did become actively involved in the Cornish Movement.

This would further confirm that the religious configuration of the Revival was not based on denominational but on class boundaries.

This historical background provides the context for studying the contemporary relationship between Methodism and Cornish identity. The second half of the twentieth century witnessed a greater popularization of the Cornish Revival as its iconography and ideology filtered out to a wider public. Paradoxically, this occurred at a time when Methodism began to go into long-term decline. Recent statistics suggest that Methodism in Cornwall has suffered a rapid decline in attendance figures over the last two decades, whereas in neighbouring Devon and Dorset the comparative figures are holding up much better: indeed attendance in Dorset is rising (refer to fig. 1). In Cornwall there has been a relative increase in Anglican attendance, perhaps assisted by inmigration to the region, but it has been the evangelical 'New' churches that have experienced the greatest gain, rising 36 per cent in the period from 1989–98.

Table 1: Methodist Percentage of Total Sunday Attendance

	Cornwall	Devon	Dorset
1979	46%	18%	6%
1989	42%	17%	7%
1998	35%	16%	8%

Source: UK Religious Trends 3, Christian Research, (ed.) Peter Brierley, 2002/3

Nonetheless Methodism seems to remain a much more prominent symbol of cultural distinctiveness in Cornwall than in Devon and Dorset. The Cornish National Minority Report published in 1999 quoted that Methodism is one of the cultural elements that continues to demonstrate Cornwall's distinct ethnicity.[26] Although regional Methodism has declined in strength, its ideological impact as a beacon of Cornish identity has lived on in both the internal and external images of Cornwall. As mentioned, even in societies where the dominant faith is declining, religion may still provide a vital lifeline for the survival of cultural or ethnic identities. Steve Bruce has drawn attention to the psychological role of religion within social mutation:

> The role of religion in cultural transition involves acquiring an enhanced importance because of the shift from one world to another . . . Modernity undermines religion except when it finds some major social role to play other than mediating the natural and supernatural worlds. Most of those social roles can be grouped under the two headings of cultural defence and cultural transition.[27]

Cornwall in recent years has been experiencing a very significant period of cultural transition, both politically and religiously. The debates surrounding a Cornish Assembly have now been accompanied by the launch of a campaign for a National Church of Cornwall. The *Fry an Spyrys* (Free the Spirit) campaign was founded by Andrew Philips, who was brought up an Anglican and became an ordained minister of the Church of England. Despite his connections with the Church of England, Philips believes that the Church has been a repressive force on Cornwall, and that it is the Methodist Church which has served as the real crusader of Cornish religious identity:

> There is a sense that the Methodist Church is the Church of Cornwall, because its a rebellion against the Church of England, which was of course imposed upon us as an alien Church . . . in order to suck Cornwall more into the United Kingdom . . . and it is still fulfilling that function.[28]

The 'new' revival of Cornish Nationalism largely centres its narrative on the Reformation period, and the subsequent repression that followed the 1549 Prayer Book Rebellion. The Church of England is perceived by many nationalists as being a political tool of the English State, instigated upon Cornwall in this period, and is still functioning in this way to the present day. Although Methodism did not arrive in Cornwall until over two hundred years later, the religious movement is seen as providing the Cornish the opportunity of spiritual and social freedom from English 'colonial' control. Philips notes that he has received considerable support in his campaign from Methodists in Cornwall as 'they do not want the English label imposed on them' by a growing association with the Anglican Church. Methodism is not just seen as a symbol of Cornish ethnicity by religious individuals, it is also asserted as a beacon of Cornish difference by atheist activists. John Angarrack, the Cornish rights campaigner, describes himself as a 'confirmed agnostic', but believes that 'Methodism has its roots in Republicanism', and provided the Cornish with a democracy that the English State did not allow them.[29] Religion being used as an ethnic emblem by secular activists is not a unique occurrence. Billing notes that although religious practice is an 'optional extra', it is often cited by secular activist as a justification for a nation's separateness or territorial rights.[30] Furthermore, territorial and religious ethnicity is often a transnational phenomena; Bruce has drawn attention to the role of religion for global Diasporas, in the protection of ethnic and cultural identity. Similarly Cornish Methodism has served as an 'ethnic' religion for many Cornish descendants overseas, as Pawley White observed:

> with the dispersal of Cornish People over the world you find that linking up and I find it wonderful that in Australia, America and South Africa—to be with the Cornish people . . . and in my lifetime this sense of being part of the dispersion [has developed much more] . . . .And very often their Cornishness is linked up with their Methodism.[31]

It would seem that for Pawley White the 'Cornishness' of Methodism has 'developed' into a more conscious symbol of current Cornish ethnicity (or 'clannishness') even though, as discussed, he does not directly connect Methodism with Cornish Celticity. Nonetheless, for him it has become a true ethnic religion, linking the Cornish People across the globe. Indeed, although this requires further research, it would appear that Methodism remains a forum for the expression of Cornish heritage and culture for many Diaspora communities. In the US State of Michigan, while the descendants of the old Cornish mining communities have now mostly dispersed, the chapel often remains the only outlet of Cornish traditions and culture.[32] But the dynamics of time and memory need to be considered here. Various oral historians have demonstrated that identities shift according to time dimensions, social environment, and the 'performance' of the interview situation itself.[33] In more recent years the growth of overseas Cornish Societies and 'homecoming festivals', such as Dehwelans, have undoubtedly propagated a renewed consciousness of transnational Cornish ethnicity. The interview with Pawley White was recorded at the time of Dehwelans 2002, which he mentioned at several points through the conversation, perhaps making the Diaspora aspect of Cornish Methodism even more relevant to him. Similarly, many American-Cornish Methodists have noted that although the chapel was a fundamental part of their forebears' 'Cousin Jack' culture, their own sense of a separate Celtic-Cornish identity (being something different from England) has only developed during their own lifetime.[34]

Nevertheless, unlike the current Cornish-American emigrant

situation, it would seem that within Cornwall itself, many Methodists have not entirely developed a specifically Celtic or Cornish (national) identity, and like many of their ancestors who migrated overseas, take their 'historical legitimacy' from an alternative era. As discussed, although Methodism may not have been connected to the idea of Celtic nation, it nonetheless 'expressed' a Cornish distinctness that was based on a more recent industrial past. As Payton has noted, due to its intellectual and 'romanticized' image of Cornwall, the Revivalist movement as a whole failed to relate to the mass of the Cornish population, which due to socio-economic 'paralysis' was itself 'fossilized' in the working-class Methodist culture of the pre-First World War period.[35] Moreover, the industrial heritage appears to still reverberate throughout Cornish Methodism to the present day:

> They [the Methodists he knows] know I'm involved with the [Cornish] language, celebrating St Piran and that sort of thing. . . . I think they are pleased to know that those sorts of things go on. There is definitely a curiosity there to find out more —so slowly, slowly—it's possible perhaps to move the Methodist Church away from that industrial revolution background—towards a more appreciative view of Cornish culture over the centuries.[36]

Ray Chubb is an active member of Mebyon Kernow and the Cornish language movement. He was brought up an Anglican, but after returning to Cornwall to live in the 1990s, he 'converted' to Methodism, as he preferred the more 'traditional' service of the local Methodist chapel, and felt there were more Cornish people attending the chapel than the local church. In part, this perhaps suggests the symbolic power of Cornish Methodism, Chubb not only choosing to *convert* to Methodism for theological reasons, but also as a act of cultural defence; the chapel being seen as more Cornish than the church. It would seem from Chubb's experience that a merger between Methodism and Cornish culture is beginning to occur in some places. Chubb mentions it may be possibly to slowly move the Methodist Church away from its 'industrial revolution background'. Despite a curiosity in 'older' customs, it would seem that that the remnants of this industrial culture still remain in the twenty-first century, and the demarcation between Celtic and Methodist culture still continues to persist. The Revivalist Movement had centred on a pre-industrial, Catholic, Cornish speaking past, but as Deacon has noted, this vision was incompatible with the more recent industrial, Methodist and Liberal identity that most Cornish people had been culturally accustomed to.[37] Indeed, it could be argued that Cornish Methodism does have its roots intertwined in the industrial revolution period, the two movements being born at about the same time in Cornwall. More-over, the role of the 'popular' Methodist culture of the nineteenth century, in the peak of Cornish socio-industrial prowess, was 'fossilized' in the collective memory of the next generation, preserving the old Cornish traditions of their forebears. Urwin has drawn attention to how the Industrial Revolution added a further territorial dimension to the political make-up of the country, due to the specialisation of regional socio-economic and the spatial independence of religious culture.[38] Although not necessarily based on Celtic distinctiveness, the Methodist-Industrial era (as Payton has demonstrated) provided another layer of distinctiveness to the periphery.[39] This could, in part, explain why the dichotomy between Cornish Celtic and Cornish Methodist-Industrial culture has persisted into the twenty-first century. Although Cornish society may no longer be 'fossilized', the oral and cultural traditions passed down from the pre-war period may well continue to dominate much of regional Methodist identity.

THE CHAPEL AND LOCALITY

Segregating factors of locality, chapel, and the individual demonstrates that both Cornish religious and ethnic identity are complex and multi-layered in character. Just as Cornish identity consists of many diverse cultural guises, Methodism has been divided by spatial and social elements. The intricate dynamics of Cornish ethno-religious identity will now be discussed in more detail to examine the various factors that can prevent national and social cohesiveness. Divergences within the sub-regions and communities which make up Cornwall are founded on diverse socio-cultural, environmental, and historical boundaries. More-over, between sub-regions and indeed *within* them, 'psychological' boundaries can exist to further polarize one group from another. As Anthony Cohen has noted, boundaries between groups are purely mental constructs'.[40] Billig has argued that 'objective variables', such as language, religion, or geography, cannot predict where state boundaries are drawn, therefore 'subjective' (or psychological) variables are the decisive ones.[41] The borders of religion are not confined to Cornwall; for example, Methodism is both English and an international faith. But psychological borders based around identity fundamentals such as locality or ethnicity, can transform a religion into a badge of difference or even nationhood, as has often been the case with *Cornish* Methodism. Whether through desire or necessity, the growing ecumenical movement has begun to blur boundaries between religious denominations. The 'coming together' of the Church of England and the Methodist Church is increasingly becoming a factor in modern religious society. Religious unity is also seen as a way forward for many Cornish Nationalists, a Cornish Church, theoretically providing both spiritual and social equality. Nevertheless, at the 'grass roots' level, chapel, community and family often take precedence over the 'macro-ecumenical' perspective. In order to understand this relationship more fully we need to look at it though the spatial perspective of locality.

The severance between religious localities is not exactly productive of a Cornish ethno-religion, and religion as a symbol of Cornish ethnicity varies dramatically between macro level and the micro level of chapel and locality. The construct of Cornish identity around sub-regional rudiments and not Cornwall as a whole has great relevance to ethno-religious culture. Joshua Fishman, in his study of a community in Western Galicia, concluded the inhabitants' identity was based around the cosmos of *this village* or *this valley*, rather than the more abstract idea of the (Polish or German) nation. Nonetheless this did not decry the peoples' 'concrete consciousness' of their surrounding culture.[42] Similarly, the majority of Methodists may have not been accustomed to an appreciation of Celtic customs associated with the Revival Movement, but for many Methodists, their understanding of Cornish culture was based on more 'recognizable' customs of the *Cornish* family, chapel, and locality.

Indeed, the basic unit of spatial identity of regional Methodism is the chapel, which is organized at a highly localized level. It would certainly seem that loyalty to chapel and locality were tenacious elements within much of Cornish Methodism, as Eric Kemp, who was born a Primitive Methodist noted: 'change was very slow in Cornwall, and people went on as before . . . they stuck to their Primitive Methodism, or New Connexion, or Wesleyan'.[43] Moreover, the remnant of this gulf between chapel and denomination is still apparent in many communities in Cornwall even today. Julyan Drew, an Ordained Methodist Minister, commented that, 'there are places in Cornwall that you would think that [Methodist] Union never happened'.[44] This is apparent to many Methodist ministers who often find it difficult to unite local congregations in the inevitable merger of chapels in the climate of declining religious attendance. Drew expanded on this issue:

> [Methodists] have supposedly been united for seventy odd years now . . . but when Union came what they didn't do is close any chapels . . . so in the various Circuits you will have a

former Bible Christian chapel, a former Wesleyan chapel, or
former Prim chapel. The people that go to those places
develop a loyalty towards those places . . . and it actually
saddens me about Methodism—that our loyalty is to a place
rather than to a movement, or a cause, or a faith—it's caught
up in this building, and there's a plague of Methodist buildings all over Cornwall.[45]

The same ideological links to chapel and the 'old faith' is again
evident. It is mentioned that in Cornwall loyalty is focused on a
building and not the religious movement; the symbolic power of bricks
and mortar within the cultural memory of Cornish Methodism should
not be underestimated it would seem. Cornwall experienced a bonanza
of chapel building in the nineteenth century, and in this sense, a chapel
can act as a mnemonic link back to a mystic golden age of the days
when Methodism, local industry and community were firmly
entrenched in Cornish society; in the same sense as many Revivalists
looked back to the golden age of Celto-Catholic Cornwall. But in
addition to being symbolically reminiscent of the culture of their forebears, the chapel is often representative of the family, community and
locality ties that reverberate within its walls:

Their parents or grandparents—it's sort of a living memory
thing—they actually built it, so there's a sense that they have
to be faithful to them . . . even if it's quite clear that that
chapel as a tool of the Church is past its sell by date. Very
many important moments in their life would have been played
out in that place . . . it's interesting to walk into a Methodist
church and see where people sit—and very often it's the same
place week in week out . . . and there are people dotted
around the place, and you think why don't they sit together
—but their sitting where they've always sat—and they're
sitting next to granny—and it's the ghosts of the people who
once attended there are there as well.[46]

Lyn Bryant has argued that family and kinship ties have acted as
a vehicle for a separate Cornish identity. These family networks
are integrated within the regional variants such as local industry,
geographical separateness, and the independent structure of Methodist
chapels.[47] The chapel, therefore, perhaps encompasses the *memory* of
the 'core values' of family, locality, and local socio-economic culture.
Chapels are also prominent 'visual' icons of Cornwall, which are
embedded within both external and internal images of the region.

Drew's comment that both buildings and people take on personalities is a very relevant argument to the assimilation between the visual characteristics and cultural memory of a chapel's congregation. For example, the modest rural chapels and the grandiose Wesleyan Churches become both architecturally and socially two poles apart as the nineteenth century progressed. In addition to differing architectural qualities, many of these chapels still have foundation stones or name plaques depicting their origins as (for example) a Wesleyan, Bible Christian, or Primitive chapel; a continuing badge of distinctiveness, separate from a purely 'Methodist Church'. Colin Allen a former Methodist Minister in the Clay Country, described an ex-Bible Christian chapel, in his Circuit, in which, 'you can still sense the cultural background of the Bible Christians in the type of hymns and worship they like'. It would seem that Methodist churches in the same community have often traditionally been divided. It is a common narrative that Anglican and Methodist congregations in the same street or village would not speak to each other, but it would seem the same is equally true within the Methodist Church. Allen can remember as a young man the 'great rivalry' between the Wesleyan and Bible Christian chapels in Porthleven, 'it was the Bryanites and Wesleyans who were almost enemies'.[48] Although Allen recalls that this rivalry petered out over the years, remarkably Drew reports that divisions still exist between churches within the same vicinity:

> My experience is that you can have within spitting distance of each other—in the same town or village two Methodist Churches of vastly different personality of congregation . . . I think congregations have personalities—psychological issues . . . in the same way as individuals do—and vastly different —you think what's going on here . . . why are they so different?[49]

Just as Cornwall as a whole may be seen as distinct from England, whether ethnically or symbolically, within Cornwall there exist symbols of distinctiveness at the level of locality which differentiate between districts or even within a community. For many Methodists, the chapel encompasses the underlying values of community and historical legitimacy; but while these are uniting factors at the locality level they are not necessarily conductive of a cohesive 'Cornish' religious movement. In addition to elements of kinship and territory, the 'simple faith' of Cornish Methodism also embraces Cornish iconography such as fisherman, miners, and hedgerow preachers' which often adopt quasi-religious status. Maurice Halbwachs first introduced the term 'collective memory', and demonstrated how the framework of a society not only influence peoples' personal memories of their own lifetimes, but also a communities shared memories of the past. He added that collective memories are a crucial element in the formation of identity for religious communities.[50] Just as 'new-wave' Cornish nationalists often use the religious martyrs of the Reformation period as a crux of their cultural memory, many 'traditional' Methodists, focus on the Cornish icons of village and community life that construct their perception of 'what Cornish is' in that particular locality. The collective memory of communities in the Clay Country for example, may contain socio-religious elements of that particular locality. This is suggested in the eastern borders of the Clay Country where the Sammy Coombe, a clay captain, Cornish wrestling champion, and Methodist preacher, is a prominent figurehead in the oral tradition of that locality.[51] The Cornish fisherman is often a powerful quasi-religious figurehead for those brought up in coastal regions. Since his 'earliest memories of Methodism', fishermen were a prolific influence on Colin Allen's religious identity, who was raised in the fishing village of Porthleven:

> I remember my grandfather taking me to chapel . . . the old fishermen would be there . . . and I used to sit there with one eye open and watch them . . . and these dear old men would pray with such fervency that the tears would run down their cheeks.[52]

Although Cornish figureheads such as fishermen and miners are synonymous with the image of Cornwall per se, it would seem that these 'ethnic' symbols are often synthesized into defenders of the values of a Cornish spatial locality rather than the Cornish nation as a whole. For many individuals this is not a specifically highly conscious assertion of their ethnicity, nor an overtly nationalist sentiment, but rather it is an almost unconscious vindication of their shared past and the bonds of kinship and locality that link all these facets of spatial identity. Billig's theory of 'banal nationalism' similarly demonstrates that nationalism is not always a conscious phenomenon, and 'ideological habits' of daily life, transmitted through visual iconography, verbal discourse, and the media, unconsciously effect how its citizens perceive their sense of place.[53] This does not necessarily denounce the Cornish ethnicity of this 'unconscious nationalism' rather it is an ethnicity formed by an individuals' perception of 'their Cornwall' which he or she transposes onto the macro view of the land. In other words, there exists a number of different Cornwalls according to various individuals' perception of what being Cornish is.

But the impact of both *macro* and *micro* views of Cornish religious identity can also survive within one individual, and of course not every person would categorically fit into the *nationhood* or *locality* model, and there exists a 'individual dimension' in which a person will take on various identity elements according to time and situation. The impact of family, chapel (or Church in this case) and locality, are still rudimentary elements within the cultural memory of certain Cornish nationalists such as Andrew Phillips:

> Simple fishermen . . . my grandfather was a simple fishermen . . . Cornwall's never far away from the sea, there's always been this fishing culture around it—and the Methodist Church did well in the fishing cultures . . . St Andrew's Church—St Peter's Church [in Newlyn], they were both fisherman—they were brothers . . . [the Newlyn fishermen] had family boats —and the Mayflower was our family boat.[54]

Although, in part, Phillips perceives Cornwall from a macro level, the importance of family and community which is indicative to the cultural memory of popular Methodism, reverberates through the con- nection placed between the two churches and family boats in Newlyn. Phillips refers to both (Cornish) locality and (Cornish) nationalist facets within the construction of his own ethno-religious identity. Although he was brought up in the Anglican Church, the Methodist ancestry in his own family appears to mould his perceptions of spatial identity within Cornwall. As discussed, socio-religious identity may not always be centred on strictly denominational lines, and the influences of family and locality can continue to shape certain aspects of an individual's personality. This raises the wider question of the transient nature of identity in post-modern society, where an individual can have numerous interchangeable identities in a global multimedia age. It has been argued that 'national' identity retains permanent homogenous elements that are not changeable,[55] but if we take Cornwall as a case study, the diversity and depth of both religious and spatial conscious- ness within groups and individuals, suggests that even national identity can shift according to time and situation. Moreover, individuals can 'select' various historical and ethnic identities in order to conceptualize their own sense of place in the modern world. In this way, Cornish Methodism can be 'manipulated' to represent a variety of cultural, spatial and spiritual identities.

CONCLUSION

Although a fusion between Cornish Methodism and Cornish Nationhood does appear to be developing, it would seem that many ideological and cultural divisions continue to exist, both from within the religious movement and from without. For some individuals, their identity is firmly entrenched in either a nationhood or locality perspective. Nevertheless, in the so called 'post-modern age' when identity is arguably much more fluid and interchangeable, individuals will often adopt different identities in various social, time and geographical dimensions, which enables them to relate to a number of spatial and ethno-religious identities. Either way, despite a rapid decline in Methodist attendance, for the religious movement still to be seen as a symbol of both Cornish locality and Cornish Nationhood, it would seem that Methodism, even if only ideologically, remains a vital part of Cornish ethnicity in the twenty-first century.

NOTES AND REFERENCES

1. James Kellas, *The Politics of Nationalism and Ethnicity*, Basingstoke, 1991, pp. 45–48.
2. Derek Urwin, 'Territorial Structures and Political Developments in the United Kingdom', in Stein Rokkan and Derek Urwin, *The Politics of Territorial Identity*, London, 1982, p. 20.
3. Ina Merdjanova, *Religion, Nationalism and Civil Society in Eastern Europe —The Postcommunist Palimpsest*, New York, 2002, p. 91.
4. Philip Payton, *The Making of Modern Cornwall: Historical Experience and the Persistence of 'Difference'*, Redruth, 1992, Chapter 7.
5. Payton, 1992, p. 132.
6. Garry Tregidga, 'Socialism and the Old Left: The Labour Party in Cornwall during the Inter-War Period', in Philip Payton (ed.), *Cornish Studies: Seven*, Exeter, 1999, p. 84. Also see Stein Rokkan, *Citizens: Elections: Parties: Approaches to the Comparative Study of the Processes of Development*, Oslo, 1970, pp. 75–144.
7. Bernard Deacon, 'And Shall Trelawny Die? The Cornish Identity', in Philip Payton (ed.), *Cornwall Since the War*, Redruth, 1993, pp. 212–4.
8. John Probert, 'Are Cornish Studies Going in the Wrong Direction?', *Cornish History Network Newsletter*, 4, March 1999, pp. 4–5.
9. Ronald Perry, 'State Uniformity, Regional Unity and Local Diversity in Cornwall, 1870–1914', *Cornish History Network Newsletter*, 6, November 1999, p. 6; Ronald Perry, 'Cornwall's Mining Collapse Revisited: An Empirical Survey of Economic Re-adjustment in Late-Victorian and Edwardian Cornwall', *Cornish History*, http.//www.marjon.ac.uk/cornish-history/0108cmcr/
10. Bernard Deacon, 'In Search of the Missing "Turn": The Spatial Dimension and Cornish Studies', in Philip Payton (ed.), *Cornish Studies: Eight*, Exeter, 2000, p. 214.

11. David Easton, 'Ceased to Meet': The Closure of Methodist Chapels in Cornwall Since 1932', unpublished MA thesis, University of Exeter, 2002.
12. See Robert Currie, *Methodism Divided: A Study on the Sociology of Ecumenicalism*, London, 1968, pp. 199–200, 205.
13. Nicholas Orme (ed.), *Unity and Varity—A History of the Church in Devon and Cornwall*, Exeter, 1991, p. 138.
14. David Luker, 'Revivalism in Theory and Practice: The Case of Cornish Methodism', *Journal of Ecclesiastical History*, 37: 4, October 1986, pp. 603–19.
15. Payton, 1992, pp. 87–94.
16. George Thompson Brake, *Policy and Politics in British Methodism 1932–1982*, London, 1984, p. 423.
17. David Adamson, *Class, Ideology and the Nation: A Theory of Welsh Nationalism*, Cardiff, 1991, pp.104–12.
18. Garry Tregidga, 'The Politics of the Celto-Cornish Revival, 1886–1939', in Philip Payton (ed.), *Cornish Studies: Five*, Exeter, 1997, pp. 126–8, 130.
19. Tregidga, 1997, pp. 135, 137–9.
20. Interview with Cecil Beer, ref: CAVA/M/G1, November 1996, CAVA.
21. Tregidga, 1997, p. 137.
22. Interview with George Pawley White, May 2002, CAVA.
23. Interview with Brian Coombes, June 2003, CAVA.
24. See E.P. Thompson, *The Making of the English Working Class*, London, 1980, pp. 385–411.
25. Interview with George Pawley White, May 2004, CAVA.
26. *The Cornish and the Council of Europe Framework Convention for the Protection of National Minorities*, 1999, p. 13.
27. Steve Bruce, *Religion in the Modern World: From Cathedrals to Cults*, Oxford, 1996, p. 96.
28. Interview with Andrew Phillips, January 2004, CAVA.
29. Interview with John Angarrack, August 2003, CAVA.
30. Michael Billig, *Banal Nationalism*, London, 1995, p. 71.
31. Interview with George Pawley White, May 2002, CAVA.
32. Interview with Flora ('Tommi') O'Hagan, May 2004, CAVA.
33. For an example of this refer to Elizabeth Tonkin, *Narrating our Past: The Social Construction of Oral History*, Cambridge, 1995; Alessandro Portelli, *The Battle of Valle Giulia: Oral History and the Art of Dialogue*, Wisconsin, 1997.
34. Interview with Carolyn Haines; Gage McKinney; Vivianne Trevithick Bradley; Jim Wearne; Susan Pellowe, April/May 2004, CAVA.
35. Payton, 1992, p. 135.
36. Interview with Ray Chubb, March 2004, CAVA.
37. Deacon, 1993, pp. 214–5.
38. Urwin, 1982, p. 29.
39. Payton, 1992, p. 87
40. Anthony P. Cohen (ed.), *Symbolising Boundaries: Identity and Diversity in British Cultures*, Manchester, 1986, p. 17; quoted in Deacon, 1993, p. 201.
41. Billig, 1995, p. 24.

42. Joshua Fishman, *Language and Nationalism*, Rowley, p. 6; quoted in Billig, 1995, p. 62.
43. Interview with Eric Kemp, April 2002, CAVA.
44. Interview with Julyan Drew, March 2004, CAVA.
45. Interview with Julyan Drew, March 2004, CAVA.
46. Interview with Julyan Drew, March 2004, CAVA.
47. Lyn Bryant, 'The Cornish Family', in Philip Payton (ed.), *Cornwall Since the War*, Redruth, 1993, pp. 182, 192.
48. Interview with Colin Allen, June 2002, CAVA.
49. Interview with Julyan Drew, March 2004, CAVA.
50. Maurice Halbwachs, *The Collective Memory*, New York, 1980; quoted in Cornelius Holtorf, *The Distant Past*, http://citd.scar.utoronto.ca/CITDPress/Holtorf/2.7.html
51. Kayleigh Milden and Garry Tregidga, 'Reflections on Rescorla: A Study of Micro-Peripheral Identity', 2001, *Cornish History*, http://www.marjon.ac.uk/cornish-history/rescorla/context.html
52. Interview with Colin Allen, June 2002, CAVA.
53. See Billig, 1995.
54. Interview with Andrew Phillips, January 2004, CAVA.
55. Billig, 1995, p. 139.

THE CONTESTED CORNISH
CHURCH HERITAGE

Graham Busby

INTRODUCTION

Cornwall has long been one of the leading tourist destinations in the United Kingdom,[1] receiving nearly five million visitor trips in 2001,[2] and possesses a linguistic and cultural heritage distinct from the rest of the country.[3] Indeed, the local authority states that 'no other county [in Britain] has such a recognizable cultural identity'.[4] The collections of Cornish folklore, made in the nineteenth century, located 'Cornishness in a "primitive", dark and wild "Celtic" culture' where ancient super-stitions were said have survived the impact of Roman, Saxon, Danish and Norman invasion.[5] This folkloric activity, so important in the Victorian era, created a genre of the 'other' and the 'exotic' which has informed almost all subsequent constructions of Cornwall and the Cornish.

These early folkloric and ethnographic studies were also con-cerned with assessing a population that was considered to be racially inferior to the English Anglo-Saxon; in other words, power relations were never far beneath the surface. Today, however, Cornish culture is recognized as exceptionally rich, a tradition that can be traced back to the medieval period when miracle plays and the lives of the saints were written in the Cornish language.[6] Whilst the population itself may have experienced material poverty, this cultural activity created a spiritual wealth which has led, in modern times, to the reification of 'Old Cornwall' as a spiritual resource: strongly influencing a number of prominent individuals in late nineteenth-early twentieth-century Cornish society as they strove to rediscover 'Celtic-Catholic Cornwall' in the aftermath of industrial collapse. This resulted in the establishment of the Cowethas Celto-Kernuak (the Celtic-Cornish Society) in 1901, the Federation of Old Cornwall Societies in 1920, and the Cornish Gorseth in 1928. Significantly, it is this reified 'Celtic Christianity'—which Bradley considers to be spiritually unique and is said to have assimilated many Pagan beliefs—that is today sought after so eargerly.[7] Indeed, it is argued here that many of today's visitors to Cornish churches come in search of precisely this: in their minds, at least, there is a precious Cornish heritage of which 'Celtic Christianity' is a central feature.

While there is now a comprehensive literature concerning heritage tourism,[8] remarkably little exists concerning visitors to ecclesiastical sites as a specific market segment. Because of the scale of visitor numbers, research has tended to focus on cathedrals[9] rather than parish churches; indeed, according to Keeling there is 'currently no published research information on the profile of visitors to churches'.[10] In fact, there is now limited data on visitors to parish churches on Exmoor[11] and in Cornwall.[12] It is argued here that Cornish churches are distinct from those in England by nature of their 'Celtic' origins, placing them in a category of their own and inviting research on them in their own right. This research is exploratory in nature, given that no previous studies have been undertaken, and is essentially atheoretical. And by incorporating responses from Cornish residents located in the immediate area of each church, the research also begins to address the 'chasm between tourism . . . and the perspectives of many Cornish people' observed by Payton and Thornton.[13]

CORNISH CHURCH HERITAGE

Cornish 'church heritage' as recognized today dates from the period known as 'The Age of the Saints', the late fifth or sixth centuries AD,[14] when missionaries from Ireland, Wales and Scotland established very small churches all over Cornwall. Whilst no buildings remain from this period, many of the extant churches were built on the same site within raised enclosures known as *lans*.[15] Cornwall is distinct from England in exhibiting these *lans*, the term itself deriving from the Cornish language: meaning a holy place. Thus, for example, Lanreath, Lanivet and Lanteglos all demonstrate the *lan* prefix—the latter featuring another Cornish-language word *eglos*, meaning church. On the north coast, the settlement of Egloshayle takes its name from the church, meaning 'church on the estuary' in Cornish.

The 'Celtic' saints are more accurately Brittonic (from Brittany, Cornwall and Wales) according to Orme,[16] and were educated individuals rather than saints as we understand the term today. Many legends have grown up around these individuals and this, undoubtedly, adds to the enduring aura of Cornish distinctiveness. The visitor to Cornwall will read of legends such as that of St Ia (Ives), who reputedly came across the sea to Cornwall on a leaf,[17] and St Austell who fought with the Devil on Hensbarrow Downs.[18] Table 1 illustrates the number of sites associated with these 'Celtic saints' in Cornwall.

Table 1: Church and chapel sites of 'Celtic' saints in Cornwall

Total number of saints venerated at sites in Cornwall		140
Total number of such sites in Cornwall		185
Relationship of saints to sites:		
Saints with	1 site	112
	2 sites	18
	3 sites	3
	4 sites	3
	5 sites	1
	6 sites	1
	8 sites	1
Approximate number of saints:		
Unique to Cornwall		78
Same with 1 site in Cornwall		70
Venerated inside and outside Cornwall		62
Same with 1 site in Cornwall		41

Source: adapted from Orme (2000)

Nearly all of the two hundred-plus Cornish churches bear distinctive names that have come down from 'The Age of the Saints', the late fifth to late seventh centuries, according to Orme: a fact that surprises and delights many visitors to Cornwall.[19] Whilst no buildings from the pre-Norman era remain, Norman work has been identified by Pevsner in 'about 140 churches and about 111 fonts'.[20] The Norman decorated doorways were frequently retained when later building replaced much else. Despite several phases of re-building, nearly half of all Cornish churches retain some trace of twelfth and thirteenth century work.[21]

Anticipating Cox and Ford's assessment of what constitutes a most distinctive tourist product,[22] Pevsner observed that 'Cornish church architecture offers a picture of unmistakable character and, especially for the 15c and 16c, of ever-recurring features. Before 1400 there was much more variety': what has been lost is an even richer built heritage.[23] Whilst the exterior architecture is, obviously, the visitor's first sight, the interiors of churches are frequently rich in craftsmanship, social history and tradition.

Hamilton Jenkin[24] identified 220 parish churches in Cornwall, almost all good examples of what Kennedy and Kingcome have termed 'serious heritage'.[25] English Heritage, the quasi-autonomous government body, 'lists' buildings of architectural or historic importance as Grades I, II* or II: and of the Cornish churches 130 are listed Grade I with a further 66 as II*, representing 58 per cent and 29 per cent of the total respectively.[26] To put the importance of the number of Grade I and II* listed Cornish churches into context, there are approximately 370,000 listed properties nationally, of which over 92 per cent are Grade II.[27] In Cornwall, these churches are seen as an important component of indigenous Cornish culture and as a potential resource for the development of tourism, a resource similar to that identified by Boissevain in Malta.[28]

Data on visitor numbers to Church of England sites is presented by the University of Exeter's Tourism Research Group, the English Tourism Council (formerly English Tourist Board) and ICOMOS. The Tourism Research Group notes that, in 1999, 19.9 per cent of all survey respondents (n=3,331) visited Truro Cathedral[29]. The English Tourism Group's[30] *Sightseeing in the UK* reports an estimated 500,000 visitors to the cathedral in 1998, with just two additional churches attracting in excess of 30,000 visitors: these being the church of St Winwalloe at Gunwalloe and St Just-in-Roseland. Additionally, the ETC's[31] *Heritage Monitor* shows a rather more precise figure for St Just-in-Roseland for 1998—some 67,400 visits—with Gunwalloe estimated to have received over 50,000 visits. The *Heritage Monitor* also lists churches receiving between 10,000–50,000 visitors in 1998; included here is another Cornish building—Padstow with 16,000. This church data is frequently calculated from Visitors' Book signatures, a method which attracts some criticism.[32]

Ease of access, in terms of the church being open or not, clearly has an influence on visitor numbers and Cornwall, in this respect, differs from areas of England: in 1982, '93% of those in Cornwall [were open compared] . . . to as few as 20% in Merseyside', according to

Hanna.[33] He has described churches as the 'Cinderella' of tourism, based on the significant difference between their intrinsic interest for visitors and the scarcity of finance for their promotion. In Cornwall, the creation of joint Diocesan/Heritage Coast Service church trail packs, covering the entire territory of Cornwall, has brought promotion of churches into the limelight, although it is argued that they are being purchased by certain types of visitor: those wishing to pursue historic, cultural, and similar tastes at an introductory level. As Winter and Gasson[34] have observed, the churches detailed in the trail packs have been drawn into the wider world of tourist boards, local authorities and businesses: although it must be noted that this is with the assent of each Parochial Church Council.

METHODOLOGY

The face-to-face survey was conducted at three churches in Cornwall, each 'typically Cornish' yet exhibiting different and contrasting features. Gunwalloe is located on the edge of a beach, surrounded by National Trust land; St Just-in-Roseland is beside the River Fal; and Lanteglos-by-Fowey is in the middle of farm land—although on the route of a popular walk. A pilot survey was conducted over four days in March 2002—two days being allocated to what was considered to be the most visited church. Permission to undertake the survey was obtained from each of the three Parochial Church Councils and was granted on the basis that further aspects of the visitor experience were investigated for their benefit. A total of forty-three variables were addressed by the questionnaire.

The *next-to-pass* method[35] of selecting respondents, whereby when one questionnaire has been completed, the next person to pass is questioned, was utilized. This approach is particularly useful when the size of the survey population is not known and when the setting of an *ad hoc* sampling fraction (every nth visitor) might entail periods of the day when researchers are under-utilized. The method also reduces interviewer bias since the interviewer does not have to choose whom to interview. It has been used satisfactorily with other visitor research in Cornwall.[36] The research took place over 48 days between March and October 2002, thereby incorporating three school holiday periods. It is considered that data collection over this period of time provides a representative visitor profile given low, shoulder and high season tourist activity.

Besides this form of data collection, a number of visitors' books have been reviewed for pertinent comments, not just for the three survey churches. A key aspect of this data concerns 'reliability' and themes identified have been independently corroborated by a

Table 2: Church survey respondent features

Respondent data	Gunwalloe	St Just-in-Roseland	Lanteglos-by Fowey
n =	286	294	145
British	266 (93%)	266 (90%)	131 (90%)
Overseas	20 (7%)	28 (10%)	14 (10%)
Day visitor	29 (10%)	18 (6%)	24 (17%)
First visit to Cornwall	17 (6%)	31 (11%)	11 (8%)
Three or more visits	217 (76%)	208 (71%)	95 (66%)
Under 25	2 (1%)	5 (2%)	0
25–34	17 (6%)	12 (4%)	8 (6%)
35–44	42 (15%)	43 (15%)	22 (15%)
45–54	73 (26%)	52 (18%)	44 (31%)
55–64	82 (29%)	99 (34%)	35 (24%)
65–74	51 (18%)	67 (23%)	30 (21%)
Over 75	18 (6%)	15 (5%)	4 (3%)
Retired (E)	123 (43%)	123 (42%)	53 (37%)
Socio-economic type A,B	82 (29%)	100 (34%)	63 (44%)
Graduate qualifications	80 (30%)	107 (39%)	68 (50%)
Household income			
Under £7,499 p.a.	15 (7%)	9 (4%)	0
£7,500–£9,999	12 (5%)	3 (1%)	2 (2%)
£10,000–£14,999	28 (12%)	27 (12%)	9 (10%)
£15,000–£19,999	26 (12%)	33 (15%)	9 (10%)
£20,000–£24,999	24 (11%)	29 (13%)	9 (10%)
£25,000–£29,999	21 (9%)	30 (13%)	12 (13%)
£30,000–£39,999	40 (18%)	24 (11%)	15 (16%)
£40,000–£49,999	26 (12%)	26 (12%)	6 (7%)
£50,000–£59,999	14 (6%)	18 (8%)	9 (10%)
£60,000–£69,999	8 (4%)	10 (4%)	6 (7%)
Above £70,000 p.a.	12 (5%)	17 (8%)	15 (16%)

Notes:
[1] Missing values predominate within the household income variable.
[2] Percentages rounded.

colleague, anthropologist Steven Butts. Words sharing a similar connotation permit the grouping of synonyms by category and can emphasize particular themes or concepts.[37]

THE CORNISH CHURCH VISITOR PROFILE

Table 2 presents the key socio-demographic data. British visitors clearly predominate although it is worth noting that a review of the visitors' books for each church suggest that the proportion of overseas visitors might be very slightly greater than is reflected here. Day visitors represent between 6 and 17 per cent of the total, reflecting the effect of large numbers of tourists rather than a low day-visitor rate as such. Particularly interesting is the loyalty factor: for 76 per cent of visitors to Gunwalloe, 71 per cent at St Just, and 66 per cent at Lanteglos, there have been three or more previous holidays in Cornwall.

An alternative perspective is that there are now few first-time visitors to the Cornwall; this could be of future concern given the age profile whereby 79 per cent of visitors to the three churches are aged 45 or over. Retired visitors represent 42 per cent and 34 per cent come from socio-economic types A, B; Thornton[38] and the Tourism Research Group[39] have suggested have suggested that the 'white collar' ABC1 categories represent about 70 per cent of visitors to Cornwall. However, as Meethan[40] has observed, such categorizations are not necessarily useful for marketing purposes although they continue to be widely used. As might be expected from these visitors, a statistically significant association exists between the possession of higher education qualifications and higher household incomes ($p = <.000$).

As Table 2 shows, in terms of party size, the majority of visitors

Table 3: Party size by church

Party size	Gunwalloe	St Just-in-Roseland	Lanteglos-by-Fowey
1	10	9	11
2	164	174	98
3	51	37	20
4	38	47	11
5 or more	22	27	5

Note: one missing value for Gunwalloe.

arrive as a couple, accounting for 58 per cent of all visitors at Gunwalloe, 59 per cent at St Just-in-Roseland, and 68 per cent at Lanteglos-by-Fowey. Lone individuals are remarkably few whilst coach-borne visitors are usually only found at St Just, predicated by the sub-tropical plants in the grounds attracting organized tours. The visitor profile indicates a predominantly middle-class, well-qualified, high-income, Cornwall-loyal market.

THE CHURCH HERITAGE EXPERIENCE

All destinations have some unique characteristics which, in turn, create place identity.[41] Cornwall is an exemplar in this respect and it is argued that this is one of the reasons for the remarkable degree of repeat visiting to the named churches. Table 4 indicates repeat visiting ranging from 28 per cent of all visitors at Lanteglos-by-Fowey to 46 per cent at St Just-in-Roseland. This level of loyalty is partially explained by the settings: Gunwalloe is almost on the beach, with rocky cliffs on either side, as Figure 1 illustrates. St Just has a graveyard full of sub-tropical plants (although this is not clear in Figure 2) and is in effect one of the many 'Cornish gardens' currently in vogue. All three churches are kept open throughout the year; Hanna's survey drew attention to the importance of this.[42]

Table 4: Church visitor loyalty

	Gunwalloe	St Just-in-Roseland	Lanteglos-by Fowey
First visit to church	178 (62%)	160 (54%)	105 (72%)
Repeat visit	108 (38%)	134 (46%)	40 (28%)
Last visit: 2002	12	12	5
Last visit: 2001	31	33	12
Last visit: 2000	14	16	3
Last visit: 1990–1999	30	41	10
Last visit: 1980–1989	12	11	2
Last visit: 1970–1979	4	6	0
Last visit: 1960–1969	1	8	0
Last visit: pre-1960	3	2	0
Cannot remember year	1	2	8

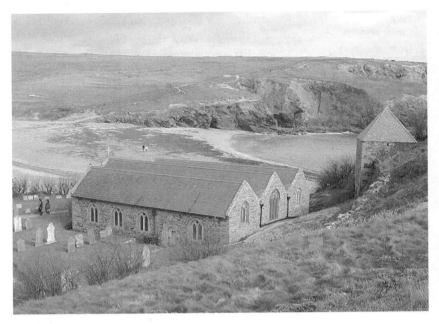

1. Gunwalloe.

2. St Just.

Amongst the unique characteristics is the perception of 'Celtic' origins. Utilizing a five-point Likert scale, whereby 1 represented 'English' and 5 'Cornish Celtic', respondents were asked to provide a score for each church. Taking the three churches as a group, 338 respondents (59 per cent), from 572 valid responses, gave a score of 5. Interestingly, faced with this choice, 121 respondents (21 per cent) gave a value-neutral score of 3. Isolating the results for each site, 68 per cent of visitors considered Gunwalloe to be the epitome of a Cornish Celtic church compared with 58 per cent at St Just and 40 per cent at Lanteglos. Ironically, the latter is a classic example of the numerous Cornish churches located within a *lan*; this site is illustrated in Figure 3. The notion of the 'Celtic' is often place-specific though chronologically vague;[43] in Cornwall this is assisted by the large number of settlements named after Cornish (Celtic) saints. When the place-names associated with a 'Celtic' saint, but where no religious building exists, are added to the list, the visitor may truly believe Cornwall to be a land of the saints, suggesting cultural uniqueness. In his two-part television programme *Kernow: Part Seen, Part Imagined*, Moffat noted the numerous Cornish road signs indicating places named after 'Celtic' saints, emphasizing their importance as visual signifiers of 'Celtic' identity in Cornwall.[44]

3. Lanteglos.

It is suggested that for most visitors the perception of 'Celticity' is based on a model of 'simplicity', where a church has relatively few elaborate features, is smaller than the norm, and in setting and presentation is almost an integral part of the landscape.[45] Added to this 'mythical' perception is the milieu in which Cornish churches exist: surrounded as they are by place-names evoking scores of Cornish saints—to which many of the churches are dedicated—and ancient artefacts such as Cornish crosses and holy wells.[46] Guide-books, and there are many, retell the various 'Celtic' legends and further elaborate this construction of Cornish Celticity: a good example here is Filbee's explicitly titled *Celtic Cornwall*.[47] Medieval hagiography and folklore collected in more modern times combine to create a powerful repertoire of cultural heritage that, for the visitor, emphasizes 'continuity with a particular past and a particular landscape'.[48] But despite the appeal of this powerful blend, many visitors—as they to struggle to interpret this romanticized, ancient past—though readily accepting the 'Celtic' label, are nonetheless confused about the meaning of the term.[49] For Harvey *et al.*,[50] the search for 'Celticity' today is often concerned with a search for individual identity and meaning in modern

Table 5: Respondents' views on how Cornish churches differ from those in the rest of England (percentages within name of church and for total of all responses)

Reason for difference	Gunwalloe	St Just-in-Roseland-	Lanteglos-by-Fowey	Total
Smaller than usual	34 (21%)	24 (18%)	4 (5%)	62 (16%)
Building materials	21 (13%)	19 (14%)	23 (28%)	63 (17%)
Architecture	22 (13%)	18 (14%)	12 (14%)	52 (14%)
Older than the norm	21 (13%)	15 (11%)	10 (12%)	46 (12%)
Remote locations	14 (8%)	9 (7%)	2 (2%)	25 (7%)
Celtic	2 (1%)	7 (5%)	7 (8%)	16 (4%)
Vaulting/ceiling	6 (4%)	3 (2%)	8 (10%)	17 (4%)
More character	8 (5%)	5 (4%)	2 (2%)	15 (4%)
Simpler	8 (5%)	6 (5%)	1 (1%)	15 (4%)
Part of the landscape	6 (4%)	4 (3%)	4 (5%)	14 (4%)
Pew ends	2 (1%)	0	1 (1%)	3 (<1%)
Lans	1 (<1%)	0	1 (1%)	2 (<1%)

4. Bench ends at Gunwalloe.

consumer society, and this may be especially so for visitors to Cornish churches.

Of the 725 respondents, 381 considered they could explain why Cornish churches appear different from those across the Tamar. However, a number of the reasons cited do not actually concern the appearance of the churches: rather they are intangible or historical aspects. Table 4 illustrates these. Pew ends are cited by just three individuals, despite their importance for social and architectural historians. Rowse[51] suggested that oak benches were one of the most distinctive characteristics of Cornish churches, and Pevsner commented on those at Launcells, Gorran and Zennor: at the latter, those depicting the Mermaid of Zennor legend having been made into a chancel seat.[52] Figure 4 shows bench ends at Gunwalloe.

For 15 per cent (111) of all respondents, the reason for visiting the church was because it was located on the route of a walk. This introduces another dimension in as much as visiting the church might be a serendipitous experience, as Visitors' Book comments indicate, or that the walk was planned to incorporate the site. In Cornwall, two walking routes are promoted because of their religious attractions. St Michael's Way—*Forth Sen Myghal*—is a twelve-mile route commemorating that possibly taken by pilgrims to Santiago de Compostela who might have disembarked at Lelant and then travelled overland to Mount's Bay in order to avoid the passage around Land's End. Involved with Cornwall County Council in establishing this route was Bredereth Sen Jago (the Brotherhood of St James), a group of latter-day individuals interested in everything associated with the Santiago pilgrimage. It is considered that members of this group—which has adherents outside Cornwall as well as within—along with those of the national Confraternity of St James are likely to form yet more examples of Keeling's[53] 'special interest visitors'. In mid-Cornwall, there is The Saints Way, which takes in a number of churches as it makes its way between Padstow and Fowey, following as it does the supposed route of 'Celtic' saints as they made their way down the Camel and the Fowey as they journeyed from Ireland or Wales to Brittany. Again, Cornwall is celebrated as the Land of Saints, and the Celtic connection is emphasized once more.

For other visitors, a significant number of the Cornish churches have literary connections, from the nineteenth century onwards, which are reflected in more than one *genre*. Daphne du Maurier was married at Lanteglos-by-Fowey—this aspect now features in the annual festival[54]—and was the reason cited by 5 per cent of visitors to the church during the survey. To illustrate another example, beyond the view of the survey, it was at St Juliot in North Cornwall that Thomas Hardy met his first wife, Emma Lavinia Gifford, in 1870, whilst drawing up plans for 'restoration' of the church—work he later regretted.[55]

As Davidson has pointed out, it was Hardy's first visit which 'inspired his romantic novel *A Pair of Blue Eyes*' and, after Emma's death in 1912, much of his finest poetry.[56] Hardie records a pilgrimage, in 1991, by novelist D.M. Thomas and 'outstanding Hardy scholar' James Gibson who travelled the same route from Bockhampton to St Juliot, 'matching their time schedules to his', as part of the Thomas Hardy Society's biennial conference.[57] St Juliot is, undoubtedly, visited by literary tourists since the nearby former rectory is now a five-diamond guest house which hosts workshops and is linked to the Thomas Hardy Association website which itself displays links to over three hundred Hardy web-sites.[58]

Also on the north coast, further west, is St Mawgan; the parish website highlights the fact that this 'classic English (sic) village was chosen by the BBC as the location for Agatha Christie's Miss Marple'.[59] The website also features St Eval and St Ervan, the latter being mentioned by church enthusiast John Betjeman in his *Summoned by Bells*. The former Poet Laureate is buried at St Enodoc and this church is certainly a recipient of literary tourist interest; for example, recitals of Betjeman's poetry take place near his grave—this author attended one on 28 September 2000, organized as one of the events in Restormel Borough Council's Tamarisk Festival. Local authorities are not the only catalyst for such events, and literary tourists are attracted to churches with particular associations elsewhere in Britain. Visitors to The World of James Herriot attraction in Thirsk, for example, visit St Mary by default as do visitors to Selborne, St Mary where 'a good relationship between the Gilbert White Museum' is reported.[60]

Noting the relationship between literary works and the screen, Busby and Klug[61] observe that 'many films and television dramas owe their existence to literature in the first place': this certainly applies to a number made in Cornwall which feature local churches. The compilation by Craig and FitzGerald[62] charts films and television dramas shot in Cornwall since 1913. Those featuring churches include: *Yellow Sands* (1938) showing St Levan and Gunwalloe, based on Eden Philpotts's novel; *Poldark*, shot in the 1970s, illustrating St Winnow and based on Winston Graham's saga; five productions, based on Rosamunde Pilcher's novels, shot between 1994–96 by Frankfurter Filmproduktion, showing Perranuthnoe church; and *Twelfth Night* (1995), presenting Lanhydrock and St Michael's Mount. The *Poldark* novels, written over a forty-year period, may well provide subliminal inspiration for visiting Cornwall and its churches; the official website (www.poldark.com) features a heavily-utilized message board, one of which has questioned whether the 'story board' of filming at St Winnow church is still available in the building—it is.

CONCLUSION

Hanna[63] has described English churches as the 'Cinderellas' of tourism because of the difference between their intrinsic interest and the scarcity of resources for their promotion. This view holds true for Cornish churches which, undoubtedly, form part of Cornwall's rich heritage. Indeed, the Cornwall Tourist Board's strategy *Delivering Distinctive Difference* indicates that 'Cornwall's Celtic heritage and culture in addition to the environment and landscape was seen as the cornerstone of "difference" which would help attract high-spend niche markets'.[64] The research reported in this article has identified Cornish church visitors as well-qualified, high income, and remarkably loyal. Taken together, retired visitors and those from socio-economic groups A and B represent 76 per cent of the survey population. Nonetheless, there is clearly a need to attract 'new blood', given the demographic profile, and those seeking to encourage further visitors to Cornish churches might do well to consider their 'Cinderella' status.

In terms of the visitor experience, the majority of respondents considered that the sites visited demonstrated 'Celtic' features although, it is argued, this had as much to do with a search for personal identity as it did with the actual identification of representations of any historical period. The evidence of *lans* at many Cornish churches suggests an early Christian (and arguably 'Celtic') influence but, paradoxically, this distinctive feature appears not to be familiar to most visitors: reinforcing the observation that their wish to identify with a particular historic period or place is motivated by a psychological construct rather than an evidence-based one. Ongoing research, such as that by Cockerham[65] into the distinctive slate memorials of early modern Cornwall, provides a steady stream of evidence that might serve as current signifiers of Cornish cultural difference. The Tourist Board, in pursuit of its strategy, might do well to note them and draw their attention to potential visitors. But ultimately, the question of whether tangible signifiers of 'difference' exist is immaterial—as destination marketeers the world over understand—because it is the perception of difference that is important for the visitor. For this reason, Cornwall's churches—as well as being important repositories of Cornish culture in a historical sense—also play a crucial role in reproducing a contemporary Cornish culture that is so attractive to the visitor. Indeed, Cornwall's religious resources may well become more important in the development of tourism over time, just as Boissevain[66] has demonstrated was the case of Malta.

NOTES AND REFERENCES

1. H. Gilligan, 'Visitors, tourists and outsiders in a Cornish Town', in M. Bouquet and M. Winter (eds), *Who from their labours rest? Conflict and practice in rural tourism*, Aldershot, 1987, pp. 65–82.
2. South West Tourism, *South West Facts 2001*, website http://www.swtourism.co.uk/html/research_statistics.shtm, viewed on 27 October 2003.
3. B.P. Andrew, 'Tourism and the Economic Development of Cornwall', *Annals of Tourism Research* 24:3, 1997, pp. 721–35; D.C. Harvey, 'Landscape Organization, Identity and Change: Territoriality and Hagiography in Medieval West Cornwall', *Landscape Research* 25:2, 2000, pp. 201–12.
4. Cornwall County Council, *Cornwall Heritage and Culture Strategy*, Truro, 2000.
5. J. Vernon, 'Border crossings: Cornwall and the English (imagi)nation', in G. Cubitt, (ed.), *Imagining Nations*, Manchester, 1998, pp. 153–72, p. 157.

6. N. Orme, '*The Saints of Cornwall*', Oxford, 2000.
7. I. Bradley, 'The Celtic Way', cited in C.H. Williams, 'Conclusion: New Directions in Celtic Studies: An Essay in Social Criticism', in A. Hale and P. Payton (eds), *New Directions in Celtic Studies*, Exeter, 2000, pp. 197–229.
8. B. Garrod and A. Fyall, 'Managing Heritage Tourism', *Annals of Tourism Research*, 27:3, 2000, pp. 682–708; S. Dutton and G. Busby, 'Antiques-based Tourism: Our Common Heritage?', *Acta Turistica* 14:2, 2002, pp. 97–119.
9. English Tourism Council, *Heritage Monitor*—quoted on ETC website, 13 November 2000; ICOMOS, *To be a pilgrim—meeting the needs of visitors to cathedrals and churches in the United Kingdom: a survey undertaken in 2000*, London, 2001; M. Shackley, 'Space, sanctity and service: the English cathedral as heterotopia', *International Journal of Tourism Research* 4:5, 2002, pp. 345–52.
10. A. Keeling, 'Church Tourism—Providing a Ministry of Welcome to Visitors', *Insights*, 2000, pp. A13–A22.
11. J. Brice, G. Busby and P. Brunt, 'English Rural Church Tourism: A Visitor Yypology', *Acta Turistica* 15:2, 2003, pp. 144–62.
12. G. Busby, 'The Cornish Church Heritage as Destination Component', *Tourism* 50:4, 2002, pp. 371–81.
13. P. Payton and P. Thornton, 'The Great Western Railway and the Cornish-Celtic Revival, in P. Payton (ed), *Cornish Studies: Three*, Exeter, 1995, p. 84.
14. A. Preston-Jones and P. Rose, 'Medieval Cornwall', *Cornish Archaeology*, 25, 1986, pp. 135–85.
15. N. Orme, 'From the Beginnings to 1050', in N. Orme (ed.), *Unity and Variety—A History of the Church in Devon and Cornwall*, Exeter, 1991, pp. 1–22.
16. Orme, 2000.
17. M. Filbee, *Celtic Cornwall*, London, 1996.
18. A.M. Kent, *The Literature of Cornwall—Continuity, Identity, Difference 1000–2000*, Bristol, 2000.
19. Orme, 2000.
20. N. Pevsner, *The Buildings of England—Cornwall*, Harmondsworth, 1951, p. 16.
21. Preston-Jones and Rose, 1986.
22. J.C. Cox and C.B. Ford, *The Parish Churches of England*, 7th edition, London, 1954.
23. Pevsner, 1951, p. 18.
24. A.K.H. Jenkin, *The Story of Cornwall*, London, 1932.
25. N. Kennedy and N. Kingcome, 'Disneyfication of Cornwall—Developing a Poldark Heritage Complex', *International Journal of Heritage Studies* 4, 1998, pp. 45–59.
26. Diocese of Truro, *Diocesan Directory*, Truro, 2001.
27. English Heritage, *Why do we list?*, www.english-heritage.org.uk, viewed 20 August 2003.

28. J. Boissevain, 'Ritual, Tourism and Cultural Commoditization in Malta: Culture by the Pound', in T. Selwyn (ed.), *The Tourist Image: Myths and Myth Making in Tourism*, Chichester, 1996, pp. 105–20.
29. Tourism Research Group, *Cornwall Holiday Survey 1999*, Exeter, 1999.
30. English Tourism Council, *Sightseeing in the UK 1998*, London, 1999.
31. English Tourism Council, *The Heritage Monitor*, London, 1999.
32. G. Busby, 'A True Cornish Treasure: Gunwalloe and the Cornish Church as Visitor Attraction', in P. Payton (ed.), *Cornish Studies: Eleven*, Exeter, 2003, pp. 168–91.
33. M. Hanna, *English Churches and Visitors*, London, 1984, p. 5.
34. M. Winter and R. Gasson, 'Pilgrimage and Tourism: Cathedral Visiting in Contemporary England', *International Journal of Heritage Studies* 2:3, 1996, pp. 172–82.
35. TRRU (Tourism & Recreation Research Unit) *Recreation site survey manual—methods and techniques for conducting visitor surveys*, London, 1983.
36. G. Busby and Z. Hambly, 'Literary Tourism and the Daphne du Maurier Festival', in P. Payton (ed.), *Cornish Studies: Eight*, Exeter, 2000, pp. 197–212.
37. R.P. Weber, *Basic Content Analysis*. 2nd Edition, London, 1990.
38. P. Thornton, 'Tourism in Cornwall: Recent Research and Current Trends', in P. Payton (ed.), *Cornish Studies: Two*, Exeter, 1994, pp. 108–27.
39. Tourism Research Group, 1999.
40. K. Meethan, 'Selling the Difference: Tourism Marketing in Devon and Cornwall, South West England', in R. Voase (ed.), *Tourism in Western Europe—A Collection of Case Histories*, Wallingford, 2002, pp. 23–42.
41. W. Nuryanti, 'Heritage and Postmodern Tourism', *Annals of Tourism Research* 23:2, 1996, pp. 249–60; D. Uzzell, 'Creating Place Identity Through Heritage Interpretation', *International Journal of Heritage Studies* 1:4, 1996, pp. 219–28.
42. Hanna, 1984.
43. J. Lowerson, 'Celtic Tourism—Some Recent Magnets', in P. Payton (ed.), *Cornish Studies: Two*, Exeter, 1994, pp. 128–37.
44. A. Moffat, *Kernow: Part Seen, Part Imagined*, Episode 2, Carlton Television, 20 April 2001.
45. W.G.V. Balchin, *The Cornish Landscape*, London, 1983.
46. Orme, 2000.
47. Filbee, 1996.
48. D.C. Harvey, 'Heritage Pasts and Heritage Presents: Temporality, Meaning and the Scope of Heritage Studies', *International Journal of Heritage Studies* 7:4, 2001, pp. 319–38.
49. C. Thomas, 'Cornish Archaeology at the Millennium', in P. Payton (ed.), *Cornish Studies: Ten*, Exeter, 2002, pp. 80–89.
50. D.C. Harvey, R.A. Jones, N. McInroy and C. Milligan (eds), *Celtic Geographies; Old Cultures, New Times*, London, 2002, cited in B. Deacon, 'The new Cornish Studies: New Discipline or Rhetorically Defined Space?', in P. Payton (ed), *Cornish Studies: Ten*, Exeter, 2002, pp. 24–43.

51. A.L. Rowse, *Tudor Cornwall*, London, 1941.
52. Pevsner, 1951.
53. Keeling, 2000.
54. Busby and Hambly, 2000.
55. A.L. Rowse, *The Little Land of Cornwall*, Gloucester, 1986.
56. R. Davidson, *Cornwall*, London, 1978, p. 39.
57. M. Hardie, Introduction, in M. Hardie (ed.), *A Mere Interlude—Some Literary Visitors in Lyonesse*, Penzance, 1992, pp. 7–12, p. 8.
58. www.yale/edu/hardysoc, viewed 17 August 2001.
59. www.stmawgan.org.uk/st_mawgan_plan.htm viewed 27 May 2004.
60. ICOMOS, 2001, p. 12.
61. G. Busby and J. Klug, 'Movie Induced Tourism: The Challenge of Measurement and Other Issues', *Journal of Vacation Marketing* 7:4, 2001, pp. 316–32.
62. S. Craig and D. FitzGerald, *Filmed in Cornwall*, Launceston, 1999.
63. Hanna, 1984.
64. A. Hale, 'Representing the Cornish', *Tourist Studies*, 1:2, 2001, pp. 185–96, p. 194.
65. P. Cockerham, 'On My Grave a Marble Stone: Early Modern Cornish Memorialization' in P. Payton (ed.), *Cornish Studies: Eight*, Exeter, 2000, pp. 9–39.
66. Boissevain, 1996.

A MATCH, A MEAL, AND A SONG: THE EARLY YEARS OF CRICKET IN CORNWALL

Ian Clarke

INTRODUCTION

An advertisement placed in *The Sherborne Mercury* read:

> Whereas the annual sale for cattle at St Teath, near Camleford, Cornwall held at the first Tuesday in July, 'has for several years being rather neglected'. This is to inform the publick, that the Gentlemen farmers etc. of the neighbourhood will produce a large show of cattle of the said day being the 3rd day of July next.
>
> N.B. the evening of the same day will be cricketed for a very handsome silver laced hat.
>
> Dated: St Teath, 14 June 1781, and signed, Nathaniel Long.[1]

This is the earliest recorded reference to cricket being played in Cornwall. It does not mean that the game had not been played before or indeed that the game was not being played at a similar time in other parts of Cornwall. The short reference implies more and needs explanation. Bowen and Underdown have shown that cricket developed quite extensively across the southern counties of England in the mid-eighteenth century,[2] whilst Goulstone has noted that the first recorded cricket in Devon was in 1773 at Teignmouth, and in Cornwall in 1814.[3] Bowen has written that in Kent at the end of the eighteenth century people talked about 'playing at crickets'.[4] This game at St Teath would not so much be a cricket match, but a single wicket competition, particularly if the prize was noted as a 'silver laced hat'. The single wicket matches were popular at the time and attracted gambling as well. The cattle market at St Teath would have been a lively affair, particularly as we find that Nathaniel Long was the publican of the White Hart, situated just opposite the village square where the market took place, and where in a field behind the pub the single wicket match could have taken place. Douch has shown that public houses were very much at the centre of Cornish recreational activity in the period and a silver-laced hat was not uncommon as a prize for wrestling.[5]

This article points to the origins of cricket in Cornwall, and shows how cricket became established in Cornwall against a background of both gentry and popular recreations and tradition in the first decades of the nineteenth century. It offers an insight into who played cricket and notes that a subtle change in those taking part in the game occurred from about 1829. The parameters of the dates for this article have been set: 1781 as the first recorded reference, and 1829–30 as the years of change. Previous assumptions had been made that cricket was first played in Cornwall in 1814. This and 1813 are indeed key dates for cricket in Truro, yet the years up to 1829 showed that the game failed to grasp significant attention as an important summer recreation in Cornwall. The location of where cricket was played is significant to the overall picture of the game in Cornwall, and factors such as travel, place and patronage are also important. John Bale's *Sport and Place* sets cricket in its rural village green idyll but also explains the diffusion of the game and its location over time.[6] Finally, there is not the space in this article to make comparisons with a wider national context (this has been made in a much larger study) but the key points of when, where, why, and how cricket in Cornwall became established are addressed in this article.[7]

CORNWALL: THE CONTEXT

Mining, fishing, and farming were the backbone of the Cornish economy in the eighteenth and early nineteenth centuries, and the quickest way to communicate was by sea through ports such as Looe, Fowey, Falmouth, Truro, Penzance, and Padstow. The inland roadways were in such a poor state that the preacher John Wesley, entering Cornwall for the first of his many visits in 1743, lost his way over Bodmin Moor. However, by the time Robert Southey, the poet laureate, left Falmouth by chaise one morning in 1802, he was able to write: 'What a county for travelling is this! We advanced fourteen leagues today without fatigue or exertion.'[8] As Payton has explained: 'Cornwall in the period 1700 to 1850 does not appear at first glance to have been a region suffering the disadvantages and marginalisation of social and economic peripherality'. Indeed, 'The Cornish economy was amongst the first to industrialise the early and successful application of steam power facilitating the development of deep mining and achieving for Cornwall a place in the forefront of technological innovation'.[9] Halliday agrees: 'It was an age of innovation and expression, a new heroic age of common miners and uncommon men.'[10]

For the upper and middle classes, profits from mining rights, land acquisition, business, and trade stimulated the Cornish economy and brought them wealth; for the Cornish mine labourer and the farm worker life was often short and tough. With the end of the Napoleonic Wars hard times came to British farming. Adding to the social and economic problems in Cornwall were retuning soldiers seeking employment. Some found work in farming: but at a low wage. As Rowe explained: 'Cornish farmers attempted to withstand the post-war slump by reducing the prices of production'. Thus, for example, 'in the Stratton district, where no mining or fishing industries competed for labour, wages remained as low as 7s until the middle of the century'.[11]

Although agriculture suffered in this period, as Palmer points out, the mines did not. The numbers directly involved in the mines, according to Heard, were about 60,000 and there were many others who benefited from their output.[12] Cornwall's population rose dramatically in the first three decades of the nineteenth century, from 192,281 in 1801 to 301,306 by 1831. Gilbert's contemporary observation serves as a reminder of the changes overtaking Cornwall in this period:

> Among the general customs of Cornwall, may be reckoned wrestling, and hurling matches, and the inhabitants of the county acquired a superior vigour and adroitness. Desperate wrestling matches, in-human cock fights, pitched battles, and, riotous revellings are happily now of a much rarer occurrence than heretofore: the spirit of sport has evaporated, and that of industry has supplied its place.[13]

TRURO: LEISURE AND CRICKET

By the end of the eighteenth century, Truro had become an elegant Georgian town, a 'Bath of the West'. Its population was 8,077 in 1801, and in the next twenty years it had increased to 12,939. Palmer explains: 'The hey-day for this social centre for the elite of the town was probably during the Napoleonic Wars . . . Regular monthly Assemblies were held [and] these rooms provided a venue for occasional balls and other entertainment for many years to come'.[14]

Clark's extensive study of British Clubs and Societies has helped us to understand the vast range of leisure interests available, particularly for the upper and middle classes. He found that, 'the

Cornish market town of Truro maintained a school society, a society of Hiccobites, Oxford and Cambridge clubs and a club of Cornish naval officers'.[15] There was also a theatre, a music festival established in 1807, and in the Assembly Rooms scientific lecturers were held. By 1813 a cricket club had been formed, followed two years later by a branch of the Geological Society, and in the 1820s the unusually named Hare Pie Club met at The Dolphin. A day at Truro Races was a major social event, with bands and a dinner and ball in the evening.[16] In addition to Truro, Penzance had also become fashionable at this time. Penzance was the home of the Royal Cornwall Geological Society, founded in 1814. The town catered for other middle-class interests, with a Gentlemen's News Room formed in 1799, a Ladies' and Gentlemen's Book Club which later became Penzance (Morrab) Library, a cricket club in 1819, and for the farming interest there was the Penwith Agricultural Society.[17]

It was appropriate that in Truro, Cornwall's premier and most fashionable town, a cricket club was established. *The Royal Cornwall Gazette* reported:

> The members of the Cornish Cricket Club, lately established in this town, were this evening highly gratified by the appearance on their ground of the fine band of the Dorset Militia (which marched in here today on their was to Plymouth) which continued through the whole of the evening to enliven the 'Olympic Field' by playing several lively and national airs.[18]

Interestingly, the new body called itself the Cornish Cricket Club, not necessarily because it was the first in Cornwall, but because it saw itself as the most prestigious. Similarly, at different times during the nineteenth century Penzance and Hayle cricket clubs also claimed the right to be called the Cornish Cricket Club, because they had remained unbeaten over a period of time. A later reference to cricket in Cornwall has mistakenly assumed that the Cornish Cricket Club meant the Cornwall *County* Cricket Club: certainly, Truro's first club was meant for the gentlemen of the town and surrounding area but it did not necessarily have Cornwall-wide pretensions.[19] There is evidence that Bodmin—another Cornish centre with a developed sense of civic pride —also had a cricket club in the same year that Truro's was formed, but no evidence to show that these two clubs played each other.

Commenting on this new Bodmin club, the *Royal Cornwall Gazette* observed that: 'The Bodmin Cricket Club finished their annual sports on Thursday last, after which the members partook of an excellent dinner at the Queen's Head in that town and concluded the day in the most perfect harmony and conviviality'.[20] It is important to consider the context in which this observation was made. First, it was 1813 and Cornwall was fortified in preparation for the ever-present threat of a French invasion. Various regiments and militia were either garrisoned in, or embarked from, Cornwall. Links between the military and cricket were important, and in Cornwall as elsewhere increased military activity—not least the presence of regiments from outside —may have acted to promote the growth of cricket. The Artillery ground in London was the principal venue for metropolitan cricket in the eighteenth century, and in 1799 the West Kent Militia played a match against Plymouth Garrison.[21] Bodmin, too, was a garrison town —and so not surprisingly an early home of Cornish cricket.

Secondly, the journey from Truro to Bodmin, a distance of twenty-two miles, remained difficult in the early nineteenth century, despite the improving turnpike roads, and this may have prevented the two cricket teams from having met. Indeed, early references to cricket matches in Cornwall appear to allude to competitions among club members themselves, rather than the playing of games between opposing teams. Thirdly, clubs in regional centres such as Bodmin or Truro were seen as important vehicles for gentrified sociability, a means of enhancing elite cohesion at a time of uncertainty and social and political unrest. As Ford has pointed out: 'it is not surprising that this was the period in our history when sports clubs were formed, and cricket clubs were perhaps the most numerous of sports clubs.'[22]

Fourthly, the 'annual sports' referred to by the *Royal Cornwall Gazette* meant not only cricket but other games too: particularly athletic exercises such as running or throwing the ball. At Bodmin, however, these exercises were unlikely to have included the traditional Cornish sports of wrestling and hurling. The gentlemen cricketers would have avoided participation in what was seen as lower-class— and, after 1815, potentially subversive—recreation, although on occasions they may have patronized such activities. Additionally, older forms of gentry recreation—such as gambling—had become less popular, and cricket was now firmly established as the leading participatory leisure pursuit for the gentry.

Finally, there was the important link between sport and place. Heard has written that the [Truro] Cornish Cricket Club played, 'in the ground for that purpose near Michell Road to the north of the town'.[23] There are references to cricket being played there as early as 1813 and as late as 1830.[24] In 1813 the ground was described as the 'Olympic Field', the classical allusion suggesting that the site had also been used for wrestling and other 'ancient sports' in the past as well as more recently, an assumption confirmed by the *Royal Cornwall Gazette* which concluded that the Cornish had learnt this 'classical and manly art from the Greeks'.[25] Despite the anxieties of the gentry, cricket and wrestling—both summer activities—could coexist sometimes in traditional community recreation areas: such as 'The Beacon' at Bodmin or on 'The Downs' at Helston. On such occasions there was rarely mention of the performance of the players or indeed the results. However, the one constant theme was the sociability, and the matches or meetings were invariably concluded with a meal. 'On Tuesday last the Members of the Cornish Cricket Club concluded their meeting for the present year', noted one newspaper report, '[t]he party afterwards partook of a sumptuous dinner at The Red Lion Inn, and concluded the day with the greatest harmony. Several good songs and duets were sung adding much to the pleasures of the evening.'[26] The Red Lion, Truro's main coaching inn, was the venue for the club dinners in 1816 and 1817. However, in 1820 the club 'dinned in a tent pitched in the field for the purpose'.[27]

CLASS, CRICKET AND LEISURE

Heard's contemporary commentary gives an appropriate, if not a entirely accurate, picture of sporting activity in Cornwall in 1817:

> Hunting, shooting, fishing and other rural sports occasionally divert the leisure hours of the higher ranks . . . Cricket Clubs have recently become very numerous . . . The lower classes are addicted to athletic and pugilistic exercises, and their seasons of peculiar festivity are generally distinguishes by feats of wrestling, cudgelling &c in which they excel.[28]

When Heard was writing there was evidence of only three cricket clubs in Cornwall, with cricket being played at just five localities: Bodmin, Launceston, Torpoint, Truro, and Whiteford (sic).[29] More popular was hurling, yet Heard failed to mention it, despite its long-standing reputation as a quintessentially Cornish parish sport. Hurling was, however, an activity for the lower classes, which gentlemen avoided but for which nonetheless—as tradition demanded—they often provided prizes and patronage.[30] Tradition is a difficult barrier to break down. If the gentry had their hunting and fishing, and patronized for the sake of tradition—and to ensure social cohesion—some of the 'sports' of the lower classes, who themselves had wrestling and hurling, then where was cricket going to fit into the pattern of leisure? Even at the races all walks of life seemed to come together, the lowly rubbing shoulders with the great: 'Notwithstanding the threatening aspect of the day, and the discoursing state of the roads, persons of all classes, some on foot, some on horseback, and others in almost every species of carriage known in this county from the gay barouche to the dung cart hastened to the sport.'[31] Cricket, by contrast, though already a pan-class leisure activity on the village greens of eighteenth-century rural south-east England, had failed to take hold in Cornwall in the period before 1830.

Tradition, time, patterns of work, and the slow diffusion of ideas, fashions, and tastes were all factors that may have retarded the development of Cornish 'village' cricket in the eighteenth century. But issues of religious cultural identity were also significant in late eighteenth- and early nineteenth-century Cornwall, as Methodism began to take hold, and religion was one influence that did begin to challenge traditional sporting practices. Rule has pointed out that the Anglican Church in Cornwall had rarely confronted the conduct of popular amusements. William Carvosso, for example, who became a prominent Methodist class leader, recalled that 'I was borne down by the prevailing sins of the age, such as cock-fighting, wrestling, card playing and Sabbath breaking.'[32] In the absence of a lead from the Established Church, Carvosso and like-minded Methodists were determined to oppose such 'evils'. Thus the *West Briton* newspaper, noted for its reforming zeal, commented in 1823 on the annual feast at Germoe: 'On the present occasion, a body of Brianites, a sect lately sprung up from amongst the Wesleyan Methodists, made their appearance at the time of the hurling, and attempted to put a stop to the diversion.'[33] Such interventions were often successful. But as well as saving individuals from these 'evils', the Methodists—in opposing and even eradicating hurling and other activities—had created a space in which the more 'civilized' 'village' cricket might eventually appear.

As we have seen, in the case of the gentry, the pace of change and the consequent introduction of cricket as a leisure activity was some-what quicker, the gentleman of Cornwall taking the lead in introducing the game west of the Tamar. Yet, as Table 1 indicates, there was not a significant growth in the number of cricket matches until 1828.[34]

Patronage remained an important factor in sport throughout Britain in this period, as Malcolmson observes: 'while some of the traditional popular recreations were concluded fairly autonomously and their fundamental roots in the common people's own culture of social inter dependence, many others were at least dependent on the patronage, usually of the gentry'.[35] Cornwall did not have the large cricket promoters active elsewhere, such as Lord Sackville or Earl Winchlesea, and—paradoxically—the Cornish gentry (often no friends of the new Methodist activists) continued to patronize traditional sports. There is, for example, a two-column report in the *West Briton* of

Table 1: Cricket Clubs and Teams 1815 to 1830: matches reported in the newspapers

Club	1815	1816	1817	1818	1819	1820	1821	1822	1823	1824	1825	1826	1827
Bodmin (formed 1813				1		1							
Bude													
Callington		1											
Camelford													
Crowan													
Helston													
Lanhydrock												1	
Launceston			1										
Liskeard							1						
Looe													1
Lostwithiel							1						1
Penzance													
Redruth													
Sancreed													
St Buryan													
St Columb													
Stoke Climsland		1											
Stratton													
Torpoint			1										
Truro (formed 1813)	1	2			1								

Sources: *Falmouth Packet & Cornish Herald, Royal Cornwall Gazette*, and *West Briton.*

the celebrated wrestling match in 1826 between James Polkinghorn of Cornwall and Abraham Cann of Devon, where the importance of gentry patronage is made plain. As the *West Briton* noted, gentlemen were prominent amongst the spectators at this great event: 'The nobility and gentry of both counties [Cornwall and Devon] were seated in boxes in the upper tiers.'[36]

However, in the same year as the Polkinghorne-Cann contest, there was an important reference to Thomas Agar-Robartes and cricket. In the previous year, Agar-Robartes had gone up to Christ Church, Oxford, and he had no doubt encountered and even played cricket there: a gentleman's sport that he was anxious to see encouraged in Cornwall. The *West Briton* reported: 'A match of cricket was played on Thursday last in the pleasure grounds at Lanhydrock between Thomas Agar-Robartes esq. and a party of young Gentlemen and the Bodmin Club.'[37] The young Agar-Robartes became a member of the Marylebone Cricket Club in 1827, and was probably the first

Cornishman to gain entry to that influential and socially exclusive body.[38] The MCC would have had little direct influence upon cricket in Cornwall at the time, except in the dissemination of the rules of the game that filtered down through the channels of conversation or within the newspapers of the day. Although Robartes appeared to be a keen cricketer there was no noticeable expansion of the game at Lanhydrock until his son Thomas Charles established a 'club' there in 1859.[39]

Of greater significance in the development of cricket in Cornwall in the 1820s was the patronage shown by the St Aubyn family at Clowance. In 1829 Sir John St Aubyn, 5th Baronet of Clowance, hosted a match in his park where the team took the name Crowan: from the parish in which Clowance was situated. Sir John and his two sons had been to public school at Westminster, and would have seen and probably played cricket there.[40] Like Agar-Robartes, they wished to encourage the game in Cornwall. But there were important differences between the recreational cricket established at Clowance and the match previously mentioned at Lanhydrock. The Clowance participants were still noted as 'gentlemen' but their team initiated a series of matches of a more competitive nature between three newly formed clubs: Crowan, Helston, and Penzance. The *West Briton* noted: 'On Tuesday last the match of cricket so long pending between the Gentlemen of the Helston and Crowan Cricket Clubs came off at Clowance Park.'[41]

THE CHANGING FACE OF CORNISH CRICKET

i) Crowan, Helston, and Penzance: 'the triangular series' 1829 and 1830
In 1829 the *Falmouth Packet* newspaper went out of its way to 'congratulate the County on the late revival of the noble and ancient game of cricket'.[42] As Table 1 indicates, more matches were being played by 1829, and the establishment of clubs at Crowan, Helston, and Penzance —that played each other twice in 1829 and once each again in 1830—added considerably to the volume of activity.[43] All three places were within a ten-mile radius, and proximity helped to spread the game. There was also a deep-seated rivalry in trade, commerce, and civic pride between Helston and Penzance: and what better way to settle differences amongst the middle classes than by a manly game of cricket? The first match between the two took place upon Helston Downs, and the *West Briton* commented: 'The weather was so fine that a great concourse of people attended to witness the sport.'[44] The contest ended in a close victory for Helston by one notch, with the paper adding: 'The play on each side was excellent and well contested, not a disputed notch occurred during the whole day.' The same paper

concluded: 'Each party were so highly gratified by the day's sport that we are informed the Helston Club are to pay the Penzance Club a visit in a few weeks.'[45] The return match took place in September where numerous spectators were again reported, and although Helston won on the first innings, Penzance won the match by thirty-two notches:

> At five o'clock both clubs adjourned to Clarke's Union Hotel, where about 40 sat down to a very handsome dinner provided for the occasion. Several appropriate toasts and excellent songs contributed to enliven the evening and the party separated with regret at about ten o'clock after the enjoyment of a day replete with harmony.[46]

The full report of the match is twenty-seven lines of one column, including nine lines for the scores and eight lines upon the dinner: so as much importance was given to the social occasion as to the scores or skills shown in the match.

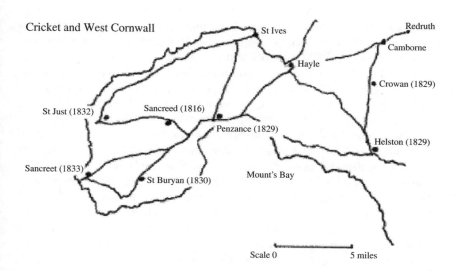

Helston and Crowan opened their encounters in the 'triangular series' of 1829, with the first match in August: 'On Tuesday last the match of cricket so long pending between the Gentlemen of the Helston and Crowan Cricket Clubs came off at Clowance Park.'[47] Crowan defeated Helston, 'by 47 runs . . . At the conclusion of the game there was much badinage and good humour reported on both sides'.[48] Penzance and Crowan managed to play each other three times in 1829. The first two matches were played within a few days at the end of August; Penzance winning at Clowance Park, and Crowan winning the second match at Penzance. Unfortunately, the third match was rain-affected but, undaunted, the players of both clubs left the ground, travelled into Penzance, had a meal and returned for a friendly game until dark: 'The Clubs dined together at Henwood's Hotel at three o'clock, but the weather clearing about five o'clock they again proceeded to the field and played a friendly game, which was soon put an end to by want of light.'[49]

A closer examination of the players from the Crowan, Helston, and Penzance Clubs provides an interesting insight into who played the game. The newspapers on more than one occasion refer to the players of Crowan and Helston as 'gentlemen', whereas the Penzance team are referred to as merely 'members of the Penzance Club'.[50] The Crowan Club was a mirror image of those well established up-country teams whose participants stemmed from the gentry.[51] The teams that played in 1829 and 1830 consisted of two St Aubyns, son and nephew of the owner of Clowanc Park; two Ustickes whose parents were minor gentry at Mawnan; Stephens and two Hills who were tenant farmers of Sir John St Aubyn. The local surgeon, John Vivian of Townshend, was invited to play in 1830, as was Willaim Millet, a yeoman farmer from Hayle. The clergy were represented by Revd Samuel Symonds, curate of Crowan in 1817, who by this time had become vicar of Philleigh, near Truro, and Alexander Vawdrey, a student at St John's, Cambridge who was soon to take Holy Orders to become curate of St Erth, a nearby parish to Crowan. The opening bowlers and key members of the club were Thomas Rutger a noted horticulturist and head gardener at Clowance, and George Becket, the estate gamekeeper.[52] One report commented on: 'The excellent bowling of those experienced players, Messers Rutger and Becket who are certainly superior to any in the western part of the county.'[53] Dennison recorded that there were three professional cricketers playing for Surrey and Sussex in the 1840s whose occupations were gardeners.[54] Neither Rutger nor Becket was a professional cricketer, nor were they 'gentlemen', but their country-house background and their cricketing prowess gave them entry to the gentry club of Crowan.

From the team sheet of the Gentlemen of Helston it can be seen that whilst the majority of the team that played against Crowan and Penzance in 1829 were indeed 'gentlemen' according to the definitions of the time, three of the players were not. They were tradesmen of the town, coming from the growing number of cricketers from the lower middle classes who were now taking part in the game—not as the professional cricketers noted by Dennison—but as amateur groups playing cricket in their leisure time. Of the players who have been identified, H.M. Grylls Esq. opened the innings as befitted his status as a senior player in age and his importance as a banker and solicitor from a notable local family. There were three other players from the legal profession, including Frederick Hill, later Mayor of Helston and Chairman of the cricket club in the 1850s. The three players from trades occupations were John York, a draper; Henry Sleeman, a chemist; and George Lanyon, an iron monger. They were in their early twenties and listed as assistants in their fathers' businesses, so were able to obtain time off work when matches were played on Tuesdays and Fridays.[55] The team included the remarkable Edward Shaw, born in Essex in 1785 and steward to Sir Rawlinson Vyvyan of Trelowarren. The *Cornish Telegraph* wrote in 1858 that 'amongst the Helston team was a cricketer many had heard about but few had seen, Mr. Edward Shaw, seventy years of Trelowarren, still has an arm and an eye that younger might envy'.[56] Many of the players were leading citizens of the town, the very people who were likely to form a cricket club. Although York, Sleeman, and Lanyon were from a lower tier of the middle class, Helston was a town club that built upon the town's foundations in trade and commerce, resulting in a more inclusive and broader range of people from within the wide spectrum of the middle classes. Cricket in Cornwall was no longer the exclusive preserve of the gentry.

The origins of the beginnings of cricket at Penzance are unknown. However, two of the town's early cricketers—George Beare, a banker, and Thomas Beare, a master printer—came from Norfolk: in-migrants who brought with them an enthusiasm for the game. Cricket had been played in Norfolk for much longer than in Cornwall, and Bale has identified no fewer than forty-two clubs playing there before 1837.[57] It is possible that the Beare brothers introduced the game to Penzance. The first team included three Coulson brothers: Charles, a hardware and general furniture dealer, Nathaniel, an ironmonger, and Thomas, a timber merchant who became an Alderman in 1839. There were two painters, a tin merchant, a blacksmith, a spirit merchant, a chemist, and Richard Dennis, a gentleman ship owner and land proprietor. All except Richard Dennis and Jonathan Higgs, the blacksmith, were under thirty.[58] Seven of the players lived within the borough of Penzance and, significantly, all were tradesmen: the social group described by Hobsbawm as 'the great mass of men, rising from modest, though rarely from really poverty stricken beginnings to business affluence'.[59] The growing prominence of this class was one factor in the changing picture of who played cricket, the lower middle class taking an increasing role on the cricket field, a pattern that was observable in

Cornwall as the changing pattern of leisure in other parts of the country was replicated west of the Tamar. The cricket matches as sporting events, together with the local rivalries they played out, were important in the development of the game in Cornwall but the social dimension remained equally salient. Meals were taken on the ground or held in the towns' hotels, and were important elements in the leisure life-style of the gentry and, increasingly, the middle classes who met together for after match feasting and male sociability: 'The toast; the song: the jest and beguiled the time to a late hour . . . The wine, so superior produced encore, when swift flew an order for six bottles more.'[60]

ii) Recreation and Feast Days
The second major factor in the changing face of Cornish cricket was that the game was played increasingly as a part of rural festivals and in an emerging network of village matches. For the Cornish, feast days were an important feature in the rural calendar. Each parish had its own particular saint—to which its Church was often dedicated—and the feasts or fairs held in his or her honour were kept on the nearest Sunday or Monday. In many parishes, sport formed part of the recreational activities held on those days and much has been written about this.[61] Miss Courtney, writing in 1886, recalled:

> St Just feast (which, when the mines in that district were prosperous, was kept up with more revelry than almost any other) is always held on the nearest Sunday to All Saints'-day. Formerly on the Monday, many games were played, viz—'Kook, a trial of casting quoits, farthest and nearest to the goal, now all but forgotten' (Bottrell), wrestling, kailles, or keels (ninepins).[62]

The extent to which cricket was being co-opted as part of these feast-day games is indicated in a report of St Buryan feast in 1830, by which time the changing nature of recreation in Cornwall—especially participation in cricket—was increasingly apparent:

> On Monday last a grand cricket match was played in the parish of St Buryan between the St Buryan Cricket Club and the club of the parish of Sancreed. The novelty of the game and being also the parish feast, a vast concourse of spectators assembled. It is worthy of remark that this parish on the Feasting Monday have been remarkable for their cock-fighting and badger beating, but the manly game of cricket

seems now completely to have superseded those cruel sports
. . . We are informed the return match is to be played at
Sancreed on Whitsun Monday.[63]

There are several points here that require comment. First, a glance
at the map shows the location of the parishes of St Buryan and
Sancreed in relation to Penzance, as well as to Helston and Crowan.
Cricket in Penzance had been revived in 1829 and there was a thriving
club, so that the 'novelty of the game' in the far west of Cornwall could
well have spread from there. Indeed, the concluding statement from
the newspaper report noted that 'cricket clubs are now forming in most
of the western parishes',[64] indicating the extent to which the game was
expanding at this time. Secondly, St Buryan Cricket Club was unlikely
to have been overwhelmingly gentry-biased and may well have included yeomen farmers, their sons, farm labourers, craftsmen, and
tradesmen. It is probable that, as the cricket match was played on feast
day—an event that was socially inclusive—then the emerging 'village
cricketers' of St Buryan (and other communities in Cornwall) were
becoming more like the archetypal village cricketers of south-east
England. Finally, although the newspaper alluded optimistically to the
decline of 'cruel sports', the *Royal Cornwall Gazette* in 1854 noted
the survival of badger-bating in Redruth.[65] The traditional features of
Cornish parish feasts did not die out as swiftly as Methodist detractors,
middle-class improvers, or gentry patrons had expected or hoped.

CONCLUSION

By 1830 cricket was being played across Cornwall, although its
popularity did not begin to equal that of the game in south-east
England. But, as Table 1 indicates, the number of matches played and
the number of clubs active had increased in the last three years of the
1820s. The table also shows the embryonic stages of networks based
upon locality: Liskeard, Looe, and Lostwithiel in south-east Cornwall;
Launceston, Camelford, and Bude in north Cornwall. In the early
years of the 1830s the west Cornwall network widened to include St
Just-in-Penwith and Sennen. As the networks became more complex,
so cricket was reinforced as a summer activity, its players from an
increasing mixture of classes. There were the gentlemen cricketers of
Truro and Crowan; the tradesmen cricketers of Helston and Penzance;
and the socially mixed villagers of St Buryan and Sancreed.

Cornish society did not embrace cricket rapidly, and although the
gentlemen cricketers of Truro adopted the game as early as 1813, it did
not expand as a popular leisure activity in Cornwall until the 1830s.
The development of cricket at Crowan was clearly the influence of one

family, a picture that fits the national pattern, but in Cornwall such influence was rare rather than commonplace. Instead, it was those cricketers from trade and commercial backgrounds in Helston and Penzance who made the really significant contribution to the development of the game in Cornwall. They were outside the gentry circle, so the town-based clubs that emerged were essentially middle-class and were tailored to their needs. It is probable, as we have argued, that the cricketers in the villages of Sancreed and St Buryan were from a mixture of classes: but for them cricket was still a novelty, in marked contrast to the game's status over the Tamar as the epitome of rural England.

As with all traditions, recreational activities did not change overnight. In Cornwall, despite the best efforts of their opponents, old ways did not die out: wrestling and hurling continued throughout the nineteenth century and beyond, while cricket took until 1850 to become established as a major leisure activity. In many places the season lasted from March to October, providing numerous opportunities for matches within the networks that had emerged. However, one significant feature of cricketing established firmly in Cornwall in the years from 1815 to 1830 was the game as a social occasion: a tradition that did not change with time—a match, a meal, and a song!

NOTES AND REFERENCES

1. *Sherborne Mercury*, 2 July 1781. See also H.L. Douch, *Old Cornish Inns and Their Place in the Social History of the County*, Truro, 1966, p. 59.
2. R. Bowen, *Cricket: A History of its Growth and Development*, London, 1970. See particularly a map: The spread of cricket to the end of the 18th Century, p. 50.
3. J. Goulstone, *Early Club and Village Cricket*, 1973, n.p.
4. Bowen, 1970, p. 35.
5. Douch, 1966. See p. 47, references to a silver-laced hat and wrestling, and p. 59 for Nathaniel Long and the White Hart.
6. J. Bale, *Sport and Place: A Geography of Sport in England, Scotland and Wales*, London, 1982, pp. 68–72.
7. See I.D. Clarke, 'The Development and Social History of Cricket in Cornwall 1815–1881', PhD thesis, De Montfort University, 2004.
8. F.E. Halliday, *A History of Cornwall*, 1959, repub. Thirsk, 2001, p. 306. By 1800 there were fourteen Turnpike Trusts operating in Cornwall greatly enhancing the quality of the roads.
9. P. Payton, *The Making of Modern Cornwall*, Redruth, 1992, p. 73.
10. Halliday, 1959/2001, p. 307.
11. J. Rowe, *Cornwall in the Age of the Industrial Revolution*, 1953, repub. St Austell, 1993, p. 238.
12. J. Palmer (ed.), *Truro in the Age of Reform 1815–1837*, Truro, 1999, p. 4. See also J. Heard, *Gazetteer of the County of Cornwall*, Truro, 1817, n.p.

13. C.S. Gilbert, *An Historical Survey of the County of Cornwall*, Vols. 1, 2, and 3, London, 1817, p. 104.
14. Palmer (ed.), 1999, p. 46.
15. P. Clark, *British Clubs and Societies 1580–1800: the Origins of an Associational World*, Oxford, 2000, p. 136.
16. An excellent description of the Truro Races is given in *Royal Cornwall Gazette*, 3 September 1825.
17. J. Palmer (ed.), *In and Around Penzance*, Penzance, 1997, p. 6 and p. 89. See also J. Thomas, *Ancient and Modern History of Mount's Bay*, Penzance, 1823, n.p. , lists the different societies and when they were formed in Penzance.
18. *Royal Cornwall Gazette*, 29 May 1813.
19. See G.B. Buckley, *Fresh Light on Pre-Victorian Cricket*, Birmingham, 1937.
20. *Royal Cornwall Gazette*, 23 October 1813.
21. Goulstone, *Early Club and Village cricket*, n.p.
22. J. Ford, *Cricket, A Social History 1700–1835*, Newton Abbot, 1972, p. 46.
23. Heard, *Gazetteer of Cornwall*, n.p.
24. *Falmouth Packet*, 8 May 1830.
25. *Royal Cornwall Gazette*, 27 June 1807.
26. *Royal Cornwall Gazette*, 8 October 1818.
27. *Royal Cornwall Gazette*, 27 May 1820.
28. Heard, *Gazetteer of Cornwall*, n.p.
29. See Table 1: Cricket Clubs and Teams 1815 to 1830: Matches reported in the newspapers.
30. J. Palmer (ed.), *Truro During the Napoleonic Wars*, Truro, 1992, p. 26. She makes reference to a prize of 2s 6d for each goal scored at the Truro Parish Fair.
31. *West Briton*, 8 October 1824.
32. J. Rule, 'Methodism, Popular Beliefs and Village Culture in Cornwall 1800–1850', in R.D. Storch (ed.), *Popular Culture and Custom in the 19th Century*, London, 1982, p. 54.
33. *West Briton*, 7 May 1823. See also *Falmouth Packet*, 7 September 1833, which reported that 'Lanson Races were attempted to be stopped by the Wesleyans stating the practices of racing as frivolous, cruel, impolite and unchristian.'
34. See Table 1.
35. R.W. Malcolmson, *Popular Recreations in English Society 1700–1850*, Cambridge, 1973, p. 56.
36. *West Briton*, 27 October 1826.
37. *West Briton*, 29 September 1826. A letter from the Archivist at Christ Church, Oxford confirms, 'Thomas James came up to Oxford in October 1825 aged 17', Judith Curthoys, 27 March 2003.
38. His personal account book shows an entry, 'June 16 sent to MCC £3', 1827 and subsequent years up to 1846 show the same amount. National Trust, Lanhydrock Archive.

39. Thomas Charles Agar-Robartes, 'Notebook, Cricket 1859–1861', National Trust, Lanhydrock Archive.
40. See D. Hartley, *The St Aubyns of Cornwall 1200–1977*, Chesham, 1977.
41. *West Briton*, 7 August 1829.
42. *Falmouth Packet*, 8 August 1829. See also Buckley, *Fresh Light on Pre-Victorian Cricket*, p. 46.
43. See Table 1.
44. *West Briton*, 12 June 1829.
45. *West Briton*, 12 June 1829. A notch was a run scored. A notcher was the scorer, runs scored by the team were notches/carved on to a wooden stick. See R.S. Rait-Kerr, *The Laws of Cricket, Their History and Growth*, London, 1950, pp. 32–3 and engraving.
46. *West Briton*, 16 September 1829.
47. *West Briton*, 7 August 1829.
48. *West Briton*, 7 August 1829.
49. *West Briton*, 16 September 1829.
50. *West Briton*, 4 September 1829.
51. Underdown, *Start of Play*, see chapter 3, pp. 44–66.
52. *Census Returns*, Crowan 1841, H/107/141, and 1851, H/107/1917. *Pigot's Directory of Devon and Cornwall*, London, 1830. D. Ellory-Pett, *The Parks and Gardens of Cornwall*, Penzance, 1999, p. 326.
53. *Falmouth Packet*, 5 September 1829.
54. W. Dennison, *Sketches of the Players*, London, 1846, n.p.
55. *Census Returns*, Helston, 1841, H/107/139. *Pigot's Directory*.
56. *Cornish Telegraph*, 21 July 1858.
57. Bale, *Sport and Place*, p. 72.
58. *Census Returns*, Madron and Penzance, 1841, H/107/143 and 1851, H/107/1918.
59. E. Hobsbawm, *Industry and Empire*, London, 1999, p. 61.
60. *West Briton*, 2 October 1829. Report upon the end of season dinner for Helston Cricket Club.
61. See A.K. Hamilton Jenkin, *Cornwall and its People*, Newton Abbot, 1983, and T. Deane and T. Shaw, *The Folklore of Cornwall*, London, 1975.
62. M.A. Courtney, *Cornish Feasts and Folklore*, Leeds, 1973. Reprinted from *The Folklore Journals 1886–1887*, Penzance, 1890, p. 3.
63. *Falmouth Packet*, 22 May 1830. See A.A. Clinick, *The Cornish Year*, Truro, 1926, pp. 12–13 for feast days and festivals in May.
64. *Falmouth Packet*, 22 May 1830.
65. *Royal Cornwall Gazette*, 27 October 1854.

RADON AT SOUTH CROFTY MINE: THE SOCIAL CONSTRUCTION OF AN OCCUPATIONAL HEALTH AND SAFETY ISSUE

Sandra Kippen and Yolande Collins

INTRODUCTION

In the 1980s South (Wheal) Crofty, an ancient tin mine situated at Pool, between Redruth and Camborne in Cornwall, became the centre of a controversy that was never properly resolved, and that demonstrates the conflict that may arise when discourses around an occupational health and safety issue are in competition. At the time of our story the site on which South Crofty is placed had been actively worked for centuries: firstly for tin, then copper, and finally for tin again. The mine under discussion was formed by the gradual amalgamation of about a dozen interrelated nineteenth-century mines in the area (themselves the products of innumerable earlier amalgamations), and had a history that reflected the vagaries of world tin markets, finally ending with its closure in 1998.

In early 1972 testing for radon gas at the mine was recommended by the Mines and Quarries Inspectorate as a routine precautionary measure. The presence of radon at this particular mine had not been seriously considered and the management did not appear to have any fears, directing the survey team to those areas of the mine, some of which were dead ends or far from usual workplaces, that they thought might contain high concentrations of the gas and its daughters.[1] But the management's confidence in the ultimate safety of the mine was misplaced, and this was the beginning of a turbulent time for both the mine management and the workers. There was a lack of clear

information about the meaning of 'exposure to radon', but the
management, nevertheless, was required to ensure that workers were
not subjected to greater levels than those prescribed and defined
as 'safe' by the International Commission on Radiation Protection
(ICRP). This powerful body, established in 1928, regulates the tech-
nicians of radon control and 'since its inception has been the one
internationally recognized body responsible for recommending dose
values for ionising radiation'.[2] These recommendations are
implemented in the form of legislation or codes of practice by other
organisations in different countries. In the UK, legislation in the area is
monitored and enforced by the National Radiation Protection
Board (NRPB). The NRPB had been established by the *Radiological
Protection Act 1970* 'to advance knowledge and to provide information
and advice about radiological protection'.[3] It is advised by the International Commission on Radiological Protection (ICRP), but modifies
that advice in line with the particular UK definitions as defined by
itself.

This article examines the events at South Crofty in relation to the
medical and scientific knowledge about radon gas from the 1970s
onwards. We see that this knowledge was used by the ICRP and the
NRPB to set workplace levels of radon exposure deemed as safe and to
monitor and enforce these safe levels measures at South Crofty. However, when miners developed symptoms suggesting over-exposure to
radon, the same medical and scientific knowledge (or, in this case, the
lack thereof) was used to deny them compensation.

The biomedical model has long dominated the occupational health
and safety area. If a doctor says a person is sick by virtue of their
occupation, then they are sick. If the medical profession decrees that
there is doubt of the relationship between the worker's condition
and their occupation, then the compensatory advantages of having a
disease caused by work are denied the sick person. Acknowledgement
of factors other than ones understood as 'scientific' would create
enormous difficulties in the management of the financial and legislative
business of society. It is much simpler to rely on the biomedical model,
through which disease can be clearly defined in physical terms.

Ever since the publication of Berger's *The Social Construction of
Reality*[4] sociologists and others have worked on the premise that
the answer to the question so ably put by Pontius Pilate—'What is
Truth?'—is that truth is whatever is constructed by those able to make
the best use of it. Nowhere is this more strongly demonstrated than in
medical field, yet it took considerable time for Berger's work to be
applied to the reality of medical knowledge. Once the realization hit,
however, medical knowledge became fair game for analysis by social

constructionists. The focus of the critique has been mainly the medical profession's use of its knowledge to validate its own particular favourite views or to further its profession in some way. Throughout this analytical process, the area of Occupational Health and Safety has been somewhat neglected, with a few exceptions which have a leaning to Marxist critique of employer-employee relationships; i.e. how medical knowledge is used to further the agenda of employers in their exploitation of employees. Thus has the social constructionist approach taken issue with the medical model.

This article does not propose a critique of medical knowledge as such (the 'facts' as already known should provide their own critique of that area). It builds on the theories already disseminated to propose that the same medical knowledge, and the same readiness of access to it, can be used very differently by different groups through their own discourses to further their own agendas.[5]

THE PROPERTIES OF RADON AND ITS EFFECT ON HEALTH

Radon is a colourless, odourless, tasteless gas, one of the noble elements. It is a by-product of uranium and occurs naturally, usually in crystalline rock, most notably in granite. It is diffused into the air in the proportions relative to the surface of rock exposed, or through dissolving in water. The solubility in water is inversely proportional to temperature, i.e. the colder the water, the greater the amount of radon dissolved. As water heats up the radon is released. In metalliferous mines radon may emanate from crushed ore or be carried in water and, where ventilation is poor and temperatures high, can be retained in areas of a mine in large quantities. The gas itself is harmless, but its decay products, commonly known as its daughters, attach themselves to aerosols or particles of dust or other impurities in the air and are breathed in by people in the environment—in our case, miners.[6]

Data about the effects of radon on health have been, to say the least, confusing. Early information was related to the effects of radio-activity from follow-up research on the results of the Hiroshima and Nagasaki bombings. This has been soundly criticized by some as inappropriate, as the predictions for other populations have been extrapolated using largely linear methods, and the possible differences between large, short-term exposure, as in a nuclear explosion, and small, long-term exposure, is claimed not to have been properly accounted for.

Various international studies have shown that there is an excess of lung cancer among uranium miners and even amongst some metal miners,[7] but the picture here is also confusing. Lung cancer is strongly associated with smoking and the histopathological challenge of differentiating between cancers resulting from different causes has, to date, largely not been met.[8] Most miners are, or at least were, smokers and to determine whether cancer is the result of that or of being exposed to radon is at present speculative, although crucial to the miners' claim for compensation. Evidence that smoking will greatly increase the risk of lung cancer through exposure to radon further complicates the picture.[9] However, there is increasing evidence of a link between radon exposure and lung cancer, if smoking habits are assumed to be in line with the rest of the community.[10]

Radon has been held responsible for a variety of other conditions. Considerable controversy was created by an article in *The Lancet* which hypothesized a relationship between radon and myeloid leukaemia.[11] There has also been some debate about links between radon exposure and prostate cancer.[12] A more recent study, however, correlated incidence of several major cancers with radon levels for postcode sectors of South West Britain. Non-melanoma skin cancer was the only one of the fourteen major cancers studied to show a significant increase with high radon exposure.[13] The authors of this study, whilst claiming to have shown that household levels are not dangerous, do not deny the 'substantial evidence' linking radon exposure of miners to lung cancer. Bernard Cohen questioned the scientific bases on which predictions about lung cancer and exposure to household radon are based.[14] *New Scientist* claimed that he had 'stirred up a hornet's nest' and quoted the UK's Sarah Darby and the USA's Jonathon Samet as criticizing both method and conclusions.[15]

An intriguing counter-view of the nature of radon in relation to health is that which defines it as a miracle cure. For example, Eben Byers, a well-known American industrialist, was known to have ingested four half-ounce bottles of a popular commercial tonic called Radithor, every day until he died of radium poisoning in 1932.[16] Although this is a historic view,[17] the use of radon is still prevalent in many areas. In 1997 the UK newspaper *Express on Sunday* described a visit to a mountain spa in Badgastein, Austria where, the author enthuses:

> Infused with a magical element called radon, the air and water here are famous for their healing properties. Arthritis and rheumatism sufferers report Lourdes-style after effects, particularly after a visit to treatment rooms in the tunnels under the mountain.[18]

The radon health mines of Montana are another well-known radon resort. These old mines, opened in the 1950s, now do a thriving business in offering 'natural' healing to tourists.[19] When South Crofty was struggling with falling tin prices and threatened closure during the 1980s and 1990s, the recurring joke (recounted in the mine's in-house magazine) was that it could always re-open as the Pool Radon Health Mine.

SOUTH CROFTY MINE

By the 1970s health and safety at work in the UK was well regulated, culminating in the *Health and Safety at Work Act 1974.* South Crofty miners, more than ever before, were in a position to know that their work was as safe as could reasonably be achieved or, if not, that they had the means to bring about change through union action and enforcement of legislation. They were confident in their ability to balance risk with benefit. The dangers of miners' disease, for example, were well known and had been for centuries. In the late nineteenth and early twentieth centuries miners' disease had been identified in metal miners as silicosis, sometimes associated with tuberculosis, and by the second decade of the twentieth century a high incidence of lung cancer was beginning to be recognized.[20] The link of the lung diseases with vitiated air became even clearer, and efficient ventilation was re-inforced as a preoccupation in mine planning. The efforts of employers to maintain healthy environments led to expectations in the miners of life expectancy similar to that of the rest of the population.

Genuine alarm was created by the revelation to the miners, through the 1972 testing by the Mines and Quarries Inspectorate, that the very air they breathed (which did not seem different from any other) was likely to cause cancer through exposure to radioactive gas. Some miners work in uranium mines, and there the risk is known and dealt with, but tin miners do not generally expect to work in radio-active areas. The South Crofty miners were understandably taken aback to find that they were at risk in a way similar to that experienced by uranium miners. The feeling about the sudden appearance of this new danger was put into words by a miner. 'Radon? I'd never heard of it. We were stunned when they told us. Normally you know the risks you take. But this was different. We were in danger without knowing it'.[21]

The South Crofty miners were familiar with risk. They may have even be perceived to thrive on it—if some anecdotes of 'daredevil' underground exploits are to be believed. They worked with explosives; they were not unlikely to be hit by falling rocks or involved in cave-ins; they sometimes worked in areas with poor air and even poisonous gases and the maxim stated by a nineteenth-century doctor that 'he is a miner and he must die'[22] has not entirely faded from popular wisdom. In spite of this, the radon discovery created a furore at South Crofty. Why? It has been suggested that radiation produces special fears because of, first, its association with the A Bomb, thereby linking it with terror and destruction; second, the publicity that attended the cancer cases at Hiroshima, linking it with cancer—'the greatest fear word in the US'—and finally that it is 'unsensed' and therefore mysterious and unknowable.[23]

The lack of clear information about the meaning of exposure to radon led to an uneasy silence, with the mine management taking action to improve and maintain ventilation and to monitor levels of ionizing radiation in the air using the fairly inaccurate, but convenient and speedy method Kusnetz method. Later, in 1976, a model of the 811 Instant Working Level Meter (WLM) was introduced. This was more accurate and allowed the ventilation engineer to measure levels of radon and to track the sources.[24]

The issue reached crisis point in 1980 when the *West Briton* newspaper[25] quoted a claim by a union member that a reading of radon gas levels in part of the mine were 'up to 60 times above the American permitted standard'. One of the most confusing things to the non-scientist about radon is its measurement as discussed in scientific journals. The measurement used at South Crofty was Working Level Month (WLM) i.e. the amount of radon gas to which the worker was exposed for the period of a calendar month. This was calculated by regular monitoring with the WLM meter, which measured levels of α and β radiation levels in the air in occupied parts of the mine, and by then requiring workers to log their movements. In the 1980s, when a radon technician, as distinct from the ventilation engineer, was employed, he set up a computer program to calculate the radiation experienced by each worker over a period of a month. Prior to this, calculations were carried out manually. Workers had access to their WLM score and if it was getting high over a period of twelve months measures were taken to put them in low-radon or radon-free workplaces. Should they exceed the safe working level set by the ICRP and enforced by the NRPB, they were subjected to a medical examination. (As the symptoms of lung cancer and other cancers do not appear for ten years or more after the exposure to the carcinogenic source, the role of the medical examination seems questionable—but such is the power of the medical model). Every effort was made by the mine management to keep the workers informed. Even the medical examiners (local General Practitioners) were required to question the workers they examined about whether they had any concerns or not and to record them on the medical sheet. Almost unanimously, the medical sheets showed that the miners represented themselves as content and not in any concern for their health.

The measurement of WLMs is in Becquerels/sq meter—a unit that has little relevance for any but radiation scientists. Other measurements are picoCuries and millirems. Some measure the amount of gas in the air, some measure the breakdown of the gas to radiation particles, others measure the biological consequences of the radiation.[26] They cannot be compared. It seems unlikely that when the miners came up with the levels of radon being 5, 10, 40, or 110 times higher than safe working levels they could have much idea of what those figures actually meant.

The other issue in measurement is how they the figures are calculated. The statistics pulled with morbid epidemiological interest from the radiation-induced cancers following the A-Bomb holocaust have been used to calculate probability of developing various conditions from a very high-intensity, short-lived exposure to radiation. Mainly linear extrapolations have then been done to determine the health effects of low-intensity, long-lived exposure. Bernard Cohen[27] has been a strong critic of the Linear No-threshold (LNT) theory which, he says, despite evidence to the contrary, 'continues to be accepted and used by all official and Governmental organizations'.[28] It may be that the relationship is not linear and that low exposure over a long period of time is more or less harmful than high exposure over a short period of time. Cohen's work has been reinforced by experiments carried out with mice in the USA which purport to show that low dose domestic exposure carries little or no risk of lung cancer. Sarah Darby of the USA refutes this approach and quotes her follow up studies of lung cancer victims which show a link between lung cancer and domestic radon exposure.[29]

If, as Lubin *et al*[30] hypothesize, the Inverse Dose Rate is diminished or disappears for low total doses, low exposure over a long period of time is harmless (or may even be therapeutic) and the setting of WLMs is largely pointless. It is much more important to know whether people have been exposed to high, short-lived doses. In South Crofty this was controlled for the miners, who normally were not allowed to go into high radon areas. However, other workers, such as the ventilation engineer or the radon technician, whose work of testing and maintaining good air carried them into all areas of the mine, would routinely come into some contact with high radon levels. It may only have been for a very short period, and their WLMs would remain well within safe levels, but the danger of their exposure to high, short-lived doses was unknown and, apparently, unrecognized.

In March 1980 the claim of dangerous radon levels at the South Crofty was reinforced by allegations of 'at least five deaths involving lung and stomach cancer'.[31] After a short period of industrial action, the company responded by doubling ventilation and issuing, at the miners' request, ventilation helmets to the workers. These so-called air stream helmets were the idea of the UK's National Coal Board's Safety in Mines Research Establishment and were manufactured by Racal-Amplivox.[32] The principles on which it was based were later shown to be sound[33] and the helmet, as well as filtering the air, provided ear muffs and goggles for further protection. However, its use in the mine was short lived due partly to the restrictions it placed on movement and mainly to its weight—about double that of normal safety helmets—an expensive exercise at approximately £50 per helmet.

Soon afterwards, further publicity was generated about some thirty-five miners who, in the early 1970s, had broken into old workings later shown to have high radon contamination. Ten years later nine of them had died of various cancers, there were three others suffering from cancer, and several others with what appeared to be pre-cancerous growths. The concern was obvious in a published photo of the union boss holding a 'fistful of death certificates'.[34]

The union maintained a high level of interest. In 1983 the General and Municipal Workers Union put out a newsletter with the headline 'New evidence on Lung Cancer Risk in Non-Coal mines'. It claimed that over 40 per cent of non-coal mines were exposed to dangerous levels of radiation before 1973 and that, although the number of over-exposed miners had dropped considerably, non-coal miners 'are one of the most heavily exposed radiation workers in the country, and the most heavily exposed non-coal miners in the world'. They then quoted new evidence from a study of Swedish iron miners showing that they were likely to double their risk of contracting lung cancer after less than four years exposure to the maximum dose limit.[35] This had prompted them to ask the NRPB to reduce the maximum safe level enormously and to ask the Department of Health and Social Security 'to make lung cancer in underground miners a prescribed industrial disease, so that benefit can be paid'.[36]

Although there was an enormous amount of concern locally, there was little discussion at a legislative level. An early approach in Parliament was made by Mr Street with a question to the Secretary of State for Employment asking him to list the mines in the UK which were affected by radon gas, and the current practice for protecting underground miners. The response was that only some Cornish tin mines had concentrations that regularly approached maximum levels recommended by the NRPB and that management and workpeople had been advised by the Mines and Quarries Inspectorate.[37]

This lack of interest was soon to change. In the 1980s there was gradually burgeoning awareness of the presence of radon in houses built over uranium tailings and some investigations were taking place. The radon 'scare' did not accelerate, however, until 1984, when the world heard the intriguing story of the American nuclear power-plant worker who set off a radiation alarm on his way *in* to work, having been exposed to more radiation in his home than he usually experienced at work.[38] Europe and the UK picked up on the issue and made the alarming discovery that Cornwall and Devon were particularly high radon areas and that many people were living (and had been living for generations) in homes that had what were perceived to have dangerously high levels of radon. It was at this stage, when radon was perceived to be a health threat to larger groups than miners, that the monitoring bodies took a more wide-ranging interest.

The discovery of radon in the domestic sphere increased the powers of the NRPB. Following recommendations from the ICRP and *Euratom Directive* 80/836 the *Ionising Radiations Regulations 1985* were introduced into the UK by 1986. Some felt that the advice from the ICRP used by the NRPB underestimated the risks posed by radon. In September 1987 at an ICRP meeting at Como, Italy, a signed declaration outlining areas of concern about the ICRP's current evaluation of risk, drawn up by Friends of the Earth and signed by over eight hundred scientists, was presented to members.[39] It claimed that, based on studies of A-Bomb survivors and occupationally exposed radiation workers, the risk of fatal cancer was currently underestimated by between two and five times, and that the issue of non-fatal cancers was not adequately addressed. It stated that 'although the epidemiological data shows inconsistencies, it is clear that recommendations should err on the side of caution'. It concluded that ALARA (As Low As Reasonably Achievable) should be rather ALATA (As Low As Technically Achievable).

Others have been critical that the evidence from the 1940s onwards used by the NRPB is based on research that is no longer relevant and thus overestimates the risk, placing unnecessarily draconian restrictions on both work situations and households. Philip Abelson is one such critic. He says of early research:

> Much of the mining was carried out in tiny openings so small they were locally called 'dog holes'. In many of the mines there was little or no ventilation. Thus radon and its daughter products accumulated in the holes together with excessive

silica dust. Typically the miners did not wear respirators. The
men had a macho attitude and respirators interfered with
efficient work. About 72% of the miners were smokers. Non-
smokers with them could not avoid heavy passive smoking.
From 1948–1960 inadequate ventilation was common, even in
large company-owned mines.[40]

Nevertheless, the NRPB used this data and methodology, mainly relating to miners and lung cancer rates, to determine risk for households.

Under the *Ionizing Radiations Regulations 1985*, firms were
obliged to appoint a Radiation Protection Adviser (RPA) who was
required to be an expert with appropriate qualifications in radiological
protection. This, of course, provided an opportunity for many consult-
ancy bodies to offer their services as RPAs to small firms whose
resources would be better used in employing outside consultants than
in adding yet more to their salaried personnel. The NRPB was quick to
offer its services here. Under the *Radiological Protection Act, 1970* the
NRBP had a role in keeping people responsible for radiation protection informed and advised. However, during and following the
Chernobyl disaster their role extended to also informing and advising
the public, a task that fitted well with those required of RPAs.

South Crofty was required to notify the Health and Safety Executive (HSE) about excess radon daughters, as well as take further
measures to restrict exposure of employees, to monitor all personnel
and classify those who received high levels of exposure. Classified
personnel then were required to undergo regular medical surveillance.[41]

The collapse of the tin price in 1985 increased the difficulties for
management, although this was partly offset by funding support
for essential mine modernization from the Department of Trade and
Industry. That funding was withdrawn in 1991, leaving it necessary to
open old levels with increased exposure of workers to radon. Despite
the continued application of the ALARA (as low as reasonably
achievable) principle, the figures show that maintenance of low
exposure was not always possible.[42]

Compensation for miners was not forthcoming and when the mine
closed in 1998 there were a number of outstanding compensation cases,
unresolved because of the lack of available medical evidence. Most of
the men were smokers and there was only one case of lung cancer in
the group, although there were several cases of tracheal and stomach
cancer, which some medical theorists claimed could be closely related
to radon exposure. The difficulties of making definitive links between
disease and exposure were reflected in the case of the death of a

sixty-six-year-old miner who suffered from lung cancer after reportedly working in a mine area contaminated with radon. The inquest was held with a nine-person jury to determine whether radon was responsible for the death. The local paper reported: 'The outcome of the inquest is being looked on as important as it could lead to a precedent with Cornwall tin mines possibly facing compensation claims from families from other miners who died similarly'.[43] The jury returned an open verdict in spite of evidence presented that research suggested a link between lung cancer and the mining occupation. The family solicitor expressed disappointment that no representatives from the NRPB or the HSE were called to give evidence, obviously believing that the bodies responsible for monitoring radon levels and ensuring workplace safety would support the case that long-term exposure to unsafe radon levels could be held responsible for lung cancer.[44]

CONCLUSION

As we examine the story of South Crofty we find that, following the discovery of radon gas, the understanding and use of the medical and epidemiological evidence evolved in different directions for different parties. This article has not made any attempt to solve the scientific riddles of radon. Whether short-term, high-exposure or long-term, low-exposure to the gas is dangerous or therapeutic is unanswered. The evidence to date indicates a link between radon exposure and lung cancer. But the management of confounding factors such as smoking makes the evidence less clear than we would like, and research and speculation about links with other cancers are contradictory.

In spite of this, the monitoring bodies put in place regulations and codes of conduct, prescribing in detail safe levels of radon exposure to which industries and households were committed. South Crofty mine was obliged, in a time of financial difficulties due to falling tin prices, to put in place expensive and complicated procedures to monitor and manage radon levels.

In sharp contrast, when the miners used the same evidence to demonstrate that they had been exposed to unsafe levels of radon (as prescribed by the monitoring bodies) and to claim compensation for symptoms relating to their past work (even symptoms of lung cancer, which link had been demonstrated), they were unsuccessful because of the uncertainty about the medical effects of exposure.

We see in this story that social and political use was made of the 'facts' as they were known. The more powerful organizations with international support gained power and status through using the facts to their advantage whilst the less powerful workers of a financially struggling tin mine were unable to support their case with the same facts. This is not a criticism of either party. It may be necessary here to put in the disclaimer that all but the earliest social constructionists found essential to prevent the misuse of their findings by turning them into a 'blame the victim' perspective. From this view, on the one hand, organizations are suspected of a conspiracy against disadvantaged groups or, on the other hand, physical symptoms have their reality questioned and purveyors of power claim that people suffering those symptoms are nothing more than malingerers. We do not claim that scientific organizations have conspired to misuse medical knowledge. Nor do we maintain that the suffering felt by people with symptoms described here is not real. Rather, the argument is that the social and political use made of medical knowledge is not necessarily in a direct relationship with the 'facts' as known and propagated by medical science. Facts are selected and emphasized in accordance with the social and political function of whichever group is using them. The story of South Crofty is only one of innumerable stories, providing a micro-view of the wider social perspective of power and use of knowledge.

NOTES AND REFERENCES

1. C. Dungey, J. Hore, and D. Waller, 'An Investigation into Control of Radon and its Daughter Products in some Cornish Mine Atmospheres', *Mining Industry* 88, 1979, p. A35.
2. K. Bowker, 'Proposals for Changes in Radiation Protection Standards', *Occupational Health Review*, August/September, 1990, pp. 21–22.
3. NRPB pamphlet, 'Living with Radiation', Reading, 1981.
4. P. Berger and T. Luckman, *The Social Construction of Reality*, London, 1966.
5. E. Willis, 'RSI as a Social Process', *Community Health Studies* 10:2, 1986, pp. 210–19; and R. Gillespie, 'Accounting for Lead Poisoning: The Medical Politics of Occupational Health', *Social History* 15:3, 1990, pp. 303–31; and K. Figlio, 'How does Illness mediate Social Relations? Workmen's Compensation and Medico-legal Practice, 1890–1940', in P. Wright and A. Treacher (eds), *The Problem of Medical Knowledge: Examining the Social Construction of Medicine*, Edinburgh, 1982, pp. 174–217.
6. D. Smith, 'Radon in British Coal Mines: Measurement and Distribution and Control of Risk', in *Safety, Hygiene and Health in Mining*, Harrogate, 1992; I. Lowndes and C. Sensogut, 'Computer Simulation of Radon Contamination Levels around Controlled District Recirculation Circuits', *Mining Science and Technology* 10, 1990, pp. 177–89.
7. M. O'Riordan, S. Rae, and G. Thomas, 'Radon in British Mines— A Review', in *Radiation Hazards in Mining: Control, Measurement and Medical Aspects*, 1981; J. Lubin *et al.*, 'Quantitative Evaluation of the Radon and Lung Cancer Association in a Case Control Study of Chinese Tin Miners', *Cancer Research*, 50, 1990, pp. 174–80; and C. Edling and O.

Axelson, 'Quantitative Aspects of Radon Daughter Exposure and Lung Cancer in Underground Miners', *British Journal of Industrial Medicine*, 40, 1983, pp. 182–87.

8. Edling and Axelson, 1983, p. 186.

9. C. Bowie and S. Bowie, *Radon and Health: The Facts*, Taunton, 1991.

10. J. Hodgson and J. Jones, 'Mortality of a Cohort of Tin Miners 1941–86', *British Journal of Industrial Medicine*, 47, pp. 665–76.

11. D. Henshaw, J. Eatough, and R. Richardson, 'Radon as a Causative Factor in Induction of Myeloid Leukaemia and Other Cancers', *The Lancet*, 335, 1990, pp. 1008–101.

12. J. Eatough and D. Henshaw, 'Radon and Prostate Cancer', *The Lancet* 335:8700, 1990, p. 1292.

13. D. Etherington, D. Pheby, and F. Bray, 'An Ecological Study of Cancer Incidence and Radon Levels in South-West England', *European Journal of Cancer* 32A:7, 1996, pp. 1189–97.

14. B. Cohen, 'Test of the Linear – No Threshold Theory of Radiation Carcinogenesis for Inhaled Radon Decay Products', *Health Physics*, 68:2, 1995, pp. 157–74. and B. Cohen, 'Problems in the Radon vs Lung Cancer Test of the Linear No-Threshold Theory and a Procedure for Resolving Them', *Health Physics* 72:4, 1997, pp. 623–8.

15. F. Pearce, 'Breathe Easy: The Threat from Natural Radon May Have Been Overstated', *New Scientist*, 16 January, 2169, 1999, p. 13.

16. R. Macklis, 'Radithor and the Era of Mild Radium Therapy', *Journal of the American Medical Association*, 264:5, 1990, pp. 614–8.

17. P. Frame, 'Natural Radioactivity in Curative Devices and Spas', *Health Physics* 61:6, 1992, pp. 580–82.

18. L. Thomas, 'Peak Fitness: A Visit to a Mountain Spa in the Land of the Von Trapps leaves Lesley Thomas on a High', *Express on Sunday*, 5 October 1997, pp. 59–60.

19. D. Kirby, K Smith, and M. Wilkins, *Radon Health Mines*, Roadside America, 2004, accessed 2 February 2004, available from http://roadsideamerica.com/attract/MTBASradon.html.

20. J. Samet, 'Radiation and Disease in Underground Miners', in R. Wheeler (ed.), *International Conference on the Health of miners*, Ohio, 1986, pp. 28–35.

21. J. Dale, 'The Mysterious Chapter of Death among South Crofty's Miners', *NOW!*, 4 July 1980, p. 13.

22. G. Rosen, *The History of Miners' Diseases*, New York, 1943.

23. R. Lapp, 'Cancer and the Fear of Radiation', *New Scientist*, 91, 1981, p. 1260.

24. Dungey, Hore, and Waller, 1979, p. A36.

25. 'Gas Fear Leads to Tin Mine Stoppage', *West Briton*, 20 March 1980.

26. D. Smith, 'Radon in British Coal Mines: Measurement and Distribution and Control of Risk', in *Safety, Hygiene and Health in Mining*, Harrogate, 1992, p. 499.

27. Cohen, 1995, pp. 157–74.

28. Cohen, 1997, pp. 114–19.

29. Pearce, 1999, p. 13.
30. J. Lubin, J. Boice, C. Edling *et al.*, 'Radon-Exposed Underground Miners and Inverse Dose-Rate (Protraction Enhancement) Effects', *Health Physics* 68:4, 1995, pp. 494–99.
31. 'Mine-Gas Talks Are Successful: Crofty Row is Settled', *West Briton*, 27 March 1980.
32. Author Unknown, 'U.K.-Developed Anti-Dust Helmet Poised for Large-Scale Production', *Mining Journal*, 20 February 1976, p. 141.
33. D. Wake, R.Brown, R. Trottier and Y. Liu, 'Measurements of the Efficiency of Respirator Filters and Filtering Facepieces Against Radon Daughter Aerosols', *Annals of Occupational Hygiene* 36:6, 1992, pp. 629–36.
34. Dale, 1980, p. 13.
35. Edling and Axelson, 1983, pp. 182–87.
36. General and Municipal Workers Union, 'Health and Safety: New Evidence on Lung Cancer Risk in Non-coal Mines', *News Service* 17, June, 1983.
37. Parliamentary Debates, Vol. 986, 18 June, 1980, p. 508.
38. V. Hutchings, 'Natural Borne Killer?', *New Statesman*, 30 August 1996, pp. 28– 29.
39. P. Green, 'The Response of the International Commission on Radiological Protection to Calls for a Reduction in the Dose Limits for Radiation Workers and Members of the Public', *International Journal of Radiation Biology and Related Studies in Physics, Chemistry and Medicine.* 53:4, 1988, pp. 679–82.
40. Hutchings, 1996, p. 28.
41. T. Morrison, *Cornwall's Central Mines: The Southern District, 1810–1895*, Redruth, 1983; and M. Howes, 'Exposure to Radon Daughters in Cornish Tin Mines', *Transactions of Institute of Mining and Metallurgy* 99, 1990, pp. A85–A90.
42. F. McAllister and M. Howes, 'Exposure to Radon in Cornish Tin Mines', in J.V. Bramley (ed.), *Proceedings of Health and Safety in Mining and Metallurgy Conference*, held in London 14–16 May 1996, London, 1996, pp. 111–23.
43. L. Hall, 'Dilemma in Death of Miner: Doctors Unsure whether Radon is to Blame', *Camborne Packet*, 16 September 1987.
44. *Camborne Packet*, 16 September 1987.

THE NATIONAL DOCK LABOUR
SCHEME IN CORNWALL

Terry Chapman

INTRODUCTION

The desperate and degrading scenes around the gates of Britain's major ports in the later nineteenth century, with hundreds of under-employed men fighting for the few jobs available, are well documented.[1] Movement towards national control of the dock-land's then casual labour force began during the First World War, made some progress between the Wars, and reached fruition during the Second. After the War, like much of the Attlee Government's sweeping social and economic reform, the National Dock Labour Scheme (NDLS) established in 1947 grew from its pre-war and wartime predecessors. Following pre-war voluntary schemes, winning the War had required compulsory central control of manpower in the vital port transport industry. The perceived benefits of such were to be continued in peacetime. State control of other key industries—transport, tele-communications, power—would improve their efficiency and social accountability. So too on the docks, where in particular a national control scheme would, in aiming to end casual employment, also seek to end the deprivation that had accompanied it since before the Webbs. At its height, before abolition in 1989 as part of the arguably equally far-reaching reforms under Thatcher, the NDLS applied to over eighty of Britain's ports, thirteen of which were in Cornwall. This article forms part of an examination of the workings of a scheme—designed mainly for ports such as Liverpool and London—in harbours such as Par and Portreath.

Writing recently in the series *Cornish Studies*, R. Perry has shown how 'economic options in one period result from events and decisions in previous'.[2] He used this path-dependent model to show how politically-influenced decisions in the nineteenth century regarding Falmouth's rail link could have helped reinforce the regional importance of Plymouth that continues to this day. Arguably and apart from the railways, development of the region's transport system is an illustration of what Perry sees as a mining-biased 'serious imbalance' in the research of Cornwall's economic history.[3] In small part this article offers some of the called for redress. Conventionally and chronologically 'reconstructionist', this is not an attempt to use Cornish experience merely as data to 'inform wider perspectives and contexts and test generalisations, models and theories'.[4] Nor can it really claim to be an attempt to contextualize Cornwall's experience to qualify as part of the 'New Cornish Studies'.[5] Rather the endeavour here is more the inverse: to illustrate the broader context by 'valorizing' or centralizing Cornish difference.[6]

As the decades since the Second World War mounted, so critics came to attribute much of Britain's relative post-war economic decline to Attlee's reconstruction package. The organization of dock labour in Cornwall is taken to show that as part of the post-war reconstruction programme, the NDLS grew inevitably from experience before, expedience during and expectations after the Second World War. With hindsight it may indeed be possible to argue that fulfilling promises of social reform made during the War did eventually slow Britain's post-war economy. But as this study will first seek to show, the period's 'political imperative' made a social reform package including the NDLS inevitable as well as necessary.[7]

The article is primarily a study of the NDLS itself: its origins, its rules, its organization. But while examining the Scheme, the three contexts in which it operated, the political, the industrial, and the local are also discussed. Each of the four threads will be shown to have followed its own, albeit linked-dependent path where events and decisions in one period influenced those in successive. The beginnings of Cornwall's port transport industry are first briefly outlined. Then, from their origins in the period of Victorian industrial horror, the NDLS and its political, industrial and local contexts are followed to the end of the First World War. The inter-war years of economic depression that affected Cornwall, and political re-alignment which did not, are next examined. The first half of this article ends with the organization of dock labour during the Second World War, particularly in Cornwall. This, it is hoped, will help to illustrate the fusion of necessity and social conscience that formed the Welfare State and managed economy, which characterized British society for more than the next thirty years.

Having shown how important and inevitable was Attlee's recon-struction package of which the NDLS was part, the second half of the article examines the post-war period. The same four threads will be followed, culminating in the dismantling of much of what had been put in place, including the NDLS, by the Thatcher administrations.

THE PORT INDUSTRY IN CORNWALL

The history of Britain's—and Cornwall's—maritime trade is a long one. There is, for instance, evidence that the Romans traded through a harbour near St Enodoc.[8] But as will be seen by 'fast forwarding' across the centuries, ports began to develop beyond the needs of purely localized trade to meet those of emergent industrialization. Hence-forth, a port's fortunes would be bound to those of the industries that it served. Like their umbilical railways, the ad hoc propagation of the nation's ports during industrialization would complicate later attempts to impose strategic direction.

Noall conveniently groups nine of Cornwall's trading ports into three groups of three.[9] In the east Charlestown, Par and Fowey expanded with china-clay extraction. In the west Hayle, Portreath and Truro were linked to the rise then fall of copper and tin mining. Finally, for Noall, the established ports of Falmouth, Penryn and Penzance emerged as general trading ports in the early twentieth century. Mousehole, St Ives, Porthleven, and Newlyn made up the rest of the thirteen Cornish ports originally under the Scheme.[10] But, traffic through them was such that they rarely featured in discussions of the Area Dock Labour Board (Cornwall); nor, therefore, do they feature in this article. These other ports do, however, confirm Roddis's observation that later in the twentieth century, 'What was once a full blooded flow from every port became confined to the export of china-clay from St. Austell Bay and Fowey'.[11] Under 'extra-Cornwall influences', an 'intra-Cornwall difference' becomes apparent.[12] The two main clay ports continue to reflect the fortunes of the parent industry. Mining and its ports on the other hand have all but dis-appeared, along with coal as a domestic and industrial energy source. As a result, and with other sea-borne freight moving almost entirely to roads and containers, all Cornwall's western ports remain at the point where Roddis found them in 1951: that of having almost ceased trading altogether. The shipping concerns that served Cornish ports followed much the same divergent pattern. While some local firms, such as HTP Ltd, examined below, once operated their own small fleets, there were also general freighting lines offering a service similar to that provided by road hauliers today. Hain's of St Ives was probably the most prominent among such locally, while Coast Lines and Everard's seem to have been the main national fleets to have plied Cornish ports. With waterside offices in Falmouth, Penzance, and Truro, Coast Lines—like Hain's—continued to trade under their own name for many years after being taken over by P & O. But both disappeared during the 'shipping revolution' of the 1970s discussed below. Family-run Everard's specialized in bringing in much of the coal for Cornwall's gas and electricity generating stations, when operating, and are still thought to carry china-clay to UK and European ports.[13]

DOCK LABOUR IN CORNWALL UP TO THE OUTBREAK OF THE SECOND WORLD WAR

Having very briefly outlined the history of Cornwall's port transport industry, attention can now turn to its inclusion in the NDLS. However, it is first necessary to establish the origins of the Scheme itself. As already seen the process started in late nineteenth century industrialization. Ironically 1989, the year the NDLS was abolished, was to have been marked by the TUC as the centenary of an important milestone in British industrial history.[14] The 1889 'Dockers' Tanner Strike', when London dockers united to force an increase in their daily rate from 5d to 6d (2.5p), is widely regarded as among the earliest stirrings of the modern Labour Movement. Then, in the years of widespread industrial unrest before the First World War that even reached the local china-clay industry, a strike in Liverpoool in 1912 spawned the first attempt to register dock labour.[15]

Into the story then comes Ernest Bevin (1881–1951): a man whose history it is almost impossible to disentangle from that of dock labour. From an impoverished background, before the Great War Bevin worked as an unskilled carter on Bristol docks before becoming a full-time official of his union. Part of his union role in the west was to seek new members including from among workers in 'decaying ports like Falmouth and Fowey'.[16] During the War the Government made dock-work a reserved occupation and established centrally co-ordinated local joint committees to run each port area, just as their successors would during the Second World War. Bevin helped represent his union on the Bristol committee. He later earned the sobriquet the 'Dockers' KC' for his appearance before the 1920 Shaw Inquiry into the port transport industry. Not only did he win acceptance of the two fundamentals of decasualization and registration underpinned by maintenance payments when there was no work; he also successfully publicized the plight of the labouring poor far beyond those on the docks.[17]

The problems faced by the industry then can perhaps be illustrated by brief examination of a strike on Hayle docks in 1916. Once the patriotic fervour accompanying the War's outbreak had dissipated, the numbers of days lost to strikes rose to reach just below six millions in 1918.[18] Most were over pay, as in the Hayle dispute between Bevin's Dock Wharf Riverside and General Workers' Union and Messers Hosken Trevithick and Polkinghorn. Always contentious, 'tallying' or load-counting errors had compounded the men's dissatisfaction with piecework rates in the face of war-induced increases in the cost of living. Any disruption to supplies of nitrate of soda for the National Explosives Company would, according to a press report, be 'a national and local calamity'. HTP, whose initials can still be seen above a 1911 date-stone on Truro's recently refurbished Poltisco Wharf, diverted cargoes to Penzance where there were no union men. A union-sponsored conciliation seems then to have brought about a temporary return to work at the previous rates of pay, so small wonder that the correspondence shows wrangling reopening a scant two months later.[19]

The Hayle dispute illustrates several of the themes recurring in this examination of the NDLS in Cornwall. Firstly, there is the impact on the national economy (taken as analogous with the war-effort). There is also a local economic impact on both employers and employees involved. Some 120 men were in dispute, most of whom were permanent, but the twenty-five 'slingers' at its centre were casual. Then cargoes could be redirected and worked, something that with the future solidarity of dockers would become increasingly difficult. The disappearance of HTP Ltd, complete with their small shipping fleet, confirms previously discussed changing transport patterns. Piecework rates underlay the dispute, and would remain a source of friction right up to their rancorous abolition in the 1960s. Finally, and while no contemporaneous comparison is offered, rates of 6d (2.5p) for the back-breaking effort involved in loading a ton of grain, or 7d for a ton of tin, seem by today's standards pitiful.

After his successful appearance before Lord Shaw, Bevin went on to forge the mighty Transport and General Workers Union of which he was the first General Secretary. In 1931 the second Labour Government had to re-inaugurate an Inquiry under Sir Donald Maclean with Bevin a member, to progress Shaw's stalled recommendations for registration and maintenance. By then 86,000 of the country's dockers, about two-thirds of the total, were in voluntary registration schemes in over thirty ports, including most of the major ones and three in Cornwall.[20] H.W. Whyte records that by 1934 Falmouth, Fowey, and Penzance had a registration scheme for dockers who by 1938 numbered 91, 170 and 90 respectively.[21]

Having traced the origins of dock labour registration, and in view of later criticism, attention can turn to the inclusion of smaller ports

such as Cornwall's in national schemes. The question of small port
inclusion might even be used to illuminate how other pre-war requirements needed to be consolidated during the Second World War and
became post-war realities. Local historian J. Higgans says of pre-war
Hayle dockers, 'Rarely were there sufficient ships to ensure employment for all and . . . there was hardship among them'.[22] While Whyte
does not list Hayle as having a pre-war registration scheme, he does say
that all docks at that time tended to attract 'Casualties from other
trades'; a floating population of the 'undesirable and unemployable'.[23]
Employers in ports such as the three in Cornwall may therefore have
wanted a registration scheme to prevent those displaced from elsewhere by the Depression swamping those reliably employed on what
dock-work there was. Subsequent wartime correspondence found
regarding the ports of Lowestoft and Yarmouth shows some of the
thinking on the other side of the industry, among employees, on
smaller ports' inclusion. As well as putting forward a by then strategic
need, their union also argued that men in such non-scheme ports were
disadvantaged through lower pay and no paid holiday: even costing the
disparity at 1/- (5p) a day.[24] It seems likely, therefore, that in smaller
ports such as Cornwall's both sides of the industry saw benefit in
belonging to the schemes that preceded the NDLS.

As will be discussed later, the popular and political mood at the
end of the Second World War when the NDLS was established was
hardly conducive to the withdrawal of ports from arrangements that
the war had demonstrated effective, both industrially and socially. That
is not to say, however, that there was not opposition—including from,
among others, the dockers themselves. Glasgow's dockers who, for
instance, left the T&GWU before the War because they disliked
Bevin's autocratic leadership style, apparently decried the efforts
towards decasualisation then being made by, 'Employers, trades' union
officials, or even well-meaning social reformers'.[25] The latter, of course,
probably including the above-cited H.W. Whyte.

Having struggled, the resurrected Maclean Committee could not
agree on how to make the pre-war Unemployment Insurance Scheme
work on the docks. Employers on the Committee insisted that benefits
should be met by contributions but the trades' unions argued that the
scale of the problem was by then far beyond that originally envisaged
for the Insurance Scheme. They wanted a special scheme within the
industry. The Government was finding similar problems across much of
depressed industry. Reflecting the then current wisdom, an Inquiry
into its finances recommended increasing revenue while reducing ex-
penditure, including cutting unemployment benefit. Fiercely contested
in Cabinet, C.L. Mowat decries as 'paltry' the £12.25 million difference

over which the second Labour Government split and fell. He also very neatly summarizes the result. For the next nine crucial years, 'British politics were dominated by depression and military aggression: the former leading to weakness in face of the latter.'[26] Bevin's opposition to both strands of the process needs final brief consideration.

Before doing so, however, and in continuance of this article's aim of where possible illustrating the national through the local, it is necessary to briefly sketch the period's local economic and political landscape. An important insight into the inter-war economy of Cornwall and thereby the national can be gained from the Murray Team's post-Second World War Survey of Devon and Cornwall: hereafter referred to as the Exeter Survey.

In the years leading to the Second World War, depending on whether involved in the newer, lighter, domestic or older, heavier, exporting industries, some parts of Britain fared better than did others. So too Cornwall. Here men were being laid off in agriculture, mining, and quarrying (together with their associated engineering): in other words the exporting port-dependent industries. With a familiar ring, the Exeter Survey found some compensation in employment growth in the less-well-paid service sector supporting wealthier in-comers and tourists. But, when the rest of Britain had recovered from the worst of the world trade slump, Cornwall's underlying economic and unemployment problems remained. The Survey's patronizing principal critique seems to be of the 'Proclivities exhibited by business enterprise' in Cornwall for investing in 'Purveying services [rather] than towards other types of production'.[27] Such caustic observations have subsequently drawn accusations of the Survey's 'undisguised contempt for much of what then defined Cornwall'.[28] But, it will be argued, such censure might at least in part also be attributed to a preference, prevalent at the time, for that very antithesis of Cornishness: centralism. How the War affected Cornwall's more 'onerous and significant' structural unemployment, and how the Survey thought it could be redressed, will be discussed later.[29]

Searching for the origins of the inter-war socialist movement in Cornwall, G. Tregidga links such to the growth in trades' union membership associated with the efforts of pioneers such as Bevin. Having increased during the Great War in the more industrialized parts of Cornwall, and among four groups in particular, 'railwaymen, quarrymen, *dockers* and lorry drivers' (emphasis added), union membership—and therefore numbers of potential Labour voters —continued to grow throughout the 1920s.[30] But these were desperate times, when unemployment in Camborne, Redruth, and Hayle averaged around 30 per cent.[31] Consequently, confidence in the Labour

Movement weakened and any hopes of an electoral breakthrough evaporated. Without the breakthrough seen as 'inevitable' in urbanized industrial areas up-country, Cornwall did not undergo the political realignment experienced elsewhere.[32] At the outbreak of the Second World War, Cornish politics were thus 'fossilized' in the traditional Liberal versus Conservative era.[33] Finally in this section, it is important to return to Bevin, with a brief examination of his career in the years leading to the Second World War. He was involved in economics and politics far beyond those of the port transport industry through the Maclean Committee. Serving on another Governmental Committee, that providing financial advice, bought Bevin into direct contact with John Maynard Keynes, with whose influential thoughts Bevin was 'fascinated'.[34] Then, at the 1935 Party Conference, he attacked the popular Leader of the Parliamentary Party, George Lansbury's pacifist support for disarmament through the League of Nations. Lansbury resigned, and leadership of the Party passed to Clement Attlee. Subsequently, in light of the worsening situation in Europe and under pressure from among others, Bevin (still General Secretary of the T&GWU and by then President of the TUC Congress), the Party dropped its opposition to re-armament in 1937.[35]

On the eve of the Second World War Bevin was, therefore, the most powerful trades' unionist in the land. On the docks, with which he retained a personal affinity and despite some opposition, voluntary registration schemes were operating in most major ports, and at least three in Cornwall. From near collapse the country's economic base was beginning to recover thanks in part to the belated rearmament programme. Cornwall, however, remained in the economic doldrums with its political landscape frozen in an earlier era. Playing a pivotal role in winning the war would require Bevin to introduce as an expedient the improvements to dock-land employment for which he had fought so long. As will be seen, it would also let him (with others again as a wartime necessity) try to help all those from among whom he sprang. From experiences before the war, compounded by those during, there grew inevitably a post-war social reconstruction package that included the NDLS.

DOCK LABOUR IN CORNWALL DURING THE SECOND WORLD WAR
When Churchill became Prime Minister in May 1940 Attlee, having indicated his willingness to serve in a coalition, became his Deputy. Other key ministerial positions also went to Labour, with perhaps the most significant (not least for the purposes of this study) being Bevin's becoming Minister of Labour and National Service. By voluntarily

inviting him to fill such a vital post, Churchill confirmed the importance of the trades' unions to Britain's war effort. Some might say that their importance to the peacetime economy, while somewhat dented of late, remains to this day.

Bevin's swift and effective taking control of the nation's wartime manpower was remarkable. Within days of taking office, the relieved War Cabinet had agreed to confer on him the unprecedented power to make anyone between fourteen and sixty-four years of age do anything he ordered. But he was surely right to believe that by ensuring that it was 'force by consent', or to use his own idiosyncratic 'voluntaryism', he would avoid more than infrequent use of compulsion.[36] His approving principal biographer, A. Ian Bullock, puts the approach in broader context. Unlike the regimes against which they fought, the 'right way' was to rely on people's willingness to make greater sacrifices than those into which they could be compelled.[37] But, by accepting the State's obligation to recompense sacrifices willingly made, the influence of his Ministry spread beyond health and safety in factories into workers' living conditions even their leisure time. Attlee's administrations would later recognize the need to compensate, on a broader scale, the demands that had been made.

From 1941 responsibility for controlling dock labour was vested in a specially formed independent body, the National Dock Labour Corporation—except in Glasgow and Liverpool which operated under a different Government Department. The Minister appointed the NDLC Chairman, with the rest of its National Board being drawn equally from each side of the industry. Under the National, a chain of similarly balanced Local Boards maintained a pool of registered labour from which employers could engage twice a day as they had always done. Dockers were required to attend eleven calls a week, with the Corporation guaranteeing payment for attendance in return for the men working anywhere required, including if necessary ports other than their own. By establishing as a wartime necessity the principles that Bevin had been fighting for since before the 1920 Shaw Inquiry, sometimes against the dockers themselves, were laid the foundations of the post-war National Dock Labour Scheme.

Addressing the first board meeting of the wartime NDLC, Bevin outlined the reasons for the Cabinet's decision to control dock labour through such. The primary need, he said, was strategic. But while it was vital that the docks had sufficient labour, by making the most efficient use of it the Corporation would also be helping to 'Resolve the major problem of casual work with which the industry had been concerned for so many years'.[38] Reporting to the House on the Corporation's formation, Bevin again first emphasized the scheme's strategic importance before again bringing out its social dimension. Interestingly, in light of recent experiences in the re-privatized railways, he also affirmed that as a Government guaranteed non-profit making Corporation it, 'Avoided the rigidity of State control yet gave State backing, and secured a certain amount of flexibility . . . without destroying initiative or enterprise'.[39]

Later that same month, when invited to address the Corporation's first AGM and with the need for shipping increased now that Japan and the USA had entered the war, Bevin could give the scheme's strategic need even greater emphasis. Nothing, including 'privileges', could be allowed to hinder shipping and any 'concessions' made should be recorded for restoration after the war. But he again concluded, 'A great social reform has been inaugurated.'[40] That the industry was therefore facing conflicting priorities is made clear in the Chairman's subsequent letter of thanks. In it he asked the Minister to write to the whole industry further disseminating the points he had made. The Chairman found it 'lamentable' that the eyes of 'some reactionaries on either side' were focused too much on 'The past or the future rather than the overwhelming needs of the moment'.[41] On a broader scale it might be argued that much post-war social reconstruction hinged on the dilemma then confronting the port transport industry. To meet the overwhelming needs of the present, future prospects had to be mortgaged in attempts to resolve problems of the past. The alternatives were too awful to contemplate.

By 1941, registers in the three main Cornish ports had fallen: Falmouth's was down to 82, Fowey to 102 and Penzance to 59. Hayle and Portreath, and Par and Charlestown had been added to the Scheme, with each pairing holding a register of 62 and 50 respectively. Therefore, despite the addition of four more ports, Cornwall's total of registered dockers fell during the early years of the War, from 351 to 305.[42] Continued national tightening of manpower had combined with a local fall in demand as a result of the reduced export of china-clay. It was a process that was to continue. In 1943 when operating experience was reviewed, and by which time a further seven Cornish ports had been swept into the scheme, Cornwall's total register remained at 299. By then, incidentally, on the other side of the industry thirty-two firms were registered as employers of dock labour in Cornwall.[43]

As already stated, the Corporation's wartime organization paved the way for much of the subsequent post-war National Dock Labour Scheme. The Corporation's joint National Board operated through a series of similarly balanced local boards. Cornwall's wartime NDL Corporation's offices were in Cross Row, The Moor, Falmouth (telephone Falmouth 888). During the War again as later, each area had a

Manager to allocate workers and who also acted as Secretary to the Area Board. And just like the Scheme that followed it, costs of the wartime scheme (including attendance money set initially at 5/- (25p) per turn proved) were met by a levy charged on the wages paid to workers by employers. The Corporation's first Cornish Board included some well-known local names, several of whom were still involved in 1947 when the post-war Scheme's Local Board first met.[44] The same process of wartime expediency influencing post-war planning can be found way beyond the port transport industry.

Assisted by enthusiastic observers such as the Exeter Survey, various official post-war planning bodies were working almost from the outbreak of the war. A full Cabinet Committee was then formed in 1943, with Bevin reportedly providing much of its 'driving power and ideas'.[45] The basis for the post-war Welfare State was laid in a series of White Papers issued by the Reconstruction Committee as the War ended. Of the series only two, however, need discussion here. To one, that on employment policy, this study will return. The other, that on social insurance and published in 1946, embodied much of the famous wartime Beveridge Report. Seen to have played a crucial part in winning both the war and the 1945 election, the Report warrants at least brief examination here.

On its publication to an enthusiastic reception in December 1942 (just as the tide of war turned at EL Alamein), many are thought to have glimpsed the future for which they were fighting.[46] Later, the differing commitment of the two main political parties to the proposals came to largely determine the outcome of the first post-war General Election. Unquantifiably but undoubtedly, Labour's concentration on Beveridge's adage the 'people's peace' helped secure their numerically massive win.[47] Later still, critics to the right argue that the Report and other nostrums of Attlee's bid for New Jerusalem were to contribute to Britain's relative post-war economic decline. What they may be overlooking, however, was the possibility that, 'The dynamic for social reconstruction lay in the politics of class: the price of working class participation was working class welfare'.[48] Without the promise of reconstruction, at least some doubt might have been cast over the extent of that participation. Their champion Bevin's main personal and ministerial concern was employment. In the House in September 1944 it was he who moved the White Paper that committed all future Governments to the pursuit of full employment. Keynes's ideas for the state's stimulating demand to grow the economy and absorb unemployment had of course provided much of the Paper's intellectual basis.

Bevin's approach to post-war employment, once the Normandy landings were successfully underway, can be illustrated by a return to the port transport industry. On the docks he started the demobilization process by calling a meeting between representatives of his Ministry and both sides of the industry. He told the meeting that, 'The Government [he?] had decided that it was impossible to return to pre-war casualism', and invited delegates to submit proposals for a post-war scheme. While supporting the decision, the employers' side believed that the post-war scheme should not include the 'very small ports'. Their principal objection however was to the continuation of joint control. The trades' union side also welcomed a permanent scheme, but they wanted its scope maintained and signalled the main sticking point by insisting that 'Workers must share equally in its administration'.[49] In their 'very helpful letter' responding to the proposals with some detailed points, Cornwall's Board sided with the trades' unions in opting for the continuation of joint control.[50]

Broader attitudes at the end of the War can perhaps be found in the report of the Forster Inquiry set up to arbitrate on proposals for a post-war dock labour scheme. In general terms on the vexed question of joint control, Forster thought it inadvisable to abandon such when the 'Need for closer co-operation of employers and work people in industry is much in the public mind'. In particular, and since the industry's workers had 'quite clearly expressed' their willingness to only work jointly, any other alternative was unworkable.[51] As will be seen, although joint control was retained, Forster's were not the last words on post-war dock labour proposals. Earlier in the War, Chairman's Reports to Corporation AGMs had not only illuminated the present but unwittingly perhaps, also foreshadowed the future: both on the docks and beyond. At the end of 1943, reporting a worrying increase in the number of unofficial stoppages (most not very long, but cumulatively disruptive to the war effort), the Chairman thought it important in an organization 'as democratic as industry today' to remember that 'democratic freedom carries with it a duty to observe obligations'.[52] He called for union support in dealing with such disruption. The same tension between state, management, union, and men will be seen during the later discussed post-war corporatist period. On a more positive note, as well as tangible improvements such as the introduction of welfare and training schemes, he could also proclaim the Corporation's National and Local Boards as, 'Pioneers . . . showing that labour and management sides of industry can both associate successfully in the direction of an undertaking'.[53] On the docks and beyond, it has now been shown how thinking during the war that addressed problems from before came to shape Britain after. Critical of the Conservatives' pre-war record, enough of what today might be termed 'middle Britain' tentatively joined the customary support in accepting what Labour politicians and their intelligentsia were proffering. But based mainly on the urban industrialized areas, Labour's huge Commons majority in 1945 (393 seats to the Conservatives' 213) tended to mask the 'more modest nature of its popular support'.[54]

As before the war, locally the electoral outcome differed from that up-country. Although the ten years of momentous change between elections spanning the war make comparison difficult, some challenges were bring made to the 'isolated world of Southwest politics'. Younger voters in Falmouth and Penryn, when added to those of the unionized industrial workers drafted in to expanded factories around Camborne probably helped Labour to their famous first Cornish win in the Falmouth and Camborne constituency.[55] Elsewhere, the county continued its pre-war ossification with the Liberals and Conservatives dividing the four remaining Cornish seats between them.

Finally and briefly, it is necessary to turn to the local economic picture at the end of the war, as depicted by the Exeter Survey. Having forced an increase in manufacturing and corresponding contraction of the service sector the War had, 'Profoundly re-cast the pre-war shape and structure of the survey region's economic life'.[56] Continuing to show its patronizing but prevalent preference for centralism, the Survey claims that it was in the 'highest interests of this country —indeed essential' for Devon and Cornwall to be 'modernising and extending capital equipment'. On port transport, with which this study is primarily concerned, what today would be termed a cost-benefit analysis would decide the 'reasonably strong' case for expanding the port of Plymouth together with its road and rail links. A similar process could also be applied to the region's minor ports: all of which they list incidentally being in Devon. Cornwall's ports, notably Padstow and St Ives, apparently only needed consideration in support of fishing.[57] Their ignoring the clay ports is surprising, since as will be seen, exports including clay would be vital in paying for what the Survey somewhat disdainfully dubs 'The social reforms to which the nation has committed itself, the chief of which is the raising of the living standards of *the* poorer people' (emphasis added).[58]

In later decades of the twentieth century a body of opinion, articulated by the historian C. Barnett, attributed much of Britain's relative post-war economic decline to the Attlee reconstruction package. The Barnett school of thought suggests that a short-term policy of 'parlours before plant' had disastrous long-term consequences.[59] This article, through the medium of dock labour in Cornwall has so far supported the rebuttal of the first part of such a view, in that it overlooks the period's political imperative.

Always vulnerable, casually employed dock-workers had suffered particularly during the depressed inter-war years. Dockers and their contribution to winning the war have been taken here to represent much of Britain's then labouring poor. Crucial as Minister of Labour their champion Bevin helped secure decasualization for dockers, with the process again being taken to represent social improvement for the whole strata from which he sprang. Thankfully it is impossible to know how long or well British working people would have fought without the promise of social reconstruction. Without such, however, it is at least possible that the alternatives offered by their Axis enemies or Soviet allies might have been considered. Even on American tick, reconstruction including the NDLS must have been better than defeat or revolution.

THE NDLS IN CORNWALL: AN ILLUSTRATION OF THE POST-WAR PERIOD
As well as arguing that Barnett paid insufficient attention to the period's political realities, the previously cited P. Addison also criticizes the Barnett thesis for its selectivity in centring on one factor, the Welfare State, and one Government, Attlee's. Notwithstanding early accusations of narrowness, the remainder of this article will be seen to perhaps offer more support for the later-stated broader Barnett view that the efforts of successive post-war Governments to sustain full employment, 'Retarded modernisation' by 'Enabling unions and workers to resist technological change'.[60]

To argue the economics of such a proposition would exceed the scope of this study. Rather the endeavour here will be to illustrate it at the local, political, and industrial level: in other words, the three contexts in which the NDLS has been seen throughout this article. It will first be shown that Attlee's economic and social aims were almost wrecked on the docks. Then, after a few years of relative economic growth, dock-land disruption—both local and national—confirmed the need for modernization attempted by Wilson after 1964. Dock labour's modernization followed an Inquiry by Lord Devlin, but resistance to change again resulted in massive disruption. The Heath Government's failed attempts to deal with such contributed to their downfall, as it had to Wilson's. Labour's second attempt, the Social Contract under first Wilson again then Callaghan, while sunk on a wider sea will seen to have at least been harried by dock-side reaction. Increasing mechanization's slashing numbers needed on the docks had reduced the impact of such. Consequently, once Thatcher had 'dealt' with the miners, dockers were not the force they had been when confronting Heath. Major changes in its national political and industrial contexts can therefore be seen through the local workings of the NDLS in Cornwall.

The balanced NDLS Boards acted as a two-way conduit linking dock work with dock-workers. As such, their first concern was always to ensure that the number of workers matched the work available. Both locally and nationally, the story of the NDLS is therefore largely one of declining numbers in the face of increasing mechanisation. The process reached a point where Colonel Oram called his review of a lifetime in the industry *The Docker's Tragedy*.[61] By the early 1970s, when Devlin finally provided the security that dockers had so long sought, technology was all but doing away with the need for them. That is not to say, however, that there were no further attempts to extend the Scheme.

THE NDLS IN CORNWALL: FROM ESTABLISHMENT TO DEVLIN 1947–1965

Unprecedented levels of state involvement in the economy had helped win the Second World War. Following their ambiguous 1945 election victory, and with an ideological commitment also stretching back to the Webbs, Labour would take into public ownership the evocative if ill-defined, 'Commanding heights' of the economy. However, other than the ultimately diluted attempt to nationalize all transport, the original nationalization programme did not directly affect dock labour. The complementary railways were of course nationalized, as were two of the then major port users, gas and electricity production. Added to such indirect influences, the make up of the Dock Labour Scheme's Boards, both national and local, called for worker involvement in its administration.

A complete set of the minutes of Cornwall's Area Dock Labour Board has been retained in the Cornwall Record Office and forms the basis for the remainder of this study.[62] Assistance in gaining access is gratefully acknowledged; as is that of other agencies accredited in the endnotes of this chapter.

The Area Dock Labour Board (Cornwall), made up of one employers' representative and one employees' from the western ports and a similar pairing from the eastern, first met in November 1947. Having elected chairmen from among themselves, the Board agreed to alternate their monthly meetings between Falmouth and Fowey. They also purged the wartime registers of dormant dock-workers and employers. The first firm post-war statement of the number of dock-workers in Cornwall was in October 1949: when there were some 80,000 dockers in total, Cornwall's were reduced from 275 to 260. A total of thirteen original port employers have been inferred from the

Board's early minutes. Among early discussion of various minor works were a new call-stand at Fowey, and improvements to the mess-rooms at Par and Hayle. Two new, identical headquarters buildings were also proposed locally, and eventually approved by the National Board. Of the two substantial buildings, that in Trevethan Road, Falmouth, has recently been repainted and re-let, the other is believed to be still in use within Fowey Docks.

Variations in demand for labour among the ports of Cornwall, and Plymouth, were met by transferring workers between them. Initially, the Board considered transfer to and from Plymouth, 'Impractical . . . [and] . . . very expensive' (10/49). But travel between any port by early 1950s public transport cannot have been easy. In addition, the requirement was fraught with organizational difficulties. Fowey men, having risen at 0500, refused to work over-time beyond 2100 at Falmouth (11/49). 'Not desirable' was how the Board viewed Charlestown men who had also worked beyond 2100, being required to transfer to Plymouth or western ports early the next morning (3/51). Plymouth men were transferred to Par, releasing others to transfer to western ports (7/53). Ten years later, with presumably improved transport links, the Board noted the first ever transfer of Plymouth men direct to west Cornish ports (6/63).

In those areas to which it applied, the Scheme defined both dock-workers and dock-work. As will be seen, the Scheme's geographic and practical scope was later to become increasingly contentious. The Scheme never applied to liquid cargoes or to the landing of fish catches by the crew, but there arose plenty of local 'definition disputes' to illustrate its original scope. The Board decided that timber stacking at Par came within the definition, but the landing of shingle from 'self-trimmers' at Truro did not (1/55; 11/56). Rowe and Co. had to register as port employers in Hayle when the Ministry of Food gave up responsibility for importing potatoes (10/55). Penryn Council was reminded that although fish catches were outside the definition, the landing of boxed fish came within (2/58).

The Local Board's minutes also provide a useful insight into the period's more general world of work. One noticeable feature is a difference in attitude to what today might be termed health and safety issues. Harvey's were informed that it was not the Board's responsibility to provide protective clothing for the working of cargoes of cement (9/52). While safety boots were available on signature for work at ICI in Hayle, a later price list of industrial gloves and goggles needed only to be '[b]rought to the workers' attention' (2/52; 5/57). In an extraordinary incident, following complaints by other bus passengers, the men were asked to exercise 'reasonable care' with their clothing, and the Truro employer agreed to provide shovels rather than have them carry their own (11/54).

Costs of the Scheme, including the provision of 'attendance money' when there was no work, were met by a levy on the wages paid by employers to their allocated workers. In 1955 the levy was 13 per cent of wages paid for handling overseas cargoes, and 9 per cent for coastal.[63] One of the reasons for the Scheme's not being introduced until 1947 was opposition to its costs and complexities among port employers. Locally, such opposition is known to have been largely overcome by the influential and respected Mr M.J. Kenna.[64] For his work in preparing Cornwall's ports for the Scheme, and then as its first Area Manager who also acted as the Board's Secretary, Mr Kenna was subsequently recognized with its Meritorious Service Award (12/62).

But it was not only employers who objected to the Scheme. Its introduction coincided with a series of major unofficial stoppages, forcing the Attlee Government repeatedly to use troops to keep vital imports and exports moving during the austere early post-war years.[65] While there were many other factors, at the centre of the disputes M.P. Jackson identifies the dockers' unwillingness to cede control.[66] For instance, the Scheme forced the breaking of the prevalent 'Three days on the hook; three days on the book' outlook.[67] Added to which, its system of joint control, including the exercise of discipline, led some workers to question on whose side were their supposedly representative members of Local and National Boards. Consequently, as the gap between union membership and its leadership widened, there arose in the industry a powerful 'unofficial movement'. At the local level, a study of papers from the Scheme's introductory period revealed other causes of discontent, but only a half-day strike at Penryn involving the new Scheme's terms. The Board had suspended a worker for refusing to work overtime.[68] While, as has been noted, the docks were something of an exception, one reason for the success of the Attlee Governments in achieving their policy goals was the support given by the trades' union movement. 'Informal rules' were observed that saw wage restraint exercised by one side in return for full employment and social reform by the other.[69] The benefits of acquiescent trades' unions were not lost on the incoming Conservatives who put the emollient Sir Walter Monckton in charge of keeping the unions sweet.[70] But, as Britain's economy grew during the 1950s, so too did pressure for change within the labour movement. R. Taylor interprets left-wing Frank Cousins's TUC address in September 1956 denouncing pay restraint as '[m]arking the end of the era' of industrial relations consensus.[71]

Following further national disruption on the docks, Mr. Justice

Devlin's (a name also to become closely linked to the story of the NDLS) first Inquiry into the industry in 1956 was highly critical of the employers' attitude to the Scheme. Rather than one of patronage, they were encouraged to accept it as 'a partnership of equals'.[72] The employers subsequently dropped their continuing quest to end joint control, with application of the Scheme's disciplinary powers relaxed and disruption consequently reducing.

Locally, the number on Cornwall's register of dockers remained stable between 1952 and 1957 at around 250. This five-year 'boom' period of never-repeated stability was only 4 per cent down on the 1949 figure. Over the following five years Cornwall's register fell to 200: a drop of 20 per cent on the 1957 figure (12/62). At the start of the decade, R. Perry reports unprecedented levels of employment in Cornwall. By its end, when journalist G. Moorhouse set out to find *The Other England*, he found Cornwall with the highest unemployment rate, singling out Falmouth as the worst in the country.[73] Throughout this study the operation of the NDLS in Cornwall is taken to represent wider applicability. So, while the impact of an economic downturn might be greater in Cornwall, it reflects the national picture.

Prime Minister Macmillan's 1957 claim that many people had 'Never had it so good' came with a caution that such a position might not last.[74] Concern about the nation's apparent prosperity but paradoxical decline in comparison to others, sparked a number of official and unofficial investigations. Indeed, the title of one of the latter is now often taken to delineate the last years of Macmillan-style one-nation Toryism. In his *The Stagnant Society*, M. Shanks attributed much of the perceived stagnation to Britain's still antediluvian industrial relations.[75] Retrospectively, K. Jeffery sees much of the electorate's dissatisfaction with the Tories at the 1964 election stemming from their failure to modernize themselves and the country.[76]

But before going on to examine the changing political context, we shall return to the industrial with a brief examination of one of the period's self-critical official inquiries. Among the shortcomings identified by Lord Rochdale's 1962 assessment of the efficiency of Britain's major ports was the continuing volatility of casual labour.[77] Within months of coming to power in 1964, the Wilson Government commissioned the by then Lord Devlin to follow up Rochdale's earlier observations on dock-labour. Having quickly settled the pay dispute that actually triggered their establishment, the Committee reported on the two other parts of their remit, decasualization and dissent, in August 1965. The nine main reasons they identified for the industry's ills need not detain this narrative, suffice to say that at their heart was the conclusion that it was still casual labour that fostered casually disruptive attitudes.[78]

Local evidence in support of that conclusion can perhaps be inferred from some of the problems then associated with the transfer of workers between ports. Three Plymouth men were involved in an 'altercation' over meal times at Fowey, and although found in breach of the Scheme, were still entitled to 'Dead-time Money' for the turn in question (12/59; 2/60). Harvey's twice complained about the handling of MV *Vectis Isle* in Truro by combined gangs of Truro and Falmouth men (8/61; 5/62). Another Truro employer (Waters & Son) complained about the number of stoppages for a smoke, while ICI at Hayle thought it unreasonable to be required to take men back to the mess-room for tea-breaks (10/62;6/60).

Devlin aimed finally to end dock-land casual employment, and its consequential disruptively casual attitudes, by first of all doing away with the casual employer. In future, employers had to be deemed capable of discharging the Scheme's obligations to be licensed as such. Dock-workers, rather than pooled as hitherto, would then be permanently attached to individual licensed employers. In this allocation of workers to specific employers, Devlin marked the biggest revision of the NDLS. But while introducing that major change, Devlin retained the Scheme's original system of controlling recruitment, registration, discipline, and termination through Local Boards under the National. Critically, as will be seen, despite impending massive changes in handling techniques, the definition of dock work was also left untouched. Decasualization of employers came first with the Docks and Harbours Act of 1966, followed by that of employees under the 1967 Dock Labour Order. Before decasualization, there had been some 1,200 employers operating in Britain's then 83 Scheme ports. With licensing under the 1966 Act, employer numbers reduced to 428 of which London alone still had 165, four of whom employed over 1,000 men each.[79] In Cornwall on the other hand, there were only nineteen employers licensed initially who, after the voluntary redundancy that accompanied the 1967 Order, employed 145 between them (10/67).

Initially, employers in Cornwall's ports requested exemption from the 1966 Act through their respective professional associations (5/66). Of the local authorities required to license employers in Cornwall's municipal ports (Truro, Penryn, and Penzance), Truro's reaction was examined in detail and confirms that they too balked at the arrangement's costs and complexities.[80] In three of Cornwall's privately owned ports (Par, Charlestown, and Hayle) the only operating company was anomalously required to license itself. But Sir George Honeyman, who considered reactions to Devlin, did not accept such peripheral objections, nor the trades' unions' counter-argument for extending the Scheme to all Britain's three hundred or so ports. In his view, Devlin marked such a departure that its impact needed to become clearer before the Scheme's scope was altered in either direction.[81]

The docks were to be 'modernized' (watchword of the incoming Wilson Government) through the implementation of Devlin's two-part recommendations. As has been seen, the first part had finally ended casual labour in the industry, and as will be seen, the second part completely restructured its pay system. But, at the same time as the industry faced such organisational upheaval, it was also facing an equally far-reaching technological revolution. The size of the task can be seen when Colonel Oram speaks of his disbelief in 1967 at seeing, 'Ships that took a week to discharge with 200 men being turned around by 13 in one tide.'[82]

THE NDLS IN CORNWALL: FROM DEVLIN TO ABOLITION 1965–1989

So far the post-war section of this article has traced the operation of the NDLS, both nationally and locally, through its changing political context from Attlee's nationalization to Wilson's modernization. It has also touched upon impending technological change. In the final section, industrial change continues and coincides with further changes in the political context, from Wilson's reforms to Thatcher's abolition. But the section starts with changes at the local industrial level. As has previously been suggested, the primary function of the Local Dock Labour Boards was to ensure that the number of dockers registered matched the work available. In the early 1960s, Cornwall's Board's minutes show that numbers in the west were falling as demand in the east was rising.[37] The reasons for the differing demand, seen more clearly once dockers were attached to specific employers as required by Devlin, serve to illustrate something of a disparity in the local industrial climate throughout the period.

One of the reasons for the falling demand for dockers in western ports was the move away from coal for power production. Hayle and Falmouth's sea-supplied coal-burning gas-works were closed in the late 1950s, those in Penzance and Truro, in the mid-1960s. Hayle's power station went in the next decade. A number of national carriers also disappeared from local ports, their trade probably switching to road, while traffic through Portreath fell to a point where its register was closed and the two remaining dockers transferred to Hayle (4/64). The dockside in Portreath was given over to local needs housing and car parking, while filling in part of the harbour itself provided parking in Penzance. It was of course an up-turn in china-clay that fuelled the opposite increasing requirement for men in the eastern ports. The modernization of Par at the start of the 1960s, coincident with the upswing, had extended its clay-ship handling capacity to eleven. Deep-water Fowey and tiny Charlestown were later also modernized, in 1968 and 1971 respectively. Just like the introduction of the Scheme itself, Devlin's changes were met nationally by an upsurge in unofficial strike activity.[83] Again, just as during the turbulent early post-war years, a search of the period's papers did not find the national pattern repeated locally. In a study trying to use the local picture to illuminate the national, this repeated difference perhaps needs some explanation. One analysis has suggested that while port size and complexity may account for some of the disparity, reactions to the Scheme also con-tributed. In the larger ports, the 'costs' of the NDLS (forfeiture of right to work when/where/for whom liked, formalized disciplinary code, and so forth) outweighed its 'benefits' (security even during periods of underemployment, physical amenities, and so forth). The result was high levels of unrest. In the smaller ports, such as Cornwall's, the opposite was of course the case. Benefits were perceived as out-weighing the costs, and relations were correspondingly less torrid.[84]

Even so, there is evidence of difficulties in the clay ports over modernizing the industry rather than the Scheme. A dispute was apparently preventing the requested recruitment of five more men each for Par and Fowey until an 'experimental productivity agreement' was introduced following investigation by the T&GWU's Dock Officer (Tom O'Leary) (8/69; 10/69). Soon afterwards the Local Board was to note that without recruitment, 'Previous acute labour shortages had been effectively reduced' (6/70). But, just over a year later after ECC (Ports) Ltd had warned of a 'continuing recession', the Local Board agreed to recommend a reduction of six at each main clay port through voluntary redundancy (9/71; 11/71).

The local 'modernization' dispute, illustrating volatility in the china-clay port's labour requirement, blurs with a national dock strike in 1970: the first such since the 1926 General Strike. Protracted pay negotiations following Devlin are seen at the heart of the 1970 strike, with a failure to adjust labour levels quickly enough in face of increas-ing containerization behind the second which came in 1972.

At the outbreak of the 1970 strike, the *West Briton* forecast rising prices of imports, a 'fertiliser famine' for farmers, and 'serious consequences' for china-clay exports.[85] The *Falmouth Packet*, on the other hand, found some solace in the dispute, with local boat-owners supporting the dozen or so large ships anchored 'waiting for orders', which were also acting as a considerable draw for holiday makers.[86] The following week's *West Briton* reports panic buying of sugar as news of the dispute's settlement came.[87] Local papers said nothing about the causes or resolution of the dispute: with no responsibility for pay or industrial relations, neither did the Local Dock Labour Board.

Initially, local reporting of the second strike followed the same pattern as that of the first. There are warnings of shortages of imports and difficulties for exports, together with news of interesting convoys of delayed shipping. Two weeks into the strike, and the *West Briton*'s headline is much more pointed: '6000 Clay Men March Against the Striking 100'. The 'grimly determined protest' organized by the claymen's unofficial Joint Industrial Shop Stewards' Committee was headed by the local MP (Piers Dixon/Conservative) and Managing Director of ECLP (Alan, later Sir Alan Dalton), and stretched three quarters of a mile through St Austell.[88] Alarmingly, there are also reports that their alleged jeopardizing of local jobs in pursuit of national aims had led to threats to dockers' families and refusals to serve them in shops.[89] Having made 800 redundant the previous year, ECLP later said that the dock strike ended just in time to prevent further lay-offs.[90]

These local effects of national reactions to Devlin can perhaps now to be placed in political context. Following Devlin, it was the collapse of fragmented and protracted pay talks that triggered the 1970 national strike. Resumption was through a complex formula linking pay rises to the end of 'restrictive practices', and which thereby did not break the government's then statutory incomes policy.[91] Earlier, Wilson himself had linked a seamen's strike to the July 1966 sterling crisis, while commentators such as K.O. Morgan subsequently link unofficial dock strikes to devaluation, finally conceded in November 1967.[92] Little wonder therefore that industrial relations reform became a political priority. But Lord Donovan's 1968 report advocating a continuance of voluntarism was a 'sad disappointment' to Wilson and his new Secretary of State for Employment and Productivity, Barbara Castle.[93] Subsequent rejection by the TUC forced the abandonment of more radical proposals following her *In Place of Strife*—at enormous political cost.

Heath's Conservatives had promised a comprehensive Industrial Relations Bill before their unexpected 1970 election victory.[94] As if to endorse their plans the first national dock strike, while not of their making, occurred within two weeks of them taking office. The promised Act was, however, doomed from the start as employers avoided its use, and the trades' unions manoeuvred its neutering.[95] The 1972 national dock strike, another fall-out of Devlin, was perhaps the most prominent example of how unworkable the Act was. The National Industrial Relations Court established under the Act had jailed five dockers for contempt in refusing to stop 'blacking' a cold store in east London. Amid industrial uproar far beyond the docks, the argument that the action should have been against their union soon secured the men's release.[96] But the committal of the 'Pentonville Five', as they became known, brought Britain's docks to a stand-still for the second time in two years.

A number of cold stores, container depots and non-Scheme ports were being picketed in protest at their threat to dockers' jobs. Increasing mechanization saw the number of registered dockers almost halving from 60,000 in 1967 to 32,000 in 1975.[97] Writing in the Report's aftermath, D.F. Wilson sees that in concentrating on improving the Scheme, Devlin had not reviewed the proscriptive definition of dock-work. Consequently, as mechanization eroded old demarcations, instead of protecting them as intended the Scheme came to, 'Stand between dockers and the new jobs'.[98] Constrained by the Scheme to work only in ports, after Devlin dockers for whom there was no work were placed on the Temporary Unattached Register. Although triggered by the imprisonment, it was '(ab)use of the TUR' that precipitated the 1972 national strike.[99] Recommendations for dealing with the TUR made by the non-statutory Aldington-Jones Committee eventually ended the strike. But the Committee's effective exchange of the TUR for 'no compulsory redundancies' introduced the contentious 'jobs for life' commitment.[100]

However unstable, resolution of the two national dock strikes opens the local effect of Devlin to closer examination. While one important feature needs further work (the ending of piecework in china-clay ports), work so far has shown something of a paradox in the post-Devlin Scheme's local application. Locally, and by extension therefore probably nationally, there appears something of a con-tradiction when the Scheme's expanding organization is set against its contracting numbers.

Looking first at the Scheme's expansion, smaller authorities such as Truro City Council and Harvey's had to be pressed to provide the required new statutory levels of physical amenities (ablutions) (1/71; 3/71). Training can be seen as becoming more important, from the establishment of a two-day local introductory course in 1963 to the point where eight national training centres were providing training for registered workers and others from port authorities and larger operators. University weekend schools were organized and there was a distance learning scheme (8/72; 12/75). Sporting activities included football, cricket, golf, bowls, darts, and sea-angling, with evidence of Cornish involvement in most (9/75; 9/78). National arts and crafts exhibitions were also held between 1968 and 1984, with again evidence

of Cornish success (5/79; 8/82). However, against the Scheme's professional and pastoral expansion can be seen the continuing decline
in numbers. Locally, Devlin's attachment of dockers to individual
employers revealed a problem with 'light-duty' men previously
invisible in aggregated numbers (10/70). Following confirmation of
incapacity, the release with replacement of almost 14 per cent of
Cornwall's register was negotiated over two years. The Board then
decided to continue considering the china-clay ports individually, but
to group up the western ports (6/72). Traffic patterns seem to have
allowed manpower levels to stabilize until the mid-1970s, with Par and
Fowey around 50 each, Charlestown 2, and the combined western ports
just below 30. Then came the withdrawal as port operators of the once
mighty foundry-men come timber and builders' merchants, Harvey's.
At first the loss was ameliorated by using their men on non-dock
work for Wheal Jane in Truro, and to remove the coal dump on
closure of Hayle's power station (3/76; 5/76). Eventually, the four
Truro workers were transferred to Falmouth and, with Harvey's parent
firm contributing, the five Hayle men took voluntary severance (12/77;
2/78).

There was a series of National Voluntary Severance Schemes
from decasualization onwards, costs of which were initially met by a
1 per cent increase on the levy paid by employers (8/75). But, in
an effort to speed reduction of the work force, Special Severance
Schemes part-funded by the Government were introduced. Over 45,000
dockers took voluntary redundancy in the Scheme's second half of
existence.[101]

While technology was drastically reducing the required number of
dockers, the broader economy was also under pressure. Britain's, along
with most of the developed world's, economy was reeling from a
quadrupling in the price of oil. The local impact saw some 2,000
Cornish manufacturing jobs and 1,000 extractive (mainly clay) jobs lost
in the late 1970s.[102] Falmouth's ship-repair yard had bordered on
complete collapse following a devastating boilermakers' dispute.[103]
Hopes of Falmouth becoming a container port had been raised in some
quarters with the passing of the 1971 Falmouth Container Terminal
Act, and later of its supporting offshore oil work, but both came to
nothing.

In its paradoxical expansion while declining, further changes to the
Scheme were in motion. The Heath Government had fallen, blamed by
some on the 'brutal exercise of trade union power': notably that of the
miners.[104] Mindful of that, and of their own earlier defeat over *In Place
Of Strife*, Labour formed a minority government. Facing an Opposition
Motion rejecting earlier nationalization proposals, the then Secretary

of State for Employment Michael Foot believed that the government had either to, '[e]xtend the [National Dock Labour] Scheme . . . or . . . discard it'.[105] The era of the Social Contract between Labour and the trades' unions was hardly conducive to the latter.

But following vigorous employer-sponsored opposition in the Lords, the Government's proposed cargo handling zone within five miles of the sea, the so-called 'dockers' corridor', was reduced to 0.5 miles around harbours.[106] Inside the 'defined dock area' all handling of cargo (further defined), including the stuffing and stripping of containers, was considered dock-work. Cornwall's Dock Labour Board therefore 'monitored' later proposals for containers in Falmouth (10/81;8/86) and, right to the end of the Scheme, Cornish Calcified Seaweed Ltd. were being reminded that their wharf came within Truro's defined dock area, and therefore the Scheme (4/84; 6/87).

Curiously like 1967 decasualization, 1976 modernization merged with disputes in the main china-clay ports. After stoppages in both ports, a compromise over new handling arrangements at Fowey was accepted by the company only '[u]nder the strongest possible protest and in the interest of other workers'.[107] In Par, after years of argument it took an industrial tribunal in Exeter to decide that crane and conveyor driving was *not* dock work (1/79). The following year's NDLB Report bemoans the number of similarly handled definition disputes, seeing the results for the industry as, 'invariably un-favourable'.[108]

Perceptions of a 'Winter of Discontent' did little to improve the likelihood of a continuance of the Social Contract. But, on coming to office and unlike Heath with his over-ambitious Industrial Relations Act, Thatcher's approach would be 'step by step' with no less than eight Enactments taken to tip the balance away from organizations and towards individuals.[109] Having tacitly made the fateful break with the post-war commitment to full employment, the new government's industrial policy has been usefully encapsulated as: 'Denationalization, decentralization and deregulation'.[110] If the compression is accepted, then clearly the days of the NDLS were numbered.

Early signs of the shift can be found in the minutes of Cornwall's Dock Labour Board. Specialist training was now being done on site, for which the mechanical handling equipment had to be hired by the employer (5/79; 10/80). Weekend courses were stopped, although the distance learning scheme continued (12/81). Two large national sports competitions were suspended but several smaller ones survived, with Fowey twice later runners-up in the national bowls championships. Of the remaining local premises, the amenity block at Penryn was sold to the Local Authority, and one floor of the Falmouth office rented to a financial company (4/82; 5/82). Nationally, the Board disposed of six of its training centres, its two London sports-grounds, and the 'land-ship' training facility at Liverpool.[111]

The same spread of issues—numbers, amenities, definition, and discipline—continued to confront the Local Board. Manpower levels, more or less stable after the severance schemes, dropped to 94 with another release following introduction of new rolling stock in the main china-clay ports (1/87; 10/87). Problems included the taking of three months to screen one recruit for Penzance (4/85 to 7/85) and 'months of disruption' between workers transferred from Falmouth to Par/Fowey (3/88; 5/88). Licensing Authorities were still having to be pressed to provide facilities (12/85; 3/86; 1/88), and the owners of at least three ships were suspected of breaching the Scheme at Penzance. (6/87; 4/88; 8/88) Falmouth's best year in the Scheme, also its last saw a definition dispute over the handling of 'risers' when the drill-ship *Pacnorse 1* dry-docked (5/88; 10/88). Local concerns led to only partial support for the national strikes called over alleged attempts to circumvent the 1984 miners' strike.[112] Writing in the immediate aftermath of the Scheme's abolition, and the defeat for the dockers in the strikes that accompanied it, the Turnbull team believe that, in the government's sights, dockers were second only to the miners.[113] Even if so, Thatcher herself knew better than to confront both simultaneously.[114] But having dealt with one, attention could turn to the other. Announcing a Bill to abolish the Scheme, the then Secretary of State for employment, Norman Fowler, described it as 'A statutory monopoly . . . a total anachronism . . . the biggest obstacle to a modern port industry.' For the opposition, Michael Meacher saw the announcement coming more from 'Thatcherite dogma' than any real concern for the nation's economy.[115]

Four years after the Scheme's abolition, consultants were tasked to evaluate the impact of having done so. They found that major ex-Scheme ports were the main beneficiaries, largely at the expense of smaller ex-Scheme ports. The industry had slimmed, working practices and relations had changed, with the T&GWU having lost both membership and influence. Port users were seen to have benefited from increased service and choice. Some investment in ports was also found to have been inhibited by the Scheme, citing among other examples the post-Scheme introduction of new handling equipment and warehouses in the main china-clay ports.[116] Ten years later, three articles in the journal of the *Institute of Economic Affairs* reflected on abolition. One, written by a former employer, concluded that there had been no return to the bad old days of casualism. Of the other two, written by pertinent academics, one examined broader effects, concluding that to sustain the benefits of greater flexibility the industry needed to develop longer-term strategies to cope with continuing change. The last took Liverpool as a case-study. As well as revitalizing the port transport industry both nationally and locally, P. Stoney saw its abolition as 'such an influential source of wealth creation', adding impetus to the whole local economy.[117]

But even as the axe was rising, Local Boards taking their cue from the National continued to function normally. Cornwall's Board had planned all their 1989 meeting dates. Fowey had again entered the bowls championships. Training was in the process of being reorganized on a regional basis. However, at their 492nd meeting held on 6 June 1989 on the Scillies, the Area Dock Labour Board (Cornwall) agreed that unless anything came from the National that needed their attention, no further meetings were necessary.

CONCLUSION

By centralizing the story of dock labour in Cornwall, this article has sought to show that as part of the Attlee Government's social reconstruction programme the NDLS grew inevitably from a mix of experience, expedience, and expectation before, during, and after the Second World War. In examining the subsequent influence of previous events and decisions along four interlinked paths, it has also sought to show the origins of Cornwall's port transport industry and its inclusion in the NDLS. Post-war planning in the port transport industry reflected that way beyond the docks. Cornwall was found to have only partly mirrored the ambiguous electoral support given elsewhere to Attlee's post-war plans. With the decline in general freight, particularly coal, the county's port transport industry became concentrated on china-clay.

Immediately after the Second World War, dockers' resistance to the NDLS was found behind a series of major disputes forcing the repeated use of troops to keep vital cargoes moving. Growing concerns regarding comparative inefficiency then fuelled pressure for modernization, but when introduced on the docks by Wilson in the mid-1960s it was again met with disruptive resistance. Dock-land's subsequent opposition to Heath's industrial relations policy was seen to have had a particularly divisive local impact. Resistance to industrial relations reform was compounded by the dockers' mistrust of major changes in cargo handling technology. So stiff was their opposition that some claim that the NDLS that had previously protected their jobs came to de-bar them from the emergent new ones. The pursuit of further restrictions therefore added pressure to Labour's fragile social contract. A changed political backdrop and reducing numbers under increasingly generous severance terms then meant that dockers could not deflect Thatcher as they had done Heath.

The first half of this article showed the need and inevitability of the NDLS for the whole post-war reconstruction package. The second half has perhaps shown more support for the subsequent criticism that the pursuit of full employment begun in that package came to hamper industrial modernization. As a general result K.O. Morgan claims that, in its break with industrial regulation, '[t]he Thatcher revolution was considerable, almost complete'.[118] In particular, in the port transport industry, the M. Thomas team report that, 'Any return to the NDLS would be seen as undesirable'.[119]

In July 1948 eighteen Penryn dockers went on a week-long strike over the stacking of 380 tons of cement from the *Fixity*.[120] Exactly forty years later, two teams of ten men worked over the weekend in Falmouth to unload 5,000 tons of cement from the *Balsa 34*.[121] This local comparison, spanning the life of the NDLS, shows some of the many changes in the Scheme's political and industrial context. Industrially, the handling capacity had clearly changed but men were still needed to shift the cargoes from ship to shore. Politically, achieving a balance between abuse of and abuse by the dockers' pivotal position in a maritime trading economy has been shown to have been at issue throughout much of the post-war period.

Almost regardless of political judgements, it could be said that, however inevitable and necessary it originally was, the Scheme was flawed from the outset. On the one hand, it never encompassed all ports. Consequently, throughout its life the Scheme was chasing changing traffic and technology. On the other, the Turnbull team points to the inherent tension across the industry's 'frontier of control'. Sympathetic to the Scheme, they see the workers' acceptance of terms that replaced it being more 'coerced compliance' than 'co-operative commitment'.[122] Some might say that, during the Scheme, it was the other side of industry who faced the same dichotomy. A few years ago in Australia, the balance apparently settled more in favour of the workforce. After massive disruption in ports there, the High Court directed *insolvent* Sydney firms to re-employ at least some of 1,400 sacked dockers.[123]

This article has offered an analysis of the NDLS in Cornwall, and its other operating contexts, as a microcosm of the whole. While it is hoped that to some extent the analogy has been served, there remains at least one important difference between the local and national picture. Nationally, traffic moved from Scheme to non-Scheme ports, from old conventional to new specialized, from west coast facing the Empire to east coast facing Europe. Locally, there was either nowhere else for cargoes to go, as in Cornwall's eastern ports, or—as befell the western ports with the relentless march of road transport—sea-freight dwindled to near zero. A coarse analysis of registered strengths confirms the difference. At the start of the Scheme there were some 80,000 dockers, of whom almost 300 were in Cornwall. By the end there were 9,500 nationally, and just under 100 in the county. But it is too simplistic to compare the almost 90 per cent national reduction to the 66 per cent local. When the Local Board first broke down their register in the early 1970s, there were 132 dockers in Cornwall of whom 103 were employed in only two ports. Twenty years later, at the Scheme's end, the main china-clay ports' proportion of the total had fallen by 'only' 30 per cent to 73. Cornwall's register of dock workers became, and perhaps always was, as much a function of the china-clay industry as that of port transport.

On the Scheme's abolition, those of the dock labour force who remained in Falmouth and the two main clay ports were absorbed into parent organizations. Elsewhere, it is likely to have been compensated redundancy. Of the ports themselves, the future of Par and Fowey seem inextricably linked to extraction. Indeed, traffic through Par looks set to increase with a hoped for increase in the output of aggregates.[124] Charlestown looks likely to continue quietly, and perhaps appropriately, catering for visitors, the world's square-sail fleet, and film-makers. The opening of the National Maritime Museum in Falmouth might herald a move towards the 'cultural consumerism' seen on a small scale in Charlestown, and on a larger in the regeneration of dock-lands in cities such as Cardiff, Glasgow, and Liverpool.

Authorities behind all Cornwall's ports have to balance the often conflicting cultural, residential, recreational, and commercial potential of their valuable water frontage. In trading terms R. Perry, with whom this study started, has recommended with others a 're-centralizing' strategy for Cornwall based on the 'Atlantic Arc', rather than an eastward-heading centre.[125] While he sees the award as confirming the 'failure of 3 decades of regional development', European Objective 1 is aimed at revitalizing Cornwall's economy.[126] The County Council's *Connecting Cornwall* summarizes the transport input for Objective 1 consideration. Among other strategic aims, improvements needed include links to the Isles of Scilly, and both Fowey and Falmouth as a cruise-ship call with the latter becoming a 'major marine industry port'. Future development of the county's road and rail haulage should also be integrated with ports.[127] Having eluded earlier Administrations, (New) Labour's promised 'joined-up' national transport policy might yet emerge. However, unless directed from elsewhere, future control of manpower in British trading ports seems unlikely to bear the currently unfashionable corporatist stamp of the National Dock Labour Scheme.

NOTES AND REFERENCES

1. G. Phillips and N. Whiteside, *The Unemployment Question in the Port Transport Industry*, London 1985, cites both Booth and Webbs's reports of deprivation among dockers' families. Reports on dock-gate melees by contemporaneous journalist H. Mayhew are quoted in R.R. James, *The British Revolution 1880–1939*, London, 1978.
2. R. Perry, 'The Making of Modern Cornwall 1800–2000: A Geo-Economic Perspective', in P. Payton (ed.), *Cornish Studies: Ten*, Exeter, 2002, p. 167.
3. R. Perry, in P. Payton (ed.), 2002, p. 185.
4. B. Deacon, 'The New Cornish Studies: New Discipline or Rhetorically Defined Space', in P. Payton (ed.), 2002. Page 35 cites definition of 'reconstructionist' history: 'seeking the most probably truthful . . . interpretation inherent in the documents of the past'. See page 26 for arguments against using the 'local . . . to illuminate broader academic generalisations'.
5. B. Deacon, in P. Payton (ed.), 2002. Page 28 lists three 'central concepts' of New Cornish studies: 'Interdisciplinarity, comparison and context'.
6. R. Perry, in P. Payton (ed.), 2002, p. 185.
7. P. Addison's *The Road to 1945* is highly regarded among works on British politics of the Second World War. He concludes his *The Road From 1945* contribution to P. Hennessey and A. Seldon, (eds), *Ruling Performance* Oxford, 1987, with a rebuttal of C. Barnett's *The Audit of War*, to which this study will return. In page 20 of *Ruling Performance* Addison claims to identify 'simplifications' underlying Barnett's thesis: one being the failure to acknowledge fully 'political imperatives behind the reconstruction programme'.
8. P. Payton, *Cornwall*, Fowey, 1996, p. 66.
9. C. Noal *The Story of the Ports and Harbours of Cornwall*, Truro, 1970, pp. 21, 29 and 34.
10. National Archives (NA) BK1/296 11.01.43.
11. R. Roddis, *Cornish Harbours*, London, 1951, p. ix.
12. R. Perry, in P. Payton (ed.), 2002, p. 185.
13. For fleets discussed see: K.J. O'Donoghue and H.S. Appleyard, *Hain of St Ives*, Kendal 1986; K.S. Garret, *Everard of Greenhithe*, Kendal, 1991, and Fenton *Ships' Monthly* Oct–Dec 1985. For changes in cargo handling technology see: E. Corlett, *The Ship: The Revolution in Merchant Shipping 1950–1980*, HMSO, National Maritime Museum, 1980.
14. P. Turnbull *et al.*, *Dock Strike: Conflict and Restructuring in Britain's Ports*, Aldershot, 1992, p. 1.
15. Although commentators find some revolutionary syndicalist undertones in the pre-World War One upsurge in strikes, most agree with A. Bullock. In Vol. I of his massive *Life and Times of Ernest Bevin: Trades'*

Union Leader 1881–1940, London, 1960 (p. 33) he locates their main cause in rises in prices and profits outstripping those of pay. R.M. Barton, in *A History of the Cornish China-Clay Industry*, Truro, 1966 (pp. 153–154) found local issues including pay being fuelled by up-country discontent.

16. A. Bullock, Vol. I, 1960, p. 36.
17. A. Bullock, Vol. I, 1960, p. 116.
18. J. Stevenson, *British Society 1914–1945* London, 1990, p. 197.
19. Unindexed papers in CRO Truro file DDX401/68.
20. A. Bullock, Vol. 1, 1960, p. 462.
21. H.W. Whyte, *Decasualisation of Dock Labour with Special Reference to the Port of Bristol*, Bristol, 1934, p. 24 and NA BK 1/54 01.10.43.
22. J. Higgans, *The History of the Cornish Port of Hayle*. Unpublished, held in CSL Redruth file C/387, p. 38.
23. H.W. Whyte, 1934, p. 17.
24. NA BK1/54 07.06.44 and 19.10.44.
25. W. Kenefick, *A Struggle for Recognition and Independence: Dock Unionism in Glasgow 1853–1932* in S. Davies *et al.*, (eds), *Dock Workers*, Aldershot, 2000, p. 338.
26. C.L. Mowat, *Britain Between the Wars 1918–1940*, London, 1984, pp. 392, 400.
27. J. Murray, *Devon and Cornwall: A Preliminary Survey*, Exeter, 1947, p. 186.
28. P. Payton, 1996, p. 254.
29. J. Murray, *et al.*, 1947, p. 245.
30. G. Tregidga, 'Socialism and the Old Left', in P. Payton (ed.) *Cornish Studies: Seven*, Exeter, 1999, p. 79.
31. P. Payton, 1996, p. 249.
32. G. Tregidga, in P. Payton (ed.), 1999, p. 81.
33. Payton, 1996, p. 254.
34. Bullock, Vol. I, 1960, p. 426.
35. Mowat, 1984, pp. 552, 632.
36. S. Stephens, *British Society 1914–1945*, London, 1984 p. 100.
37. A. Bullock, Vol. I, 1960, p. 100.
38. NA BK1/196 19.10.41.
39. *Hansard Parliamentary Debates* 04.12.41.
40. NA BK1/141 30.12.41.
41. NA BK1/141 31.12.41.
42. NA BK1/68 28.07.41.
43. 1943 figures for both employees and employers from NA BK1/54 01.10.43.
44. NA BK1/296 11.01.43 shows the original members of Cornwall's NDLC Board as: S.F. Hough, Chairman, R. Jose, G.H. Bennetts, B.C. Opie, J.J. Richards, W.E. Cavill, C.R. Harvey, J. Hill, M.J. Kenna, Secretary.
45. Bullock, Vol. II, 1967, p. 284.
46. On the Beveridge Report see Stevenson, 1984, p. 454: 'Captured mood of optimism and articulated ideas which already commanded considerable

support.' K.O. Morgan, *The People's Peace: British History 1945–1990*, OUP Oxford, 1992 p. 14: 'Close to embodying a national consensus about the purposes of the War'. Remarkably, over 800,000 copies were sold (Barnett 1986, p. 28). Abbreviated copies were distributed in Occupied Europe and even dropped with RAF bomb-loads: a seemingly odd way to disseminate 'Britain's master contribution to a better world', (Stevenson, 1986, p. 456; Morgan 1992, p. 37).

47. K.O. Morgan, 1992, p. 27.
48. P. Addison, in Hennessey and Seldon (eds), 1987, p. 21
49. NA BK1/162 06.10.44.
50. NA BK1/162 19.10.45.
51. Forster Inquiry HMSO 21.11.46.
52. NA BK1/146 17.12.43.
53. NA BK1/143 15.12.42.
54. S. Fielding, P. Thompson and N. Tiratsoo, *England Arise: The Labour Party and Popular Politics in 1940s Britain*, Manchester, 1995, p. 68.
55. G. Tregidga, *The Liberal Party in the Southwest Since 1918*, Exeter, 2000, pp. 113–15.
56. J. Murray *et al.*, 1947, p. 253.
57. J. Murray *et al.*, 1947, p. 304.
58. J. Murray *et al.*, 1947, p. 300.
59. C. Barnett, *The Audit of War: The Illusion and Reality of Britain as a Great Nation*, London, 1986, p. 246.
60. C. Barnett, *The Lost Victory: British Dreams, British Realities 1945–1950*, London 1995, p. 353.
61. R.B. Oram, *The Dockers' Tragedy*, London, 1970.
62. CRO Truro X/900 Series. Subsequent detailed entries referenced by date only, thus: 10/49.
63. A.H.J. Bown, *An Introduction to Port Working*, London, 1955, p. 49.
64. L.A. Smith (retired member of Cornwall Dock Labour Board) to author.
65. See P. Hennessey and K. Jeffery, *States of Emergency: British Governments and Strike Breaking Since 1919*. In response to dock-land disruption during the period they list two full States of Emergency, use of troops on two other occasions and planning for another. London, 1970.
66. M.P. Jackson, *Policy Making in the Trades' Unions: The T&GWU's Policy on the Decasualisation of Dock Labour*, Aldershot, 1991, p. 95.
67. R.B. Oram, 1970, p. 155.
68. *Falmouth Packet*, 30.04.48.
69. J. Phillips, *The Great Alliance: Economic Recovery and the Problems of Power 1945–1951*, London, 1996, p. 131.
70. A. Seldon, *Churchill's Indian Summer 1951–1955*, London, 1981, p. 203.
71. R. Taylor, *The Trades' Union Question in British Politics: Governments and the Unions since 1945*, Oxford, 1993, p. 362.
72. Quoted in D.F. Wilson, *Dockers: The Impact of Industrial Change*, London, 1972, p. 105.
73. G. Moorhouse, *Britain in the Sixties: The Other England*, Harmondsworth, 1964, p. 18.

74. Quoted in K. Jeffery, *Retreat from New Jerusalem: British Politics 1951–1964*, Basingstoke, 1997, p. 65.
75. Cited in K.O. Morgan, 1992, p. 199.
76. Jeffery, 1997, p. 111.
77. *Report of the Inquiry into the Major Ports of Great Britain*, London, 1962, p. 213.
78. Jackson, 1991, pp. 102–3.
79. M.P. Jackson, *Labour Relations on the Docks*, Farnborough, 1973, p. 109, Jackson L., 1991 p. 104.
80. CRO Truro B/TRU 340 and 341.
81. Jackson, 1973, p. 88.
82. Oram, 1970, p. 169.
83. J.W. Durcan *et al.*, *Strikes in Post-war Britain: A Study of Stoppp. of Work due to Industrial Disputes 1946–1973*, London 1983, p. 308.
84. Turnbull P *et al.*, *Persistent Militants and Quiescent Comrades: Intra-industry Strike Activity on the Docks 1947–1989*, *Sociological Review* 44:4, Oxford, 1996, p. 709.
85. *West Briton*, 23.07.70.
86. *Falmouth Packet*, 24.07.70
87. *West Briton*, 30.07.70.
88. *West Briton*, 10.08.72.
89. *Cornish Guardian*, 17.08.72.
90. *West Briton*, 17.08.72.
91. S. Hill, *The Dockers: Class and Tradition in London*, London, 1976, p. 7.
92. Morgan, 1992, p. 299.
93. Taylor, 1993, p. 157.
94. Morgan, 1992, pp. 313–14; R. Taylor, 1993, pp. 186–87.
95. R. Taylor R, 'The Heath Government and Industrial Relations: Myth and Reality', in S. Ball and A. Seldon (eds.), *The Heath Government 1970–1974: A Reappraisal*, Harlow, 1996, p. 173.
96. Stoppages highest in national newspapers, engineering and building with planning made for a one-day General Strike. *Union Man: The Autobiography of Jack Jones*, London, 1986, p. 251.
97. P. Turnbull *et al.*, *Dock Strike: Conflict and Restructuring in Britain's Ports*, Aldershot, 1992, p. 47.
98. Wilson, 1972, p. 151.
99. Turnbull, *et al.*, 1992, p. 28.
100. For the Turnbull team the term has a 'hollow ring' given that over 50,000 dockers left the industry after Devlin (Turnbull, 1992 p. 25).
101. Individual severance payments rose from £2,000 in the early 1970s to £35,000 by the late 1980s. Turnbull P *et al.* 1992, p. 49.
102. Payton, 1996, p. 282.
103. *Falmouth Packet*, 11.08.72.
104. Douglas Hurd (Heath's Parliamentary Secretary and later Foreign Secretary in Thatcher's Cabinet), quoted by R. Taylor in Ball and Seldon (eds), 1996, p. 189.
105. *Hansard Parliamentary Debates*, 14.04.75.

106. G. Adams, *Organisation of the British Port Transport Industry*, London, 1973, pp. 229–30; and *Dock Work Regulation Act*. HMSO 1976 Clause 4 (3).
107. *West Briton*, 01.04.76.
108. *NDLB Annual report and Accounts*, 1980, p. 4.
109. See Taylor, 1993, pp. 269 and 321–25.
110. P. Turnbull, *Docks*, in A. Pendleton and J. Winterton (eds), *Public Enterprise in Transition: Industrial Relations in State and Privatised Corporations*, London, 1993, p. 197.
111. *NDLB Annual Report and Accounts*, 1982/1983 pp. 2–4.
112. *Falmouth Packet*, 17.08.84 & 31.08.84 and *Cornish Guardian*, 19.07.84 & 30.08.84.
113. Turnbull *et al.*, 1992, p. 119.
114. M. Thatcher, *The Downing Street Years*, London, 1993, p. 362.
115. *Hansard Parliamentary Debates*, 06.04.89.
116. N. Evans *et al.*, *The Abolition of the NDLS*, London, 1993, pp. 66, 49.
117. P. Stoney, 'The Abolition of the NDLS and the Revival of the Port of Liverpool', *Institute of Economic Affairs*, p. 22.
118. Morgan, 1992, p. 470.
119. M. Thomas *et al.*, 'The Strengths and Weaknesses of Dock Labour Reform: Ten Years On', *Institute of Economic Affairs June 1999*, p. 17.
120. *Falmouth Packet*, 09.07.48.
121. *West Briton*, 14.07.88.
122. Turnbull *et al.*, 1992, p. 228.
123. *The Times* 05.05.98.
124. I. Bowditch (spokesman for Imerys') to author.
125. R. Perry, 'Economic Change and Opposition Economics' in P. Payton (ed.), *Cornwall Since the War*, Redruth, 1993, p. 81.
126. R. Perry, 'The Making of Modern Cornwall 1800–2000: A Geo-Economic Perspective' in P. Payton (ed.), *Cornish Studies: Ten*, Exeter, 2002, p. 183.
127. Cornwall County Council. *Connecting Cornwall: Regeneration Through Better Communication*, Truro, *Action Programme 3*.

POSITIONS, PATRONAGE AND PREFERENCE: POLITICAL INFLUENCE IN FOWEY BEFORE 1832

Helen Doe

INTRODUCTION

Feelings ran high in Fowey in 1817 with the arrival of a candidate for one of the town's two Parliamentary seats. One poster from 'A Tradesman' announced a meeting of the Blue party at which they would proclaim that 'Slavery has breathed its last breath in Fowey' and that they would use all lawful means to drive out of the town 'every man who wishes by Tyranny and Bribery to bend their necks to the Yoke of a foreign invader'. The earnest promise was that they 'have already coupled Trade with the name of Blue—and henceforth forever they will couple together Grey and Poverty. And swear eternal hostility to the one, which ever will, as they know from 60 years of bitter experience, produce the other'.[1] The invader referred to was not the recently defeated Napoleon, but George Lucy, the prospective M.P. from Warwickshire and the opposing party for whom he was the preferred candidate, were known as the Greys. The poster's words laid out the two main themes of the battle, bribery and trade.

This battle between the two groups, the Greys led by the Corporation of Fowey and the Blues led by J.T. Austen, was bitter and expensive.[2] It lasted for much of the early nineteenth century until Fowey lost her franchise under the Reform Act of 1832. Such political disagreements were not unknown in Fowey; there had been previous fiercely contested elections in the late eighteenth century. Bribery in various guises was a regular part of such elections and Cornwall had a reputation for its 'rotten' boroughs. Trade was an important factor for the town. Fowey had been in decline for some years, the port, one of the largest natural harbours in Cornwall, was under-utilized, and access, other than by sea, was difficult due to the poor state of the roads. Fowey was a considerable distance from Parliament and the circles of power and influence in London. Yet the town and its inhabitants were of real interest to the government and to men of power or those who sought power because the borough could send two M.P.s to London.

The purpose here is not to detail the long and highly complex battles over who should represent Fowey, but to consider the benefits that the electoral system and, in particular, the contested elections, brought to Fowey. There were many advantages in a political system that encouraged favours. There were three main areas where a grateful M.P. or a prospective candidate could assist the inhabitants of Fowey. They could assist with positions, particularly those within the gift of the government, such as the Customs and Excise. They might become patrons and find a place for someone's son in the navy or help to further the career of an officer. Thirdly, they could assist by offering preference in trade contracts. Voters and key influencers were lured by the image of a thriving port with busy shipyards, and plenty of business for the favoured few—in this case, the shipbuilders.

THE POLITICAL BACKGROUND

Before the 1832 Reform Act, Cornwall had twenty-one electoral boroughs and could return forty-four M.P.s, so that the county was 'grossly over-represented in the House of Commons'.[3] A traditional view of Cornish politics is of a series of 'rotten' boroughs, controlled by local landed interests who decided who would be the MPs and told the small number of voters how they must vote. More recently this view has been challenged and has shown that there were 'elements of consistently independent political behaviours well before 1832'.[4] This was certainly true of Fowey. A classification of pre-Reform Act Cornish boroughs attempted to define them as primarily venal, corporation, patronage, or 'open'.[5] Fowey could be classified in any of the first three; voting rights were jealously guarded, and the extension of any franchise was an anathema to those who wished to retain their influence. Votes were bought and sold, properties that had voting rights were left empty to reduce the number of voters and 'faggots' were brought in to become temporary residents claiming voting rights. Expensive appeals were lodged with Parliament if the results were not to a party's liking and large sums were spent to sway matters: £20,000 was one figure suggested as an influencing factor.[6] There were 'always eager buyers of borough properties, men wishing to ingratiate themselves with the government of the day by offering the support of "their" members sitting for "their" boroughs. Alternatively they regarded them as financial propositions; selling the seats and sometimes seeking control of government patronage in return'.[7] It was an understood part of the electoral system during the Hanoverian period, and all the parties in Fowey used it to their advantage.

POSITIONS

The Government had within its gift many local positions, and a government-supported candidate or sitting M.P. could influence the appointment to some senior positions and would have the direct gift of some of the junior ones. In 1764 Charles Crokatt was such a prospective candidate. He had prepared his ground and ensured that his supporters in Fowey knew that he was close to the government. He had 'waited on Mr Grenville, (who was before apprised of my business) who cordially honours me with his countenance and recommendations, a proof of which I shall be able to show you on Monday next'. He then requested them to 'promote our interest by communicating it to those voters with whom it will have to wait and this additional interest will I hope insure our success'.[8]

Crokatt was a London merchant and was highly desirous of taking one of the two seats at Fowey, but he was pitting himself against the traditional nominees. The nomination of the two M.P.s was previously held either by a member of the Rashleigh family of Fowey or the Edgcumbe family. Crokatt used every means at his disposal. As a government-supported candidate he had been given the right to some local appointments as he had hinted in his letter. However, he overplayed his hand and caused a serious complaint to be lodged against him with the Lords Commissioners of the Treasury in February 1765.

Walter Polgrean had been appointed Deputy searcher in the Customs in 1762 and had also been fulfilling the position as a Landwaiter since 1763. He was waiting for the official warrant to confirm his position, which would enable him to collect his pay arrears. As he informed their Lordships, 'Your Petitioner is so happy to find, that your Lordships have been pleased to sign a warrant appointing him to the said office of Landwaiter, Your Petitioner having seen the said warrant in the Hands of one Mr Crokatt.'[9]

Joy was turned to outrage when Crokatt 'refused to deliver the said warrant to your petitioner unless your Petitioner would promise to vote for him at the ensuing election . . . The said Mr Crokatt has also told your Petitioner that he thought proper to say how your Petitioner would behave, and he threatened also to give the said place away to another person, pretending that he was sufficiently autonomous and empowered so to do.' Polgrean's indignation glares though every sentence and he was confident in support for his complaint. 'Your Petitioner being fully persuaded that your Lordships have not given the said Mr Crokatt authority to treat with him for his vote in your Lordships name.'[10] Polgrean was right about their Lordships being concerned, but their concern would be more for the challenge to their authority than Polgrean's woes. There is no copy of their reply, just a brief note stating that letters were written to both Polgrean and Crokatt. In the event Crokatt lost a very close election with twenty-four votes to Philip Rashleigh's twenty-seven votes. It is significant that Crokatt never did achieve his ambition to become an MP; he may have lost government support or found the whole process far too expensive.

The offer of Customs positions would continue to be of import-ance in elections in Fowey since 'Every employment in the gift of the Customs, Post Office or any other branch of government was needed to conciliate local interests and aid in electing Members of Parliament who would support the ministry of the day.'[11] During the electoral battles in 1820 Colonel Campbell, the father of a candidate, used his gift of twenty junior Customs appointments to help his son.[12] But for some the Customs posts were more than just vote influencers as a friend in Customs was a potentially valuable contact. An ally who might interpret the rules to the advantage of a merchant as the ex-associate of a timber merchant explained: 'he [had] complained he could do nothing with the present set of men in office and said he would get them changed, he would have regular clearance that the advantage would gain from having them all changed was that he should have the timber measured as he liked.'[13]

While allowance must be made for the sound of axes being ground by the ex-associate, a friendly Customs official was a big asset to merchants as Campbell's fellow candidate, Baillie, knew from unhappy experience. As a member of Bristol's West India Association, he and his colleagues had protested at over-zealous Customs officers. These officers had been impounding ships and cargoes on the grounds that the marking of the consignments had been incorrect. This caused 'in many cases the loss of the sale, and the detention of ships have proved serious injuries to the parties concerned', while the Customs officers gained whether it was genuine fraud or not since the owner had to pay to retrieve his property.[14]

Places in both Customs and Excise became a lure to voters during these years and were freely used by both sides. 'Campbell was very open in his expressions and went so far as to tell the parents and friends of those who were made Excisemen that they were in duty bound to give him their votes. Reports that places even from a Night man to Permit writerships are promised.'[15] In 1828 Austen, the leader of the Blue party, put pressure on George Lucy, by then the Fowey MP and his partner in the battle against the Corporation of Fowey, whom he felt was not doing all he could to find suitable government sweeteners. 'But considering you have represented Fowey nearly nine years as a known friend of ministers without any patronage to bestow on them they complain, and certainly not without reason . . . and it is a notorious fact that the abuse of power that some of the Officers in that Service possessed prior to the General Election in 1826 caused the return of Mr Eden and yourself to be petitioned against.'[16]

It was not just positions in Fowey the East India Company was also a target. When John Godber of Fowey wrote to Campbell hoping to obtain a nice secure position as a tea warehouse keeper, he naturally finished with an offer 'to oblige him at the next election'.[17] All of these offers whether Customs positions or in the East India Company, amounted at most to twenty at any one time, and in many elections the number of positions on offer were far fewer. These might, however, be just enough to make the difference in elections that numbered between 120 and 150 electors.[18]

NAVAL PATRONAGE

Patronage was an accepted and integral part of naval life. Nicholas Rodgers quotes a letter in this respect, from Captain Lord Egdcumbe to Newcastle in 1761: 'one of the electors [of Fowey] has a son on board my ship who has passed his examination, and if he could be made a lieutenant; the father's vote would be secured'.[19] Edgcumbe's family was the holder of one of the two seats in Fowey. However, Rodgers argues that the Navy resisted too much political influence in positions, and that civilian politicians were carefully excluded from real influence on naval promotions.[20] There was, however, one Royal Navy officer who had a different view on how to achieve his promotion.

William Rashleigh, as Fowey MP from 1812, was subjected to heavy pressure from a locally based naval officer, who clearly believed with good reason that his best route was to put pressure on his local politician. In December 1813 Lieutenant Thomas Willcocks Nicholls had heard that the position as Lieutenant of the Gribben Head signal station was vacant. Rashleigh had strong influence as the signal house was on his land. There is on the face of it nothing unusual in Nicholls's request; however, the final sentence of his letter deserves attention: 'Your Uncle Mr. C Rashleigh has always told me I should have the preference and could the wishes of a greater part of the inhabitants of Fowey procure the situation I am sure I should have it.'[21] Rashleigh's uncle was Charles Rashleigh, solicitor, banker, builder of Charlestown harbour, and political agent to the Earl of Mount Edgcumbe who held the other seat at Fowey. Nicholls was playing the voting card and promising his influence on the voters in the town of Fowey. An easy matter to suggest, but Nicholls's later behaviour indicates that he did indeed have such power.

The position at the signal station did not happen, but Nicholls's need for posting was taken seriously. At Rashleigh's request, Nicholls wrote again to give full details of his background and experience. Nicholls had served in the navy for fifteen years and had achieved a lieutenancy from Sir Alexander Cochrane in the West Indies. He had been invalided out three years previously from the Mediterranean, 'My length of servitude when backed by your interest I think will induce their Lordships to give me a good command.'[22]

Being out of service and located some distance from the seat of power in London was a major disadvantage to a man keen to get back into the Service. While internal patronage was the 'spring that drove the machinery of promotion', Nicholls's previous patron, Cochrane, was still at sea in the West Indies.[23] Timing was critical, as in April 1814 Napoleon abdicated and soon there would little or no chance of being appointed to a command. Nicholls applied extra pressure with a more detailed and specific request and he made sure to mention Rashleigh's fellow M.P., Wigram:

> Things having taken a material change since I had pleasure of seeing you, and as in all probability a Peace will soon take place and must again request again you'll solicit Lord Melville in my behalf and as His Lordship has promised you Sir, that he will appoint me to a vessel of the class I so much desire (that is a cutter or schooner) I must beg leave to acquaint you Sir that unless the vessel his Lordship is pleased to appoint me the command of is to be kept in the service after a Peace takes place it would be little or no use to me to accept of her. Should His Lordship not be able to immediately comply with this request he certainly can do one thing and that is promote me to the rank of Commander as a very large promotion will take place in the event of a Peace with France and as you Sir are on the spot to make this application with the assistance of Mr Wigram should you Sir think it necessary, he having on a former occasion promised to get me promoted. Should you Sir agree with me in this I have no doubt of obtaining it. I cannot conclude this without returning my sincere thanks as well as those of my friends for the trouble you have already taken on my behalf.[24]

While Nicholls had been careful to include mention of Wigram (and his promise) in his letter, it was not he who worked on Nicholls's behalf, but Reginald Pole Carew, M.P. for Lostwithiel. Pole Carew, was a member of the Edgcumbe family and had previously been the M.P. for Fowey and was now Fowey's Recorder. He was a man with close connections in government, having held several senior ministerial positions. He was also a good friend to both Rashleigh and Fowey.[25]

Nicholls achieved his aim and was appointed to command HMS *Bramble*.[26] However, such was his confidence in his political power in Fowey that he pushed for more, just days after he received the welcome news:

Yours of 29 June I duly received and in answer beg leave to return you my sincere thanks for what you have done. I must also request you'll have the goodness to convey my best respects to Mr Pole Carew and say if I can at any time be of any service to him in the Borough of Fowey I shall find a pleasure in doing so. And if it's not troubling you too much I should wish to know if the vessel I am to be appointed to is to remain some time in commission, otherwise it would be folly for me to accept of her as it would be attended with great expense my joining her. Should you feel inclined to inform me on this head as soon as possible I shall feel greatly obliged.[27]

Pole Carew's reply to Rashleigh was brisk, somewhat irritated and included a clear warning not to overstretch the mark:

My Dear Sir, I think I should inform Lieutenant Nicholls that I can by no means undertake to ask a question of the Admiralty which would seem to imply a suspicion that when they are doing a kind act by appointing him to the command which he has solicited they mean to do so unkind a thing as to put an end to his command as soon as he has incurred the expense of his outfit. He should rely upon them having all due consideration for the circumstances in which he may be placed, and accept with cheerfulness and thankfulness what he has appeared to receive, if he wishes to make and keep fair weather at the Admiralty or elsewhere—and after all I think it very improbable that the Board could pretend they know how long they may now hereafter find it expedient to keep any particular ship in commission.[28]

Nicholls took the hint, and did not try this route again, so his next approach was a subtler request via his friends in the Fowey Corporation, suggesting a command near to home. Rashleigh passed this on to Pole Carew who replied:

> Your note accompanying the application from the Corporation of Fowey respecting the *Bramble* schooner did not reach me at this Place till yesterday, and I have this day written to Mr Hay to express our joint wishes that in the Event of arrangements being made for stationing such vessels for the prevention of smuggling along the coast, the *Bramble* may be stationed at the Port of Fowey under the command of Lieut. Nicholls. You shall know the result so soon as I receive the answer.[29]

Nicholls duly received his orders and was sent, not to the Cornish coast, but with despatches to his previous patron, Cochrane, now Vice Admiral of the American Atlantic and Gulf Coasts. Cochrane himself was no stranger to politics or Fowey, having been the M.P. for Stirling Burghs from 1800 to 1806 and an unsuccessful candidate in the Fowey election of 1806.[30] By October 1815 the *Bramble* was back in Plymouth and Nicholls had his big reward. The *Royal Cornwall Gazette* reported the sale of the Prize *Triton*, captured by Lieutenant Nicholls of the *Bramble*: 'A brig of 278 tons, captured while bound from Bordeaux to Guadeloupe complete with her cargo of 274 hogsheads of claret, seven casks of white wine, plus other consumables.'[31]

On his retirement to Fowey, Nicholls threw himself into politics with gusto and showed that his talk of his friends in Fowey was more than just words. He and a fellow officer, Hearle, were highly visible political activists for the Fowey Corporation. Nicholls was an effective rabble-rouser, demonstrating his real worth to Pole Carew and Rashleigh. In a crucial election of 1818 he successfully drowned out an opposition speaker by holding 'a speaking trumpet through which he brayed hideous and unremitting discord', a feat that had him labelled as a 'pot valiant son of Neptune'.[32] Much propaganda in the power struggles was done via posters. One poster in March 1827 had a distinctly naval touch to it and reflects Nicholls strong-minded view of the rights of the supporters of the corporation. It was a call to arms of the supporters of the Greys; 'the last effort resorted to was Treachery, but you still remain firm and unshaken, bearing with manly fortitude the multiplied Evils which have been heaped upon you and your Children, and resting your Sheet Anchor on the Crisis which is fast approaching'. Nicholls continued to be a thorn in the side of the Blues right up to the disenfranchisement of Fowey in 1832. A letter in 1830 to Austen, the leader of the Blue party, suggested the need to 'lay up a plan of removing the firebrands [referring to Hill, another activist and Nicholls] who will, more or less, always keep Fowey in a flame and excite opposition'.[33]

PREFERENCE
The twelve-ton sloop *True Blue* was registered in Fowey in 1790. It was built more for pleasure than serious business and was under the fifteen-ton legal requirement for registration. For such a small craft it had a wide group of shareholders: Thomas Mein surgeon, Thomas Orchard gentleman, Joseph Adams of Liskeard surgeon, Joseph Smith gentleman, Susanna Treffry widow, John Harvey of Liskeard attorney at law, and Dr John Wolcot of London.[34] The *True Blue* was a political statement. The Blues were challenging the comfortable arrangement by which the Rashleigh and Edgcumbe families had shared the two seats. Mein, Susanna Treffry (otherwise known as Mrs Austen, mother of the eight-year-old Joseph Austen), and Wolcot were all leading members of the party.[35]

While positions or patronage helped to win a few votes, greater effort was needed to influence the rest of the voters. Pitt's survey of Cornish boroughs in 1747 noted that candidates were welcome in Fowey if they could bring 'some kind of trade to it'. There had been promises before. Mr Crokatt, Polgrean's tormentor, had vowed in 1761 that he would bring 'a number of Carolina ships there every year, and offered a bond of ten thousand pound for the performance of it' and another prospective candidate in 1766 suggested the fitting out of two ships for the Newfoundland trade. One commentator described the town as 'three parts ruined, without spirit or power to relieve herself' and trade continued to feature as a political issue into the nineteenth century for Fowey.[36] The town was moribund and seemed unable to capitalize on its deep harbour. Lostwithiel Corporation, who controlled the Fowey waters, was uninterested in the port other than the collection of harbour dues. This was the stagnant situation that Joseph Austen, leader of the opponents was determined to break when he became of age and he blamed the Corporation of Fowey for their vested interests and parochial views.

Attempts were made to attract new opportunities. There was a failed attempt by Austen to get the Packet vessels based there during a temporary strike at Falmouth. Rashleigh and the Corporation wanted to establish Fowey as a bonded port, and they tried to enlist the support of Pole Carew. The latter, however, expressed doubts about the lack of suitable warehousing and did not give it his support.[37]

Austen and Lucy, the M.P. from 1818, also continued to try, but the Customs in London produced an unfavourable report.[38] Both parties also used charts as a way of promoting the town and its harbour. Pole Carew published a chart by a Mr George Thomas in 1811. Austen was to follow two years later with a more detailed chart addressed to 'The Merchants of the United Kingdom'. It showed details of watering spots, shipyards, and ropewalks to tempt more vessels to use the harbour.

Fowey shipbuilders stood to gain from improved trade, not just from the investment in new building, but also from increased repair and maintenance business as more vessels traded to and from Fowey. At the beginning of the nineteenth century the major shipbuilder was Thomas Nickels, based at Caffa Mill Pill. The locally built ships were sloops, barges, lighters, and an occasional barquentine with the average tonnage for 1790–94 being forty-eight.[39] This average increased by 1800 to seventy-two tons. But in 1803 there was a significant step change in Nickel's activity: 'launched at Mr Nickels' yard, at this place, a fine ship, called the *Twins of London* admeasuring between 300–400 tons, but will carry about 500: perhaps the largest ever built in Cornwall'.[40]

She was registered as 308 tons and among her shareholders were Thomas Plummer, John Bareham and John Plummer of Fenchurch Street merchants, plus Joshua Rowe of Torpoint.[41] Her size and the London investors make her stand out. There are no previous Fowey registered ships with London merchant involvement and these men were also politically active. For a vessel of this size work would have started in 1802, an election year and the commissioning discussion before that. Thomas Plummer became the M.P. for Ilchester in Somerset in 1802, before being unseated for bribery in 1803. Bareham represented Stockbridge and Okehampton at various times between 1793–1822, and Rowe of Torpoint was to be a key player behind a challenge to the Fowey Corporation in 1806.[42] The coincidence is suspicious.

Nickels next turned his attention to navy contracts. No vessels had been placed with ports further west than Dartmouth, so he wrote to the Admiralty on 16 December 1805 offering to 'build Brigs or other vessels'.[43] Nickels achieved his objective and was awarded a contract for a vessel of 421 tons. He continued to write to the Admiralty, however, in a vain attempt to improve a tough contract. In his letters he showed clear knowledge of more favourable contracts placed elsewhere, referring to a friend who was being paid more.[44] The identity of Nickels' friendly informant is a mystery. He may have been another shipbuilder, such as Davey of Topsham who was a regular builder for the Admiralty or there is a possibility that it could have been Wigram, the Fowey M.P.

Sir Robert Wigram was a man of considerable influence and wealth, a Director of the East India Company and the owner of one of the biggest shipbuilding yards on the Thames. He had fitted out four ships as troop transports for government in 1795 and was a staunch supporter of Pitt. On applying to Pitt for a baronetcy in May 1805, he reminded him that his 'political loyalty' was well known to Pitt and claimed to have spent £300,000 much of it to benefit the navy.[45] Since Nickels was a strong supporter of the Corporation of Fowey and another election was due, the awarding of the navy contract was timely. 1806 saw a challenge to the Corporation's control of the M.P.s for Fowey when Joshua Rowe supported John Teed and Sir Alexander Cochrane as candidates. In the event Wigram's son, another Robert, became the M.P. for Fowey and Sir Robert senior became M.P. for Wexford.[46]

Nickels had his prize, the Royal Navy contract to build the brig HMS *Primrose* on 25 January 1806, but at a lower price per ton and with a short timescale. By 1807 he was bankrupt and the contents of the yard were offered for sale in the *Royal Cornwall Gazette* including 'The Slabs and Offals being left from the construction of a large Brigantine for Government'.[47] The cause of his bankruptcy was launched by his trustees one month later. It was the first and last Royal Navy contract awarded to a Fowey builder in the nineteenth century. Nickels survived and set up business again with his son, George.

Nickels had previously had very little competition in Fowey, At the turn of the century there were Collum and Willcocks who built a few vessels, average size twenty-eight tons and fifty tons respectively. This situation changed in 1809. Austen in his business dealings required ships, but since the main builder Nickels was a supporter of the opposing party, he turned to William Brokenshaw, who had recently moved from Mevagissey to set up his shipbuilding business. Brokenshaw had married the daughter of George Beer, a close political ally of Austen. Brokenshaw became Austen's ship agent, both helping him to buy ships from elsewhere and building ships in Fowey.

By 1817 the battle between the Greys, the corporation party, and the Blues, Austen's party, was intense. Austen decided to take more direct action to influence the Fowey voters writing to Adam Thomson, a close friend, on 8th February 1817:

Mr. Beer and self have just had a little talk about the best method of keeping people here in the right path . . . We are decided that one pound laid out in trade which will cause

employment here will do more than ten pounds given to
them for corrupt purposes. Whatever is done should be done
quickly for any stir in trade now would make our inhabitants
unanimous in petitioning against any attempt get a new
charter.

As part of his battle he had opposed a new town charter to Fowey
which he saw as only serving to put the same vested interests back in
power in the town.[48] One month later, in another letter to Thomson, he
wrote, 'There is no doubt of this town having once been a place of very
large trade, and from facilities which its fine harbour and situation
afford the revival of its commerce may be regarded as successful
speculation.' He sought two 'honest and independent men' who could
represent Fowey and support the trade of Fowey. Thomson's brother
was a London ship and insurance broker and well placed to introduce
ship owners and merchants to the town.[49] This route introduced a
wealthy West India merchant as a candidate and in 1818 Thomson was
able to tell Austen that 'Mr. Wildman wishes to lay down a vessel of
360 tons immediately for the Jamaica trade and would fit out and
sail her from our port [with] other ships.'[50] This did not happen as
Wildman was elected for Colchester in a by-election.

Meanwhile one of the opposition candidates, George Lucy, was
also persuaded to invest in Fowey shipping, buying a quarter of the
shares in one of Nickel's earlier vessels, *Yeomans Glory*, which had
been launched in 1813. The agent for the transaction was John Bennett,
a leader of the Corporation, and a keen supporter of Lucy's candida-
ture. Nickels was back in business and launched the *Henry* for London
owners in 1819, perhaps with help from Lucy or his fellow 'Grey'
candidate, Stanhope.

In the long, drawn-out battle between the Greys and Blues there
was some shifting of allegiance as men moved to work with former
rivals if they saw an advantage. The most significant change was when
Lucy, after being elected with the Corporation's active assistance,
formed a pact with Austen against them in 1819. The political battles
continued with increased bitterness and Lucy wrote to Austen in July
1824:

I think we are just as far from having a snug quiet borough as
we were in 1818 . . . You thought the building of five ships on
our concern would, by giving employment satisfy the people
. . . and I must say while there are such people in Fowey as
Hill, Hearle and Nicholls . . . there must be opposition.[51]

The vessels, all built by Brokenshaw, were the *Emerald, Lucy, Hero, Union*, and *Susanna*, launched between 1819 and 1821.

The Corporation, while severely wounded by Lucy's defection, was not lying down and fought an intensive campaign to attract other candidates who could influence the electorate. In 1824 they introduced Alexander Glynn Campbell and Colonel Hugh Duncan Baillie to Fowey. Campbell's father, as seen earlier, had customs places to bestow and Baillie was a partner in Evan Baillie and Company, merchants of Bristol. Baillie and Company were sugar merchants with trading interests in the West Indies and were regular purchaser of ships in Bristol, the average size being 300 tons. A ship was commissioned for them in Fowey, to be built, of course, by Nickels. It would be the largest ship to be built in Fowey for twenty years, 281 tons. Colonel Baillie insisted on the ship being insured during building 'in order to guard against the remote possibility of the Agents of the Opposite Party being wicked enough to attempt the destruction of the property by fire'.[52] The *George* was launched in 1826 with great ceremony watched by a 'numerous assemblage both on sea and land'.[53] The launch occurred, with excellent timing, just one week before the election.

The 1826 election was the last contested election in Fowey, with Austen and his candidates, Lucy and Eden, versus the Corporation's candidates, Baillie and Campbell. Both parties had sought to influence the electorate with shipping investment and proposed Government patronage, Campbell had customs posts to offer and Eden was a

Table I: Tonnage and number of new vessels built in Fowey 1786–1835

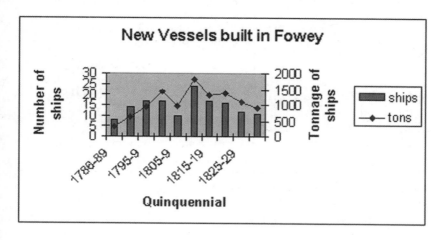

Table II: 'Political' ships and their shareholders

Date	Name	Ton	Type	Builder	Shareholders
1790	True Blue	12	Sloop	Unknown	Thomas Mein surgeon, Susanna Treffry widow (mother of J. T. Austen)
1794	Dolphin	51	Lugger	Nickels	W. Colmer, Thos Nickels
1795	Fowey	49	Sloop	Nickels	Sold to Navy Board (Wigram fitted 4 ships as troop transport 1795)
1803	Twins	309	Ship	Nickels	London merchants, Plummer & Bareham, & J. Rowe of Torpoint)
1807	HMS Primrose	384		Nickels	
1810	Ann & Elizabeth	87	Sloop	Brokenshaw/ Smith	Thomas Breed, Griffins Wharf London
1811	Elizabeth Ann	68	Sloop	Brokenshaw	Geo Beer & Adam Thomson
1813	Jane & Elizabeth	55	Sloop	Brokenshaw	Geo Beer & Adam Thomson
1813	Heed	101	Schr	Brokenshaw	Wm. Brokenshaw, Adam Thomson and George Beer
1815	Duke of Wellington	60	Schr	Brokenshaw	R. Leane, William Lane, J. T. Austen
1816	George	101	Schr	Brokenshaw	William Norway, George Beer, Adam Thomson
1819	Mary	65	Schr	Brokenshaw	Adam Thomson
1819	Henry	123	Bargtn	Nickels	for London owners, Lloyd
1819	Place	38	Sloop	Brokenshaw	George Beer & William Brokenshaw
1820	Emerald	92	Schr	Brokenshaw	Brokenshaw, Joseph Ham, J. T. Austen, Richard Leane, Wm Borlase
1820	Lucy	36	Smack	Brokenshaw	all J. T. Austen
1820	Hero	59	Smack	Brokenshaw	all J. T. Austen
1820	Union	85	Schr	Brokenshaw	all J. T. Austen
1821	Susanna	131	Snow	Brokenshaw	all Austen
1821	William	67	Schr	Nickels	Nickels, Brownfield of Greenwich,gent
1824	Hector	125	Brigtn	Nickels	James Hill, R. Hearle, George Nickels
1826	George	281	Ship	Nickels	Baillie & Co of Bristol
1828	Eliza Wolsley	37	Sloop	Nickels	all Joseph Sowell
1830	Hydra	25	Sloop	Brokenshaw (?)	all J. T. Austen

Source: Transcription of Fowey Ships registers by C. J. Ward Jackson
Cornwall Maritime Museum ships database, courtesy of Captain G Hogg, R.N.
PRO: BT 107/17 1804

protégé of Robert Peel. The shipbuilding yards of Nickels and Broken-shaw had both gained benefits from their respective parties. In the election on 13 June, Baillie and Campbell lost by 122 to 153 votes and there was much accusation of bribery by both sides.

An analysis of the ships built in Fowey between 1786, the start of ship registration, and 1832 shows a distinct pattern of political invest-ment. There were two categories: vessels where the main investors were local Blue or Grey party activists and those where the com-missioning of the vessel can be linked to prospective or sitting MPs. In the first category, some investment decisions may merely have been a preference for a shipbuilder who shared the same politics. In the second category there were deliberate attempts to influence voters. Two of the three largest vessels built in the port at this time all come into the second category, these were the *Twins* and the *George*, built by Nickels. The passage of the contract for HMS *Primrose* may had been smoothed with some political assistance since the Navy was often very reluctant to have ships built so far away, preferring sites that could be closely supervised.

The shifting allegiances of this period led to some strange alliances. Joshua Sowell had been an agent for Austen working with him for some years; he had been openly critical of Nickels's building methods, accusing him of using bad timber.[54] He subsequently fell out with Austen and in 1824 was seen as a supporter of the opposition. He was even able to overcome his previous doubts about Nickels by 1828 to commission a vessel, the *Eliza Wolsley*.

Politics did, in the event, bring trade to Fowey. By examining the registered shareholders in the vessels, it is possible to see which yards gained. Seventeen per cent of all the vessels built by Fowey based shipbuilders can be attributed to political motivations or influence (see

Table III: Nickels and Brokenshaw political and non-political ships

	Niclels non-pol	Nickels political	Brokensh non-pol	Brokensh political	Other builders	Total built in Fowey
No. of ships	46	9	6	14	71	146
Total tons	3,438	1,426	457	1,003	4,380	10,704
Average tonnage	75	158	76	72	62	73

Source: as Table I

Table III). By examining the vessels attributable to Nickels and Brokenshaw the influence of the 'political' ships is evident. In the case of Nickels, this contributed to 18 per cent of his vessels, but 32 per cent of the tonnage built by him. The percentages for Brokenshaw are highly significant, 88 per cent of the vessels built by him are linked to the Blue party and 84 per cent of tonnage.

Without the support of Austen, Brokenshaw might well have been forced out of business such was the dominance of Nickels. However, while the shipbuilders feature here, there were benefits, too, for the workforce at both yards, and for other Fowey businesses such as the sailmaker, ropemaker, blockmaker, and blacksmith. There was, in addition, work from the maintenance or repairs of those vessels remaining in the port.

CONCLUSION

While some individuals benefited from preferment or customs positions, the wider community of Fowey looked in vain for other opportunities. From the late eighteenth century to the last contested election in 1826, the people of Fowey watched the political sideshow where the motivations of the various parties encompassed the desire for power, personal advancement, and business growth. The gains were limited to a small number of people: the electors represented just 1 per cent of the 1801 population of 1,155.[55] Some individuals gained positions through the candidate's promises, but many of the grander promises proved to be empty. The wider populace no doubt became jaundiced by the electoral promises of so many candidates, all of whom announced the great benefits they could bring to the business of the town.

Once elected, the MPs—with the exception of Rashleigh and Pole Carew—were disappointments to Fowey. Lucy, when pushed by Austen about the lack of benefits flowing to Fowey, complained that 'the Government, if they have interfered it has certainly not been in our favour on any occasion that I can recollect, and considering the support given them in parliament I think their behaviour is scandalous'.[56] Special criticism, possibly to deflect criticism away from himself, was reserved for his fellow MP, Peel's favoured candidate Eden: 'Then the disappointment that Mr Eden has caused. I hope at your late interview at Whitehall Place you touched on this subject and whether Mr Eden considered it no part his bargain to serve his Fowey friends.'[57] If Austen had been able to raise the subject it would have had little effect, Eden was wholly unimpressed with Fowey. He wrote to Peel, 'You will be happy to hear that I am returned after three days very arduous Contest . . . almost every vote was contested which accounts for so great a space of time being wasted on so inconsiderable a place.'[58]

In Fowey, the main parties were too busy fighting elections and spending large sums of money on the electoral battles to assist the town in capitalizing on its geographic benefits of a large deep-water harbour and closeness to the mines. The political rivals, Austen and Rashleigh, were unable to come to an agreement on a route that would have enabled the output from Austen's copper mines to be shipped from Fowey. Austen was forced to spend money building a new harbour at Par in 1830, which rapidly became the competitor to Fowey's facilities both in shipbuilding and trade.

The political investments in shipping certainly helped Brokenshaw, who was able to challenge the virtual monopoly of Nickels. Up to 1832 Brokenshaw was heavily dependent on Austen and his party. While for Nickels, the investments were an additional way to get customers and his business was not wholly reliant on his political connections. His big benefit was in gaining larger contracts that might otherwise have been possible, even if in one case it brought near collapse.

For many of the key players the stakes were high. The whole period was high risk, large sums of money were spent and the continuing loyalty of any man could not be assumed as shifts in allegiance were frequent. One individual who seemed to relish the opportunities that came his way was Thomas Willcocks Nicholls. He remained loyal to the power base that enabled him to exert unusual leverage to gain his appointment. His reward came from his capture of a prize ship and enabled him to retire to Fowey to continue as a thorn in the side of Austen for many years. While there is scepticism about the ability of politicians to have any real influence on naval promotions, Nicholls seems to be the exception. When the government needed the Fowey seats for it supporters, Nicholls was confident he, and his friends in the Corporation, could deliver the votes helped by a sprinkling of positions in the Customs service.

Positions and patronage did help to win some votes, but the Blue party's determination to oppose the status quo meant that both groups had to make greater efforts to demonstrate the benefits their party could bring to trade in the town. In Fowey, trade equated with ships. But if bribery and some trade brought limited benefits, one noisy and colourful aspect of the electioneering scene was lost after 1832, and that was the campaigning. One example of a campaign procession of the prospective parliamentary candidates in 1826, organized with naval precision, features T.W. Nicholls as 'Triton', the name of his prize ship. The proceedings were reported in a letter to Austen:

About dusk their landau was drawn through the town by a parcel of boys and candidates for situations in the Excise, proceeded by a grand display of flags bearing different mottoes, what I could not decipher, and a few musical instruments —they were supported in their carriage by a trio, viz. Bottlemarker, Tight-Lie and Triton, and the rear was brought up by at least 50 virgins (not one of whom I should imagine exceeding 12 years of age) and a few boys.[59]

NOTES AND REFERENCES

1. Cornwall Record Office [hereafter CRO]: R 5507/4 21 November 1817.
2. J.T Austen changed his name to his mother's maiden name, Treffry, in 1838.
3. E. Jaggard, 'The Political World of Sir Christopher Hawkins', *The Journal of the Royal Institution of Cornwall*, 2000, p. 99.
4. E. Jaggard, *Cornwall Politics in the Age of Reform*, Cambridge, 1999, p. 3.
5. Jaggard, 1999, p. 49.
6. R. Thorne, *History of Parliament: House of Commons, 1790–1820*, Vol. II, London, 1986, p. 57.
7. Jaggard, 1999, p. 55.
8. CRO: R/5690.
9. The National Archives: Public Record Office (hereafter TNA:PRO): T 1/451 1 February 1765.
10. TNA: PRO: T 1/451.
11. N.A.M. *Rodgers, The Wooden World*, London, 1986, p. 328.
12. J. Lewis, 'J T Austen and the Struggle for Power in Fowey 1816–1833', unpublished paper, n.d., p. 79.
13. Lewis, n.d., p. 85.
14. Society of Merchant Venturers of Bristol: West India Association Miscellaneous papers, 15 February 1815. Memorial to Treasury re seizures of property by customs officers.
15. Lewis, n.d., p. 105.
16. Lewis, n.d., p. 134.
17. Lewis, n.d., p. 125.
18. Thorne, 1986, p. 53.
19. Rodgers, 1986, pp. 330–31.
20. Rodgers, 1986, p. 335.
21. CRO: R/5083, 17 December 1813.
22. CRO: R/5083, 13 January 1814.
23. Rodgers, 1986, p. 301.
24. CRO: R/5083, 13 April 1814.
25. Thorne, 1986, p. 845.
26. CRO:R/5083, 28 June 1814.
27. CRO: R/5083, 2 July 1814.
28. CRO: R/5083, 6 July 1814.
29. CRO R/5083, 6 August 1814.

30. Thorne, 1986, p. 457.
31. *Royal Cornwall Gazette*, 30 March 1816; quoted in I. Pickering, *Some Goings On*, Fowey, 1995, p. 46.
32. J. Keast, *The Story of Fowey*, Exeter, 1950, p. 98.
33. Lewis, n.d., p. 136.
34. CRO: MSR Fowey Registers 13/1790.
35. Keast, 1950, p. 89 and Thorne, 1986, p. 53.
36. L. Namier and J. Brooke, *The House of Commons 1754–1790*, Vol. II, p. 228.
37. CRO: R/5083, 6 August 1814.
38. Lewis, n.d., p. 133.
39. Bartlett Library, National Maritime Museum Cornwall: Ships database.
40. *Royal Cornwall Gazette*, October 1803.
41. TNA: PRO: BT 107/17 1804/13.
42. Thorne, 1986, p. 54.
43. TNA:PRO ADM 16/1587.
44. TNA:PRO. ADM 16/1587.
45. Thorne, 1986, p. 555.
46. Thorne, 1986, pp. 54–55.
47. *Royal Cornwall Gazette*, 18 July 1807.
48. Lewis, n.d., p. 16.
49. Lewis, n.d., p. 17.
50. Lewis, n.d., p. 39.
51. Lewis, n.d., p. 103.
52. Lewis, n.d., p. 105.
53. *Royal Cornwall Gazette*, 10 June 1826.
54. J. Keast, *The King of Mid Cornwall*, Redruth, 1982, p. 57.
55. Thorne, 1986, p. 53.
56. Lewis, n.d., p. 103.
57. Lewis, n.d., p. 133.
58. Lewis, n.d., p. 118.
59. CRO: TF 916 quoted in Lewis, n.d., p. 124.

'AS CORNISH AS POSSIBLE'—'NOT AN OUTCAST ANYMORE': SPEAKERS' AND LEARNERS' OPINIONS ON CORNISH

Kenneth MacKinnon

AN INDEPENDENT ACADEMIC STUDY ON CORNISH

On 22 December 1999 I was remitted by the Secretary of State for the Environment, Transport and the Regions (DETR) to undertake in January and February 2000 an Independent Academic Study on Cornish. As the result of Parliamentary representations by Andrew George, M.P. for St Ives, on an adjournment motion on 23 February 1999, the United Kingdom government considered signing the European Charter for Minority or Regional Languages with respect to the Cornish language. The study was to provide a body of factual information on Cornish which would guide the government in its decisions. The study was managed by the Government Office for the South West, and reported to DETR on 24 March 2000.[1] By this time the government had signed the Charter—but without the inclusion of Cornish—and ratified it on 27 March 2001, again without inclusion of Cornish. Subsequently, however, the Government announced that it would include Cornish in the provisions of the Charter.[2] In this it was doubtless guided by the Academic Study, but representations had also been made by Scottish and other sources through the Council of Europe Committee of Experts to the UK government in 2002 concerning delay in its recognition of Cornish. The Government subsequently made an official declaration on 11 March 2003, which was registered by the Council of Europe on 18 March 2003, that the UK recognizes that Cornish meets the Charter's definition of a regional or minority language for the purposes of Part II of the Charter.[3]

In the course of the Study three focus groups were held for speakers, learners and members of organizations of each of the three major language-varieties:

- for Common Cornish—Kernewek Kemmyn—on Saturday 19 February 2000 in St Austell Church Hall 12:30–14:00;
- for Unified and Unified Revised Cornish—Kernewek Ünys—on Saturday 19 February 2000 in Church Rooms, Lostwithiel 15:00–16:30; and
- for Late/Modern Cornish on Tuesday 22 February in Conference Chamber F116, Truro College, 19:00–20:30.

These meetings followed a common structure, prompted by a questionnaire exploring:

- The Language Revival and its significance
- Resources and financial support for the language movement
- Problems arising out of the language varieties
- Cornish in social life
- Cornish in public life
- Cornish in economic life
- Cornish and its future

Full verbatim transcripts of these meetings, and summaries, together with a copy of the questionnaire, have been deposited in the Cornish Studies Library, Redruth, and in the libraries of the Institute of Cornish Studies and Royal Cornwall Institution, Truro. These transcripts are reported and commented upon below in sequence of their date order. These texts provide a perspective on speakers' and learners' opinions and attitudes on Cornish, and current concerns regarding the language. This paper identifies salient issues arising out of this body of opinion and attempts further to discuss their implications.

KEMMYN (COMMON) CORNISH FOCUS GROUP: OPINIONS, ATTITUDES, ISSUES

1) Language Death?

The Prayer Book Rebellion of 1549 was seen as a major initial factor of language death. This was regarded as 'The Cornish Holocaust' in which, it was alleged, 11 per cent of the population—half the able-bodied male population—was killed. The language was also weakened by the ensuing severance of links with Brittany, and the refusal of a Cornish liturgy and scriptures by the Church. There had been substantial decline during the seventeenth century, and cessation as community speech in the eighteenth. Nevertheless, there was evidence for some continuity of knowledge of Cornish throughout the nineteenth century, such as oral tradition (counting in Cornish, knowledge of the Lords' Prayer), literary competitions, and continuing awareness of the existence of the language.

2) Revival

The revival of Cornish, led by Henry Jenner and Robert Morton Nance, seemed to come at a time when the British Empire and its associated attitudes were at their height. This seemed to be a period of widening awareness at least, and if the revival did not 'take off' at that point, it was 'taking off' now in circumstances when there was some crisis of confidence in 'being English' and what it was for. The revivalists could give direction and focus but they had not invented the consciousness or knowledge of the language. In the past the language had been a badge of peasant ignorance, of 'west-country yokels'. But now it was a measure of self-worth and community values, and a means of motivating people to do things they might never otherwise have thought themselves capable of.

Evidence of demand for information about Cornish was forthcoming, and there had been changes of attitudes over the past twenty years. One lady reported that, 'The attitude changed very subtly over the years from the hostile.' There was rising demand for attention to the language in the schools, going back to initiatives by Edwin Chirgwin in the 1930s, E.G. Retallack Hooper's school at Mount Pleasant, and pupils' demands at Helston in the 1970s. Several of the informants were themselves involved in Cornish language activities in schools. These demands were now being met in many instances.

3) Speakers and Users Today

There was a greater measure of consensus in this group than others on the numbers of actual speakers, and those with some knowledge of the language. Twenty years ago, maybe twenty to forty persons might have an effective everyday ability in Cornish. Today that number was around 200. Knowledge at the level of a few words and phrases might be shared by about 3,000. This was fairly consensual too.

Cornish was also now used for special registers (such as a lecture on the eclipse), and there was evidence produced of bilingual homes, and families where children were being brought up to speak Cornish.

The point was emphasized that a Cornish community in the home had to be created in order for children to maintain the language.

4) Media and the Arts

Respondents were themselves involved in a number of media and cultural activities, involving Cornish poetry readings, theatrical productions, video and film, live music, song contests, festivals, and record production. There was lively discussion on whether Objective One status might be able to assist these initiatives further. The view was emphasized that there existed a wealth of actual talent using the Cornish language for all these activities. But it was not getting its due measure of recognition, nor official financial support.

5) Language Varieties

People were aware of enmities in the past, but a more tolerant view now seemed general. Concerning the different varieties, one lady said: 'It's up to them to produce their books, to support their classes, to resource their need.' Some negative views were expressed about the role of academics regarding the language. But more positive notes were sounded on providing music for another group's activities, and good conversational relations with folk there. The spelling argument had produced increased awareness of the language, and had not hindered mutual intelligibility.

6) For the Future

Tourism and the influx of newcomers were seen as a risk of 'Cornwall becoming sterilized and appearing the same as everything else.' The language and culture 'should be assisted and helped in every way so that we can keep up part of our uniqueness and . . . it does not become another area that is . . . just the same as anywhere else, which certainly it's not', was one man's view.

Another felt: 'The best is yet to come.' And the final word summed up the best hope for the future: 'Children learning *Kernewek*.'

UNIFIED (REVISED) FOCUS GROUP: OPINIONS, ATTITUDES, ISSUES

1) Continuity

Several members of the group provided evidence of known speakers and users of the language from the end of the eighteenth and throughout the nineteenth century. Thirty-two such people were known, including a case of transmission from a nurse *c.* 1790–1800 to an old man still living at the end of the nineteenth century. The Kelynack family of Newlyn also preserved traditional Cornish sayings and lore. There were even attempts to teach Cornish at the Cathedral School before the First World War.

Everyday knowledge of Cornish—especially in farming contexts —was attested by knowledge of the local names, field names, etc., and their meanings. There did seem to be some sort of 'apostolic succession', as this tradition became taken up by early revivalists, such as Lach-Szyrma, Jenner, Allin-Collins, and Morton Nance. There was awareness too that Cornishmen had played a part in the revival of English in the later Middle Ages—and a feeling that it was appropriate now for the favour to be returned.

2) Identity

Motives for this revival echoed Jenner's famous rhetorical question: 'Why should Cornishmen learn Cornish? . . . the answer is simple. Because they are Cornishmen.'[4] One man said, 'It defines who we are.' One lady said that 'in an ideal world . . . people would come up with what is their local language, what they feel to be their language, and ideally maybe a world language as well. In an ideal world everyone would have one that gave them their sense of personal identity and ability too.' My own view that this was the case for most of the world's inhabitants, was rejoindered by one lady: 'It's only the English who can't!' Other points made in discussion focused on a sense of common Celtic identity: a helpful Irish enterprise adviser and a pilgrimage to Galicia.

Interest in Cornish was no longer seen as a nationalist or anti-English issue, more a case of asserting cultural identity as opposed to being militant. Bilingualism is being seen not just as ideal—but normal. One view was that French, Spanish or German bilingualism was not going to involve people in Cornwall—'the only other language in which the Cornish people will become bilingual is Cornish'.

3) Power Relationships

Cornish seemed, at least to one man, to enjoy 'a colossal reservoir of goodwill'. Many people showed interest and encouragement to people learning the language. But there were still people who were not just indifferent but hostile: 'some people in senior positions who are definitely hostile and are on record as saying fairly unkind things about the language'. Cases were cited of Cornish welcomes being removed from successful tourist literature and signage. One participant identified three distinct issues which he termed 'the elite dominance effect . . . of a few people who are exerting undue influence by the positions they hold . . . the state education system which is not structured in a way which can engage with Cornish and . . . the fear of being seen as a second rate citizen'. One lady saw problem as, 'a power thing, isn't it?, If you have no language, you have no power . . . consequently if we lost our language, then we're powerless.'

This unequal power relationship was seen, historically, as beginning with the replacement of Cornwall's Cornish-speaking aristocracy by unsympathetic English or Anglicized gentry in the Civil War period, and the insistence on using English in social relations. A lady added: 'The interesting thing is that the language probably partly died out for the same reason people weren't speaking the accent either. English has really become the language of power. You would have had to have learnt English to have got on.' There was stigma even today in using a Cornish accent or dialect. Hostility could still even result from passing a bilingual cheque.

4) Resources

Improvements in cultural infrastructure over the past twenty years were seen as: 'Not a jot' or 'very few and far between', 'all bottom up—nothing top hand whatsoever'. 'If you doubled the number of teachers . . . you double the number of people taking Cornish . . . It is as simple as that . . . because the demand is so great'. But 'people teaching Cornish have no infrastructure to keep classes going', and if a teacher who receives no support has to move house or retire, or becomes too old or too ill to continue, things tend to collapse. Others blamed the National Curriculum for failing to provide for Cornish in the schools.

Another view was: 'It's got to come from the state education system . . . It's the only infrastructure that's capable of transferring the language to that number . . . I think we do extremely well as a language movement . . . every time someone runs a class . . . there's always people to populate it.' One lady felt that most parents would like their children to have the chance to learn some Cornish. Another felt children might choose Cornish instead of French. Others were critical of the education authority for refusing a survey and for failing to provide for the needs of already bilingual children.

On the question of funding for language initiatives, one man said: 'We contribute mightily to the Treasury, how about the Treasury contributing mightily to us?' He also compared the situation in Cornwall with that in Wales. There was discussion too on the prospects for better funding as the result of Objective One moneys becoming available. Raising the precedents of language-related initiatives in the Highlands and Islands being similarly funded, respondents thought that the South West Development Agency structure would result in the funding and jobs going to Exeter and Plymouth. However, one respondent's Cornish-related business initiative had been funded by Plymouth Enterprise. This respondent reported buoyant demand for his products—from all parts of the language movement.

Cornish was seen to suffer from having no official recognition, and that 'we seem to be coming to the end of the things that we can do off our own back. If we've written to people, we've lobbied people, we've given them documentations, we've spoken to them and we've looked for ways of trying to get funding and tried reasonably hard. And none of this is happening for us. So we are coming to the end of reasonably doing [things] to just help jolly things along on their own.'

5) Numbers of Speakers

There was considerable variability in the group's impressions of how many people could manage an everyday conversation in the language, or speak on their own special field. There was even greater variability on how many people might know a few Cornish words and expressions. There was much better knowledge about the cases where people were actually using the language in home life and bringing up children to speak the language.

One of the factors was seen as the geographical spread of speakers and the difficulties of developing registers for everyday life without geographically tight-knit communities. One lady thought that: 'It's not quite yet a critical mass.' One man had taught himself to swear in Cornish. Others reported the use of Cornish on building jobs and mending cars. One participant felt that the problems of inhibitions in the uptake of Cornish, in the media, and in calculating the numbers of speakers, clearly called for a rigorously controlled census.

6) Language Varieties

Relations between speakers and users of the different language-varieties was reported generally as unproblematic. There had been difficulties arising out of 'language-politicians' in the past 'in stirring things up'. But such personalities were seen now as individuals without a great deal of widespread support. One lady said: 'ultimately the survival, the nourishing of the language is bigger than anything these problems cause'.

One lady saw differences getting 'smaller and smaller'. There might be problems with organizers but actual speakers of the different varieties come to our events and we go to theirs. The annual Cornish-language Carol Service was a unifying event for all. The Gorseth provided an institution which was thoroughly Cornish and where the language reigned supreme.

Differences were not always hard-and-fast: for example, both Kemmyn and Modern/Late users might speak with Unified pronunciation whilst using their own orthographies. The different language-varieties were seen as 'regional dialects' by another respondent, who had an interesting view of the future of the language in these terms. One respondent explained: 'What's actually happened . . . political events have rumbled on . . . but people have tended just to get on . . . you have got this kind of upper, lower kind of thing going on . . . if left to its own devices . . . would settle down . . . and you'll probably be left with a west Cornwall dialect that would . . . sound . . . a little bit like Late Cornish, crossed with Unified, and probably written like a cross between the two. And in the east you'll proabably have something that sounds a bit like a cross between Unified and Kemmyn . . . maybe written like that.'

7) Public Life and Media

Cornish was reported as having featured in broadcasting and television. Since the end of Westward Television, and later the takeover of West Country by Carlton, Cornish was reported as having disappeared from local television. But TSW—who had held the franchise in the intervening period—was thought to have done some Cornish-language work. BBC Southwest was criticized as a public service broadcaster for not doing anything much for Cornish. Big events for Cornwall and Cornish were ignored. There had been more coverage for *Keskerdh Kernow*—the commemorative march to London in 1997—in Wales and other broadcasting areas than in Cornwall. There was, however, a five-minute news broadcast in Cornish on commercial radio.

The use of the language in public events was discussed. Local press dominance by the *Mail* group was criticized for trivializing the language, and regarding it as academic, a little bit weird, ancient, historical, or nationalist. The millennium and the eclipse were discussed. Eclipse t-shirts in Cornish were reported as doing 'a roaring trade'. The prospects for a new higher education campus in Cornwall were not anticipated as an opportunity for the language.

8) For the Future

Respondents saw the language as an opportunity for children. There were requirements for teachers and publications. The language might also benefit tourism. The last word was, however: 'I think it's the children thing.'

MODERN (LATE) CORNISH FOCUS GROUP: OPINIONS, ATTITUDES, ISSUES

1) Decline
Amongst the reasons put forward for the decline of Cornish were the Prayer Book Rebellion and loss of population which ensued, land-owners and loss of a Cornish-speaking aristocracy, loss of people overseas, and second-class citizen status. Some thought pockets of actual speakers survived. It made a lot of difference to perceptions whether you regarded the last native speaker as a Mousehole fish-wife speaking a quaint peasant language, or a scholar who taught mathematics to mining engineers. There might have been a vested interest in nineteenth-century antiquarians pronouncing survivals as 'the last', or languages as dead.

2) Revival
Revival was seen by one lady as claiming our right to a heritage which had been taken away. Jenner's original justification for learning the language was echoed in such responses as: 'Because I'm Cornish'; 'Because I'm not English'; 'Identity, really'; 'I just want to be as Cornish as possible'; 'Tradition'; 'Because it it's there to be learnt'.

Now there might be employment reasons for learning Cornish. One respondent sang Cornish in a choir when young. Now he wanted to know the meaning of what he sang. Respondents reported prejudice when they were at school. In the past, knowledge of and interest in Cornish might have made one a subject of prejudice—but not now. In the past there were few opportunities to learn Cornish. One respondent complained classes were so dull he fell asleep.

3) Language and History
Many complained of the neglect of Cornish history in their education. For example, the Industrial Revolution, in which Cornwall had played a leading part, was completely overlooked. Similarly, the Tudor period had also been ignored, in which there were several Cornish rebellions —with a language dimension—and in which there was great loss of life: up to half of Cornwall's able-bodied male population in 1549, it was claimed. This was seen as an important initial cause of the language's decline.

4) Identity
At one point there was a lively discussion whether closer political identity with Europe was in Cornwall's or the language's best interests. One respondent saw the English as having an identity crisis. He said:

'They don't like that now because their identity is getting lost.' One lady did not want some German or Frenchman giving out silly directives. Another did not want 'all those . . . people in Brussels earning an incredible amount of money tax free'. Discussion then turned to Objective One, and the ways in which new opportunities from Europe might help the language. Help came to Cornwall as the result of Breton M.E.P.s supporting Cornwall because they were aware of the language connection.

Respondents reported on awareness amongst those they knew of the language and its significance. People with knowledge of the language were no longer hiding it away. Speakers might openly use it at work and when they met. One lady said: 'When I was growing up people were hiding it away from them.' Another said: 'Made an outcast. Whereas now you're not an outcast any more.'

5) *Language in Education*

There was much discussion on the Cornish language at both school level and in other sectors of education. It had once been taught in a private school. It had also been a GCSE subject but changing regulations had meant that the Mode Three scheme had been lost. Adult classes had increased. A schools survey had once been refused. However, a survey on what was happening now was going ahead. Some adult classes were being held in people's homes.

Children were being brought up to speak Cornish: 'A couple of dozen', according to one man. Lack of opportunity to follow this up at school was blamed upon the National Curriculum. However, there were ways round this, and opportunities within it were discussed.

6) *Present-Day Speakers and Learners*

There was a great deal of variance on how many speakers and effective users of the language there might be. However, the group seemed fairly representative of present-day learners. One man said: 'We've got a real cross-section . . . the obvious people that are missing tonight are all the ones who've got babies . . . that's quite a high proportion.' This was seen as the commonest reason for dropping out of classes.

One lady said: 'Many of us are shop workers.' Others reported being in other 'working-class' jobs, and using Cornish with work-mates. One man said: 'My Cornish came on in leaps and bounds with that.' Another reported a similar experience and added: 'People were stopping and listening to us.' A man and a woman reported using Cornish in their social club. Many had experienced unemployment, and about three-quarters of the class had spent periods away from Cornwall as a result of crossing the Tamar in search of job opportunities.

7) Economy and Public Domain

Europe's 80 million speakers of lesser-used languages were discussed in relationship to cultural tourism. Cornish in public signage, and house and street naming, were both seen as increasing since the 1970s. One lady said that: 'it was more like a middle-class thing, and now it's anybody and everybody who wants to'.

Cornish was also reported as being used in choirs, in festivals such as Lowender Peran, and in theatrical productions such as Knee-High Theatre and its play 'The Riot'. This had been taken beyond Cornwall, and one man said: 'If it projects Cornish inside Cornwall, the more it's projected outside of Cornwall, the stronger it is likely to get in Cornwall.' There had also been co-operation between the various language groups in the Cornish committee of the European Bureau for Lesser Used Languages, in television initiatives, and in the County Council and local authorities' framework agreement on the language.

8) Tripartite Split

Place names and road-signs led into discussion on the three present-day forms of the language Many felt that it was quite usual for languages to have different dialects. North Welsh and South Welsh were very different, and English had many dialects and standard forms. Communication between the different forms of Cornish was not seen as a problem. There was discussion of signage for English Heritage sites and what form of Cornish should be used. One man said: 'Why haven't the three lots got together and gone to English Heritage and said, "Look, there are three kinds of Cornish here. Can we sit down and work out how it's going to be?"' A more realistic view was added by another, ' We don't really need to . . . we've just kind of almost agreed to differ now between ourselves in a short time, because we have tried desperately hard to reach an accommodation with each other and we've not been able to, and so we've just had to . . . live with each other's difference in terms of writing Cornish . . . so when a group is approached by a body . . . and they want to translate something then the person . . . the group they approach is [the one] who provides the translation, and other people don't complain about it'. Others agreed that it was more important to see Cornish in the public domain than to argue what form should be used.

A standard form was seen by one man as a *raison d'être* to sort it out. Another thought that 'there would be lots of practical advantages in having one written standard, but I don't think it's going to happen . . . That's the real problem.' There was extensive discussion on the problem, and one lady said: 'But then, natural progression in time, people can only use one version or find it easier to use one version, that one is going to become more popular no matter what is chosen as being official. So, common usage will dictate it eventually anyway.'

9) The Institutional Abolition of Cornwall

A real present-day problem was identified in the loss of Cornwall's institutions and public services 'up country', with police, vehicle-breakdown, and ambulance services not knowing where places were, protracted inquiry into how place-names were spelt, resulting not only in much inconvenience but also in life-threatening situations. As a result distinctively Cornish place-names were simply being removed from maps. Examples were cited. The possible future loss of the education authority was also seen as threatening the prospects of the language in the schools.

10) For the Future

Establishment of the language in schools remained the most salient way in which the future of the language could be secured: 'What would ensure the future of the Cornish language? Teaching it to kids at school.'

IMPLICATIONS AND CONCLUSIONS

The announcement of the government's intent to sign the Charter on behalf of Cornish was read popularly as an indication that the Cornish language was now to enjoy 'official status'. This was probably the first occasion that there has been any sort official recognition given to the language at governmental level. Whether that constitutes actual recognition of Cornish as an official language is a moot point, as Rob Dunbar's view on this makes clear (See endnote 2). In contrast, Scots Gaelic had enjoyed mention in crofting, land court, education, broadcasting, and nationality legislation going back to the nineteenth century, as well as an acceptance of its equal validity with English by the then Secretary of State, and Scottish Home and Health Department in 1970.[5] Nevertheless, in the absence of specific language status legislation, the official status of Gaelic continued to be challenged until UK Parliamentary statements were made earlier in 2003,[6] and draft bill measures were announced for implementation in the Scottish Parliament in the session 2003–04.[7] As a next step on that route, Cornish needs to advance to Part III recognition under the European Charter.

Discussion in the three focus groups threw up a number of salient issues. Several of these deserve some further consideration. These are examined more closely below, in sequence from the prompts in the questionnaire.

Revival and Identity

The late nineteenth and early twentieth centuries were the heyday of the British Empire. Yet this was seen as the point in time where the Cornish Revivalists initiated a centrifugal, as opposed to a centripetal, movement. The language became symbolized as the most salient feature of a local identity. It is no surprise that this led, a half-century later, to the emergence of a political nationalism and the sense of Cornwall as a nation in cultural as well as political terms. Jenner's 'simply because we are Cornish' was taking other dimensions. I have taken one respondent's reason for learning Cornish, to be 'as Cornish as possible', as a headline for this article. It epitomizes much of what several others said.

The respondents who identified today as a period of opportunity for language revival tied this in with an awareness of decline of Empire and a sense of identity crisis about being English. To parallel Ireland's earlier situation, England's adversity is Cornwall's opportunity.

However, other issues were tied in with language: community, individual self-worth, recovery of pride, and emergence from second-class status. Interest in things Cornish, and in the language in particular, was seen by observers as being 'weird' and 'peculiar' not so very long ago. Not only language, but also accent and dialect were seen as stigmas, and as the badge of country bumpkinhood. Not so now. Quite the converse, in fact: there was a demand for Cornish in public life and education, and a thirst for knowledge. The lady who reported that things were being concealed in her earlier life felt she had been 'Made an outcast. Whereas now you are not an outcast any more.' This echoed the case I had encountered earlier, outside the focus groups, of a house-keeping lady without formal qualifications or any prestigious job who had learned Cornish and achieved a good standard. She said: 'Now I can speak Cornish I really think I am a somebody. I'm not a nobody any more.' This very much epitomizes the highest aims of further and adult education.

A very sophisticated view was put by the lady who said that in an ideal world everyone would have their own language and a world language as well. My view that this might be quite normal for most of the world's inhabitants was rejoindered by the insistence that it is only the English who have not achieved this desirable status. There may be several insights here. Anglophone societies—the Anglosphere—are notorious in resisting other languages and insisting everyone speaks theirs. Without Cornish, Cornwall is just one other amongst many English-speaking societies. With its own language it is distinctive, and (like 'Galway Bay') has its own ethnolinguistic culture and a metalinguistic awareness that the monolinguals do not know.

Bilingualism is perhaps not so much an ideal as normal in the wider world. Cornish-English bilingualism was seen as a much more likely scenario than bilingualism involving our immediate continental neighbours.

Language, Community and Power

Cornish was seen to possess a 'colossal reservoir of goodwill'. It functioned too as the language of community—and not only in the past. However, there were still some inimical attitudes to be encountered—in some cases in positions of power and influence. Cornish signage might be resisted, Cornish welcomes cut out from tourist publicity, and Cornish in public places removed. One respondent identified three distinct issues relating to the inhibiting of Cornish in public life. These were:

1. the elite dominance effect: a few exerting influence by their positions;
2. the state education system which is not structured to engage with Cornish; and
3. the fear of being seen as a second-class citizen.

Language was seen as the key to power by one lady: 'If we lost our language, then we'd be powerless.'

The Celtic dimension was identified as a source of strength. Assistance for Cornish enterprise had come from an Irishman in the case of a small one-person business, and from Breton MEPS in the case of Objective One. It is tempting here to recall Edward Lhuyd, who three hundred years earlier on his peregrinations through Cornwall formulated the concept of a common Celtic identity shared by the very disparate non-English peoples of our archipelago. In 1707 his *Archeologica Britannica* gave these peoples a means of resisting assimilation as the Act of Union inaugurated the British state—and stole their ethnonym. Cornwall played its part in that.[8]

The Tripartite Split

The three current varieties of revived Cornish pose continuing problems. This study was conducted at a time when the very intense differences arising from this matter were certainly in abeyance. Some saw the protagonists as having lost a certain amount of sway, as people met across language-variety boundaries, and shared one another's events. Such institutions as the church services—especially the Carol Service—were uniting factors. So was the Gorseth—the one institution where pre-eminently Cornish took pride of place.

How the situation might resolve itself in the future was explored by some. One man thought that regional dialects of Cornish would emerge, with a West Cornwall dialect that would sound a bit like Modern//Late Cornish crossed with Unified, and in the east something that sounded like a cross between Unified and Kemmyn, and probably written like it. Another lady thought that a more 'natural' process would occur, whereby in time people would come to find it easier to use one version, and that is what would prevail.

But the lack of a common written standard is a real problem if the issues of increasing public use of Cornish is to be addressed. This was to some extent skated around by views such as that which imagined that should English Heritage approach a Cornish scholar in one movement or another, then his/her preferred form would that would be used on that occasion. Some people thought the real issue was to get any sort of Cornish into public view, irrespective of its form. But when Cornish does achieve this visibility, the realities of the issue will arise, and maybe spark off controversies once again. The issue of name-signs in Cornish is already arising. In some cases the forms being used have no traditional spelling basis. Maybe a start could be made by trying to get an agreed policy on place-signs. In this regard the use of the placename archive would be valuable, as would the long-overdue revision and publication of Gover's study for the English Place Names Society. Some such authority is essential for authentic forms of place-names for signage—and for blue plaques and mapping for *Forth an Yeth*, the Cornish Language Trail.

One voice expressed reservations with regard to academics and Cornish. Yet the linguistic issues of corpus planning have not yet been addressed in scholarly debate. So far this too has been quietly muted in view of past controversies. As a basis to this, the scholarly editing of the corpus of written Cornish of all periods needs to be advanced. It is putting the cart before the horse to attempt status planning before the spade-work of corpus planning has been thoroughly accomplished.

Education

Discussion focused on the setback for Cornish in education of the Mode Three GCSE scheme some years ago. School students are presently undertaking Cornish Language Board examinations, which are of course essentially adult-level in character. Subsequent developments since the study, such as at Hayle, are to be watched with great interest. But the present tripartite nature of Cornish presents its difficulties. The County Council may accept Cornish as a 'plural language'—but will all three varieties get a place in any future school level provisions?

The National Curriculum was seen as a major cause for the marginalization of Cornish in the schools. The present law of education in England regarding languages which may be taught greatly vitiates against Cornish. In the hierarchy of English first, then other European Union member-state languages (which includes Letzebürgisch), and other world and classical languages, Cornish simply has no place. This needs attention if Cornish is even to have the toe-hold of being taught as a second language, leading somewhere in terms of recognized qualifications. Cornishmen had once helped England to retain its language.[9] Now was the opportunity for the favour to be returned.

Further problems result from lack of resources and infrastructure, discontinuities as teachers (many voluntary) withdraw for all sorts of good reasons, and lack of good-quality teaching schemes, language packs, audiovisual resources, and books. There should be ways of utilizing the National Curriculum to work in favour of rather than against the Cornish language, for example, by using its provisions for minority time, local studies and the like. But if Cornish is to have some real advance in these areas in the short-to-medium term, planning, in-service training and production of teaching materials is essential. Modern technologies, inter-site video, internet, and new advances in distance-learning techniques could all play their part here.

One of the big problems for Cornish in the schools is critical mass. Demand is growing—but is widely spread out. That is why, so far, preschool initiatives have been hindered: not enough takers in any one area.

The Numbers Game

The methodology of the study was insufficient to make up for the lack of a census question, or in its absence a properly-funded research study of speakers, learners, users of the language and of public attitudes towards it. The lack of a census was specifically identified in one group. Subsequent to the study, a Cornish question on the 2001 Census was refused through 'lack of space' on the form It may be recalled however that there was in fact a blank space where the Welsh question was printed in Wales. Much of the discussion on language problems both by respondents in this study and in wider forums is uninformed without a census or a properly-resourced study on these lines. The Independent Academic Study was a useful initial inquiry. It now needs to be followed up by a language-use and public attitudes study.

Public Life and Media

Since the Independent Academic Study, several initiatives it identified have ceased. One was the biggest slice of the funding cake. I do not know whether anything else in its field has replaced it. This type of 'adhockery'—turning taps on, turning taps off—is no way to develop cultural infrastructure. The identification of much talent being exercised in the media, arts, and cultural life sphere calls for a study and a policy for the Cornish Language Arts. It is a resource that Cornwall needs to nurture, and is moreover of considerable economic significance. Unfortunately, without its own institutions, this is difficult.

The language has enabled Cornwall to punch above its weight internationally. The Inter-Celtic Film and TV Festival, the Inter-Celtic Song Contest—and securing Objective One status—are all good examples. The language means that Cornwall is not 'just another English county'. Today Cornwall faces another set of problems. We now turn to that challenge.

The Institutional Abolition of Cornwall

The land that is 'Cornwall, as an entire state, hath at divers time enjoyed sundry titles, of a kingdom, principality, duchy and earldom': Richard Carew's words from 1602.[9] It has subsequently enjoyed, and still does, the status of a shire county—but if prospects for further local government reform and for an elected South West Assembly come to fruition, Cornwall faces the prospect of becoming a mere district whose council will exercise few indigenous powers.

There are language-dimensions of this issue from both perspectives. The loss of police, vehicle-breakdown, public utilities, and emergency services—from being based in Cornwall to relocation in remote centers of power elsewhere—has resulted in delays as people try to identify locations and spell names: all utterly unfamiliar to their remote hearers. If these services are to take responsibility for local services they will need local familiarization. They do not get it. There is a language dimension to this. In 2003 the anticipated fatality resulting from this situation finally occurred.

Likewise cultural infrastructure is controlled by institutions outside Cornwall, over which Cornwall has no say or sway. Cornwall does not even have its own dedicated M.E.P. Luxemburg, of similar size, has six. Names are being taken off maps because they are un-English, and difficult for English speakers to spell or pronounce. We had that too in Scotland before devolution. If there is a case for enhanced rather than downgraded status for Cornwall, the language dimension may be one of the trump cards to play.

For the Future

The language could increase tourism. Prospects for cultural tourism have widened with the European Union. The language and culture could save and enhance the character of Cornwall. But above all other issues, each focus group saw the prospects of the language as lying crucially within the schools. They all concluded on that note. 'Children learning *Kernewek*', education seen as the only institution which could effectively deliver revival 'Teaching kids at school'; 'It's the children thing.'

For my own part, I would finally echo those who said that we have done very well as a language movement in making provisions, but we have come to the end of what we can do from our own resources. The language movement over the past century has raised itself by its own bootstraps, and has performed small miracles on a shoestring—often self-financed. The movement is progressing and it has reached the stage where it can legitimately claim a share in the provisions which modern society make for its cultural infrastructure. Languages and cultures are today supported by massive investment in the media, mass communications, education and the means of public administration. That this may be done for a majority language and culture is very much taken for granted, and maybe not seen as such—but it occurs nevertheless anyway, and everybody pays for it. Cornish speakers, learners and supporters also pay taxes, both local and national. They too are entitled in an open and participating democracy for their share of contributions be spent on their fair share of the cake. One respondent said that, 'We contribute mightily to the Treasury. Now it is the time for the Treasury to contribute mightily to us.'

The Cornish language movement can justifiably expect its own fair share to be returned to it. Such measures, if forthcoming, will need some form of co-ordination and planning. This calls very clearly for the creation of a language development agency, and that implies too a language planning body. These are questions not for a far-distant future. They are already upon us, as Cornish is being increasingly assisted from public funds.

I return in the end to the issue of self-value and self-worth, and recall the lady who was reported to me as nothing out of the ordinary, but having learned the language to a good standard, she felt 'Not a nobody any more!'

Acknowledgements

I am grateful to the Institute of Cornish Studies, University of Exeter, for inviting me to present this paper as the annual Caroline M. Kemp Memorial Lecture at the Royal Institution of Cornwall, Truro, on 1st December 2003.

I wish to thank Dolina MacLeod of Lews Castle College,

Stornoway, for undertaking transcription of the three focus group recordings, for which I am very grateful.

I am very grateful also to Dr Bernard Deacon, Lecturer at the Institute of Cornish Studies, University of Exeter, for assistance with Modern/Late Cornish expressions in the relevant transcript.

That said, I must emphasize that in the small number of instances where inferencing of the actual words spoken was difficult, the final interpretation has been my own, and my own responsibility.

I am also very greatly obliged to Mr Rob Dunbar, Senior Lecturer in Law at the University of Glasgow, for his information and advice on the legal status of Cornish.

Finally, but essentially, I thank DETR and GOSW for enabling this study to be undertaken in 2000.

NOTES AND REFERENCES

1. A full version of the report can be accessed on GOSW website at: www.gosw.gov.uk/gosw
   And on my own at: www.sgrud.org.uk
   A summary, with commentary and recommendations of the principal author, is published as: K. MacKinnon, 'Cornish at its Millenium: an Independent Study of the Language Undertaken in 2000', in Philip Payton (ed.), *Cornish Studies: Ten*, Exeter, 2002, pp. 266–82.
2. *Western Morning News*, 22 July 2002.
3. Concerning the legal position of Cornish under the Charter, Mr Rob Dunbar, Senior Lecturer in Law at University of Glasgow, and an international specialist in the law of language and civil rights observed in a personal communication of 27 October 2003: 'The UK made a declaration by letter from the Permanent Representative of the UK to the Council of Europe, dated 11 March, 2003, and registered at the Secretariat General on 18 March, 2003 that the UK recognises that Cornish meets the Charter's definition of a regional or minority language for the purposes of Part II. The declaration is effective as of 18 March, 2003. This would not constitute either a further act of signature or ratification. Strictly speaking, I am of the view that this declaration has no real legal effect. While the Charter requires States to designate which regional or minority languages are to benefit from Part III, it does not require States to indicate their views on which languages are "regional or minority languages" for the purposes of the treaty. I have taken the view that on ratification, the Part II provisions of the Charter-the general commitments in Article 7 which apply to all "regional or minority languages" as well as "non-territorial languages"—automatically applied to all of the UK's regional or minority languages, as that term is defined under Article 1 of the Charter itself. As the Charter does not require States to take any views on what are its regional or minority languages, and as it defines how these languages are based on objective principles, I am of the view that the Charter applied in

respect of Cornish from the date that the UK's original ratification became effective. The subsequent declaration of 11 March, 2003 by the UK government is helpful in that it indicates that the UK accepts this obligation, but I am of the view that the obligation pre-existed and, indeed, existed independently of the UK's declaration, which has unclear legal value in any case.'

4. *Henry Jenner, A Handbook of the Cornish Language*, London, 1904, p. xi.
5. Communications from T. D. Ewing, Scottish Home and Health Department, dated 22 April 1970; and Gordon Campbell, Secretary of State for Scotland, dated 10 July 1970.
6. Informal statement by Mike Watson, Minister for Gaelic in 2002, and official statement in House of Lords, 12 June 2003 On question whether HM Government has any plans to give the Gaelic language legal or official status within the United Kingdom. [HL3159], Lord Evans of Temple Guiting replied: 'The United Kingdom Government ratified the European Charter for Regional or Minority Languages in March 2001. As a signatory to the Charter, the Government have signalled their clear commitment to maintain and promote the use of indigenous minority languages across the United Kingdom, including Gaelic. The Gaelic language has, therefore, official status within the United Kingdom, although the Scottish Executive has devolved responsibility for the development of the language within Scotland.' *Ipso facto* it must be concluded that Cornish likewise has official status in the eyes of the UK Government. Much more could be made of this newfound status, and much more could flow from it.
7. Announced by Peter Peacock M.S.P. 10 October 2003 The Gaelic Language Bill—Consultation Paper, Scottish Executive.
8. S. James, *The Atlantic Celts—Ancient People or Modern Invention?*, London, 2000, p. 47; D.S. Williams, *Prying into Every Hole and Corner —Edward Lhuyd in Cornwall in 1700*, Redruth, 1993.
9. John of Trevisa (*c*.1340–1402), Richard Pencrych, and John of Cornwall. In 1385 John of Trevisa 'observed that some forty years earlier two Oxford grammar school masters, both Cornishmen, named John of Cornwall, and after him Richard Pencrich, had taken the lead that boys should translate . . . Latin . . . not into French but English'. Quoted by L.C.J. Orchard, 'John of Trevisa *c*.1340–1402' *Old Cornwall* VIII:5, Autumn 1975, pp. 227–35. Also see: Professor J.L. Fowler 'Notes on John Trevisa' *Old Cornwall* VIII:6, Spring 1976, pp. 298–300; and Peter Berresford Ellis and Seumas Mac a'Ghobhainn, *The Problem of Language Revival*, Inverness, 1971, p. 36.
10. Richard Carew of Antony, *Survey of Cornwall*, 1602; cited in Philip Payton (ed.), *Cornwall for Ever! Kernow Bys Vyken!*, Lostwithiel and Redruth, 2000, p. 118.

REX DAVID, BERSABE, AND SYR URRY: A COMPARATIVE APPROACH TO A SCENE IN THE CORNISH *ORIGO MUNDI*

Brian Murdoch

INTRODUCTION

There are various justifications for selecting for examination the scene in the medieval Cornish-language play *Origo Mundi* (itself part of the *Ordinalia* cycle) in which David seduces Bathsheba and has her husband, Uriah, killed. The story is told in the Vulgate II Reg. 11-12 (II Samuel in the *Authorised Version*, the names from which will be retained here in the light of the bewildering variety of forms for that of the lady in vernacular writings, although the Septuagint variation Bersabee, a possible confusion with the place-name Beersheba, is found in the Cornish text and other medieval works). The narrative is brief and begs a number of questions, principally of the characterization of Bathsheba, who is hardly even sketched, and of the justification of David, who has patently committed adultery and effectively murder.

The whole story is told, effectively, in two chapters of the Bible. In the first (II Reg. 11) we hear how Joab leads David's men into battle, whilst David, still in Jerusalem, sees a beautiful woman bathing, and discovers that she is Bathsheba, wife of Uriah the Hittite. He sends messengers, she is brought to him, sleeps with him, and becomes pregnant. Her only words in the entire passage are when she tells David that she is with child (II Reg. 11, 5). David sends for Uriah and gives him food and drink, urging him to return to his wife, but Uriah refuses even to go into his house when his comrades are still on the battlefield. David's immorality is compounded, therefore, by the attempt to send Uriah home and thus to provide a cover-up for the child, and had the strategy worked, presumably the relationship might not have continued. Only later does the question of succession become important, after the birth of the more technically legitimate Solomon.[1] As a second strategy, David now writes a letter to his general, Joab —cynically giving it to Uriah himself to deliver—telling him to place Uriah in the forefront of battle. Joab initiates a deliberately dangerous action and Uriah is killed, something which a messenger then reports to David, to the latter's satisfaction. The last two verses of the chapter are very brief in terms of content. First, Bathsheba mourns for her husband; and when the mourning is over, David marries her and she bears him a son, but, we are told, God is angered by this. The following chapter constitutes a response to this tale of adultery and murder. Nathan the prophet, David's advisor, tells him a parable of a greedy rich man who takes the single lamb from a poor man, and when David makes the appropriate response, that the rich man deserves to die, Nathan reveals the sense of the parable as a condemnation of David's treatment of Uriah. David repents, and Nathan pronounces the judgement that the child, rather than David, shall die, which duly happens. Bathsheba then bears Solomon, and is not heard of again until the next book of Kings in the context of Solomon's succession.

Even within the immediate biblical narrative, David is, if not exonerated, then at least forgiven: Nathan, after making clear to David the immorality of his acts, says that David shall not die, which is what he deserves, and although the first child of the union dies, the second child is Solomon. We are also told later in the Bible, in the opening to Vulgate Psalm 50, that that Psalm—the *Miserere*, Lord have mercy— was composed by *David cum venit ad eum Nathan propheta, quando intravit ad Bethsabee*, and so it is presumably a reflection of David's contrition. In III Reg. 15: 5 (I Kings 15: 5) David is praised, but with a specific exception made about his behaviour towards Uriah the Hittite, although that qualification may be a later gloss, and he is praised without any such qualification elsewhere (III Reg. 11: 34 and 38). The incident is not mentioned in Chronicles. As the mother of Solomon, Bathsheba acquires a new importance, and is honoured by her son as Queen Mother (III Reg. 2: 19); in the New Testament she is afforded a different importance (though she is not named), within Matthew's geneaology of Christ: *David autem rex genuit Salomonem ex ea quae fuit Uriae*, of her that had been the wife of Uriah (Matthew 1: 6). The memory of Uriah's name, then, seems to have lasted rather better than hers. The importance of David and Bathsheba and indeed of their union contrasts, then, with the actual presentation of events, and if David's actions have to be afforded what might now be called spin, those of Bathsheba leave things open, with virtually no biblical help with the answers. Uriah's role is honourable, but he is a Hittite, and therefore not a Jew. Bathsheba may be viewed as the victim of regal rape, as a seductress whose self-display whilst bathing is a provocation, or as one who acquiesces with David's demands for reasons which are also unknown. It is no surprise that feminist theologians have exhibited particular interest in the incident.

A complex story already, in biblical terms, the version offered by the *Origo Mundi* has two further points of interest. First, it has a tangential connexion with the Holy Rood Legends, which play a significant and unusual part in the play as a whole. The story, however, does not in fact figure very prominently in most versions of the Holy Rood legend as such, and Bathsheba is not even named in every version, so that whether the story should be seen in Cornish as an expansion of the Bible or of the Rood legends is a matter of debate. And secondly, the story is rare in medieval drama as a whole, although it is treated fairly regularly in other genres. Of course, David is in briefer references often simply praised as the divinely inspired composer of the Psalter, or as the great king and prophet, without reference to the incident at all, which is, admittedly, something of a distraction to his image as a type of Christ.[2] We do not find it in the middle-English play-cycles, although it is there in the French *Mistére du viel Testament*, and also plays from the time of the Reformation: in the Protestant context, it provides a valuable demonstration of salvation by Divine grace alone, since whatever David's other good works might have been, this is not amongst them. There are later dramatizations, from George Peele's drama of 1599 down to a modern Yiddish play by David Pinski and a Hollywood film of 1951, both discussed by Alice Bach[3] as offering yet more literary methods of interpreting a biblical story at the centre of which is such an 'openly constructed character' as Bathsheba, of whom the lack of biblical detail allows 'the reader the freedom to move beyond the printed page', which presumably means that the interpreter can make up more or less anything he or she likes.

The story leaves much scope for augmentation, and it is problematic in theological terms. I cite H. W. Hertzberg's recent commentary in John Bowden's transation: 'the story of David and Bathsheba has long aroused both dismay and astonishment; dismay that King David, with his manifest piety, could stoop to such an act, and astonishment that the Bible narrates it with such unrelenting openness'.[4]

Even early commentators offer readings which exonerate David, however. Talmudic commentary interprets the whole incident as a testing of David, who is tricked by Satan, and other rabbinic texts play down the effective murder of Uriah, seeing it either as a judicial error, a proper punishment for disobeying David and failing to visit his wife, or indeed pointing out that a Hittite should not be married to a woman of Israel.[5] In Christian exegesis the blame is sometimes shifted onto Bathsheba for the whole thing; the *Glossa Ordinaria* cites Ambrose, but is of course a widely disseminated text, noting that David would not have committed adultery, *nisi nudam et lauantem mulierem de domus suae interioribus vidisset*. Bathsheba's brazenness, what has been called her "unchecked animal appetites" may lie therefore at the root of it all.[6] The same idea is used to exonerate Reuben's presumed seduction of his father's concubine Bilhah (Gen 35: 22): it is claimed in the apocryphal *Book of Jubilees* that he does so when he sees her bathing, and presumably this is a back-interpretation from the David story.[7] Against this, modern literary criticism of the biblical text points out that there is nothing to support this reading of Bathsheba in the original, and that the emphasis is on David's sexuality, with Bathsheba an object of desire, leading to murder.

The extensive iconographical history of the scene is instructive. The scene can be visibly critical of David, emphasising his role as voyeur, looking down, usually, on the apparently unrealising Bathsheba from his palace as she bathes. The configuration of the narrative element in art is important. As a medieval example, in the so-called Bible of St Louis, the huge thirteenth-century illustrated Parisian manuscript, the relevant roundel is laterally divided between David gazing from his palace and the naked Bathsheba in a tub, but some representations avoid the nakedness. The painting by Lucas Cranach the Elder (1526) has her clothed, with maids washing only her feet, and David is less prominent, but present nevertheless, on the roof with his harp. In a tapestry from the Rhineland dated 1550, David is pictured with his harp, within the walls of his city whilst Bathsheba is bathing this time by a stream.[8] Against this, other celebrated examples present the observer precisely (and exclusively) with the naked beauty of Bathsheba, and reduce further or remove David altogether, so that in some cases we, as observers, become the king within the iconographical narrative, as in Hans Memling's 1485 picture, or the paintings in the Louvre by Rembrandt, where she is reading David's letter, and by Willem Drost, both of 1654.[9]

THE SCENE IN *ORIGO MUNDI*

What, then, does the *Origo Mundi* do with the scene?[10] David has found the rods that will become the Cross, and they have already performed several healing miracles. Suddenly, however, we have a new scene as David addresses Bathsheba who is, if the later augmentation to the Latin stage direction is to be accepted, on this occasion washing clothes, rather than herself, and specifically in a stream, where the

Bible is somewhat vague. If she is indeed washing clothes, this is doubtless a change for dramatic reasons, since she cannot actually be portrayed naked. But it is an odd adaptation, and is solved elsewhere by having her washing her feet or hands—the painting by Cranach the Elder has been mentioned. Even these lose the point of ritual purification (after menstruation) mentioned in the biblical text. David addresses her directly—there is nothing of the biblical questioning of who she is, and no intermediaries—and he declares in courtly fashion that he wishes to be her husband—*vethaf the wour* (OM 2111). She agrees heartily in words that are, of course, not in the Bible, but is fearful only of being found out, because Uriah, who is not named yet, but who is characterized by her as hateful, *casadow* (OM 2119), and liable to kill her if he found her out. Nevertheless she returns with David, who now swears that Uriah shall be killed: *syr vrry a fyth lethys* (OM 2123), something which Bathsheba reinforces bluntly: *ov arluth whek ol lath e* (OM 2133), 'my dear lord, kill him'.[11]

The suddenness of the switch of address on David's part in his next speech from a promise to Bathsheba that *ef a vyth . . . marow* (OM 2137f.) 'he shall be dead' to an address to Uriah has led to the speculation that something is missing here, the more so as David's words to Uriah come at the top of a folio in Bodley 791. But there is no real reason for thinking this, nor indeed is it clear what might be missing.[12] It is presumably a simple, if abrupt, scene-change. Uriah has not been (as in the Bible) away in battle, because the syncopated version of the story offered here moves to what is biblically a later part of David's subterfuge. Bathsheba's pregnancy is omitted, as is therefore the attempt to cover it up, and the business with Joab and the letters is also obviated. By sending Uriah away directly into battle personally, however, and claiming that he himself is too unwell to go, David's guilt is far more direct. Uriah appears throughout as loyal, just as he does in the Bible, and to David's less than subtle comment that Uriah should be in the forefront of battle so as not to be deemed afraid, he agrees that *ny'm pref den war gowardy* (OM 2161), no one will take me for a coward, the words used, almost, by heroes such as Roland at Roncesvalles. His honesty counterpoints David's (and indeed also Bathsheba's) duplicity. Having acquired David's blessing he claims that he must bid farewell to his wife, or else *hy holon hy a torse* (OM 2174), it would break her heart, an irony indeed. Bathsheba's next, and indeed final speeches are of great interest, though textually not entirely clear, in heightening this irony still further. First she claims that she will die if he leaves, to which he responds that it is the will of the same lord to whom she has already, in fact, protested her love. As he leaves, she expresses her sorrow, almost as in the biblical passage after she hears of his death; but when, presumably, he is out of earshot, she adds that she will pray that he may never return. The text is not entirely clear at this point, and Norris (followed by some later editors) has her assert that she will always pray that he *does* return. This loses some of the dramatic effect, and the reading adopted by Nance and Harris of *byner (re)* as 'never' seems in any case more plausible. Without that reading, her farewell is just as hypocritical, but less markedly so, and might even be ambiguous.

Uriah (with David's butler, who has earlier been a comic but negative character) rides out of the play (*extra ludum*) and a messenger then reports that he has fallen, with great honour. Joab is not present of course, but more significantly, neither is Nathan, and the reform of David—Bathsheba does not appear again, and it is important to this version of the story that she be remembered only for her wickedness —is accomplished entirely by divine means, as Gabriel delivers the parable. Full of regret that he has sinned with a wicked woman (*gans corf a'n debel venen*, OM 2251), there is no question of David's being condemned to death beyond his own statement that the man in the parable (who represents David himself, of course), deserves to die. Gabriel draws the parallel, but David is neither condemned, as in the Bible, nor indeed given any specific punishment at all, since there is no reference to the first son born to Bathsheba. In accordance with the comment in the Psalm itself, he utters the *Miserere*, which will, we presume, later become part of the Psalter. A little later on, in fact, he asks one of his counsellors (*consultor*, the nearest we get to a Nathan-figure) to teach him a penitential song. Now, though, after David's final condemnation of Bathsheba and expression of regret, we return in fact to the Holy Rood idea as he composes the entire Psalter, starting with the first Psalm, the *Beatus vir*, seated under the tree that will become the Rood: that tree is not, incidentally, the Tree of Knowledge, something which rests upon a false expansion of the stage direction *sub arbore sc _* as *sc[ienti]a[e]* rather than *sancta*, the normal designation in the Holy Rood text, from which this is pretty well a quotation; this has proved misleading for translators and commentators, including myself.[13] Nor, indeed, is the story quite over. David (as in the Holy Rood narratives) begins to build the temple, but God himself tells him that he shall not finish it—this picks up the Divine will in an earlier part of the biblical narrative. Here, though, God is clear on the reasons, and it is the killing of Uriah, a man in the image of God, which of course breaks one of the commandments:

> the vos den lath yv anken
> ty re thyswrug eredy

                    hevelep tho'm face vy
                    vrry nep o marrek len. (OM 2335–58)

'To be a man-killer is grievous: thou has destroyed, verily, the
likeness to my face, Uriah, who was a trusty knight', in the Norris
translation. This is the final reference to the narrative, and Bathsheba
is not mentioned in the Solomon parts.

The ultimate source is clearly the Bible, but the adaptation is
skilfully done. Some of this is technical: Bathsheba is washing clothes
because nakedness could not be shown on stage, and the pandering
butler of an earlier scene is neatly written out of the play with Uriah.
The reduction of the range of characters by the omission of Joab and
Nathan may also fall into this category. These points aside, though, the
changes to the essential narrative are also radical, and the links with
the biblical verses sometimes tenuous. Bathsheba mourns her husband
in the Bible, but only after his death, and the fact that the play makes
the act into one of hypocrisy is striking, but the whole reading of her
character as wicked through and through is scarcely biblical. David's
wickedness might be biblical, but hers is not. It might be noted, too,
that the development in this way of the tale of David and Bathsheba
has little to do with the Holy Rood story, however important that is to
the *Origo Mundi* as a whole. Most versions of the Rood legend follow
the various healing scenes worked by the rods that will become the
Rood tree with a simple and unusually unspecific reference to David's
past sinfulness; Latin texts omit Bathsheba, and vernacular adaptations
rarely even name her.

SOME COMPARISONS
That this is a fairly radical biblical adaptation invites comparison in
characterization and narrative content with other medieval writings
and raises the question, too, of the function and integration of this
unusual scene in the play.[14] In medieval vernacular adaptations of the
story in forms other than the drama, the Bible is usually followed fairly
closely, though with small embellishments and variations. Thus to take
examples in verse from three different languages—these could be
multiplied—Jansen Enikel, who wrote a German biblical chronicle
in the thirteenth century, keeps close to the Bible, stressing only
the loyalty of Uriah. His focus is on the death of the first child and the
birth of Solomon, however. The great French Bible of Macé de la
Charité again stresses the *grant chevallerie* of Uriah and the *grant
beauté* of Bathsheba, and criticises David. The English *Cursor Mundi*
also remains close to the Bible, and Bathsheba is once again simply a
passive object: 'Whil þis kny3t was away', we are told, 'þe kyng bi þat

lady lay'. In the English work, David composes the *Miserere* Psalm as a penance—it is called the best Psalm of all—and then the *Cursor* returns to the Holy Rood story without mentioning the other psalms. This is a small difference from the Cornish play, and it is of interest that none of these works mentions that Uriah is a Hittite and therefore in some way different. Caxton's prose version of the *Golden Legend*, finally, which includes a biblical history, also has David compose the fiftieth Psalm for the sins of adultery and homicide, but Bathsheba is not named. In all these works the interest and focus is upon David.[15]

As indicated, the Legends of the Rood do not foreground the incident as such, although it serves there as a justification for David's penance. In the basic version of the story—referred to by Wilhelm Meyer as the *Legende*—David has found the three rods which have grown from the seeds planted with the dead Adam, and they have grown together to a single tree, an *arbor sancta*, around which he places silver rings, and which work miracles of healing. Then we are told that David, because of his sin (which is described as great or serious, *grande* or *graue*, but not specified) begins a penance under that holy tree, first with the *Miserere*, and then after he has completed the entire Psalter, with the desire to build the temple. In a version now in Cambridge University Library:

> post peccatum grande quod commiserat, Dauid cepit sub
> arbore sancta penitendo flere peccatum quod commiserat,
> dicens domino: Miserere mei deus et cetera. Peracto ergo toto
> psalterio, cepit Dauid edificare templum domini in expiacione
> peccatorum commisorum.[16]

[After the great sin which he had committed, David began to weep, beneath the Holy Tree, in penance for the sin he had committed, saying to the Lord: Lord have mercy upon me, etc. When he had composed the entire Psalter, David began to build a temple to the Lord in expiation of the sins he had committed.]

The Latin matches the Cornish text and stage direction well; the sin is not specified, but the building the temple (the next stage in the Holy Rood story) is in expiation of all his sins. The Rood legends are widespread in Latin and in vernacular languages, and the generalized reference to sin is usually (though not always) reproduced. In the middle-English *Canticum de Creatione*, for example, of 1375, David weeps tears for *synne þat he hadde wroȝt*, and then *wiþ sorwe and herte vnglad/þis salme 'miserere' he mad*, before completing the Psalter and moving on to the temple. He behaves the same way in the Cross-Legend from the Northern Passion, when he realizes *þat he a synfull man had bene*.[17] Elsewhere in vernacular adaptations, the brief reference is expanded a little. In a prose English version there is a reference to David's *avoutrie*, his adultery as the great sin, this time without reference to the murder of Uriah, and a French prose text also says of the sin that *cest a sauoir de la femme Vrie*,[18] of lying with Uriah's wife. Slightly fuller again is the metrical *History of the Holy Rood* found in parallel versions in thirteenth- and fourteenth-century manuscripts, both in the Bodleian. The earlier, Ashmole 431, notes that David had committed þe *sunne of lecherie/And manslau3t*, the latter for having Uriah killed. The later Vernon manuscript is one of the very few Holy Rood texts actually to name Bathsheba.[19] The Cornish play is following the Holy Rood story fairly closely at this point; however, since that tradition does not always even give a motivation for David's penance, and rarely even names Bathsheba, let alone include the whole story, this is a considerable addition to the immediate source. Possibly the dramatist, whilst following the Rood story, added this narrative in detail for effect, but worked from memory of the Bible text to do so.

Medieval plays rarely include the story, but there is at least one example, albeit somewhat later than the *Origo Mundi*, and there are more in the Reformation period and later, down to George Peele's *The Love of David and Fair Bethsabe* in 1599, several of them discussed in Inga-Stina Ewbank's study of the 'House of David in Renaissance Drama'.[20] Amongst these, John Bale's somewhat undramatic play of 1538 known usually as *God's Promises* refers only in passing to the story when God accuses David of having *mysused Bersabe/The wyfe of Vrye, and slayne hym in the fyelde*.[21] A German play from the same year, by the virtually unknown Valten Voith, of Magdeburg, is fuller, and is used to make the Protestant point that repentance can lead to grace. Bathsheba, with her maidens, comments about the heat of the day (in the Bible it is the evening), and wishes to wash her feet; the non-biblical point probably derives here from Cranach's painting.[22] Abisai (David's general, in fact) is sent to her, and she seems innocent of why she has been summoned, agreeing out of pure obedience, placing far more emphasis upon David's iniquity. As in the Cornish play, the biblical narrative is telescoped, although here Joab gives Uriah a message for the king, Uriah hands it to David, who gives him another letter to take back at once, which loses the strategy of having Uriah sleep at home. We do not see the content of the letter, but David wonders about the battle until the death of Uriah is reported. The encounter with Bathsheba is not developed and there is no mention of the marriage, so that the emphasis is on the removal of Uriah. Only after the parable from Nathan is David accused directly of killing Uriah and of having shamed Bathsheba, for which he repents. Since this Bathsheba is clearly wronged, her indistinct biblical figure may clearly be interpreted in any way. However, it is noticeable that she usually seems to be the victim, and even in Peele's play of 1599, although she is initially willing, she repents after the event.[23]

The most complex version of Bathsheba, and hence the most interesting in comparative terms is found in that great compilation, the French *Mistére du Viel Testament* of the latter part of the fifteenth century.[24] Where thus far we have seen in the Cornish play a uniquely wicked Bathsheba, in contrast with most other early and medieval versions, and even some later ones, where she is either sidelined or treated as a victim, in French she is developed in more detail. Bathsheba appears in several scenes, in the first of which she tells her ladies (and us) how much she owes to her noble husband Uriah, whom she misses. Her scenes alternate with battle discussions between David, Uriah and Joab, so that next we see Bathsheba suggesting to her ladies a visit to a rather public-sounding *belle fontaine*, although her words perhaps betray more of her state of mind than simply that she is hot:

> Irons nous point nous sollacer
> Et ung petit nous delasser
> Auprès de la belle fontaine?
> Je sçay bien que suis toute plaine
> De humeurs; certes, si me lavoie,
> Il me semble que je seroye
> Plus a mon aise (vv. 30980–86)

[Let us go and take our ease a little by that fountain; I know that I feeling out of sorts, and if I bathe I shall feel better].

She is ill-at-ease, then, and seeking solace; David is in similar case when he sees Bathsheba and her ladies and is told that this is wife of Uriah, who is away at the war. Captivated by her, David is immediately warned by Nathan, and the Bathsehba-scenes as she completes her toilette alternate with Nathan's increasingly urgent warnings to David, reminding him that Uriah is away fighting for him, and stressing the sin of coveting another's wife: *C'est le commandement de Dieu./Fuy toy, depars toy de ce lieu.* (v. 31148f. 'It is God's commandment, go, leave this place.') Suddenly a *chevalier* is sent to summon Bathsheba to the king, and, when she is assured that he will not harm her, she goes, curious (and reprehensibly so) as to what he wants, but justifying things with the statement that *contredire ung roy on n'ose* (v. 31175 'no one dares refuse a king'). Nathan warns him again, but when David encounters Bathsheba he makes his intentions clear. She at first insists upon her honour, but eventually agrees to go with him into his private chamber. We have been shown her beauty and her own awareness of it, and the repeated motif that Uriah is away has made it clear that she is at least open to possible dalliance. This is not rape, but seduction, however. The play now interpolates a scene at the battlefront, and we assume that in the meantime Bathsheba has acquiesced to David's will, since now she voices her one regret, namely that she is pregnant.[25] This is all she says in the Bible, of course, but here she links it with the idea that Uriah will kill her, a motif that is present in the Cornish work: *S'il le sçait, j'ai peur qu'il me baille/Le cop de la mort* (v. 31383f. 'If he finds out I'm afraid he will strike me dead'). The pair now plot a way out together, and David is blunt: he will recall Uriah so that he may sleep with his wife. Bathsheba readily agrees *car nous couvrirons en effect/Nostre cas en ceste matiére* (v. 31393f. 'and that will have the effect of covering up our affair'). David spells it out to the audience in a soliloquy, too, almost like a pantomime villain. But Uriah refuses to go home, remembering his comrades in the field; David invites him to a feast, but again he fails to return to Bathsheba, so David now gives him the fatal letter to take to Joab. Bathsheba, meanwhile, continues to fear the outcome, but a maid assures her that *nostre seigneur vous aydera* (v. 31654 'our lord will help you'), which may mean that God will find a solution or, more probably, that David will do so. Joab reads the letter, agrees that he has to obey orders, and this time Uriah does not just ride out of the play, but is killed by a Philistine. Bathsheba is distraught when she sees that Uriah is not with the returning soldiers, but the ambiguity of the whole is by now established: is this sorrow for Uriah, or for her own exposure? In fact she expresses her regret for the way she has behaved towards him. David, however, marries her, and this concludes Bathsheba's role. Precisely as with the Cornish play, we have experienced the setting-up of an interesting character, only to turn, in the event, again exclusively to David. Victim or predator, in dramatic terms Bathsheba is merely an agent of sin. God himself notes that David has committed *deux grans maulx* (v. 31829), and must be taught a lesson, so that Nathan now tells the parable. This is done by Gabriel, God's messenger, in the Cornish play, but Nathan's words are also shown to be divinely inspired. David's self condemnation is present in the French play, but not the loss of the son, and Nathan says that God has forgiven David:

> Dieu t'a ton peché pardonné
> Car encor pas tu ne mourras.
> Ton régne pas ne lesseras:
> Dieu a congneu ta repentance. (v. 31914–7)

This is at once fuller and less straightforward that the Cornish, though the end-result is the same: David is pardoned by grace. Bathsheba is subtly treated throughout, and that she is ill-at-ease and out-of-humour at the absence of Uriah is presented as part of the blame. In the *Origo Mundi* Bathsheba is very much the willing, even eager accomplice, whereas even if she was ripe for seduction in the *Mistère*, she knows that she had done wrong. Even in the modern Yiddish play by David Pinski discussed by Alice Bach she is a victim, and it is interesting that not until the 1951 Hollywood film is Uriah placed again into a plausibly negative light. What Bathsheba says of him in the Cornish play is only her word on the matter, while the actual evidence of the play is that he is as noble as she is wicked. In the film (which starred Gregory Peck and Susan Hayward) Bathsheba claims that the marriage to the Hittite was an arranged one and is lacking in love, and this provides exoneration of a different sort for the relationship with and more importantly the marriage to David.[26]

In the Cornish play, the reduction of the biblical story to its essentials has led to the loss both of characters (Nathan and Joab) and of motifs (the attempt to cover up the pregnancy by having Uriah return home, the letters, the first-born son); against this has to be set the expansion and indeed provision of a character for Bathsheba. Other elements, too, are heightened, such as Uriah's heroic behaviour and David's more direct deceit. No reasons are given for Bathsheba's attitude to Uriah beyond that she finds him hateful, but for good or ill, any ambiguity in a biblical text which says so little about her has been resolved. Bathsheba is not a victim of royal rape, nor even of seduction, but an all-too-willing accomplice, not only sexually but also in the matter of having her noble husband killed. In hypocrisy she is the equal of David, too, although of course David repents. To present her consistently and unequivocally is unusual.

How is the story integrated into the *Origo Mundi* and indeed the *Ordinalia* as a whole? In essence, it provides the ultimate reason for why Solomon will build the temple and not David, because the last reference—and it is to Uriah, rather than Bathsheba—is to David's only real punishment, by which time Bathsheba has become irrelevant. She is an object of sin, and the killing of Uriah takes precedence over the adultery. Any comparative approach has to observe what has been omitted, and if Bathsheba has been striking reshaped, her absence later on is just as striking. In III Reg. (I Kings) we see Bathsheba again, pleading for the succession of her son, Solomon. David agrees, and announces to her: Solomon, your son, shall be king, before doing the same thing before Zadok, Nathan, Jehoida and the rest. In the *Origo Mundi* only the latter presentation is there, coming from David:

> arlythy my agas pys
> salmon ov map koroneugh (OM 2346f.)

'Lords, I pray you, crown Solomon my son', matching III Reg. 32–34.

CONCLUSION

Evelyn Newlyn sees the role of Bathsheba as that of a new Eve, and there is something in this idea, since she has proved to be David's downfall. And yet he initiates the affair, which leads him to murder, and though forgiven, is punished by not being allowed full participation in the temple that will be sanctified, so to speak, in the last scenes of the *Origo Mundi*, in the Maximilla episode which prefigures Christ in her death because of the cross. There has been a double effect if we compare the text with other medieval and later versions. Bathsheba may have been given a character, but she is not in the last analysis important, and her only role is as part of David's crime. She is not even a temptress in the proper sense, not really a new Eve, just a function, and she has lost the one absolutely positive role afforded to her in the Bible, namely that of Solomon's mother. Uriah has been boosted in the play, but there is some biblical support for his nobility, even if here he is not Uriah *the Hittite*, but a very noble, even heroic *syr Urry*, who rides out of the play when he, too, has fulfilled his function. These are not major characters: David is in the forefront all the time. But in the Cornish play they are both important because they are consistently and unusually presented, something which the biblical text permits, and they add substance and human interest to the bare narrative of the Holy Rood *Legende*. The vague reference to David's *peccatum grave* is made real and memorable, even if his own blame for the wicked woman is, in all conscience, a little on the facile side.

We have touched on early painting and on the Hollywood film already, so it is perhaps permissible to end with a slightly frivolous quotation with the serious end of demonstrating the way in which the essence of the story has been maintained in popular thought. The lines I wish to quote crop up with variations in the Glasgow street song known usually as 'Johnny Lad', but reference works ascribe the original to James Ball Naylor. They tell how 'King David and King Solomon led very merry lives', something which rhymes in some versions (though not Naylor's), with a reference to time spent 'with other people's wives'. However: 'when old age crept over them, their conscience gi'ed them qualms, King Solomon wrote the Proverbs and King David wrote the Psalms'.[27] This is precisely the point made at the moment we come back in the Cornish play from the Bathsheba story to that of the Holy Rood, both literally, as David sits beneath the *arbor sancta* to compose the Psalter, and figuratively, as he repents and is forgiven.[28]

NOTES AND REFERENCES

1. See J.P. Fokkelman, *Narrative Art and Poetry in the Book of Samuel I. King David*, Assen, 1981, pp. 41–70, esp. p. 53. On the question of succession, see R. A. Carlson, *David, the Chosen King. A Traditio-Historical Approach to the Second Book of Samuel*, Stockholm, 1964, pp. 140–62.

2. Thus for example, in slight and indeed derivative work, see *The Sex Werkdays and Agis*, ed. L.A.J.R. Houwen, Groningen, 1990), p. 45 (vv. 567f.).

3. Alice Bach, *Women, Seduction and Betrayal in Biblical Narrative*, Cambridge, 1997, pp. 132–65 is very good on modern literary parallels; quotation p. 136. Bach also summarizes recent feminist critiques of the narrative. See Mieke Bal, *Lethal Love. Feminist Literary Reading of Biblical Love Stories*, Bloomington, 1987.

4. H.W. Hertzberg, *I and II Samuel. A Commentary*, trans. John Bowden, London, 1964, p. 309 (from the second edition, 1960); Hertzberg notes that Chronicles omits the incident. Robert P. Gordon, *1 and 2 Samuel. A Commentary*, Exeter, 1986, p. 252 refers to the whole as a 'scabrous story'.

5. See Bach, *Women*, p. 145 (she does not mention Psalm 50) and Athalya Brenner, *A Feminist Companion to Samuel and Kings*, Sheffield, 1994, pp. 129–42. See also Louis Ginzberg, *The Legends of the Jews*, trans. Henrietta Szold and Paul Radin, New York, 1961, p. 546f. (the single volume abridgement).

6. The *Glossa Ordinaria* is in Migne's *Patrologia Latina*, vol. 113, but I cite from a glossed printed Bible of the late sixteenth century (of which there are several): *Biblia Sacra cum Glossa Ordinaria*, 1589, II, col. 522f. The passage is linked with Matthew 5, 28 and the notion of lust of the eyes. There is a curious modern reflex of the idea in the satirical poems of Eugen Roth in German, where David is looking out from his rooftop 'mit vergnügten Sinnen/doch gänzlich harmlos' (happily and harmlessly) until he sees a naked woman, '0sündhaft ihn erregend' (stirring him up to sin). The example is a comic and hence ambiguous one (David regrets the Uriah letter, but only because he had intended Bathsheba as a plaything, but she remains his wife for decades), but the idea is the same: Eugen Roth, *Die Frau in der Weltgeschichte*, [1944], Munich, 1956, p. 18f.

7. See James C. Kugel, *The Bible as it Was*, Cambridge, Mass., 1997, p. 272. The passage is in Jubilees XXXIII, 2, in H.F.D. Sparks, *The Apocryphal Old Testament*, Oxford, 1984, p. 102. On Bathsheba's sexuality in general see Raymond-Jean Frontain and Jan Woycik, *The David Myth in Western Literature* (West Lafayette, Ind., 1980, referred to by Evelyn Newlyn (below, note 10), p. 155.

8. Having David present with his harp is either an indicator of who he is., or a syncopation, since in interpretations and in literature David composes the Psalter as penance for his affair. See Betty Kurth, 'A Middle-Rhenish Bible Tapestry'. *Burlington Magazine* 75, 1939, 210f. where there is a picture of the tapestry, which is in the Burrell Collection in Glasgow.

There is a colour picture in *The Guide to the Burrell Collection*, Glasgow, new. edn. 1990, p. 104f. The tapestry is mostly typological, but the David-Bathsheba story has little in the way of typological potential. In the *Biblia Pauperum* tradition, Nathan admonishing David can prefigure the Magdalene (as a sexual sinner) washing Christ's feet, and this presupposes knowledge of the story; so too Bathsheba honoured by Solomon is used as a prefiguration of the coronation of the Virgin: see as an example *Die Armenbibel des Serai. Rotulus Seragliensis Nr. 52*, ed. Adolf Deissmann and Hans Wegener, Berlin and Leipzig, 1934, plates 13 and 34. In the handbook *Pictor in Carmine* David's fasting for the first child by Bathsheba prefigures the fasting in the desert, David confronted by Nathan is linked with John the Baptist, Herod and Herodias; oddest of all, Bathsheba observed whilst bathing by David prefigures Christ baptising the apostles: see M.R. James, '*Pictor in carmine*', *Archaeologia* 94, 1951, 141–66, pp. 154–7.

9. A facsimile of the *Bible of St Louis* has been published by Moliero in Barcelona, 2000–2001 and examples of the double-columns with eight-roundels to a page have frequently been reproduced (there are more than five thousand in the whole Bible). Cranach's painting is in the Berlin Gemäldegalerie, Memling's in the Staatsgalerie in Stuttgart. The tradition of painting Bathsheba continues down to such painters as Jean-Léon Gérôme in the nineteenth century and beyond. Hugo Steger's study of medieval images of David focusses upon his role as the ideal king and does not discuss earlier images of the Bathsheba story: *David Rex et Propheta*, Nuremberg, 1961. There is a significant illustration of the conflict between image and pictorial interest in the first volume of the folio *History of the Old Testament . . . for the Government of our Actions*, transl. From Le Sieur de Royaumont by John Coughen and Anthony Horneck, London, 1690, where a folio full-page engraving is headed 'Davids Crimes', but he himself is a tiny figure, crowned and playing the harp, in the distance, whilst the foreground is filled with the semi-naked Bathsheba and her attendant ladies. Working out what his crimes might be from the picture alone would be somewhat difficult.

10. Edwin Norris, *The Ancient Cornish Drama*, Oxford, 1859, repr. London and New York, 1968, I, 158–71 (OM 2105–2254); see also Markham Harris, *The Cornish Ordinalia. A Medieval Dramatic Trilogy*, Washington, 1969, and F. E. Halliday, *The Legend of the Rood*, London, 1955. A teaching text of the episode edited by R. Morton Nance and A.S.D. Smith version appeared as one of the *Extracts from the Cornish Texts in Unified Spelling* VI: *Davyd hag Urry* (OM 2105–2254) (Penzance: repr. by the Cornish Language Board, 1973). Nance's brief preface draws attention to the variety in the verse here, as does Halliday. The relevant portion of the *Origo Mundi* is included in the collection *Looking at the Mermaid*, by Alan Kent and Tim Saunders, London, 2000, pp. 46–55, following Norris's Cornish text (with some line-adaptation). The last three texts give proper emphasis of the unusual nature of the Holy Rood story and of the David and Bathsheba story in Cornish drama. Norris's text is cited here (with

reference to any emendations he makes), with his line-numbering, which is matched by Nance even though the layout if changed.

11. Jane A. Bakere, *The Cornish Ordinalia. A Critical Study*, Cardiff, 1980), p. 57 seems to say that the first impetus for the murder comes from Bathsheba, but this is not the case. Evelyn S. Newlyn, 'Between the Pit and the Pedestal: Images of Eve and Mary in Medieval Cornish Drama', in Edelgard DuBruck, *New Images of Medieval Women*, Lampeter, 1989, pp. 121–64, p. 155 n. 10 discusses this, but it does not seem to be supported in any translation, in fact, and thus is presumably a simple slip. Norris properly emends the text to *lath e*, 'kill him'.

12. Harris notes in his translation (p. 253) the possibility of a hiatus here, as does Halliday, *Rood*, p. 78.

13. Thus Nance's point in the brief introduction to the text-extract that this indicates that the Tree of Knowledge from the earlier scenes is still there must be dismissed. Norris does not expand the abbreviation, but Nance does, and it is also treated that way in Kent and Saunders, *Mermaid*. I made the same slip in my *Cornish Literature*, Cambridge, 1993), p. 55f., where, I regret to say, the Vulgate Psalm 50 is also misprinted as 56. Markham Harris translates the stage-direction correctly.

14. In recent criticism, Jane Bakere, *Cornish Ordinalia*, p. 57 notes the freedom of the adaptation and stresses the ultimate repudiation of Bathsheba, whom she sees as a victim of her own lust; Robert Longsworth, *The Cornish Ordinalia. Religion and Dramaturgy*, Cambridge, MA, 1967, p. 58f. sees the passage as am embellishment of the Holy Rood story; Crysten Fudge takes it as a lead-in to David's building of the temple as an atonement, which again he does in the Rood legends: 'Aspects of Form in the Cornish *Ordinalia*', *Old Cornwall* 8 (1973–79), pp. 457–64 and 491–8, see p. 495 (though it is not true to say that the story is found nowhere else in medieval drama); and Evelyn Newlyn, 'Between the Pit and the Pedestal', p. 126 stresses the misogynistic view of Bathsheba as a wicked seducer, and—interestingly—the fact that the fall for David is a fortunate one, in that the end-result is good.

In my own *Cornish Literature*, p. 55f. I stress the role of Gabriel and the omissions. See also Nance's introduction to the extract.

15. Jansen Enikel, *Weltchronik*, ed. Philipp Strauch, Hannover, 1891–1900) p. 223f. vv. 11829–60; the *Cursor Mundi*, ed. Richard Morris, London, 1874–93, repr. 1961–66 = EETS/OS 57–68) II, 454–61, vv. 7869–7972; William Caxton, *The Golden Legend*, ed. F.E. Ellis, London, 1900, II, 31–3; Macé de la Charité, *La Bible, III. Rois*, ed. A.M.L. Pragsma-Hajenius, Leiden, 1970, pp. 45–47, vv. 12811–12953.

16. Cited from Betty Hill, 'The Fifteenth-Century Prose Legend of the Cross Before Christ', *Medium Aevum* 34, 1965, pp. 203–22, see p. 219. See also Wilhelm Meyer, 'Die Geschichte des Kreuzholzes vor Christi', *Abhandlungen der bayerischen Akademie* (München), philos.-philol. Klasse 16/ii (1882), 101–66, 143f. Hill has the English text above the Latin, and Meyer prints a matching text in Provençale.

17. The *Canticum de Creatione*, vv. 1049, 1051f., cited from Brian Murdoch

and J. A. Tasioulas, *The Lives of Adam and Eve. The Canticum de Creatione and the Auchinleck Adam*, Exeter, 2002. *The Northern Passion* (Supplement) ed. Wilhelm Heuser and Frances A. Foster, London, 1930 = EETS/ OS 183), from the expanded version, p. 110, v. 2313.

18. Hill, 'Prose Legend', p. 219. J. Ph. Berjeau, *History of the Cross*, London, 1863, p. 10.

19. Richard Morris, *Legends of the Holy Rood*, London, 1881 = EETS/ OS 46), pp. 30f., v. 137.

20. Inga-Stina Ewbank, 'The House of David in Renaissance Drama', *Renaissance Drama* 8, 1965, pp. 3–40 with reference to Bale, Peele and Hans Sachs and Montchrestien. The medieval plays fall outside her scope, and she does not mention a further German play by Valten Voith.

21. *A Tragedye or enterlude manyfesting the chefe promyses of God unto man by all ages in the Old Law from the Fall of Adam to the Incarnacyon of the Lorde Jesus Christ*, in *The Complete Plays of John Bale*, ed. Peter Happé, Cambridge, 1985–86, II.

22. I have discussed the play in a forthcoming paper: '*Ein armseliger Versschmie?* Valten Voith and his Redemption-Play of 1538', in the *Festschrift for John Flood* (in press).

23. For Voith's biblical play (of which the incident is only small part), see *Dramen von Ackermann und Voith*, ed. Hugo Holstein, Tübingen, 1884, pp. 207–316. For Peele, see *The Minor Elizabethan Drama*, ed. Ashley Thorndike, London, 1910, I, 125–82.

24. *Le Mistére du Viel Testament*, ed. James de Rothschild, Paris, 1878–1891, repr. New York, 1966; the relevant part of the text is in IV (1882), pp. 145–213 (vv 30360–31919). See pp. xxiii–xxv for an introduction, noting how the writer clearly enjoyed the Bathsheba story (vv. 30867–31919). Rothschild notes other early versions (including oratorios), but does not list the Cornish play amongst the many David-plays.

25. I have discussed the notion of seduction whilst the soldier is away as a literary motif from the Odyssee and the David story to the wars of the twentieth century in 'War, Identity, Truth and Love; Leonhard Frank's *Karl und Anna*', *Forum for Modern Language Studies* 38, 2002, pp. 49–62.

26. Bach, *Women*, p. 145 on Pinski (*King David and His Wives*, trans. Isaac Goldberg, New York, 1923), and pp. 158–65 on the Darryl Zanuck/ Twentieth Century Fox film, in which the twenty-third Psalm is played at the ultimate wedding of the king, an interesting variation on the motif of composing either of the *Miserere* or of the whole Psalter.

27. *The Oxford Dictionary of Modern Quotations*, ed. Tony Augarde, Oxford, 1991, p. 159 (and other similar works) cites James Ball Naylor (1860–1945) writing in *Vagrant Verse*, 1935. Naylor's text actually has 'with many many qualms', but the variation cited here from a version of the song 'Johnny Lad' makes the point rather more clearly.

28. This is a revised version of a paper given at the Twelfth International Congress of Celtic Studies held at Aberystwyth in August 2003.

REVIEW ARTICLE

MEBYON KERNOW

Adrian Lee

Bernard Deacon, Dick Cole, and Garry Tregidga, *Mebyon Kernow and Cornish Nationalism*, Welsh Academic Press, 2003, 139pp., ISBN 1 86057 0755

In providing the first and long-awaited definitive academic study of Mebyon Kernow and its position in the wider Cornish movement, this timely book provides a valuable addition both to the growing literature on Cornish politics, and to the now significant literature on European sub-state nationalist movements. In so doing, it also stands as a worthy product of the 'New Cornish Studies' advocated by Bernard Deacon and his co-authors. It is written, in Philip Payton's words, from an 'uncompromisingly "insider" perspective'. Indeed, one of the authors, Dick Cole, is Mebyon Kernow's current Leader.

The main body of the resulting 'insider' study will stand as the definitive—indeed the only—detailed historical record of the development of Mebyon Kernow and its role in Cornish nationalism. However, it is not simply a chronicle. The authors' intimate association with the movement has produced new insights and historical appreciations not easily obtained by 'outsiders'. The historical record is set within the context of both wider academic work on the phenomenon of sub-state nationalism and identity, and what the authors call the 'Cornish paradox'. The record is consistently subjected to critical analysis, culminating in an assessment of contemporary Cornish nationalism which is part political analysis, and part critical political prognosis.

For this reader (whose first contact with matters Cornish occurred when as a schoolboy he was set lines in the language by the late Richard Jenkin in Totnes in 1955) the book's main value lies in its original and systematic treatment of the emergence and development of Mebyon Kernow from 'nationalism before MK' to the present day. Its establishment of the historical record and its mapping of MK's development are its most valuable features, and indeed these lie at the heart of its structure.

The preceding theoretical framework briefly connects the study of Cornish identity and its political expression to the wider literature on sub-state nationalism. The particular value of this discussion lies in the way in which it sets MK firmly within the general corpus of European sub-state nationalist movements. The authors have successfully resisted the temptation to regard the Cornish national movement as *sui generis* and without historic parallel. Instead, the opening chapters on the 'Cornish paradox' and the historical legacy of nationalism before MK place Cornish nationalism firmly within a style of analysis which emphasizes and uses such ideas as the distinction between ethnic and civic nationalism, the centrality of the invention and reconstruction of history to nationalist movements and the articulation of national identity, as well as the relationship between economic change, shifting lines of political cleavage, and changing party systems.

The charting of the subsequent development of MK, its various phases of development, its campaigns and its electoral record provide, if at times albeit almost unwittingly, ample evidence of the similarities between the movement and other European sub state—or as the authors would have it 'decentralizing' (p. 3)—nationalist movements. As a relative latecomer to the political scene—later than the Scottish National Party, Plaid Cymru and the first real Breton political party, the *Union Régionaliste Bretonne*—Mebyon Kernow found it even more difficult to build political support than did its sister parties. The fourth chapter is titled 'Looking for Votes 1960–1970' and details the real problems the party faced, particularly in an era when a renascent Liberal Party had begun to play the anti-metropolitan card again with, as Garry Tregidga has detailed elsewhere, considerable success.[1] Ever since its emergence as an electorally competing political party MK has always faced the problem of extending its coalition of support beyond its small core of activists, and of converting temporary support gained from its stance on single issues into a more lasting electoral base. The presence and increasing strength of the Liberal Party, and later the Liberal Democrats, coupled with the electoral weakness of Labour outside the Falmouth and Camborne areas served to ring-fence MK's electoral ambitions. Conversely, a temporary weakening in the

Liberal/Liberal Democrat position provided temporary opportunity for smaller parties—as evidenced in MK's best electoral performance ever: in the European Parliament election of 1979 (p. 71). Similarly, in 1989, the main beneficiary of the weakness of the newly-formed Social and Liberal Democrats was to be the Green Party.

With electoral breakthrough elusive, the authors analyse a pattern of development in MK that bears remarkable resemblance to that in other sub-state nationalist parties. Questions about the party's existence, role, strategy and stance in relation to its competitors (or potential allies) remain central to the party's whole existence. It is then unsurprising for such a party or movement to face constant splits— whether over ideology, policy goals, or whether its aims can best be secured as a fully-fledged political party or as a pressure group eschewing electoral campaigning in favour of the politics of influence. Bernard Deacon and his colleagues provide us with ample evidence of and analysis of MK's reaction to the pressures of competing in an unfavourable electoral environment, the leadership crises and the splits that beset the party. Like other similar parties—and size does not seem to matter—MK is a coalition that is prone to split on ideology, strategy and tactics (pp. 76–77). The cement provided by power or the necessity of supporting a significant number of elected members has meant that the imperative of maintaining unity for the next electoral contest has been absent.

The authors provide a fascinating and detailed history of the development of various tendencies within the nationalist movement, well-informed by the framework for analysis set out in the intro- ductory chapters. The transition from 'ethnic' to 'civic' nationalism, from antiquarianism through cultural defence to party formation and electoral contestation itself serves to establish MK as a political move- ment in the European mainstream. Appropriate comparisons with Scots, Welsh and Breton experiences are frequently made, but in addition to this emphasis on Celtic comparison, useful parallels and contrasts exist with other European parties and movements, such as the Savoyard and the Alsatian within France, and with some of the smaller decentralist movements within Spain. The characteristic conflicts of this pattern of development are fully analysed, including the tensions between ethnic and civic nationalism that emerged over the case of the Stannary Parliament and its descent into 'farce' over the issue of Fred Trull's birthplace (p. 66). The constant debates over policy, strategy, tactics and the party's own assessment of its support is a constant theme that is painstakingly analysed (see, for example, pp. 76–77) as is the continuing question of electoral politics versus pressure-group politics (see pp. 90–91). Again, like most movements for whom electoral breakthrough on the state-wide scene has not materialized, the political context makes it rational to seek a judicious combination of both forms of activity.

MK's difficulty in deciding upon and sustaining an electoral strategy are well documented. Whether the party 'changing direction' in the 1970s, experiencing the 'decade of doubts' in the 1980s or 're-awakening' in the 1990s, the authors accurately chronicle the often intense debate that gripped activists as a general election approached. The move into the electoral arena in the 1960s was initially unpopular with the 'large proportion' of members who wished MK to remain as a pressure group and remained a matter of debate, particularly when a weak electoral performance exposed the party's core support as 'woefully weak' (p. 57). Relationships with other parties were central to this debate, as was the MK leadership's assessment of where the party's support lay—or ought to lie. The main issue, which the book charts comprehensively, was that of the off–on relationship with Liberals and later Liberal Democrats—both as parties and as individual candidates. MK's recently agreed pact with the Green Party may open yet another chapter, although in the European Parliament elections of 2004, the new alliance was completely eclipsed by the rapid rise of the populist and firmly anti-devolutionist United Kingdom Independence Party, which—in contrast to the Greens—came from nowhere. Despite a markedly poor performance so far in local elections in Cornwall, it is possible that UKIP's sudden rise to prominence may make the assessment of MK's chances in an increasingly volatile electoral environment and a PR system (p. 120) look over-optimistic.

The presentation and discussion of MK's electoral record is marred by two significant and related aspects. Firstly, electoral results are treated inconsistently. For example, we are simply told that 'good results were achieved in the 1981 County Council elections in Penzance' (p. 80) and on the succeeding page informed that in 1985 'Colin Murley polled a strong second for MK in St Just with over 40 per cent of the vote in a straight fight' (p. 81). Secondly, following and understanding the detailed discussion of MK's electoral performance throughout the book is made more difficult by the absence of summary tables of election results. For example, the pattern of political contestation, particularly in Cornwall's local elections, varies widely both between and within districts. Nor is there a clear urban/rural divide in patterns of contestation across Cornwall. While these points are acknowledged and partly developed (pp. 104–6), even those readers who are not electoral anoraks may be left frustrated.

Without the systematic presentation of the electoral evidence, the interpretation and evaluation of particular MK candidates' per-formances over time is rendered extremely difficult. The discussion of the 1970 local elections (p. 56) provides an example with its judgement that the three CNP candidates 'were no more successful than the two from MK'. Where straightforward comparisons can be made, as in the case of the two MK candidates in the 1983 General Election, they are rendered impossible by an incomplete presentation of percentages (p. 80). All too often, MK's electoral performance in the absence of full competition from the major political parties is treated in much the same way as performance in its presence, thus making it difficult to judge its relative success or failure, and making the identification of longer term electoral trends well-nigh impossible. While it may be tempting for nationalists to regard their opponents as representing an undifferentiated bloc of 'London-based parties', such an approach makes it difficult to assess MK's real electoral impact.

One other aspect of MK's electoral performance might be worthy of attention, as one of those elusive 'windows of electoral opportunity' (p. 120). The authors rightly point to the fact that under the simple plurality electoral formula, MK candidates may be advantaged by the multi-member ward system in local elections (p. 124), particularly, one might add, where other parties do not field as many candidates as there are seats. However, in recent years opportunities for split-ticket voting in different elections have increased. In both the 1997 and 2001 General and County Council elections were held on the same day, and there is evidence from both Cornwall and beyond that some electors took the opportunity to vote for different parties for Westminster and county. In 1997, for example, up to 20 per cent of voters did so.[2] A cursory examination of the 2001 Cornwall County Council election results would seem to indicate that MK candidates, while still finding it 'difficult to achieve success in single-seat elections' might well benefit from this trend. If, as widely expected, the next General Election is called for the same day as those for County Councils, MK strategists might do well to consider their electoral tactics.

Secondly, the study draws on a wide range of primary and published sources, the former including MK's archive, interviews and recollections by participants. In particular, the illustrations are a well-chosen supplement to the book, as well as inadvertently providing a fascinating record of changing late twentieth-century fashions in facial hair. While a complete record of the sources used is provided by the end of chapter notes, it is a pity that the opportunity to present a comprehensive bibliography on Cornish nationalism has not been taken. Historians of sub-state nationalist movements, particularly of their small beginnings, are constantly bedevilled by the paucity of sources and the disappearance of key documents. If this definitive work had been accompanied by the definitive bibliography which only Bernard Deacon and his colleagues could provide, then the complete work would form a much better springboard for further research on the prognosis and the questions posed in the conclusion and postscript.

CONCLUSION
The detailed analysis of growing support for devolution within Cornwall and MK's specific contribution to that movement is well-made. However, the analysis of the response of central political elites stands on shakier ground, and downplays the extent to which the movement for further devolution has been less a response to peripheral pressure than a movement driven initially by the Labour government's 'modernization' agenda. The conclusion that mixed messages over Cornwall's status and aims 'allow central government to continue blithely ignoring Cornwall in its policies on regional government' (p. 119) takes little account of association of the policy with one particular figure in government. Combined with the relative unimportance of the issue to others in government, the extent of both Labour and Conservative opposition to further devolution, and looming problems over the reform of local government finance, devolution south of the Trent is—probably—a dead issue.

This political reality should be seen against the backdrop of a more or less profound metropolitan indifference. In what is still one of the most centralized European political systems, metropolitan indifference may well be informed by an elite perception of Cornwall shaped through the lenses of the second home, the Padstow restaurant and the St Mawes luxury hotel. The resulting view of Cornwall and its economic and social issues and problems is manifestly unlikely to coincide with the perspective of a decentralizing nationalist party.

Despite these caveats, the authors' largely optimistic prognosis of the future of nationalism and of Mebyon Kernow as the main nationalist organization is delivered with some justification. After all, despite the fact that electoral breakthrough still appears to be as elusive as ever, MK has survived for over fifty years as an organization and a significant and influential part of the Cornish political scene. Survival has meant that the party has successfully renewed itself, in terms of its leadership, its activists and membership, and its wider support. As a result, Cornwall still remains the only part of the United Kingdom, beyond Scotland and Wales, to have sustained a sub-state nationalist or decentralist movement that is neither ephemeral nor lacking in a core of support. Whereas substantial electoral breakthrough in local elections, and certainly at Westminster, will continue to be elusive, MK's influence on the Cornish political scene is unlikely to abate.

In conclusion, the book succeeds in its primary aim of providing the first definitive study of the development of Mebyon Kernow and its place in the Cornish national movement. In so doing, and in their use of systematic analysis and comparison, the authors have produced a valuable addition to the literature of European sub-state nationalism.

NOTES AND REFERENCES

1. G. Tregidga, *The Liberal Party in South-West Britain since 1918*, Exeter, 2000, pp. 195–209 contains an interesting comparison of peripheral rural, nonconformist politics in South West Britain with Scandinavia, and also details the success that Liberals, and later Liberal Democrats, have enjoyed in both expressing and strengthening anti-metropolitan sentiments.
2. C. Rallings and M. Thrasher, *Local Elections Handbook 2001: the 2001 Local Election Results*, Plymouth, 2001, pp. viii–ix.

NOTES ON CONTRIBUTORS

Graham Busby is Senior Lecturer in Tourism Management at the University of Plymouth. He has published widely on rural tourism, sustainable tourism and tourism education, and is co-author of *Tourism: A Modern Synthesis* (2000).

Terry Chapman is a postgraduate student at the Institute of Cornish Studies, University of Exeter in Cornwall. After more than thirty years in the Royal Navy, he read Contemporary History with English at the University of Plymouth. Now semi-retired, he is fortunate enough to be continuing as something of a hobby the research commenced during his first degree. This is his first article for an academic volume.

Ian Clarke is a postgraduate student at De Montfort University, Leicester, where he is completing his PhD on the development and social history of cricket in Cornwall in the nineteenth century. He studied part-time for an MA in Sports History and Culture at De Montfort University in 1998, and was formerly Head of the History Department at Launceston College, Cornwall.

Yolande Collins is Co-ordinator of Social Research, Planning and Development at the Department of Arts, La Trobe University, Bendigo, Australia, where she lectures in the history and sociology of health and illness, regional history, heritage studies, and social research. Amongst her publications is (with Mike Butcher) *An American on the Goldfields: The 1861 Bendigo Photographs of Benjamin Pierce Batchelder*, and she has co-edited (with Maureen Rogers) an anthology of papers from the Future of Australia's Country Towns Conference held in Bendigo in 2000.

Bernard Deacon is Lecturer in Cornish Studies in the Institute of Cornish Studies and Department of Lifelong Learning at the

University of Exeter in Cornwall. He has written extensively on Cornish matters: recent publications include *The Cornish Family* (2004) and *A Short History of the Cornish People* (forthcoming 2005).

Helen Doe is a member of the Centre for Maritime Historical Studies at the University of Exeter where she has recently obtained an MA in Maritime Studies. She has a particular research interest in the maritime history of Cornwall, on which she has lectured and written extensively.

Lucy Ellis is Research Assistant at the Institute of Cornish Studies, University of Exeter in Cornwall, where she is field officer for West Cornwall for the Cornish Audio Visual Archive, a major Oral History project located at the Institute and supported by the Heritage Lottery Fund. She also lectures part-time at the College of St Mark and St John, Plymouth, on socio-linguistics, and has also written extensively on the subject.

Jonathan Howlett grew up in North Cornwall, was educated in Cornwall and Somerset, and holds an MA in Cornish Studies from the Institute of Cornish Studies, University of Exeter in Cornwall. He has spent the last thirty-four years equally involved in education and as a practising artist. Currently, he is Curriculum Co-ordinator for the Visual and Performing Arts in Adult and Continuing Education at Northbrook College, Worthing, where he is also Course Leader of a pre-degree Art and Design Certificate for mature students.

Alan M. Kent is Lecturer in Literature at the Open University. He is author of *The Literature of Cornwall: Continuity, Identity, Difference 1000–2000* (2000) and has published widely on the literary and cultural history of Cornwall. His most recent publications include *Cousin Jack's Mouth-organ: Travels in Cornish America* (2004), *Assassin of Grammar* (2004) and a contribution in *The Celtic Englishes IV* (forthcoming, 2005).

Sandra Kippen is Lecturer in the Department of Public Health at La Trobe University, Bendigo, Australia, where she teaches research methods, sociology of health and illness, and ethics and communication skills. She has published in the areas of health history, disability and education and is co-author with Yolande Collins of *Aprons and Arches: A History of Bendigo Hospital Trained Nurses from 1883 to 1989*. She has a research interest in occupational health and safety in the mining industry: amongst her ancestors were Cornish miners who settled in the goldmining town of Bendigo.

Adrian Lee is Associate Dean, University of Plymouth Colleges Faculty. Previously Head of the Department of Politics at the University of Plymouth, he has research interests in territorial politics and electoral behaviour within the United Kingdom, and increasingly in the politics and governance of the Crown Dependencies and other small jurisdictions. He is a frequent broadcaster.

Sharon Lowenna is a Lecturer at Falmouth College of Arts. Her research interests are in the cultural identity of modern Cornwall, with particular reference to the Cornish Revival.

Kenneth MacKinnon is Visiting Professor and Emeritus Reader in the Sociology of Language at the University of Hertfordshire and Honorary Fellow in Celtic at the University of Edinburgh. He is also an Associate Lecturer in social sciences, education and language studies with the Open University, and is the member for language planning and development on the Ministerial Advisory Group on Gaelic of the Scottish Executive.

Kayleigh Milden is Research Assistant at the Institute of Cornish Studies, University of Exeter in Cornwall, where she is field officer for East Cornwall for the Cornish Audio Visual Archive, a major Oral History project located at the Institute and supported by the Heritage Lottery Fund. She is also completing her PhD on aspects of Cornish Methodism.

Brian Murdoch is Professor of German at the University of Stirling. In addition to his German research interests, he has written widely on literature in the Cornish language, notably his acclaimed volume *Cornish Literature* (1993).

Garry Tregidga is Assistant Director of the Institute of Cornish Studies, University of Exeter in Cornwall, where he leads the Cornish Audio Visual Archive project, a major Oral History programme supported by the Heritage Lottery Fund. He has lectured and published extensively on Cornish themes, and is author of *The Liberal Party in South West Britain Since 1918: Political Decline, Dormancy and Rebirth* (2000).